Diplomacy, Society and the COVID-19 Challenge

Diplomacy, Society and the COVID-19 Challenge brings together authors from various disciplinary backgrounds to examine the impacts of the pandemic on world politics and international relations, focusing on diplomacy and national, regional, and global responses to COVID-19.

The authors adopt a critical perspective which questions the general assumption that security is only related to state security. The book's first part deals with diplomacy and COVID-19, exploring forms such as virtual, digital, and science diplomacy. The second part, on national and regional responses to COVID-19, provides a detailed evaluation of the foreign policies of states and regional actors and the national/regional impacts of the pandemic. The third part investigates the responses of international organisations, such as NATO and the OECD, to COVID-19's transformative and disruptive effects.

This book will be of interest to students, scholars, and researchers of international relations, diplomacy, security studies, global governance, political science, political economy, and global public health, especially those with a particular focus on COVID-19 and how it has changed the world.

Erman Akıllı is Associate Professor in the Department of International Relations in the Faculty of Economics and Administrative Sciences at Kırşehir Ahi Evran University, Türkiye.

Burak Güneş is Assistant Professor in the Department of International Relations in the Faculty of Economics and Administrative Sciences at Kırşehir Ahi Evran University, Türkiye.

Ahmet Gökbel is Professor in the Department of Philosophy in the Faculty of Arts and Sciences and the Department of International Relations in the Faculty of Economics and Administrative Sciences, and Vice-Rector, at Kırşehir Ahi Evran University, Türkiye.

The Politics of Pandemics

Understanding the Politics of Pandemic Emergencies in the time of COVID-19
An Introduction to Global Politosomatics
Mika Aaltola

Pandemic Response and the Cost of Lockdowns
Global Debates from Humanities and Social Sciences
Edited by Peter Sutoris, Sinéad Murphy, Aleida Mendes Borges and Yossi Nehushtan

The COVID-19 Pandemic in the Middle East and North Africa
Public Policy Responses
Edited by Anis Ben Brik

Sweden's Pandemic Experiment
Edited by Sigurd Bergmann and Martin Lindström

Diplomacy, Society and the COVID-19 Challenge
Edited by Erman Akıllı, Burak Güneş and Ahmet Gökbel

For more information see https://www.routledge.com/The-Politics-of-Pandemics/book-series/TPOP

Diplomacy, Society and the COVID-19 Challenge

Edited by Erman Akıllı, Burak Güneş and Ahmet Gökbel

LONDON AND NEW YORK

First published 2024
by Routledge
4 Park Square, Milton Park, Abingdon, Oxon OX14 4RN

and by Routledge
605 Third Avenue, New York, NY 10158

Routledge is an imprint of the Taylor & Francis Group, an informa business

© 2024 selection and editorial matter, Erman Akıllı, Burak Güneş and Ahmet Gökbel; individual chapters, the contributors

The right of Erman Akıllı, Burak Güneş and Ahmet Gökbel to be identified as the authors of the editorial material, and of the authors for their individual chapters, has been asserted in accordance with sections 77 and 78 of the Copyright, Designs and Patents Act 1988.

All rights reserved. No part of this book may be reprinted or reproduced or utilised in any form or by any electronic, mechanical, or other means, now known or hereafter invented, including photocopying and recording, or in any information storage or retrieval system, without permission in writing from the publishers.

Trademark notice: Product or corporate names may be trademarks or registered trademarks, and are used only for identification and explanation without intent to infringe.

British Library Cataloguing-in-Publication Data
A catalogue record for this book is available from the British Library

Library of Congress Cataloging-in-Publication Data
Names: Akıllı, Erman, editor. | Güneş, Burak, editor. | Gökbel, Ahmet, editor.
Title: Diplomacy, society and the COVID-19 challenge / edited by Erman Akıllı, Burak Güneş and Ahmet Gökbel.
Description: New York : Routledge, 2024. | Series: The politics of pandemics | Includes bibliographical references and index.
Identifiers: LCCN 2023022208 (print) | LCCN 2023022209 (ebook) | ISBN 9781032455631 (hbk) | ISBN 9781032455648 (pbk) | ISBN 9781003377597 (ebk)
Subjects: LCSH: International relations--Social aspects. | COVID-19 Pandemic, 2020---Political aspects.
Classification: LCC JZ1251 .D56 2024 (print) | LCC JZ1251 (ebook) | DDC 327.09/052--dc23/eng/20230725
LC record available at https://lccn.loc.gov/2023022208
LC ebook record available at https://lccn.loc.gov/2023022209

ISBN: 978-1-032-45563-1 (hbk)
ISBN: 978-1-032-45564-8 (pbk)
ISBN: 978-1-003-37759-7 (ebk)

DOI: 10.4324/9781003377597

Typeset in Times New Roman
by KnowledgeWorks Global Ltd.

Contents

List of Figures and Tables viii
Foreword by Joseph S. Nye Jr. ix
Preface xi
Acknowledgements xiii
Notes on Contributors xiv

1 **Introduction: Pandemic, Security, and Other Broken Things** 1
ERMAN AKILLI, BURAK GÜNEŞ, AND AHMET GÖKBEL

PART I
Diplomacy and COVID-19 15

2 **Transformation of the International System and Security Conundrum during the COVID-19 Pandemic** 17
FERHAT PİRİNÇÇİ AND TUNÇ DEMİRTAŞ

3 **Far-Right Movements in the COVID-19 Era** 29
DOLAPO FAKUADE

4 **Virtual Diplomacy as a New Frontier of International Dialogue** 39
ALESSIA CHIRIATTI

5 **Diplomacy 3.0 in the Pandemic: Digital Diplomacy and Beyond** 47
ERMAN AKILLI AND GÜLNİHAN CİHANOĞLU GÜLEN

6 **Science Diplomacy and COVID-19 Politics** 56
EBRU CANAN-SOKULLU AND ATAKAN YILMAZ

PART II
National and Regional Responses to COVID-19   67

7 **Global Health Diplomacy and Türkiye**   69
   İDRIS DEMIR

8 **Government Responses to the COVID-19 Pandemic: Comparative Health Policies in the US and Canada**   81
   ÇAĞRI ERHAN AND EFE SIVIŞ

9 **China's Global Health Diplomacy in the Post-Pandemic Era: Implications for Southeast Asian Countries**   97
   CEMRE PEKCAN

10 **COVID-19 and South Korea: Focusing on Cultural Public Diplomacy with *Hallyu***   110
   YUNHEE KIM AND ERMAN AKILLI

11 **ASEAN's COVID-19 Pandemic Response: Regional and Global Reflections**   122
   HATICE ÇELIK

12 **Beyond Central Asia's Chessboard: Human Movement, Policies, and COVID-19**   131
   OLGA R. GULINA

13 **The COVID-19 Pandemic and the Middle East: Changing Policies and Mindset of Regional States**   143
   MUHITTIN ATAMAN AND MEHMET RAKIPOĞLU

14 **The UK's New Migration Policy: Post-Brexit and Post-COVID Implications**   158
   AYŞE GÜLCE UYGUN

15 **Post-Pandemic World Order and Russia**   171
   FIRAT PURTAŞ

16 **South Caucasus and COVID-19: Vulnerabilities, Setbacks, Responses**   180
   F. DIDEM EKINCI

PART III
Global Responses to COVID-19   195

17 **Human Impact on the Environment and the Increased Likelihood of Pandemics**   197
    ANA-BELÉN SOAGE

18 **The World Health Organization and the COVID-19 Pandemic**   208
    HAYDAR KARAMAN AND BURAK GÜNEŞ

19 **The COVID-19 Pandemic as a Security Issue and Its Implications for NATO**   217
    ARIF BAĞBAŞLIOĞLU

20 **Post-Pandemic Effects on the Realisation of Sustainable Development Goals (SDGs) for OECD Countries**   227
    R. ARZU KALEMCI AND MEHMET GÜRAY ÜNSAL

21 **The African Union and COVID-19: Regional Coordination and Solidarity**   251
    BILGE SAHIN

22 **Europe in the Post-Pandemic World Order: A Human Rights Perspective**   265
    EBRU DEMIR

23 **Globalisation in the Era of Power Transition: Lessons Post-COVID-19 for China and the US**   278
    MATTI IZORA İBRAHIM, BÜŞRA YILMAZ, AND MURAT ÇEMREK

24 **Conclusion: Per Aspera Ad Astra**   290
    ERMAN AKILLI, BURAK GÜNEŞ, AND AHMET GÖKBEL

    Index   *292*

Figures and Tables

Figures

10.1	Associated image of Korea	116
13.1	Number of deaths in Syria (2020–2021)	145
13.2	Fall in violence in Yemen (2020–2021)	146
13.3	Civil deaths in Yemen (2020–2021)	146
13.4	Number of deaths in Libya (2020–2021)	147
13.5	Rise of non-oil trade in GCC countries' GDP	151
20.1	The countries which are shown a decrease in the Economy subheading	234
20.2	The countries which are shown a decrease in the Equality subheading	235
20.3	The countries which are shown a decrease in Sustainability subheading	236
20.4	Line graph of efficiency scores of each country in 2018	239
20.5	Line graph of efficiency scores of each country in 2019	240
20.6	Line graph of efficiency scores of each country in 2020	241
20.7	Line graph of efficiency scores of each country in 2021	242
20.8	Mapping for average efficiency values of countries in 2018–2019	243
20.9	Mapping for average efficiency values of countries in 2020–2021	243

Tables

2.1	Rate of Increase in Global Economic Growth and Defense Expenditures (2015–2022)	20
2.2	The World's Largest Weapons Suppliers (2017–2021)	22
2.3	World Bank Energy Price Forecasts	23
10.1	The Classification of Hallyu through the Years	114
16.1	Country profiles of Armenia, Azerbaijan, and Georgia	183
20.1	Classification of Goals	233
20.2	Efficiency Scores of Each Country from 2018 to 2021	237
20.3	Average (Mean) Efficiency Scores of OECD Countries in 2018–2019 and 2020–2021	244
20.4	The Projected (Target) Numerical Value Levels for Outputs of Inefficient Countries	245

Foreword

The international system has failed its Covid test. The World Health Organization has estimated 15 million excess deaths occurred thus far during the pandemic. Given these grim statistics, should leaders of wealthy countries have done more to export vaccines and help vaccinate foreigners? When former President Donald Trump proclaimed "America First," he was being consistent with democratic theory, according to which leaders are entrusted with defending and advancing the interests of the people who elected them. But as I argue in my book *Do Morals Matter?* the key question is how leaders define the national interest. There is a major moral difference between a myopic transactional definition, like that of Trump, and a broader, far-sighted definition.

Consider President Harry Truman's espousal of the Marshall Plan after World War II. Rather than narrowly insisting that America's European allies repay their war loans, as the US had demanded after World War I, Truman dedicated more than 2% of America's GDP to aiding Europe's economic recovery. The process allowed Europeans to share in planning the continent's reconstruction and produced a result that was good for them, but that also served America's national interest in preventing Soviet control of Western Europe.

Viruses do not care about the nationality of the humans they kill. They simply seek a host to allow them to reproduce, and large populations of unvaccinated humans allow them to mutate and evolve new variants which can evade the protections that our vaccines produce. Given modern travel, it is only a matter of time before variants cross national borders. When a new variant arises that is capable of bypassing our best vaccines, we then have to develop a booster targeted at the new variant and vaccinate again, which could lead to more fatalities and more strain on medical systems. Alternatively, we can try a zero Covid policy with frustrating lockdowns and grave economic damage.

Values provide the second reason that countries should take a broad view of their national interest when fighting Covid. Some foreign policy experts contrast values with interests, but that is a false dichotomy. Our values are among our most important interests because they tell us who we are as a people. It is true that most people care more about their co-nationals than foreigners, but that does not mean they are indifferent to the suffering of others. Few would ignore a cry for help from a drowning person because she calls out in a foreign language. And while leaders are constrained by public opinion in a democracy, they often have considerable leeway to shape policy – and considerable resources to influence public sentiment.

A third reason to cooperate, related to the second, is soft power – the ability to influence others through attraction rather than coercion or payment. Values can be a source of soft power when others see a country's policies as benign and legitimate. Most foreign policies combine hard and soft power. The Marshall Plan, for example, relied on hard economic resources and payments, but it also created a reputation for benignity and far-sightedness that attracted others. A policy of helping poor countries by providing vaccines, as well as aiding the development of their own healthcare systems' capacities, would increase countries' soft power.

China quickly recognized that its soft power suffered from the origin story of its mishandling of COVID-19 in Wuhan. Not only was there a lack of clarity about how the virus originated, but in the early stages of the crisis, Chinese censorship and denial made the crisis worse than necessary before its authoritarian lockdown proved initially successful. Since then, China has pursued COVID-19 diplomacy in many parts of the world. By donating medical equipment and vaccines to other countries, China has been working to change the international narrative from one of fault to one of attraction. The Biden administration has been playing catch-up, announcing ambitious plans to donate vaccines. In addition, it pledged $4 billion in funding for the World Health Organization's COVAX facility to help poor countries purchase vaccines and supports a temporary waiver of intellectual property to help poor countries develop capacity.

In short, there were good reasons in terms of values, and self-interest for rich countries to vaccinate the rest of the world now, even before the job is finished at home. Unfortunately, the world failed this Covid test. We must do better in the future. One hopes that a volume like this will educate us all so we do not fail our next pandemic test.

Joseph S. Nye Jr.
Former Dean of Harvard's Kennedy School of Government, USA

Preface

A growing body of literature recognises the importance of the COVID-19 pandemic. The COVID-19 pandemic, which emerged in China at the end of 2019, is of interest globally because that is likely to be a candidate for being a turning point in world history. In recent years, there has been an increasing interest in the impacts of the COVID-19 pandemic on international politics. This pandemic has touched, influenced, and even transformed almost every field of human life, from politics to the economy, from social relations to daily life practices. International security, one of the leading research areas of international relations, has been affected by COVID-19 and has even mutated like the COVID-19 virus.

While COVID-19 has become a security issue, it has also changed how pre-existing security issues are addressed. The pandemic, during which international cooperation is insufficient, inter-state solidarity has decreased, and the virus is defined as the number one security problem by the UN Secretary-General, appeared to end today. However, it will keep us busy for a long time regarding its effects and results. During the epidemic, states adopted a self/help approach and tried to fight a global epidemic with local/national defence reflexes. Each state has accepted its national health infrastructure and capacity as a security reference point, and health-related issues have become an element of their basic security approaches.

This volume will consist of three parts focusing on the world in transformation during/post the COVID-19 era. The first part will deal with "Diplomacy and COVID-19" by touching upon various forms of diplomacy, such as humanitarian, digital, and virtual diplomacy. The second part, "National and Regional Responses to COVID-19", is constructed to make a detailed evaluation of the foreign policies of states and regional actors and the national/regional impacts of COVID-19. The third part, "Global Responses to COVID-19", is about global actors' responses shaped by the pandemic, stretching from NATO to the OECD. This section is about international organisations and their response to COVID-19's transformative effect, which caused unrest in their respective regions and globally.

We sincerely hope that this modest contribution, *"Diplomacy, Society and the COVID-19 Challenge"*, to the body of knowledge regarding the literature on International Relations for the pandemic and post-pandemic world order will be beneficial to qualitative and quantitative researchers, academics, postgraduate and undergraduate students, as well as individuals who have an interest in understanding how the COVID-19 challenged the international system and state affairs are (re)shaped, and the pandemic redefined international relations.

Editors,
Erman Akıllı, Burak Güneş and Ahmet Gökbel,
Kırşehir
2023

Acknowledgements

As editors, this book has been quite a journey for us. Our journey was encouraged and inspired by innumerable people, their persistence and tenacity, and their deeds of support, friendship, and generosity. We are truly privileged to have them on this journey.

We want to acknowledge the following:

Routledge/Taylor & Francis – for publishing this product of international collaboration and the current need for an authoritative reference on COVID-19 and the International Relations nexus,

- **Authors** – for their scholarly contributions that formed the substance and shaped the direction of this edited volume,
- **Emily Ross** – for her specialist guidance and profound support that made this edited volume become a reality,
- **Hannah Rich** – for the technical advice in the preparation of the manuscripts,
- **Prof. Joseph S. Nye Jr.** – for showing great courtesy by writing the foreword of this edited volume,
- **Mindy Yartaşı** – for proofreading the manuscripts and providing insights for copyediting, and
- **Simay Sultan Doğan** – for providing the manuscripts' typesetting and writing guidelines checks.

Of course, we owe our families the greatest gratitude. We want to express our deepest gratitude to our families for their unending tolerance, encouragement, and support as we worked on this edited volume.

Editors,
Erman Akıllı, Burak Güneş and Ahmet Gökbel,
Kırşehir
2023

Notes on Contributors

Editors

Erman Akıllı is Associate Professor in the Department of International Relations in the Faculty of Economics and Administrative Sciences at Kırşehir Ahi Evran University, Türkiye. Lecturing undergraduate and graduate courses on Turkish foreign policy, he has given many national and international speeches and written a number of articles, single-authored books, edited books, book chapters, and papers.

Ahmet Gökbel is Professor in the Department of International Relations in the Faculty of Economics and Administrative Sciences, at Kırşehir Ahi Evran University, Türkiye. He was awarded the Service to Turkish World Culture award in 2019 with his research topics, such as Turkish cultural history, Anatolian folk culture and beliefs, Akhism, Alevi-Bektashi culture, and Turkish religious history.

Burak Güneş is Assistant Professor in the Department of International Relations in the Faculty of Economics and Administrative Sciences at Kırşehir Ahi Evran University, Türkiye.

Contributors

Muhittin Ataman is Professor in the Department of International Relations at Ankara Social Sciences University, Türkiye, teaching international relations and Middle Eastern politics. His academic studies, mainly on Turkish foreign policy, Middle East politics, and Gulf politics, have been published in different Turkish, English, and Arabic journals and books. He is also the editor-in-chief of the *Insight Turkey* journal and the *Middle Eastern Annual*.

Arif Bağbaşlıoğlu is Associate Professor in the Department of International Relations in the Faculty of Economics and Administrative Sciences at Izmir Demokrasi University, Türkiye. His field of study is international relations: international security, European security, and international organisations. He has written for a number of academic publications and contributed conference papers on NATO's partnership policy, international security, European security, peace research, and conflict resolution.

Ebru Canan-Sokullu is Professor in the Department of Political Science and International Relations at Bahçeşehir University, Türkiye, and the Director of CIFAL Istanbul, the United Nations Education and Research Institute (UNITAR) International Training Center for Managers and Leaders, Türkiye. She is also the editor of the International Relations Council Panorama Portal. Her academic interests are quantitative political science, international security studies, foreign policy, and public opinion studies.

Hatice Çelik is Associate Professor in the Department of Asian Studies at the Institute for Area Studies at the Social Sciences University of Ankara, Türkiye. Her research interests include middle powers, foreign policy of the Korean peninsula, ASEAN and regionalisation in Asia, and international relations of Asia-Pacific. She teaches Area Studies, comparative politics of East Asia, and Korean politics.

Murat Çemrek is Chair of the Department of Political Science and International Relations at Necmettin Erbakan University, Türkiye. He is the Turkish Center for Global and Area Studies Coordinator. His research interests include globalisation, Turkish foreign policy, the Middle East, Central Asia, Islam, and politics.

Alessia Chiriatti is Head of the IAI's Educational programme and a researcher at its Institute for the Mediterranean, Middle East and Africa Programme, Italy. She is a member of the Editorial Committee of "The International Spectator" and COST (European Cooperation in Science and Technology). She is a mentor for GEM-Diamond (Marie Skłodowska-Curie Doctoral Network Joint Doctorate). She also teaches at the University of Padua, Italy. Her research interests include Turkish foreign policy, diplomacy, negotiation techniques, and active learning in international relations.

Gülnihan Cihanoğlu Gülen is a PhD candidate in the International Relations Department at the Ankara Social Sciences University, Türkiye, on the topic "Digital Diplomacy as a Tool of Public Diplomacy: A Comparative Analysis on Practices in Türkiye and Germany." She has also worked as a European Union Expert at the Republic of Türkiye Ministry of Labour and Social Security since 2012. Her research interests include globalization, diplomacy, public diplomacy, and digital diplomacy.

Ebru Demir is Assistant Professor in the Faculty of Law at Ankara Yildirim Beyazit University, Türkiye. Her research interests are public international law, international criminal law, and human rights.

İdris Demir is Professor and Rector of Batman University, Türkiye. His academic interests include energy, diplomacy, and strategy studies, and he has many articles and works published in national and international publishing houses and peer-reviewed journals.

xvi *Notes on Contributors*

Tunç Demirtaş is Assistant Professor of International Relations at Mersin University, Türkiye, and a researcher in the Security Studies Department at SETA, Türkiye. Horn of Africa politics, global/regional power competition in Africa, and Turkey-Africa relations are among his research interests.

F. Didem Ekinci is Professor of International Relations, and Head of the Department of Political Science and International Relations, at Çankaya University, Türkiye. She is a member of the Board of the Faculty of Economics and Administrative Sciences. Her courses and publications mainly focus on foreign policy analysis, international relations theories, state-building, conflict transformation, politics in the Balkans and Caucasus, and Russian and Turkish foreign policies.

Çağrı Erhan is Professor and has been the Rector of Altınbaş University, Türkiye, since June 2015. In 2018 he was appointed to the Republic of Turkey's Presidential Council of Foreign and Security Policies. He is among the founding editors of the journals *Uluslararası İlişkiler* (International Relations) and *Ankara Review of European Studies*. He was awarded the Tokyo Foundation Fellowship in 1995, the Turkish Ministry of Education Fellowship in 1997, and the Turkish Academy of Sciences Fellowship in 1998.

Dolapo Fakuade is the Programme Leader for MSc Intelligence, Security, and Disaster Management at the University of Derby, UK. She holds different visiting/adjunct positions at other universities in the UK, Germany, and the USA, teaching security and emergency management content and engaging in policy and practice-informing research. She is a "Pracademic" who maintains active professional and academic careers in Security and Emergency Response. She has worked advising on different security, emergency response, disaster resilience, and community-focused projects in Europe, the Middle East, and Asia.

Olga R. Gulina is affiliated with RUSMPI UG-Institute on Migration Policy in Berlin, Germany. She publishes extensively about migration challenges in the newly independent states. Her expertise includes comparative immigration law and its enforcement, and European and Eurasian affairs.

Matti Izora İbrahim is a PhD candidate specialising in American Foreign Policy in the Department of Political Science and International Relations at Necmettin Erbakan University, Türkiye. She has presented and published on firearms and their concealed carry in university settings.

R. Arzu Kalemci is Professor in the Department of Management at Cankaya University, Türkiye. Her research interests include historical institutionalism, corporate sustainability, and work ethic.

Haydar Karaman is Assistant Professor at Kilis 7 Aralik University, Türkiye. He has researched the non-refoulement of refugees in Turkish law and conscientious objection to military service in Türkiye.

Yunhee Kim is Research Professor at Hallym University of Graduate Studies, South Korea. She served on the Advisory Committee for the Korea-Africa

Foundation. Her research areas include public diplomacy, human security, and Sino-African and Korea-Africa political-economic ties.

Joseph S. Nye Jr. is University Distinguished Service Professor, Emeritus, and Former Dean of Harvard's Kennedy School of Government, USA. He has served as Assistant Secretary of Defense for International Security Affairs, Chair of the National Intelligence Council, and Deputy Under Secretary of State for Security Assistance, Science and Technology. He is a fellow of the American Academy of Arts and Sciences, the British Academy, and the American Academy of Diplomacy.

Cemre Pekcan is Associate Professor in the International Relations Department in the Faculty of Economics and Administrative Sciences at Canakkale Onsekiz Mart University, Türkiye. Her research interests include Asia-Pacific international relations and China-US relations.

Ferhat Pirinççi is Professor of International Relations at Bursa Uludağ University, Türkiye, and Senior Researcher in the Security Studies Department at SETA, Türkiye. His field of research includes Turkish foreign policy, Middle East Politics, arms transfers, and US foreign policy.

Fırat Purtaş is a professor. He has worked as Deputy Secretary General of the International Organization of Turkic Culture (TURKSOY) from 2008 to 2019. He is the editor of the *Bilig Journal of Social Sciences of the Turkic World*. He is a member of the Cultural Rapprochement Community in the UNESCO National Commission of Turkey. He is the advisor to the Head Trustee of International Turkish-Kazaks University. His academic works mainly focus on the Eurasian continent's political history and current issues.

Mehmet Rakipoğlu has worked at Batman and Sakarya University, Türkiye, as a research assistant and a non-resident fellow at the Center for Middle Eastern Studies. He is part of Dimensions for Strategic Studies and the Center for International Relations and Diplomacy. He has written many op-eds, book chapters, analyses, and reports for national and foreign media and think tanks. His research interests include the foreign policy of the Gulf countries, Türkiye's Gulf Policy and political Islam, social movements in the Middle East, and the relationship between religion and politics.

Bilge Sahin is Assistant Professor in the Department of International Relations at Bolu Abant Izzet Baysal University, Türkiye. She is also a Research Associate in the Department of Development Studies at SOAS University of London, UK. Her scholarly work critically engages with armed conflict, peace, and security from a gendered perspective in Africa. She is a member of the British International Studies Association (BISA) and the Women in Foreign Policy Initiative in Turkey.

Efe Sıvış is Chair of the Political Science and International Relations Department at Fenerbahce University, Türkiye. His academic interests are Turkish–American relations, Turkish foreign policy, American foreign policy, and political history.

Notes on Contributors

Ana-Belén Soage is Professor in International Relations at Universidad Internacional de La Rioja (UNIR). She has written numerous articles and book chapters on International Relations focusing on the Middle East and the Islamic World and is a regular contributor to media outlets like El País, RFI, and Sky News Arabia.

Mehmet Güray Ünsal works as a Faculty Member in the Department of Technology and Knowledge Management at Başkent University, Türkiye. He is interested in operations research, applied statistics, data science, and machine learning. He has published and reviewed papers on data envelopment analysis, time series, multivariate statistics, and machine learning in scientific journals.

Ayşe Gülce Uygun is Associate Professor in the Department of International Relations at Çanakkale Onsekiz Mart University, Türkiye. Her research interests include Mediterranean politics, European integration and EU foreign policy, migration studies, and Turkish foreign policy. She has published several articles and book chapters and lectured undergraduate and graduate courses on her areas of interest.

Atakan Yılmaz is Research Assistant in the Department of Political Science and International Relations at Bahçeşehir University, Türkiye, and a PhD candidate in the Department of International Relations at Galatasaray University, Türkiye. He is also the editorial coordinator at the Panorama Platform of the International Relations Council. His academic interests are cyberspace and security, diplomacy, quantitative politics studies, and computational social science.

Büşra Yilmaz is a PhD candidate and research assistant in the Department of Political Science and International Relations at Necmettin Erbakan University, Türkiye. She has published book chapters on International Relations.

1 Introduction
Pandemic, Security, and Other Broken Things

Erman Akıllı, Burak Güneş, and Ahmet Gökbel

As editors, when we first designed this book, "curfews" due to the pandemic were a common, mandatory, and unsettling "new normal" in many countries. Now, as we look back on those dark days from the vantage point of 2023, they seem to have faded from memory. Yet the ghost of the pandemic still looms over the world today and will continue to do so in the foreseeable future. In this book, our aim is to shed light on the pandemic's impact on the international system. By examining its effects on various aspects of society – from public health and the economy to politics, society, and diplomacy – we hope to provide a comprehensive picture of what the pandemic has meant for our world. While the worst of the pandemic may be behind us, its legacy remains. It has exposed the vulnerabilities of our societies and highlighted the need for greater cooperation and resilience in the face of global crises.

Many significant and lasting changes occurred after the interference of the COVID-19 pandemic in daily life. Considering the rapid and unpredictable conditions, academic circles adopted new frameworks for changing the *status quo*. Most analyses, academic papers, and courses taught in universities have been modified to conform to this inexperienced and unfamiliar state of affairs. Security, one of the main points in the study of the discipline of International Relations (IR), has faced profound challenges as COVID-19 became a permanent aspect of daily life.

Despite having less impact than the World Wars that occurred in the first half of the 20th century, the COVID-19 pandemic has had a significant and profound influence at the international system, state, interstate, and individual levels. For instance, the COVID-19 pandemic impacted the world at large and expedited the ongoing trend of digitalisation in the international system. This caused several sectors, including education, trade, market shopping, and healthcare, to adjust to digital processes and heavily rely on the Internet. This shift, defined as rapidly transferring business processes and information to a digital environment with the extensive application of information technologies, has been experienced worldwide. For instance, the digitalisation process of states in the international system, fuelled by the pandemic, has created an environment in which new concepts, such as the Metaverse, have flourished. Research conducted by Strategy Analytics indicates that the global Metaverse market, which was worth $6 billion in 2021, is predicted to grow to about $42 billion by the year 2026 due to the rising fascination

DOI: 10.4324/9781003377597-1

with virtual spaces for both entertainment and business during the COVID-19 pandemic (Akıllı, 2022).

On the other hand, communitarianism, the opposite of cosmopolitanism, is likely to receive more attention and enable states to strengthen their power and surveillance over people. Many states have elected conservative politicians who prioritise their national will over others. Italy's prime minister in 2022, Giorgia Meloni, who holds right-wing views, exemplifies the country's communitarianism. On the other hand, economic hardship worldwide has caused social inequality and discontent, leading to widespread protests. Regardless of whether a country is democratic or not, social unrest can occur. Protests related to COVID-19 have been witnessed in numerous countries across the globe, as demonstrated by examples such as Australia to Iran, Brazil to Germany, and South Africa to the United States (US). These demonstrations have manifested in diverse ways, ranging from protests against government measures in response to the pandemic, calls for improved healthcare and economic assistance, to opposition against curfews and other restrictions.

Globalisation had previously led to the breaking down of borders between nation-states, but the COVID-19 pandemic has abruptly halted this process. Although the situation is changing day by day, it remains unclear when and in what manner nation-states will resume the free movement of capital, goods, and labour that existed before the pandemic. Furthermore, illegal migration rates have increased significantly, and while there may be various reasons for this beyond the pandemic, it is clear that the pandemic has played a role. The pandemic has not only marked a significant point in history, dividing the world into pre- and post-pandemic eras, but also influenced current and future developments. Distance learning and working have become the norm in many business and education sectors, thanks to the pandemic. Additionally, the pandemic has highlighted that the world has been facing significant natural threats, such as climate change and global warming, leading to the emergence of new viruses and other dangers to humanity.

Moreover, the challenges resulting from the COVID-19 pandemic have caused significant humanitarian, institutional, and economic difficulties in many countries, leading to migration and refugee crises. The United Nations High Commissioner for Refugees (UNHCR) notes that the COVID-19 pandemic has significantly reduced the possibilities of achieving lasting solutions (UNHCR, 2022). Even though the COVID-19 pandemic has loosened its tight grip, the global community is still grappling with a host of issues that arose and persisted during the pandemic, such as food insecurity, increasing poverty, and inflationary pressure that have hindered progress and prosperity, as well as security. The war between Russia and Ukraine is an example of how the pandemic has contributed to conflicts.

This book discusses two distinct yet interrelated time frames regarding how the pandemic has affected people's daily lives. The first one is from when COVID-19 was declared a global pandemic until the lifting of restrictions, while the second one refers to the "new normal" established due to the pandemic, which has no specific period. In various chapters, authors provide details of a specific period while also highlighting the profound changes brought about by the pandemic. Other authors focus on the inner effects of the pandemic, particularly its impact on social relations and interstate relations. However, it's important to note that there is a lack of consensus and competing interpretations regarding these effects. To study the pandemic's impact, one must consider the global health perspective. It's clear that the coronavirus is still with us and will likely continue to be, whether or not it's officially classified as a pandemic (as noted in reports from the WHO in 2023). The transformative nature of the pandemic has caused long-lasting changes, particularly in the security field, which can be examined in more detail.

Traditional security studies, in which military capacity and state power were the focal points of analysis, were unequivocally dominant until the end of the Cold War. However, post-Cold War US primacy and the unipolar trend in international relations led to a rethinking of the definition of security (Buzan, 1998). In this context, critical security studies have developed new explanatory frameworks for understanding security by expanding the concept of security to issues beyond military and state-centric affairs, e.g. individual, national, regional, and international, and by using a deeper level of analysis of the referent objects, e.g. economic, environmental, societal, military, and political (Buzan, 1998). In this regard, critical security studies have become a field of research that draws attention to new approaches to thinking about and analysing security, including constructivist theories, critical theory, feminist theory, the framework of ontological security, aspects of postcolonial security, post-structuralism, and the ideas of the Copenhagen School, Paris School, and Aberystwyth School.

Nonetheless, external factors have long undermined state sovereignty, although interstate wars are still possible, as seen between Ukraine and Russia started on February 24, 2022. Yet, environmental factors (such as climate change, refugee crises, new viruses/epidemics/pandemics, and sea level rises) have forced decision-makers to adopt settlements that may be against their national interests. Therefore, security's inner meaning must extend beyond state security. COVID-19 has had some effect on both security studies and state systems. It is evident that things once labelled as "low politics" will occupy a great place in everyday life. Pandemics, as seen in the COVID-19 outbreak, have long been considered one of the so-called issues of low politics that have irreversibly altered the way of life and international order. So, this book critically investigates and questions the current situation and security understanding by considering the pandemic. Additionally, this book introduces new security challenges and new responses to these challenges. During the pandemic, most analyses, academic papers, and courses taught in universities have been modified to conform to this inexperienced and unfamiliar situation. We can trace this trend by focusing on recently published books. Numerous new publications regarding the diverse effects of the COVID-19 pandemic have been published. For instance, in their collective work, Harper-Anderson et al. (2023) specifically investigate the COVID-19 pandemic's impact on health, justice, and the economy. Further, they shed light on the possible reflections of these problematic areas on racial equity in the US. Their theoretical standpoint comes from a school named after L. Douglas Wilder, the first elected African-American governor of Virginia, focusing on possible ways to fight against racial inequality.

Michie and Sheehan (2022) edited another volume, a collection of articles published in its 35th volume and 2nd issue of the *International Review of Applied Economics* in 2021. This volume focuses on the nature of the political economy, dealing with concrete results that peoples of the world (most notably developing and underdeveloped countries) have. Another essential publication by Koley and Dhole (2022) gives detailed insights into the COVID-19 pandemic, covering other pandemics as examples. In their work, Koley and Dhole led authors to understand, cover, and grasp the impact of COVID-19 in all aspects. Similar to Koley and Dhole, another volume, edited by Gunaratna and Aslam, also assesses the COVID-19 pandemic from different perspectives (2022a). One of the basic concerns of the book is to put forward responses in handling the pandemic. The book gives both country- and concept-based evaluations to reach the expected outcome. Gunaratna and Aslam edited another volume, specifically addressing threats to and responses of South Eastern countries. Accordingly, this book also claims that it collected essays from scholars who have field experience. In other words, this book claims to give factual data from the field (2022b).

Jakupec et al. critically approach the COVID-19 pandemic through the perspective of nationalism and global development (2022). According to them, the international world order is still in "flux," depicting it as a Western-led global order pioneered by the US, which is internally and externally under threat. They proposed that "illiberal globalism, populism, nationalism" are those internal threats, whereas China, Russia, and India constitute one side of the external threats.

There are also books dealing with the pandemic's origins and early stages of the emergence of the virus by taking South Eastern countries as cases. For instance, being the earliest book dealing with East Asia, the volume edited by Ganguly and Mistree uses South Eastern countries as samples to evaluate their efforts, struggles, and inadequacies in coping with the pandemic (2022). Additionally, the book asserts that the pandemic is the most influential and "serious tragedy" for those countries after British colonisation – this claim is worth examination.

As editors, we aim to bring together articles from various backgrounds in this book. Still, they all focus solely on the pandemic's possible impacts on international politics and relations simultaneously giving significant insights that states (international organisations and others) had taken to tackle the pandemic between 2020 and 2023. This book aims to adopt a critical perspective, goes beyond the traditional state security perspective, and tries to grasp the implications of the pandemic at different levels. Because of environmental issues (viruses, climate change, environmental-induced migration, etc.), the world is heading towards a future with varying frameworks of inquiry. The United Nations Human Rights Council and the United Nations General Assembly adopted two new resolutions entitled "The human right to a clean, healthy and sustainable environment" in 2021 and 2022, respectively. The UN General Assembly "recognises the right to a clean, healthy and sustainable environment as a human right," which imposes responsibilities on states to act diligently. Since global warming is a reality, new viruses/pandemics are indispensable parts of our world. Therefore, this book focuses on diplomacy and national, regional, and global responses to COVID-19. For doing so, this book adopts a critical perspective, which questions the general assumption that security is only related to state security. However, we did not want to restrict our contributors to sticking to only one perspective but rather to offer a critical approach. In all chapters, we aimed to give the reader the feeling that societies (peoples) are at the very core of all chapters, whether it deals with states' foreign policies, regional developments, or global responses to the COVID-19 pandemic. Hence, the book's title is *Diplomacy, Society and the COVID-19 Challenge*: the diplomacy and society nexus is the heart of the book.

Some IR scholars have also suggested that the COVID-19 pandemic accelerates existing trends in changes to the international order rather than signalling a clean break. So, where conceptually does the book stand? For sure, there has been an ongoing transformation in the international system. What role does the COVID-19 pandemic play in this transformation? Is the COVID-19 pandemic the creator of the shift or catalysing figure? These questions involve agent-structure relations in the social sciences. In his article entitled "Anarchy Is What States Make of It: The Social Construction of Power Politics," Alexander Wendt tried to bridge agent and structure and surpassed this artificial dichotomy. Nonetheless, Wendt implies, "We cannot address these empirical issues, however, unless we have a framework for doing systemic research that makes state identity and interest issue for both theoretical and empirical inquiry" (Wendt, 1992: 423).

For the aspect of COVID-19 as a catalysing figure, one should consider the "soft power" concept. In 1990, Joseph S. Nye's book *Bound to Lead: The Changing Nature of American Power* introduced the idea of soft power to the field of international relations (Nye, 1990). Nye defines the concept as "the ability to achieve what you want by attracting it rather than using orders/force or persuading it somehow (such as providing money)." In other words, exporting a country's positive image inspires other countries to reach foreign policy goals. In its broadest definition, soft power refers to the circumstance in which a state achieves its foreign policy objectives solely through its appeal to other nations, without any material, moral, indirect, or direct intervention. According to Nye, a country's soft power potential is its ability to attract people with its culture, political ideals, and policies. The soft power of a nation will expand or diminish depending on the legitimacy of its policies in the eyes of the public because Nye asserted that "soft power is needed to create peace" and that "making peace is tougher than winning the war." Some states have withdrawn into their shells within the nation-state framework during the COVID-19 pandemic. Others have provided serious assistance within the framework of humanitarian aid. In the context of their help, they have strengthened their soft power potential. Thus, the COVID-19 pandemic has allowed such states to export their soft power potential and positive image. The legitimacy of these states in the international system has been strengthened thanks to soft power.

On the other hand, Karl Marx, in the "18th Brumaire of Louis Bonaparte," also pointed out that "Men make their history, but they do not make it just as they please; they do not make it under the circumstances chosen by themselves, but under the circumstances directly encountered, given and transmitted from the past" (Marx, 2016). Therefore, we do not need to choose between agent and structure.

On the contrary, we can overcome this dichotomy by applying dialectic to our inquiry. *So, the pandemic has had emerging effects on the ongoing transformation of the international system while accelerating the change process.*

Furthermore, there are varying approaches to the COVID-19 pandemic, blaming it for giving governments a space to intervene in ordinary people's lives and seeing it as a transformative dynamic that profoundly affected global politics. Slavoj Žižek is fair to be critical while asking whether we are all in the same boat. The increasing trend in solidarity among states is because of the intention to protect the "me/we" from other's infections. In other words, if a state wants to save itself from the grasp of the pandemic, it needs to protect other states by keeping a distance (Žižek, 2020: 15). However, Žižek also points out, "The catch is that, even if life does eventually return to some semblance of normality, it will not be the same normal as the one we experienced before the outbreak" (Žižek, 2020: 78).

According to social contract theories, people build states to sustain their security. However, in Italy, Giorgio Agamben is more critical of the pandemic outbreak, accusing the state apparatus of enhancing its control and surveillance over populations, imposing a given lifestyle on people, and constructing power-knowledge relations taking the pandemic as a good opportunity. According to Agamben, "Therefore, in a vicious circle, the limitations of freedom imposed by governments are accepted in the name of a desire for safety created by the same governments that are now intervening to satisfy it" (Agamben, 2020).

Additionally, Agamben stresses the power of a pandemic to strengthen the resultant "state of exception" (Agamben, 2005). However, in addition to the power-knowledge relationship that imposes restrictions on people, there is a constant transformation in the human habitat caused by climate change. In other words, mutations are natural, and new variants of different viruses will exist. We cannot simply ignore that fact and only stick to the issue of power-knowledge relations. As George Ritzer and Paul Dean put it, there will be an increase in the number of health crises caused by global warming and climate change. According to Ritzer and Dean, "Diseases caused by animals and insects may increase" (Ritzer and Dean, 2015: 304). With the accelerating feature of global warming (along with globalisation), these diseases will increase sharply soon (Ritzer and Dean, 2015: 335). Therefore, we are on the brink of a choice; whether being critical of what we have experienced or strictly grasping the reality of pandemics is the deadlock. Alternatively, is there a middle path?

Relying upon the meta-theoretical assumptions of critical realism coined by Roy Bashkar, there can be epistemological pluralism in dealing with the social phenomenon (Bashkar, 2008). We do not need to choose between positivism and post-positivism in epistemology. For instance, there are power-knowledge relations that human beings cannot observe via their senses, but these relations exist and are independent of reason. Issues in the book will be approached by adopting different *epistemologies* and discovering the *ontological depth* of the real. In this perspective, for the book, as the editors, we did not plan to collect essays from one philosophy, i.e. post-positivism or positivism. On the contrary, we wanted to show various sides of the COVID-19 pandemic by gathering different perspectives. However, as said before, we sought contributors that are as critical as possible.

How can one define the COVID-19 era? In this book, the COVID-19 era refers to a period between the inception of the pandemic, governments' restriction enforcement, and the use of vaccines. However, we respectively address future implications of the pandemic as well. For instance, distance learning/home office working is an inseparable part of daily and business life. Students, business people, and even ordinary people have gotten used to the Internet and distance working/learning. These changes are enormous and deeply affect modern people's daily routines. However, in international politics, we have witnessed another inequality regarding vaccine allocations, which touches on "dependency theories/Marxist approaches/imperialism debates." Developed countries/states quickly access vaccines, whereas underdeveloped or developing countries have suffered from receiving such vaccines.

What about the post-pandemic era? In this book, we aim to identify the post-pandemic/COVID-19 era, beginning with the decline in the pandemic with the mass usage of mRNA vaccines, which ultimately allowed governments to remove restrictions. Therefore, the COVID-19 pandemic has short and long-term impacts even after states get the pandemic under control. Moreover, unemployment figures have risen, and states still need help to figure out these economic problems (Jones et al., 2021). For instance, studies show that if unemployment rates reach 30%, the yearly poverty rate in the US will grow from 12.4% to 18.9%, making it the highest documented figure since at least 1967 (Parolin and Wimer, 2020).

Why is the COVID-19 pandemic considered a turning/breaking point in the development of the international system? During the pandemic, states, international organisations, and individuals were compelled to alter their order of importance to establish a new norm. Furthermore, a new period will start, the post-pandemic era, and authoritarian inclinations and the influence of public authority in politics will eventually grow, as can be seen in the Russian invasion of Ukraine, which was built upon irrational foreign policy choices and violation of generally accepted norms, as a reflection of the increased authoritarianism.

Apart from that, there are also specific problems in international cooperation. International organisations still need to manage the pandemic and enhance collaboration among member states. For instance, the World Health Organization (WHO), a specialised organisation of the United Nations (UN), has long been criticised for needing more effectiveness and trustworthiness. The WHO has learnt much from the pandemic. Another debate, which is still going on, is between communitarianism and cosmopolitanism. An excellent example of this dichotomy is Donald Trump's – the then President of the United States of America – famous slogan "America First." Many states are still confused about whether they should prioritise their national interests or enshrine international cooperation.

What exactly is distinctive about COVID-19? It is not an exaggeration to say that the COVID-19 pandemic has had profound and irreversible impacts, signifying 2020 as an essential year in world history. The world has witnessed numerous pandemics in the past, namely the Black Death (1346–1353), the Great Influenza (1918–1920), and H1N1/09 Virus/Swine Influenza (2009–2010). However, COVID-19 has a particular strain of the virus that humans have not encountered before and, thus, haven't developed immunity to. Henceforth, the widespread of the virus around the globe caused governments to take harsh restrictions to protect themselves from the unknown and morbid pandemic. In our book, as mentioned above, the COVID-19 era is the exclamation of states' severe conditions and a test of their survival instincts.

The liberal world order, which envisages freedom of movement of goods, capital, individuals, and knowledge, has been challenged. Nation-states have gained more power and a central role in international politics. Yet, nation-states are aware that an external factor, i.e. environment, threatens their national interests.

Why does COVID-19 matter for international politics (and the book)? As Sara E. Davies and Clare Wenham put it, the answer is simple: "… politics is deciding how COVID-19 is spreading and whether people are living or dying" (Davies and Wenham, 2020: 1227). In other words, the various government responses to the outbreak itself, however, reveal political decisions about who should be trusted in the international arena, who should be consulted, who should offer advice, what policies should be implemented, how such policies should be enforced, and which models should be used (Davies and Wenham, 2020: 1251). The COVID-19 era raised the question of whether states' sovereign equality in the international system is an illusion, which ultimately leads – as Karl Marx implies in Capital Vol. I, "Between equal rights, force decides."

How has the COVID-19 pandemic impacted the pre-existing power dynamics and structures? First and foremost, the global crisis affects conflict-affected countries the most. Thus, in nations impacted by armed conflict, the pandemic risks amplify disparities and place additional burdens on vulnerable groups. As a result, efforts to manage the crisis and promote peace need to be improved. Second, local and outside conflict parties quickly seize the chances presented by the crisis's policy responses. Third, the effects of the economic downturn seriously strain already weakened state institutions and jeopardise governance outcomes (thus increasing the risk of conflict). Of these three factors, the pandemic's governmental responses and diversionary effects have had the most impact on conflict dynamics, too frequently in a negative way (Mustasilta, 2020).

Back to the scope, "Diplomacy, Society and the COVID-19 Challenge" will consist of three parts focusing on the world in transformation during/post the COVID-19 era. The first part will deal with "Diplomacy and COVID-19" by touching upon various forms of diplomacy, such as humanitarian, digital, and virtual diplomacy. The second part, "National and Regional Responses to COVID-19," is designed to evaluate the foreign policies of states and regional actors and the national/regional impacts of COVID-19. The third part, "Global Responses to COVID-19," is about global actors' responses shaped by the pandemic, stretching from NATO to the OECD. This section is about international organisations and their response to COVID-19's transformative effect, which caused unrest in their respective regions and globally.

In their chapter titled *"Transformation of the International System and Security Conundrum During the COVID-19 Pandemic,"* Ferhat Pirinçci and Tunç Demirbaş focused on the security conundrum in world politics. They asserted that states with more ambitious reform plans inevitably encounter more difficult obstacles.

However, the chapter also asserts that more resilient states will have an advantage over others in resolving such obstacles if they adopt flexible and adaptable policies.

Dolapo Fakuade, in her chapter entitled *"Far-Right Movements in the COVID-19 Era,"* explores the far-right movements and their intended goal, which often makes violence inevitable and a common occurrence in Europe. It further reviews far-right activities in the onset and immediate global response to the COVID-19 pandemic outbreak with the aim to identify patterns, target groups, and impacts of the far-right activities in Europe.

Alessia Chiriatti claims that the role and practices of diplomacy have changed in her chapter titled *"Virtual Diplomacy as a New Frontier of International Dialogue."* The chapter addresses the suggested topic by concentrating on a few problems: a dearth of scientific material, terminology appropriate for the reading and analysis levels, and the potential for a coronavirus pandemic. To achieve this, the chapter will examine the various definitions of diplomacy developed over the past 30 years, focusing on digital diplomacy and e-diplomacy and highlighting distinctions and practical applications.

In their chapter titled *"Diplomacy 3.0 in the Pandemic: Digital Diplomacy and Beyond,"* Erman Akıllı and Gülnihan Cihanoğlu Gülen discussed the development of digital diplomacy, including how it came about, how it was developed, and how it was used in the coronavirus pandemic. They also shed light on the advantages and disadvantages of digital diplomacy and its potential applications in the future, as highlighted by Diplomacy 4.0: AI in foreign policy.

Ebru Canan Sokullu and Atakan Yılmaz focused on the role of science diplomacy in COVID-19 global politics and provided a thorough assessment of whether or not Türkiye has a newfound interest in diplomacy, using the term "Science Diplomacy" as an empirical case study in their chapter titled *"Science in Diplomacy and the COVID-19 Politics."*

In his chapter titled *"Global Health Diplomacy and Türkiye,"* İdris Demir investigated health diplomacy in the international relations discipline through a theoretical approach and examined Türkiye's health diplomacy profile based on global health diplomacy practices. The chapter envisaged that Türkiye might boost its soft power even further by creating new partnerships across a wider geographic range, with the successful collaboration of the public and commercial sectors working in the health sector.

Çağrı Erhan and Efe Sıvış, in their chapter titled *"Government Responses to the COVID-19 Pandemic: Comparative Health Policies in the US and Canada,"* addressed the geostrategic position of Canada and the political ramifications of COVID-19 in US domestic politics. They argued in their chapter that while the pandemic caused the largest election turnout in more than a century (2020), it also increased polarisation, politicisation, misinformation, and public mistrust of the government and damaged transparency and accountability in regional state operations.

In her chapter titled *"China's Global Health Diplomacy in the COVID-19 Era: Implications for Southeast Asian Countries,"* Cemre Pekcan analysed how China's use of global health diplomacy as a soft power strategy has affected China's relationships with Southeast Asian nations in the COVID-19 era as well as whether China's image as a leading power in the region has improved relative to the US.

Yunhee Kim and Erman Akıllı analysed how *Hallyu* fuelled South Korea's cultural and public diplomacy, its institutional roots in South Korea, and the function and impact of *Hallyu* in the COVID-19 age of international relations, as well as the origins and appraisal of *Hallyu* (from 1.0 to 4.0) in their chapter titled "*COVID-19 and South Korea: Focusing on Cultural Public Diplomacy with Hallyu.*"

As in the other regions of the world, besides the coronavirus pandemic, major regional issues have arisen, exhorting additional pressure on the Association of Southeast Asian Nations (ASEAN). Hatice Çelik examined the struggle of ASEAN with the COVID-19 pandemic and explained the organisation's reactions as an actor in the region in her chapter titled "*ASEAN's COVID-19 Pandemic Response: Regional and Global Reflections.*"

The COVID-19 outbreak and the conflict in Ukraine have disturbed both internal and external affairs in Eurasia, causing nations to re-evaluate the region's geopolitical structure and reorganise the balance of power. Olga R. Gulina analysed the consequences of the COVID-19 outbreak and Russia's invasion of Ukraine concerning the future of Eurasian countries in her chapter titled "*Beyond Central Asia's Chessboard: Human Movement, Policies, and the COVID-19.*"

Since the start of the Arab Spring and revolutions, the Middle East has undergone enormous transformations. After the Arab Spring, the coronavirus was the second most significant event that affected Middle Eastern nations. The stability of the neighbouring countries is, nevertheless, under unusual threat. Muhittin Ataman and Mehmet Rakipoğlu analysed the overall impact of the coronavirus pandemic on the security architecture, economic sustainability, domestic politics, and foreign policies of the regional countries in their chapter titled "*The COVID-19 Pandemic and the Middle East: Changing Policies and the Mindset of Regional States.*"

Two challenging issues for UK foreign policy have been the COVID-19 outbreak and Brexit; dealing with both required concurrent, multifaceted, and long-term plans since they needed the government to address them simultaneously. Ayşe Gülce Uygun discussed the Global Britain vision and its implications for the post-Brexit and COVID-19 era in her chapter titled "*The UK's New Migration Policy: Post-Brexit and Post-COVID Implications.*"

Fırat Purtaş examined Russia's foreign policy during the COVID-19 pandemic in his "*Post-Pandemic World Order and Russia*" chapter. In the chapter, provisions, approaches, and dynamics of Russian foreign policy in critical areas and disputes, such as the annexation of Crimea, the war in Ukraine, relations with the US, the European Union, China, and former Soviet geography, are examined.

In the South Caucasus, multiple regional vulnerabilities and setbacks in healthcare systems and economic capacity inherited from the Soviet era shaped the regional actors' response capacity during the pandemic outbreak. Fatma Didem Ekinci discussed the impact and implications of the COVID-19 pandemic in the South Caucasus in her chapter titled "*South Caucasus and COVID-19: Vulnerabilities, Setbacks, Responses.*"

After SARS, swine flu, and MERS, COVID-19 has been the fourth pandemic to affect the world since 2000. Although scientists had been issuing warnings about the threat presented by pandemics for the previous three decades, it has been the most damaging thus far, concentrating attention on it on a global scale. In her chapter titled *"Human Impact of the Environment and the Increased Likelihood of Pandemics,"* Ana-Belén SOAGE investigated the main factors of the pandemic through the disruption of the environment, urbanisation-globalisation, intensive animal farming, and climate change.

The WHO has faced significant obstacles in carrying out its role as the global public health authority due to the COVID-19. The pandemic has shown the WHO's power dynamics and limitations in achieving its goals from a key legal standpoint. Haydar Karaman and Burak Güneş examined the major challenges and successes of the WHO in their chapter titled *"World Health Organization and the COVID-19 Pandemic."*

Through using the concepts of international society and the international system, Arif **Bağbaşlioğlu** examined whether the COVID-19 epidemic has impacted cooperation among NATO countries, contributed to the resolution of ongoing issues within NATO, and discussed the pandemic's impacts on NATO in his chapter titled *"The COVID-19 Pandemic as a Security Issue and Its Implications for NATO."*

The pandemic has significantly impacted social, political, economic, and health outcomes. For countries that are members of the Organisation for Economic Cooperation and Development (OECD), the COVID-19 pandemic was an unforeseen and unanticipated calamity. In their chapter titled *"Post-Pandemic Effects on The Realisation of Sustainable Development Goals (SDGs) for OECD Countries,"* R. Arzu Kalemci and Mehmet Güray Ünsal employed data envelopment analysis (DEA) to discuss how the COVID-19 pandemic has affected OECD nations' ability to realise their SDGs.

Due to its long-standing institutional commitment to regional public health, the African Union (AU) has shown notable proactivity in reacting to the COVID-19 pandemic. Due to the flaws in the public health systems of many African countries and the alarming financial shortfalls faced by their governments, the AU has pledged to trace, test, and track the pandemic, ensure that African states have access to a sufficient portion of the global vaccine supply, and solicit foreign aid to combat the pandemic. Bilge Sahin explored AU policies responding to COVID-19 and their challenges in her chapter titled *"The African Union and COVID-19: Regional Coordination and Solidarity."*

In the chapter titled *"Europe in the Post-Pandemic World Order: A Human Rights Perspective,"* Ebru Demir focused on the COVID-19 pandemic situation in Europe and the responses of the Council of Europe member states. Nonetheless, she examined the effectiveness with which the European human rights procedures, particularly the European Court of Human Rights, can reassert the shared European ideals inside its legal framework. The chapter analyses several challenging legal and ethical concerns that the European Court of Human Rights may soon have to address while rendering decisions related to the COVID-19 pandemic.

Scholars of international relations are increasingly in agreement that the COVID-19 pandemic has expedited the restructuring of world politics and contributed to China's development as a rival to American hegemony. According to some academics, the collapse of the world order directly results from American leadership failures during this extraordinary pandemic. Others, meanwhile, pay more attention to the continuous global transition that was already underway before the COVID-19 crisis. Matti Izora İbrahim, Büşra Yilmaz, and Murat Çemrek discussed globalisation within the post-COVID-19 transition with regard to Organski and Kugler's (1980) power transition theory in their chapter titled *"Globalisation in the Era of Power Transition: Lessons Post-COVID-19 for China and the US."*

Overall, this book questions the pandemic's possible impacts and potential responses to COVID-19 by states, international organisations, and societies. Under the framework of critical security studies, this book questions state exceptionalism in security studies by bringing the human perspective into the stage. Questions asked in this volume bring about the problem of where the world is heading: cooperation or rivalry. This book aims to give competing approaches to this fundamental question by touching upon various subject areas relating to the COVID-19 pandemic. Through this book, we hope to contribute to the ongoing conversation about the pandemic and its aftermath and to inspire new ideas and approaches for a more sustainable and equitable future.

References

Agamben, G. (2005). *State of Exception*. 1st ed. Chicago: University of Chicago Press.
Agamben, G. (2020). *The Invention of an Epidemic* [Online]. Available at: https://www.quodlibet.it/giorgio-agamben-l-invenzione-di-un-epidemia (Accessed: June 21, 2022).
Akıllı, E (2022). "The Metaverse Diplomacy: A Future Vision for Türkiye". *Insight Turkey*. 24 (3), pp. 67–88.
Aslam, M. M. and Gunaratna, R (eds.) (2022a). *COVID-19 in South, West, and Southeast Asia: Risk and Response in the Early Phase*. London: Routledge.
Aslam, M. M. and Gunaratna, R. (eds.) (2022b). *COVID-19 Pandemic: The Threat and Response*. London: Routledge.
Bashkar, R. (2008). *Realist Theory of Science*. 1st ed. New York: Routledge.
Buzan, B. et al. (1998). *Security: A New Framework for Analysis*. 1st ed. Colorado: Lynne Rienner Pub.
Davies, S. E. and Wenham, C. (2020). "Why the COVID-19 Response Needs International Relations". *International Affairs*. 96 (5), pp. 1227–1251.
Ganguly, S. and Mistree, D. (eds.) (2022). *The Covid-19 Crisis in South Asia: Coping with the Pandemic*. London: Routledge.
Jakupec, V., Kelly, M. and Percy, M. (eds.) (2022). *COVID-19 and Foreign Aid: Nationalism and Global Development in a New World Order*. London: Routledge.
Jones, L., Palumbo, D. and Brown, D. (2021). *Coronavirus: How the Pandemic Has Changed the World Economy* [Online]. Available at: https://www.bbc.com/news/business-51706225 (Accessed: June 21, 2022).
Koley, T. K. and Dhole, M. (2022). *The COVID-19 Pandemic: The Deadly Coronavirus Outbreak*. New York: Routledge.
Marx, K. (2016). Der achtzehnte Brumaire des Louis Bonaparte. 4th ed. Italy: Hofenberg.

Michie, J. and Sheehan, M. (eds.) (2022). *The Political Economy of Covid-19: Covid-19, Inequality and Government Responses.* New York: Routledge.

Mustasilta, K. (2020). *From Bad to Worse?* [Online]. Available at: https://www.iss.europa.eu/sites/default/files/EUISSFiles/Brief%2013%20Covid%20and%20conflict.pdf (Accessed: June 21, 2022).

Nye, J. S. (1990). *Bound To Lead: The Changing Nature of American Power.* 1st ed. New York: Basic Books.

Parolin, Z. and Wimer, C (2020). "Forecasting Estimates of Poverty during the COVID-19 Crisis Poverty Rates in the United States Could Reach Highest Levels in Over 50 Years". *Poverty & Social Policy Brief.* 4 (6), pp. 1–18.

Harper-Anderson, E. L., Albanese, J. S. and Gooden, S. T. (eds.) (2023). *Racial Equity, COVID-19, and Public Policy: The Triple Pandemic.* New York: Routledge.

Ritzer, G. and Dean, P. (2015). *Globalization: A Basic Text.* 3rd ed. New York: Wiley-Blackwell.

UNHCR (2022). Mid-Year Trends, UNHCR. https://www.unhcr.org/statistics/unhcrstats/635a578f4/mid-year-trends-2022.html

Wendt, A (1992). "Anarchy Is What States Make of It: The Social Construction of Power Politics". *International Organization.* 46 (2), pp. 391–425.

Žıžek, S. (2020). *PANDEMIC! COVID-19 Shakes the World.* 1st ed. New York: OR Books.

Part I
Diplomacy and COVID-19

2 Transformation of the International System and Security Conundrum during the COVID-19 Pandemic

Ferhat Pirinççi and Tunç Demirtaş

Introduction

The global system is experiencing a gradual transformation today. Although the COVID-19 pandemic is not the main reason for this transformation, it has played a vital role in its accelerating effect. The crisis has triggered transformation not only in the health field but also in many fields, such as security, politics, economy, and energy. Erosion in the power of the US in this period of negativity is seen as one of the important changes in the global system.

In the transformation of the global system, new and dynamic alliances, competitive environments within the alliance, orientation towards defence, fragmented and flexible cooperation, and complex relations come to the fore. States have exhibited more independent behaviour in the post-COVID period. Therefore, although the alliance structures formed after World War II are questioned, they can still be functional in some cases. However, states are adopting harsh policies in their search for new security.

This study aims to answer how the transformation in the global system affects the search for security of states. In addition, the policies followed by the states in parallel with the transformation of the global system will also be analysed. To better understand this process, it is necessary to examine the unusual behaviour patterns and policies of states. In this context, it is expected that states will lend more importance to "hedging" and rigid security policies.

This study aims to analyse the policies of states in search of security in world politics in the context of the transformation of the global system. By moving away from the usual patterns, the new rules and practices introduced by the transformation will be examined through various examples.

Prominent Features in the Transformation of the Global System

The global system has transformed since the 2000s but was progressing very slowly until the COVID-19 pandemic. However, the pandemic caught states off guard, and they had to respond to pressing challenges. Unfortunately, a global solution could not be found, and states had to act on a national scale in the face of the problem. The COVID-19 pandemic has caused states' policies to become more

DOI: 10.4324/9781003377597-3

mercantilist. The disruption of the international supply chain stands out as an essential breaking point for the global system during the pandemic. States have learnt the necessary lessons from this process, expanded their capacities, and taken steps to reduce vulnerabilities.

COVID-19 has shown how significant the vulnerabilities of states are. The disruption of supply chains also affected developed and industrialised countries and required states to reduce their vulnerabilities. To resolve this situation, states need to produce a multidimensional response. Every state has its vulnerabilities and states work diligently to overcome these challenges. In the post-COVID-19 era, states are aiming to increase their resilience, starting from where they feel most vulnerable. This is particularly crucial when facing potential problems and crises. However, the formation of robust responses could be faster in some cases. For this reason, some states' efforts are effective in the short term, while others are effective in the medium and long term. For example, within the scope of the energy problem, some states may diversify energy in the short term, while others can do so in the medium and long term.

Global Leadership(lessness)

The problem of global leadership has been one of the prominent agendas in the context of the coronavirus pandemic and the fight against the virus. Compared to the recent outbreaks such as SARS, bird flu, swine flu, MERS, Ebola, and Zika (TÜBA, 2020), the fact that the coronavirus raises the issue of global leadership is undoubtedly due to its global impact. However, although the problem is global, it is seen that the fight against the virus takes place mainly at the national level. From this point of view, almost all actors with leadership potential in terms of political, military, or economic indicators in the international system in the pre-coronavirus period were unable to react quickly and adequately to the emergence of the virus.

When considered at the global level, it is seen that the UN, the most critical institution symbolising the current global system, still needs to take practical steps regarding the global pandemic. For example, the first meeting of the UN Security Council with the coronavirus agenda was held on April 9, 2020, when the impact of the epidemic was already felt all over the world, and no decision was taken as a result of this meeting (United Nations, 2020a). Although it was stated that the members of the Security Council prepared a draft resolution on coronavirus after the meeting, the Security Council could only take a unanimous decision on COVID-19 on June 1, 2020 (United Nations Security Council, 2020.

On April 2, 2020, the UN General Assembly unanimously adopted a resolution titled "Global Solidarity in the Fight Against Covid-19," and this resolution referred to the central role of the UN system in the fight against the pandemic, calling for solidarity and cooperation in the fight against the coronavirus (United Nations General Assembly, 2020). Although this decision is vital in that it is the first decision of the UN during the pandemic period, it should be noted that the decision was taken at a time when the number of people infected with coronavirus exceeded 1 million worldwide (Yürük, 2020). In addition, it is a crucial handicap that the resolution contains general statements and that the resolutions of the UN General Assembly lack executive power.

It is indisputable that the World Health Organization (WHO) is the most prominent expert organisation of the UN in the fight against the epidemic. From the beginning, WHO guided the policies shaped to combat the virus at the national level with its regular meetings and statements; however, it was widely criticised for being too slow and ineffective in the implementation of steps to combat the virus (Tüfekçi, 2020). For example, on January 22, 2020, WHO announced for the first time that the virus passed from person to person. On January 28, 2020, it declared the virus an international emergency. The coronavirus was declared a pandemic on March 11, 2020, after the virus had spread to more than 100 countries worldwide (WHO, 2020). At this point, one of the main criticisms directed at WHO was that its announcements regarding the virus were delayed, and therefore states ended up implementing late measures against the pandemic.

The US, the leading actor in the current global system at the level of states in terms of economic and military indicators, has been unable to take the reins in the fight against the coronavirus epidemic. The serious problems experienced in combating the pandemic's effects at the national level caused the US to focus more on the national fight against the virus. Because, as of May 2, 2019, the US had become the epicentre of the epidemic in terms of the number of people infected and killed by the epidemic (Center for Disease Control and Prevention, 2019). In this context, then US President Donald Trump became the leading actor in the information meetings on the fight against the virus (White House, 2020a). He went in front of the cameras almost every day and explained the fight of the US against the virus at the national level, but he still needed to create a framework that would lead the fight against the virus, apart from his criticisms of the WHO and China.

The debate about global leadership(lessness) has risen to the fore in the context of the fight against the coronavirus, including in the European Union (EU). The fact that a member decided to leave the bloc for the first time since its establishment has inspired discussions about the future of the EU. When the UK officially left the EU on February 1, 2020, the coronavirus epidemic was not yet on the main agenda of international relations. By March, when the pandemic's full impact was felt, the EU, as a supra-national actor, had difficulty producing a comprehensive and integrated response to the fight against the coronavirus with its member states. In other words, in March and April, the EU struggled to develop a systematic response even for its members, let alone adopt a leading role to design a global roadmap in the fight against the virus (European Union, 2020).

It is difficult to say that China, one of the actors with global leadership potential with its population and economic indicators, is also leading in the fight against the virus. Compared to other actors, China, which has a relatively closed structure to the outside, was a country credited with relative success in the first stage of the fight against the virus. China, which created a rapid medical equipment aid mechanism for countries struggling with the coronavirus, had provided aid to 82 states by March 20, 2020, and 120 states by April 4, 2020 (Ministry of Foreign Affairs of the People's Republic of China, 2020; Xinhua, 2020). The aid was accompanied by intense global public diplomacy. However, being the country where the virus first appeared and criticised for needing to be more timely in informing the WHO at the beginning of the fight against the virus (The Associated Press, 2020; Weissert, 2020) are obstacles to the initiatives undertaken by China to produce results on a global scale.

Renaissance in Security

The most important agenda brought forward by the coronavirus epidemic in the short term has been its impact on security. COVID-19 has been a profound turning point for the global system and an accelerator of transformation. This process has made it mandatory for states to reconsider and review security. Military, economic, social, and environmental security is already in question in the traditional security understanding; however, in the post-COVID-19 period, issues related to cybersecurity, biosecurity, borders, energy, information, health, intelligence, information, and food security have also deepened and expanded.

The military security sector will be one of the most affected sectors in the medium and long term. The sector has sub-headings such as defence expenditures, armament, defence industry, counter-terrorism, and border security. When considering defence expenditures, several factors will inevitably be taken into consideration, especially the economic effects of the coronavirus.

According to the International Monetary Fund (IMF) forecasts, the world economy was expected to shrink by 3% globally in 2020 (IMF, 2020) – and in fact, it shrank by 3.1%. The world economy was expected to grow by 3.6% and 2.6% in 2018 and 2019, respectively, and then shrank by 3% (The World Bank, 2022). This retraction inevitably affected the defence expenditures of states since economic capacity is essential in determining defence spending. However, in the context of the impact of the coronavirus on defence expenditures, considering the IMF's 3% shrinkage projection from an economic point of view, Table 2.1 lists data directly related to the relationship between economic growth and defence expenditures.

Considering the 2015–2019 economic growth, it is seen that the world economy has grown continuously at different rates compared to the previous year. It is seen that defence expenditures have increased in the ratio compared to the previous year. In this context, it should be noted that the last contraction in the world economy in the pre-coronavirus period was the 0.1% contraction in 2009 due to the economic

Table 2.1 Rate of Increase in Global Economic Growth and Defense Expenditures (2015–2022)

	2015	2016	2017	2018	2019	2020	2021	2022
Rate of change in global economic growth	3.5	3.4	3.9	3.6	2.9	–3.0	6	3.2
Rate of change in global defence spending	1.48	0.51	0.84	2.72	3.52	5.9	0.7	X

Source: IMF, Datamapper, Real GDP Growth (2020)

crisis that emerged in 2008. The reflection of this economic crisis and shrinkage in defence expenditures became apparent after 2010. While the increase in defence expenditures worldwide was 0.33% in 2011, there was a 0.88% decrease in 2012 compared to the previous year. The decline in defence expenditures worldwide continued in 2013 and 2014, with a decrease of 1.51% and 9.34%, respectively (IMF, Datamapper, Real GDP Growth, 2020).

Based on this data, it is seen that the changes in economic growth do not affect the defence expenditures of the states at a consistent rate. It can be said that the positive or negative changes in economic growth are reflected in the defence expenditures of the states after two years on average. The share that states allocated to defence expenditures in 2020 was planned and implemented in 2019 before the coronavirus epidemic started. Therefore, the negative impact of the coronavirus on the global economy should be expected to adversely affect global defence expenditures in 2021 and later. How long and at what rate this negative effect will last depends on the stage reached in the fight against the coronavirus and how soon and at what rate the global economy recovers.

The effect of the coronavirus on the field of armament and the general trend of armament in the post-coronavirus period will be varied regarding buyers and suppliers. There is an inevitable relationship between the rate of change in the defence expenditures of the states and the share they will allocate for armament in the post-coronavirus period. In this context, a consecutive decrease in defence expenditures will adversely affect the global armament volume. However, although there is often a direct ratio between defence expenditures and armament, it should be noted that the two will progress at different paces. This situation is not related to the coronavirus. The changes that occur at the global, regional, or national level can affect defence expenditures positively or negatively, but how this change influences armament is questioned in the medium term. Therefore, it should be expected that the effect of the coronavirus on armament will occur later than the effects seen in defence expenditures.

In terms of the overall trend of armaments, according to the Stockholm International Peace Research Institute (SIPRI), the volume of global arms transfers increased by 5.5% between 2014 and 2019 compared to the previous five years, and the volume of arms trade peaked in the post-Cold War period (Pieter et al., 2022). It is still being determined how long this upward trend will continue in the post-coronavirus period because the contraction in the global economy and how the post-coronavirus period will be shaped will affect the armament tendencies of states in the medium and long term.

When considered in terms of arms supplier countries, according to the SIPRI, the largest arms suppliers in the world between 2014 and 2019 were the US, Russia, France, Germany, and China. Considering the data in Table 2.2, the US and Russia differ significantly from the other three. Along with France, the market share ratio between Germany and China is similar, with only a 0.1% difference between Germany and China. In this context, the US and Russia will likely maintain their position even though the global arms trade volume has decreased. The ranking between France, Germany, and China may fluctuate.

Table 2.2 The World's Largest Weapons Suppliers (2017–2021)

	Country	Market share (percentage)
1.	US	39
2.	Russia	19
3.	France	11
4.	China	4.6
5.	Germany	4.5
	Total	78.1

Source: Pieter et al. (2022)

The post-coronavirus process will likely change the ranking among gun buyers. According to the SIPRI, India, Saudi Arabia, Egypt, Australia, and China, the five biggest buyers of the last five years, hosted 38% of world arms transfers (Pieter et al., 2022). The largest arms buyers in the last five years are also expected to change, as arms purchase volumes can fluctuate over five-year periods, sometimes even from year to year.

The post-coronavirus period will also affect the armament tendencies of countries that buy weapons or whose domestic defence industries cannot yet produce advanced weapon systems. The most robust trend expected to emerge in the medium term, if not the short term, will be the postponement of purchases of primary weapons systems that are not considered vital. Associated with this delay, they will turn to the modernisation of existing weapon systems, if possible.

Another trend will be investments in domestic defence industries as buyers aim to produce long-term results by creating an alternative weapon supply channel. The biggest problem is whether the buyer countries have the necessary financial support to support their defence industries. On the other hand, this problem can be partially overcome if the buyer countries find interim solutions by citing conditions such as joint production or technology transfer in arms purchases, as their bargaining share will increase in arms purchase agreements with the seller countries in the medium term.

On the other hand, the coronavirus pandemic has affected energy security in different ways. First of all, it should be noted that the developments regarding energy security, which were already present before the pandemic, started to show their effects more intensely during the pandemic. In other words, the coronavirus has a trigger/catalyst effect in many components of energy security, although it is not a cause of the crisis in itself. The impact of the coronavirus on energy security can be addressed in four dimensions: the energy market, producers, consumers, and energy competition. Of these, especially the first three dimensions are closely related to the economic effects of the coronavirus pandemic. The fourth dimension will show its effect on the strategic equation in the medium and long term.

When considering the energy market, the emergence of the pandemic and its global spread came at a time when energy prices worldwide had begun to decline. Considering the changes in oil prices, the oil price per barrel was above $63 in

2020 (Macrotrends, 2023). Oil prices remained relatively low compared to 2018 because of the disagreement between oil-producing countries about reducing production. At this point, although the disagreement was mainly between the three largest oil producers in the world, namely the US, Russia, and Saudi Arabia, it was a reflection of the tension between Russia and Saudi Arabia regarding production and OPEC and OPEC+ policies.

However, when the effects of the pandemic were excluded, it was predicted that oil prices would remain in the band of $65–67.5 between 2020 and 2025; in other words, there would be a slight increase in oil prices, according to the World Bank (World Bank, 2019). Therefore, in relation to the pandemic, there was an expectation of price stability, even though there were already relatively low oil prices.

The first impact of the coronavirus pandemic on oil prices was quite abrasive, shattering expectations. In the first quarter of 2020, the significant and rapid decline in global energy demand due to the pandemic and the unwillingness of large producers to reduce their production at the first stage created a twin shock effect in the oil markets. For this reason, in March, the average oil price fell below $33, with a loss of value of more than 50% compared to the same period of the previous year (U.S. Bureau of Labor Statistics, 2020). Even though OPEC+ countries, including Saudi Arabia and Russia, decided to reduce the oil supply, this decision did not affect the price increase due to the pandemic.

A similar situation will likely be seen in the natural gas market as well. As seen in Table 2.3, before the coronavirus effect started to emerge, natural gas prices, which were expected to increase steadily between 2020 and 2025, started to decrease after the coronavirus spread worldwide. In this context, natural gas prices are expected to remain below 2019 prices even in 2025.

Another security area highlighted by the coronavirus pandemic is information security. What is meant by "security of information" here differs from the "information security" concept in the literature. Security of information is discussed broadly, including cybersecurity, public diplomacy, hostile social manipulation, and post-truth, and virtual social conflicts. These cases, each of which is related to the other, have gained more importance with the coronavirus epidemic (Kwok et al., 2021: 107).

Table 2.3 World Bank Energy Price Forecasts

Energy type	Period	2020	2021	2022	2023	2024	2025
Oil (dollar/barrel)	Pre-coronavirus forecast April 23, 2019	65	65.5	66.0	66.5	67.0	67.5
	Post-coronavirus forecast April 23, 2020	35.0	42.0	44.5	47.0	49.8	52.7
Gas (dollar/MMBtu)	Pre-coronavirus forecast April 23, 2019	6.0	6.1	6.2	6.3	6.4	6.5
	Post-coronavirus forecast April 23, 2020	3.1	4.1	4.4	4.6	4.9	5.2

Source: World Bank (2019)

While information security or cybersecurity refers to securing or protecting information with its technical dimension, an important dimension that should not be ignored is the reality of information and the protection of this reality in an abstract dimension. In this context, the trend that has come to the fore is the manipulation of information in many areas. This is particularly true in social media. This trend has led to waves of disinformation in the lightning-quick flow of data sharing. This phenomenon, which can also be defined as the loss of truth, has also been used extensively in classical or conventional propaganda, manipulation, black propaganda, psychological warfare, and fifth-column activities. However, today, people are exposed to hostile social manipulation through several platforms, especially social media. In this process, which can also be associated with post-truth, the aim is to strengthen a strategy through the target country or social group by cultivating a loss of trust in institutions. This leads individuals to evaluate facts with prejudices and causes the loss of truth (Kwok et al., 2021: 107).

Re-Questioning the State (Authorisation, Democratisation, Fragile States)

The COVID-19 pandemic has had various effects on democracy and human rights worldwide. While some states took steps towards democratisation during the pandemic, others tended to become authoritarian. In some countries, public participation and views have played an essential role in managing the pandemic. These states have established various mechanisms to respond to the people's needs and distribute resources fairly. However, other states tended to become authoritarian during the pandemic. Some countries, using the pandemic process as an excuse, limited civil liberties, restricted the freedom of the press, and suppressed the voice of the opposition.

On the other hand, fragile states sought more security during the pandemic. The coronavirus pandemic has further strained fragile states' already weak health systems. These states have used security forces and military units to manage the pandemic effectively. In addition, some fragile states have implemented stricter policies towards immigrants and refugees by closing their borders (Cooper and Aitchison, 2020: 3).

Immigration and Xenophobia

The coronavirus pandemic has had a variety of effects on immigrants and foreigners. The already tricky conditions for immigrants and foreigners during the pandemic became even more difficult. In addition, the pandemic process has also caused increasing xenophobia towards immigrants and foreigners. As a matter of fact, during the pandemic process, many countries have closed their borders, restricting the mobility of immigrants and refugees. This situation has led to more difficult living conditions for migrants and refugees. In addition, many have experienced difficulties in accessing health services (Leung, et al., 2023).

On the other hand, various discriminatory policies have been implemented against immigrants and foreigners. Some countries have imposed restrictions on the rights of immigrants and foreigners or suspended citizenship applications, using the pandemic process as an excuse (Libal et al., 2021: 151). Also, in some countries, there has been an increase in xenophobia towards foreigners since the beginning of the COVID-19 pandemic.

Before COVID-19, border crossings or migration was related to social or national security. However, nowadays, migration is also caused by epidemic diseases. For this reason, it can be said that COVID-19 has led to an increase in xenophobia. However, the main features of being a great state include a large population and multiculturalism. Yet, in the post-COVID-19 process, states have implemented strict visa practices. The freedom of movement for those who adopted an anti-vaccine stance and remained unvaccinated was restricted when some states implemented a strict vaccination policy. Despite the foreign national being competent and talented, visas were not issued based on vaccine status. This situation led to an increase in xenophobia.

Zones of Conflict and Tension

The COVID-19 process has affected the situation in various areas of conflict and tension. In particular, people from communities in areas in crisis, who already live under challenging conditions and have weak health systems, have been more affected by the pandemic. In addition, the pandemic has adversely affected humanitarian activities in areas of conflict and tension (Esses and Hamilton, 2021: 255). Some humanitarian activities in these areas have been halted or restricted due to the pandemic (OECD Policy Responses to Coronavirus (COVID-19), 2020: 7). For example, humanitarian aid activities that helped millions of people in Syria were adversely affected. Due to the restrictions, many humanitarian organisations in Syria have had to limit their activities. Likewise, humanitarian aid activities have been limited in conflict zones such as Yemen, Afghanistan, and Myanmar.

However, the pandemic has also increased political instability in areas of conflict and tension. In particular, the pandemic has exacerbated political conflicts. The economic crises and limitations caused by the pandemic have increased social tensions in conflict zones and further deepened political instability. Again, using Syria as an example, health services have worsened due to the pandemic since the country's health services and infrastructure were already weak.

Conclusion

The COVID-19 pandemic has significantly impacted the global system, and much of this impact is long-term. The cooperation that took place to a certain extent in the pre-COVID-19 period has become more fragile during the pandemic. Therefore, after COVID-19, states easily deviated from cooperation. With the transformation of the global system, the search for new security is focused on acting more individually rather than collectively. The developments in the new period will likely harm national interests. Therefore, while it was possible to act more altruistically in the pre-COVID-19 period, states are now less willing to sacrifice their interests and act more selfishly.

On the other hand, it is seen that the public has influenced their states in the transformation of the global system. First, citizens have criticised the health policies of anti-vaccine people in the community, regardless of their political views. This situation has challenged the implementation of health and safety policies. Secondly, economic problems have arisen due to the pandemic's effect on people's socialisation and politics. For example, in states experiencing economic problems, social support was the first issue. However, when the standard order was restored, inflation occurred. At the same time, energy prices have risen, and supply chains have deteriorated, increasing the cost of living. The inflationary pressures that emerged due to this situation led to social unrest and increased pressure on governments.

Based on these processes, states have tended to seek individual solutions. Therefore, states are now trying to be more individual and careful with the transformation of the global system. The geopolitical power struggle that emerged after the pandemic spread caused some states to act more assertively. However, assertive states may also cooperate in different fields with the actors with whom they have tension or competition. This situation also reveals fragmented collaborations in the transforming structure of the global system.

The absence of red lines in the international system after COVID-19 also makes it possible for actors with different interests to cooperate with varying intensities on several agendas. In this context, it is possible for states that are aware of the systemic transformation to continue their search for security by following individual policies, regardless of the past and the alliances they are in. The dynamic and multi-layered relations, far from the stagnation experienced in the global system, make fragmented cooperation and variable alliances inevitable in the transforming system. The current militaries have not increased their economic capacity, are reluctant to take the initiative in solving regional and global problems, cannot react to the threats that are created or intended to be created, cannot adapt quickly to changing situations, cannot produce policies for different files and agendas in the same process, and cannot show determination in the steps to be taken. Actors who are too isolated will face difficulties when confronted with challenges.

References

Center for Disease Control and Prevention, Coronavirus Disease. 2019. "Cases in the US" [Online]. Available at: https://www.cdc.gov/coronavirus/2019-ncov/index.html (Accessed: February 5, 2023).

Cooper, L., & Aitchison, G. 2020. "The Dangers Ahead: Covid-19, Authoritarianism and Democracy", LSE Conflict and Civil Society Research Unit. Available at: http://eprints.lse.ac.uk/105103/4/dangers_ahead.pdf

Esses, V. M., & Hamilton, L. K. 2021. "Xenophobia and Anti-Immigrant Attitudes in the Time of COVID-19", *Group Processes & Intergroup Relations*, 24 (2), pp. 253–259.

European Union. 2020. "The Common EU Response to COVID-19" [Online]. Available at: https://europa.eu/european-union/coronavirus-response_en (Accessed: February 5, 2023).

IMF, Datamapper, Real GDP Growth, 2020; SIPRI, Military Expenditure Database International Monetary Fund, World Economic Outlook, pp. ix–x.

Kwok, H., Singh, P., & Heimans, S. 2021. "The Regime of 'Post-Truth': COVID-19 and the Politics of Knowledge", *Discourse: Studies in the Cultural Politics of Education*, 44 (1), pp. 106–120.

Leung, D., Lee, C., Wang, A. H., & Guruge, S. 2023. "Immigrants' and Refugees' Experiences of Access to Health and Social Services during the COVID-19 Pandemic in Toronto, Canada", *Journal of Health Services Research & Policy*, 1, pp. 34–41.

Libal, K., Harding, S., & Popescu, M. et al. 2021. "Human Rights of Forced Migrants During the COVID-19 Pandemic: An Opportunity for Mobilization and Solidarity", *Journal of Human Rights and Social Work*, 6, pp. 148–160.

Macrotrends. 2023. "Brent Crude Oil Prices". Available at: https://www.macrotrends.net/1369/crude-oil-price-history-chart

Ministry of Foreign Affairs of the People's Republic of China. 2020. "China Has Announced Assistance to 82 Countries, WHO and African Union to Fight COVID-19" [Online]. Available at: https://www.fmprc.gov.cn/mfa_eng/topics_665678/kjgzbdfyyq/t1759145.shtml (Accessed: February 5, 2023).

OECD Policy Responses to Coronavirus (COVID-19). 2020. "What is the Impact of the COVID-19 Pandemic on Immigrants and their Children?" Available at: https://www.oecd.org/coronavirus/policy-responses/what-is-the-impact-of-the-covid-19-pandemic-on-immigrants-and-their-children-e7cbb7de/

Pieter D. W., Kuimova A., & Wezeman S. T. 2022. *Fact Sheet: Trends in International Arms Transfer*. SIPRI.

The Associated Press. 2020. "China Didn't Warn Public of Likely Pandemic for 6 Key Days" [Online]. Available at: https://apnews.com/68a9e1b91de4ffc166acd6012d82c2f9 (Accessed: February 7, 2023).

The World Bank. 2022. "GDP Growth (Annual %)" [Online]. Available at: https://data.worldbank.org/indicator/NY.GDP.MKTP.KD.ZG (Accessed: July 18, 2022).

TÜBA. 2020. "Covid-19 Pandemi Değerlendirme Raporu, Ankara" [Online]. Available at: http://www.tuba.gov.tr/files/images/2020/kovidraporu/Covid-19%20Raporu-Final±.pdf (Accessed: February 6, 2023).

Tüfekçi, Z. 2020. "The WHO Shouldn't Be a Plaything for Great Powers", The Atlantic [Online]. Available at: https://www.theatlantic.com/health/archive/2020/04/why-world-health-organization-failed/610063/ (Accessed: February 10, 2023).

U.S. Bureau of Labor Statistics. 2020. "From the Barrel to the Pump: The Impact of the COVID-19 Pandemic on Prices for Petroleum Products" [Online]. Available at: https://www.bls.gov/opub/mlr/2020/article/from-the-barrel-to-the-pump.htm (Accessed: July 19, 2022).

United Nations. 2020a. "VTCs of the Security Council Members and Outcomes During the COVID-19 Pandemic" [Online]. Available at: https://www.un.org/securitycouncil/content/meetings-2020-vtc (Accessed: July 19, 2022).

United Nations General Assembly. 2020. "Resolution Adopted by the General Assembly on 2 April 2020", A/RES/74/270 [Online]. Available at: https://documents-dds-ny.un.org/doc/UNDOC/GEN/N20/087/28/PDF/N2008728.pdf?OpenElement (Accessed: July 19, 2022).

United Nations Security Council. 2020. "S/RES/2532" [Online]. Available at: https://documents-dds-ny.un.org/doc/UNDOC/LTD/N20/169/84/PDF/N2016984.pdf?OpenElement (Accessed: July 14, 2022).

Weissert, W. 2020. "DHS Report: China Hid Virus' Severity to Hoard Supplies" [Online]. Available at: https://apnews.com/bf685dcf52125be54e030834ab7062a8 (Accessed: February 5, 2023).

White House. 2020a. "President Donald J. Trump Is Demanding Accountability from the World Health Organization" [Online]. Available at: https://www.whitehouse.gov/briefings-statements/president-donald-j-trump-demanding-accountability-world-health-organization/ (Accessed: February 10, 2023).

White House. 2020b. "Remarks by President Trump in Press Briefing" [Online]. Available at: https://www.whitehouse.gov/briefings-statements/remarks-president-trump-press-briefing/ (Accessed: July 19, 2022).

WHO. 2020. "WHO Director-General's Opening Remarks at the Media Briefing on COVID-19" [Online]. Available at: https://www.who.int/dg/speeches/detail/who-director-general-s-opening-remarks-at-the-media-briefing-on-covid-19—11-march-2020 (Accessed: February 20, 2023).

World Bank. 2019. "Commodities Price Forecast" [Online]. Available at: http://pubdocs.worldbank.org/en/598821555973008624/CMO-April-2019-Forecasts.pdf (Accessed: July 24, 2022).

Xinhua. 2020. "China's COVID-19 Aid is Humanitarian, Not Geopolitical" [Online]. Available at: http://www.xinhuanet.com/english/2020-04/04/c_138947125.htm (Accessed: February 5, 2023).

Yürük, B. (2020). "UN Adopts Resolution of Global Solidarity on COVID-19" [Online]. Available at: https://www.aa.com.tr/en/latest-on-coronavirus-outbreak/un-adopts-resolution-of-global-solidarity-on-covid-19/1790464 (Accessed: February 1, 2023).

3 Far-Right Movements in the COVID-19 Era

Dolapo Fakuade

Introduction

Far-right, radical right, extreme right, and right-wing, to name a few, are terms often used interchangeably to explain groups that demonstrate passionate views and advocate that the "people and the state are one." Such passionate views in themselves may not constitute a crime and may be viewed as an expression of one's right; it is the associated actions and elements of the accompanying rhetorics that may generate concerns among rival or target groups. Within the far-right ideology, unison between the state and people is historically associated with nationalism, patriotism, and commitment to one's country. When viewed from nationalism and patriotism dimensions, an overt display or demonstration of one's affiliations, nationalism, or patriotism can be difficult to police and fault, especially in the COVID-19 era. However, an overt display of nationalism accompanied by violence and hate directed at different groups cannot be mistaken and is then viewed as extreme. The realm of extreme ideological display also further reflects radicalisation, hence the link between far-right ideology and radicalisation as reflected in different studies. The far-right movement can be traced to the phenomenon of radicalisation, which dates back to the 1960s (Kundnani, 2012) and perhaps beyond when analysed from the explanation and models of radicalisation. Radicalisation is considered the process by which an individual is socialised into an extremist ideology over a period of time that can then manifest itself in different forms of terrorism (Muro, 2016). According to Malthaner (2017), radicalisation has become a prevalent analytical paradigm applied to interpret and explain violent phenomena.

The premise that associates radicalisation with violence is also supported by authors like Maskaliūnaitė (2015). Theories of radicalisation as highlighted by Maskaliūnaitė (2015) consider radicalisation as "a process by which a person adopts belief systems to justify the use of violence in order to achieve social change, as well as process by which a person actively supports the use of violent means for political purposes" (2015: 1). An explanation or view such as this presents radicalisation as a process through which a person may willingly engage in due to interest in the belief systems, while the use and support of violence to achieve social and political change may be subjective. While the theoretical view of radicalisation may appear teleological, the support and use of violence also seem

DOI: 10.4324/9781003377597-4

inevitable if and when the sociological process is completed. Further deductions are that social change and political agenda are two fundamental drivers of radicalisation, which are common realm for violence when such agendas are frustrated by governmental systems or the public. Therefore, from this theoretical perspective, it can be deduced that violence cannot be divorced from any form of radicalisation that may account for the increasing violent rhetoric and acts that go with different forms of radicalisation. A well-known example is the September 11, 2001 attack on the United States (US). While the focus on the phenomenon of radicalisation gained momentum after the September 11 attack, it was unfortunately narrowed to Islamic radicalisation rather than all forms of radicalisation. Though other forms of radicalisation such as the far-right were gaining momentum and movements in Europe and US, they were mostly excused as nationalist sentiments and underrated until the start and during the COVID-19 era. This chapter critically evaluates the trends and groups targeted by the far-right, and the implications for EU security. The EU strategy for combating radicalisation and recruitment is further examined to identify its limitation in preventing the continued socialisation of the far-right movement and the extreme violence that appears to have been triggered by the widespread impact of COVID-19. To what extent can the application of EU strategy prevent and restrict the impact of the far-right movement? In light of evolving trends, the phenomena that drive cultural, ethnic, and racial nationalism appear to be linked to the demand for fundamental human rights, which may perhaps continue to fuel the far-right movements – especially in Europe and the West.

Far-Right Movement and Intended Goal

Radicalisation is a multi-level process, as suggested by the pyramid model (Muro, 2016). It is a process that commences with an individual who gradually engages other individuals or groups with similar views who then subsequently achieve the goal of their shared ideology. This explanation can be seen in the way far-right activities and violence perpetuated in years leading to the global pandemic outbreak. Individuals are at the centre of this socialisation process but what occurs in the socio-political environment and surrounding organisations also matters. For example, the mode of operation within the far-right family tree used by Bjørgo and Ravndal (2019) to conceptualise the far-right movements shows the interactions, interconnectedness, and overlap between the ideology of the radical and extreme right. In their explanations, they presented the far-right, which supports the fundamental principle that the "people and state is one; foreigners threaten this community," as the core of both radical right and extreme right actions. Some may view the radical right advocates for democracy to be maintained and that liberal elites should be replaced (Bjørgo & Ravndal, 2019), and that the outcome of such is not much different from the extreme right, which uses violence to achieve the goal of the far-right ideology (Ravndal & Bjørgo, 2018). What differentiates the extreme right from the radical right is that the radical right adopts democracy to achieve its goal while the extreme right adopts violence and promotes it (Ravndal et al., 2020). Overall, the goal of both radical and extreme is cultural nationalism, ethnic nationalism, and racial nationalism. Muslims are targeted based on the belief that the Muslim culture is backward as well as repressive; therefore Muslims must assimilate into Western culture or return to their homeland (Bjørgo & Ravndal, 2019). It strongly advocates against Muslim immigration and Islamisation and that the Western culture must be protected against the Muslim culture. Such a strong belief system driven by cultural nationalism overlaps with ethnic nationalism in the far-right family tree. This overlap makes it challenging to identify extreme right rhetoric and differentiate it from patriotism (Botsch, 2022). This is a continued challenge for law enforcement and security entities in Europe, which remains exploited by the far-right movements and perhaps other radicalised groups.

The ideology that drives the ethnic nationalists is that people of different ethnic backgrounds should not mix, and in order for this to be possible, people from different ethnicities should return to their homelands (Baele et al., 2020). The overall goal of the ethnic nationalists is to emphasise and promote the fundamental right of white Europeans and Americans and to defend their nations from foreign people and/or cultures. Similarly, racial nationalism passionately advocates that the white race is superior and that racial mixing threatens the survival of the white race (Ravndal, 2020). It is therefore pertinent to overthrow the Jews and their dominance, while inferior races and other racial enemies must be deported, subjugated, or exterminated. When understood from these dimensions, it is seen how the adherents to racial nationalism such as neo-Nazis are the prominent drivers of terrorism in the US (Auger, 2020). Despite the patterns, rhetorics, and activities reflecting racial nationalism in the US, for example, the movements and their associated violent acts remain unregulated due to the First Amendment which protects freedom of speech, and the right to petition the government for grievances redress even when violence might seem imminent from such speeches. With the Second Amendment providing US citizens the right to carry arms, it is easy to see the association between hate speech and extreme violence in the country.

Based on the conceptualisation of the far-right ideological movements provided by Bjørgo and Ravndal in 2019, it can be inferred that the targets of any far-right strand movement will be Muslims and religious minorities, Jews, and non-white Europeans and Americans. The call for deportation or extermination of Muslims, people of different origins, Jews, and those from "inferior" races by cultural, ethnic, and racial nationalists also suggests that Muslim foreigners, Jews, and other non-white European and Americans are the potential target of far-right movements. The extreme right advocates for the replacement of democracy and that violence against enemies of the people is legitimate (Ravndal & Bjørgo, 2018). It further suggests that left-wing political views and institutions that tolerate, protect, and support Muslims, religious minorities, and non-white Europeans and Americans might also be targets of far-right movements. These deductions were further reinforced far-right activities leading to, and in some capacity during the COVID-19 era.

Far-Right Movement in COVID-19 Era

As the world grapples with COVID-19, beyond the economic impact, the social impact of the pandemic is acknowledged by experts as one that will be deep and long-lasting (Silke, 2020). The COVID-19 era appears to have provided an enabling environment and opportunity to mobilise, recruit, and echo more hate rhetoric. Pre-COVID-19 era, the far-right movement has always been characterised by two distinct periods: mobilisation and violence. Authors have mostly focused on the period when violent acts are carried out as these are evident to all. However, further in-depth analysis of different reports since the 1990s indicates that far-right movements follow a pattern of mobilisation which is followed by acts of terror, or violence used to mobilise and recruit more adherents. To sustain this pattern, the extreme right forges transnational links by connecting online, building organisational ties, conducting joint combat trainings (Asov Battalion), and convening at conferences and concerts across Europe and the US (Bjørgo & Ravndal, 2019). COVID-19, however, offered an unprecedented opportunity for the world to unify anger due to the restrictions and situation brought about by the global pandemic. The pandemic created a new source of anger and continued frustration for many. The lockdown required due to COVID-19 impact resulted in economic marginalisation, limited resources, and created health concerns that inspired COVID-19 public protests (Curley et al., 2022). Such protests around the world were also used to mobilise, recruit, and radicalise more people into the ideology. When viewed from this dimension, especially in terms of far-right mobilisation, COVID-19 may be considered to have a game-changing role in driving the global mobilisation and recruitment for far-right ideology particularly through the use of the online platform. Evidence of this emerged as a significant concern from March 2020 onwards.

The far-right ideology gained momentum with sporadic hate crime, extreme violence, and terrorism aimed at ethnic and religious minorities, as well as political opponents and state institutions in US and Europe. A conceptual review of data, publications, and reports on far-right movements during this period suggests trends of overlapping activities or interaction between hate crime and extreme violence, with more people sharing such views. As identified by Al-Jarf (2021), the spread of the pandemic across the world was seen to be associated with hate and racist speech on social media. While this may not be a new period to Covid, the frustration caused by COVID encouraged more people to share hate and racist views on social media, especially those that encourage violence in different places (Al-Jarf, 2021). COVID-19 also directly increased affective polarisation and political intolerance which are associated with extreme right ideology. Given that people were confined to their homes, and resulted in using the internet and more social platforms, different studies reveal that the far-right movements blossomed more than ever during the pandemic. COVID-19 led to the creation of a new protest movement on digital platforms aimed against government lockdowns, related measures, and mandatory vaccines (Schmid et al., 2023). COVID-19 may be seen as a game-changer in the era of the far-right historical movements when viewed in terms of level, pace, and rapid mobilisation of adherents to the movement's ideological extreme views shared by several people who would have otherwise been neutral should the pandemic not occur. The pandemic is also acknowledged to have accelerated the rise of nationalist views in the global politics (Mkonza, 2020). In a political sense, other studies found that COVID-19 provided stronger justification for the far-right to promote their ideology and was more readily embraced as a stronger conspiratorial belief, more relatable than other forms of conspiracies. As such, findings by Galais and Guinjoan (2023) suggest that the pandemic rouse a new form of niche that might become attractive to emerging far-right parties.

Many of the far-right activities during and in the immediate aftermath of COVID-19 appear driven by the mission to deliver ethnic and racial national outcomes going beyond mere passionate advocacy for ethnic and national identity. The blurry line between passionate nationalism and overt display of nationalism accompanied by violence is perhaps one of the factors that make it challenging to address far-right extremism within educational institutions, especially in the UK (Lakhani & James, 2021). While evidence shows a direct link between the pandemic and trends in violent acts across the world in the immediate and medium term of the pandemic (Silke, 2020), the number of incidents remains minimal to generalise to the extent to trigger a significant policy change in Europe. Historically, the actions and rhetoric of the far-right had been a rigid dichotomy between passionate advocacy for cultural, ethnic, and racial national identity and those who emphasise the need to promote and deliver on such outcomes. Such dichotomy is now being challenged and revisited, as the COVID-19 era appears to have normalised or tends to be more accommodating of hate rhetorics, hate crime, extreme violence, and terrorism aimed at ethnic and religious minorities. Data further shows that political opponents and state institutions are also targeted due to grievances towards the government and government institutions following online rhetorics and mobilisation.

In the 2021 *Right-Wing Terrorism and Violence* (RTV) report by Ravndal et al., it was indicated that 68% of attacks carried by the far-right in Western Europe targeted ethnic and religious minorities. The report also revealed that, based on demographic information, half of the 68% of attacks were on immigrants, asylum seekers or refugees, and foreigners. When compared to the 2020 report, which reflected on trends of attacks in 2019 (pre-COVID-19), the report by Ravndal et al. (2020) indicated that ethnic, religious, political opponents, state institutions, sexual minorities, and vulnerable groups were the majority of those targeted for attacks. The swift to the core target groups, namely immigrants, asylum seekers or refugees, and foreigners, shows the correlation between COVID-19's impact and far-right movements' ideological mobilisation motivated by the pandemic. While the lockdown and pandemic rules may have led to frustration and hostility directed at minority groups, such attacks on these groups nonetheless highlight the association between far-right movements and COVID-19 associated restrictions.

As explained by Silke (2020), lockdown measures encouraged terrorists to mobilise online, having a more far-reaching audience since people were restricted to their homes. Such online mobilisation aimed to incite violence, driven by conspiracy theories relating to COVID-19, many of which can be traced back to far-right extremism. For example, there were claims that 5G masts were aiding the transmission of COVID-19 and a UK-based anti-5G Facebook group posted rhetoric that combined far-right, anti-government, and antisemitic conspiracies asking for readers to take action (Silke, 2020). Though without substantial evidence, such rhetoric and call for action led to the vandalisation of more than 40 telecommunication masts in the UK (Silke, 2020). This evidence shows a direct link between far-right affiliations and movements to remain true to the core objectives of ethnic and racial nationalism. In the reports by Ravndal et al. (2021) and Silke (2020), the direct correlation between far-right movements and target groups reflects the continued operation of the movement to mobilise and perpetuate violence on people and institutions they consider "enemies of the state."

Though the lockdown measures were mitigating measures taken to minimise the pandemic impacts, they provided an opportunity for further online interactions among far-right adherents. As the lockdown measures persisted, so rose the level of far-right engagement and activities online, rising to 21% more than pre-lockdown levels after 10 days of lockdown (Silke, 2020). Such opportunity presented by the "stay-home" orders enforced around the world fostered an increase in online extremist activities, which further raised the risk of increasing short-term radicalisation in the medium term, especially influenced by the sustained COVID-19 measures by governments around the world. Evidence of this is seen in the 2021 RTV report by Ravndal et al. (2021) which supports the premise that the pandemic was a driver of far-right mobilisation, thereby advancing its ideology. This makes the pandemic an important turning point for the far-right movements to utilise the online platform, gain more momentum, and recruit adherents to their cause. A unique situation proffered by the pandemic and its associated restrictions encouraged more people to consider COVID-19-specific conspiracies driven by the far-right movements.

In the 2021 report, it was indicated that most of the RTV attacks were carried out in Germany (53), the UK (25), Greece (17), and Italy (17). Though not alarming numbers in themselves, the continuous and widespread attacks carried out in Western Europe in 2020, 2021, and 2022 reflect a well organised socialisation process or pathway to terrorise the target groups. The 2022 RTV report by Ravndal et al. (2022) indicated that there were 131 RTV attacks in Western Europe in 2021, of which 106 were spontaneous while 25 were premeditated. Having more spontaneous attacks than premeditated ones provides insight into a pattern to continue and that more people are being socialised into the ideology to perpetrate violence on people who resemble the target groups. In terms of fatality, most were carried out in Germany, with the UK next with 25 fatal attacks and Italy in third place with 23 attacks. Of the 131 attacks, 74% targeted ethnic and religious minorities, 18% targeted political opponents, most of which were left-wing and anti-fascist activists, 3% of the attacks targeted marginalised groups, most of which were sexual minorities, and 3% targeted other groups, including COVID-19-related target groups. Two per cent of the attacks targeted state institutions, particularly police officers (Ravndal et al., 2022: ii). Therefore, the influence (direct or indirect) of COVID-19 on far-right mobilisation and violence became more apparent and of concern from March 2020 to the present. The data and evidence suggest that the far-right movement rapidly gained momentum as the capitalised on COVID-19's widespread impact as well as the distraction of governments and law enforcement which would have otherwise not been possible should the pandemic had not occurred.

As reported in the UK, Italy, and Ireland, there were people thought to be Chinese who were attacked because the pandemic originated from China (Ravndal et al., 2021). Such direct evidence makes it difficult to ignore the continued movements of the far-right to achieve the ethnic and racial nationalism agenda of the far-right family. The means (radical or extreme) through which such an agenda is achieved remains relatively insignificant as the most important is to achieve the overall agenda of the far-right movement. In the absence of overwhelming evidence to justify the need for policy action, it is important not to ignore the link between COVID-19 as a causal factor because of the nurtured pattern of the far-right movements to utilise disruptive events to promote and achieve their agenda. Despite the low number of COVID-19-related attacks, the evidence of online mobilisation and hate rhetorics still indicates direct links between the pandemic and the far-right movements.

The evidence presented in this section from the COVID-19 era shows that the target groups of far-right movements during this period remain consistent. It is equally important to understand that the far-right in whatever form would not deviate from achieving its overall goal of racial and ethnic nationalists from the extreme right strand of the far-right family tree. Reports reviewed showed that perpetrators intended to and did cause harm to people who were perceived as ethnic or religious minorities, particularly foreigners, immigrants, and Muslims. Evidence from data sets gathered from 2020 March revealed that though COVID-19-related attacks associated with and carried out by those linked to far-right movements were minimal, the extent of online mobilisation and recruitment into the ideology is significant. Such mobilisation drive and consistency from the far-right suggest that future pandemics or emergencies might be leveraged by the movement to recruit and instigate hate and violence. A knowledge of this pattern as well as its implications for public security is important for law enforcement agencies and public safety organisations.

Implications of Far-Right Movements for Public Security

Knowing that the far-right family tree consists of those who would use democracy as a tool and those who aim to destroy is important for explaining the actions of the far-right ideology. An explanation of their fundamental goal or objective as explained in this chapter indicates that the target groups would not change no matter the situation in society. Such consistent patterns call for better measures and approaches to policing and to safeguard the target groups who also have a right to safety in the same environment in which far-right movements transpire their activities. Safeguarding the target groups as well as securing the public against some of the extreme violence that may be perpetrated by those socialised into far-right ideologies is important. The pattern and trends that were highlighted in the COVID-19 era as examined in this chapter have implications for policy and practice.

First, there is an implication for EU security policy and counter-terrorism strategies, which are based on four main pillars, namely prevent, protect, pursue, and respond. The EU security and counter-terrorism strategy acknowledges the importance of cooperation with third countries and international institutions. It does not accommodate the dynamic environment in which the three strands of the far-right family movements. For instance, the whole phenomenon of radicalisation is embedded within the "prevent" strategy pillar, which requires that radicalisation and recruitment must be combated. Did the governments in Europe and the US combat radicalisation, which is a socialisation process and its associated violence, during the COVID-19 era? The evidence provided in this chapter suggests otherwise. If anything, the attacks witnessed around the world, especially in Europe and the US, indicate that the governments in the West and security resources were severally stretched (Silke, 2020). A status that indicates a lack of preparedness, or limitation of the prevention strategy and the EU security policy.

Based on this, the ability of governments and intelligence and law enforcement agencies to focus on traditional priorities has been undermined and appears to have continued in the same trajectory since then. This practice's implication for intelligence, security, and police agencies is that it exposes lapses in the system as well as shows the inability of existing law enforcement agencies and their practices in the aforementioned places to deliver the security policy and counter-terrorism strategy against far-right radicalisation and movements. Though offenders were apprehended, the existing prevention strategy did not effectively hinder the evolving trends nor combat radicalisation and recruitment for terrorism. Since the preventative strategy failed, the protection strategy also failed to protect citizens and infrastructure that were attacked. Likewise, there was no reduction in vulnerability amid attacks on ethnic minorities and infrastructure. It appears that for far-right radicalisation, the existing strategy framework was insufficient to mitigate and prevent the movements set in motion by the far-right family. Therefore, the far-right movement in the COVID-19 era exposed the need to improve both policy and practice for countering radicalisation and its antecedent acts of terrorism.

Conclusion

This chapter has shown that there is a link between far-right movements, especially the mobilisation dimension of the movement, and the COVID-19 pandemic. Trends of attacks carried out by the far-right in Germany, the UK, and Italy over the two years of the pandemic provide evidence that should not be ignored. Though minimal, events during this period reflect the extent of online mobilisation that occurred during the pandemic and a glimpse of what is to come in terms of actual violence and extremism. The correlation between far-right movements and their intention to capitalise on emergency or disaster situations ought to be a warning for future planning and policy formulation to ensure that actions of the far-right are better managed to ensure the safety of the target groups and overall public who may be in the line of danger when acts of violence and terror are carried out by those who embraced the ideology. From time immemorial, the actions and rhetoric of the far-right had been a rigid dichotomy between passionate advocacy for cultural, ethnic, and racial national identity and those who emphasise the need to mobilise and deliver on such outcomes. It is now important to revisit this dichotomy through a public safety and security lens due to the increasing mobilisation and recruitment. Given the multiplicity of causes at play, it is not possible to identify a single causal mechanism or "terrorist mindset." It is therefore pertinent to consider a comprehensive strategy to counter radicalisation by taking into account the individual, organisational, and societal levels that may be affected in the COVID-19 era as shown in reports and evidence evaluated in this chapter.

References

Al-Jarf, Reima. "Combating the Covid-19 hate and racism speech on social media." *Technium Social Sciences Journal* 18 (2021): 660.

Auger, Vincent A. "Right-wing terror." *Perspectives on Terrorism* 14, no. 3 (2020): 87–97.

Baele, Stephane J, Lewys Brace, and Travis G Coan. "Uncovering the far-right online ecosystem: An analytical framework and research agenda." *Studies in Conflict & Terrorism* (2020): 1–21. https://doi.org/10.1080/1057610X.2020.1862895

Bjørgo, Tore, and Jacob Aasland Ravndal. *Extreme-right violence and terrorism: Concepts, patterns, and responses*. International Centre for Counter-Terrorism, 2019.

Botsch, Gideon. "Identifying extreme-right terrorism." *A transnational history of right-wing terrorism: Political violence and the far right in Eastern and Western Europe since 1900*. 2022.

Curley, Cliona, Eugenia Siapera, and Joe Carthy. "Covid-19 protesters and the far right on telegram: Co-conspirators or accidental bedfellows?" *Social Media + Society* 8, no. 4 (2022): 20563051221129187.

Galais, Carol, and Marc Guinjoan. "The ideological slant of COVID-19-related conspiracies. A new niche for the far-right?" *Representation* 59, no. 2 (2023): 347–356.

Kundnani, Arun. "Radicalisation: The journey of a concept." *Race & Class* 54, no. 2 (2012): 3–25.

Lakhani, Suraj, and Natalie James. "'Prevent duty': Empirical reflections on the challenges of addressing far-right extremism within secondary schools and colleges in the UK." *Critical Studies on Terrorism* 14, no. 1 (2021): 67–89.

Malthaner, Stefan. "Radicalization: The evolution of an analytical paradigm." *European Journal of Sociology/Archives Européennes de Sociologie* 58, no. 3 (2017): 369–401.

Maskaliūnaitė, Asta. "Exploring the theories of radicalization." *International Studies: Interdisciplinary Political and Cultural Journal (IS)* 17, no. 1 (2015): 9–26.

Mkonza, Kagiso. "The Impact of COVID-19 and the rise of Nationalism in Global Politics." Institute for Global Dialogue, 2020. https://www.igd.org.za/publications/zoonotica/12120-the-impact-of-covid-19-and-the-rise-of-nationalism-in-global-politics (accessed November 4, 2020).

Muro, Diego. "What does radicalisation look like? Four visualisations of socialisation into violent extremism." *Notes internacionals CIDOB* 163 (2016): 1–5.

Ravndal, Jacob Aasland, and Tore Bjørgo. "Investigating terrorism from the extreme right: A review of past and present research." *Perspectives on Terrorism* 12, no. 6 (2018): 5–22.

Ravndal, Jacob Aasland. "The emergence of transnational Street militancy: A comparative case study of the Nordic Resistance Movement and Generation Identity." *Journal for Deradicalization* 25 (2020): 1–34.

Ravndal, Jacob Aasland, Charlotte Tandberg, Anders Ravik Jupskås, and Madeleine Thorstensen. "RTV Trend Report 2022." C-REX Research Report. Oslo: C-REX-Center for Research on Extremism/University of Oslo, 2022.

Ravndal, Jacob Aasland, Madeleine Thorstensen, Anders Ravik Jupskås, and Graham Macklin. "RTV Trend Report 2021." C-REX Research Report. Oslo: C-REX-Center for Research on Extremism/University of Oslo, 2021.

Ravndal, Jacob Aasland, Sofia Lygren, Anders Ravik Jupskås, and Tore Bjørgo. "RTV Trend Report 2020." C-REX Research Report. Oslo: C-REX-Center for Research on Extremism/University of Oslo, 2020, pp. 6–7.

Schmid, Fabiana, Oliver Treib, and Franziska Eckardt. "The virus of polarization: Online debates about Covid-19 in Germany." *Political Research Exchange* 5, no. 1 (2023): 2150087.

Silke, Andrew. *COVID-19 and terrorism: Assessing the short-and long-term impacts*. Pool Re and Cranfield University, 2020.

4 Virtual Diplomacy as a New Frontier of International Dialogue

Alessia Chiriatti

Introduction

The concept of the border in the post-global world has been able to produce a fruitful debate, both public and academic. So much so that it has given rise to a field of study that cuts in a sagittal path across the entire sphere of knowledge and ranges from political science, geography, economics, law, theology, and urban planning. The boundary has become a diriment point on the political agenda in a global arena characterised by the profound crisis of the Westphalian image, the grain of which still structures our world. As a result, the immateriality of the formerly rigid, immovable, and non-transferable boundary and the irrelevance of space have come to the fore. In the last decades, the emergence of information and communication technologies (ICTs) has greatly accelerated this process. In contrast, the topography of globalisation has encountered various expressions that would prefer a world without borders. Yet, humanity, on the one hand, continues to put up walls and, on the other, espouse tools, such as technology, that precisely define a zone in which, between inside and outside, and between order and disorder, continuity and contact prevail. When we speak of technology, we refer to it by thinking of a frontier (thus the technological frontier), not a border, from the Latin *finis*, but a *limes*, transversal and oblique.

During the last decades, the use of technology in the political and modern governments also profoundly changed the role and practices of diplomacy, undergoing further acceleration. With the outbreak of the COVID-19 pandemic, the use of technology in several realms (such as in economy, foreign policy, and diplomacy) has represented an innovative and useful element that has helped governments and private stakeholders to encompass the critical conjuncture that the pandemic brought on the national and international scene. With the COVID-19 pandemic, in fact, online meetings became a necessity for many organisations to continue their business and no more as a poor substitute for face-to-face events. This fact changed the cultural approach and the perception of technology.

This chapter aims to understand the internet's impact on diplomacy and how technological innovations transform negotiation practices. The proposed topic will be addressed by focusing on some issues: lack of scientific literature, terminology that agrees on the level of readings and analysis, and contingency of some

DOI: 10.4324/9781003377597-5

phenomena (as in the case of the coronavirus pandemic). To do so, the text will analyse the different meanings of diplomacy that have emerged over the last 30 years (primarily those of digital diplomacy and eDiplomacy), highlighting differences and concrete applications. The impact of technology will be investigated through a progressive and historical digression. Finally, a substantial case will be discussed, with particular attention to the work of the United Nations General Assembly in which international diplomacy has encountered technology and the latter has modified practices and negotiations.

The Twilight Zone: New Definitions for Contemporary Diplomacy

This study encapsulates within it several problematic issues: lack of scientific literature, terminology that agrees on the level of readings and analysis, and the contingency of some phenomena. The present analysis, however, is intended not only to comment on a relatively recent past, as the discussion on the coronavirus pandemic might suggest, but also to attempt to analyse the evolution in the dynamics of negotiation techniques and mechanisms over the past decades, with particular attention to the phases following the advent of the internet, including following the use of technology as a tool to conduct it and the factors that have accelerated these processes.

There is not yet a structured literature on virtual diplomacy. Many texts related to the connection between technology and diplomacy can be consulted, written by experts, practitioners, and think tanks who variously advise diplomatic institutions on how to innovate and leverage technology in the new era of international relations. Moreover, the revolution in the ICTs world represents more than a technological change. The effects of such modernisation on diplomacy can be analysed on several levels. Technology and the international context to which technological innovation applies have changed throughout history in tandem. Indeed, we should not make the mistake of understanding technological progress only with the advent of the World Wide Web, with the publication of a website's home page on December 20, 1990, by computer scientists Tim Berners-Lee and Robert Cailliau. Instead, innovation is inherent in humankind, a process of adaptation and, in its way, revolution, as with the Palaeolithic paintings in the Lascaux caves in France.[1]

Much of the literature that focuses on analysing the evolution of diplomacy in its more technological format draws on the work of Robert O. Keohane and Joseph Nye who, in 1977, were unaware of the effervescent Computer Revolution generated in California (Feichtmeir, 1979), heralded the age of complex interdependence. In a world characterised by rapidly evolving communication systems, interconnectedness, and reciprocity among the parties involved in the international arena, governments are often faced with new actors who occupy an ever-increasing space on the global stage and whose actions lead them to rethink traditional notions of power, influence, and diplomacy (Keohane & Nye, 1977). In today's global politics, foreign ministers are not the only interlocutors in setting the international agenda.

Another reading, on the other hand, developed since the late 1990s, goes beyond such an analysis and the realm of public diplomacy. Such a reading seeks to understand what new technologies can mean for managing international conflicts.

Adding a prefix to the concept of diplomacy suggests that we are dealing with a specific type of diplomatic activity, as in the case of commercial diplomacy, cultural diplomacy, or even "ping-pong diplomacy" (Cooper, 2000 & Eckstein 1993). So, the prefix "virtual" to the word diplomacy refers to the era of computerisation. In 1997, Richard Solomon, who at that time was the president of the United States Institute of Peace (USIP), suggested that the concept of "virtual diplomacy" should be understood as related to social, economic, and political interactions mediated through electronic means instead of "face-to-face" communications. Solomon adds that although virtual implies an absence of reality, such diplomacy, although conducted virtually and through technology, is real in the sense of official and authoritative interactions between authorised representatives of different governments (Salomon, 1997). In the broadest sense of the term, virtual diplomacy is a modified diplomacy applied to the emergence of an interconnected world. In more detail, the definition embraces the practices of international relations related to decision-making, cooperation, and negotiation conducted with the help of information technology.

Another definition is offered by Gordon Smith (Smith, 2001). Smith said virtual diplomacy can be understood as the conduct of what was classically understood in the past but is now a practice carried out with new tools, both because of the technology available and because it is practised by people who are not necessarily professional diplomats (in this Smith also includes a reference to public diplomacy).

Although in an even more radical sense, David Ronfeldt and John Arquilla suggested the arrival of a new era, that of "noopolitik" (Arquilla & Ronfeldt, 1999a), an emerging international system that emphasises the importance of sharing ideas and values globally. The sharing is primarily through the exercise of persuasive soft power and not through classic hard power, the latter devoted to military and security actions. Similarly, Jamie Metzl suggested the name "network diplomacy" (Metzl, 2001), insisting on the end of state-centrism in international relations and the presence of numerous new actors with different influences, particularly due to globalisation and the revolution in the media. Then, cyber diplomacy represented another step forward in the terminological examination and practice of the subject. It followed the creation of the Office for eDiplomacy created by the US Department of State in 2002,[2] which was followed later by the Foreign Office of the British Commonwealth, which instead decided to use the acronym digital diplomacy (Westcott, 2008). In the early 2000s, the foreign ministries of countries such as the United States, the United Kingdom, and Canada took the first steps by welcoming technology as an integral part of the diplomatic machine. However, a distinction must be made among these states, which can be seen by observing their approach to using the virtual sphere.

EDiplomacy (Hanson, 2012) is a concept already making inroads in the United States. In Ferguson's words, eDiplomacy denotes the use of the web and new technologies to advance the goals of diplomacy; thus, the technological revolution, interconnectedness, and digitisation remain at the centre. It is a definition drafted in very broad terms to avoid confusion with public diplomacy. However, in US practice, the latter is included as it is useful in keeping in touch with the audience that has now migrated online and exploiting the new media to convey key messages and influence its targets. The US Department of State has become the world's leading representative of eDiplomacy. Its apparatus has also housed 150 full-time employees in 25 different active diplomatic offices and linked to consular functions and information management or engaged in crisis and disaster response and policy planning. Some practical examples of the scale of eDiplomacy saw an initiative by the US Embassy in Mexico, which, together with the Mexican Embassy in Washington, the Mexican Affairs Office, and the Mexican Ministry of Foreign Affairs, worked jointly using cloud-based information systems to process various protocols related to disaster management in areas on the US-Mexico border. Another area in which eDiplomacy has responded in a very promising way is the management of migrants, as was the case with the US-Haitian population helped during the 2010 Haiti earthquake through Twitter message translation. Analysing the succession of the most recent US secretaries of state and their efforts to ferry diplomacy to a more virtual approach, we can see how Colin Powell (with George W. Bush from 2001 to 2005) paved the way, in part because of his experience in the military as a general and chief of staff during the Gulf War and the Somali Civil War. Condoleezza Rice (with George W. Bush from 2005 to 2009) then launched an initiative called Transformational Diplomacy. It was a plan to reinvigorate US foreign policy, which contained the innovative creation of Virtual Presence Posts (VPPs),[3] which are very small diplomatic structures, usually run by a single officer or consul, and which thus become virtual. Hillary Clinton (with Barack Obama from 2009 to 2013) then capitalised on what had been achieved up to that point through her far-reaching project named *21st Century Statecraft*. This was a profound technological modernisation of the US administrative and diplomatic machine, a phase also referred to as "the internet moment in foreign policy" (US Department of State, 2017).

US governance in foreign policy thus realises how crucial the tool of the web is and that it may represent the real turning point in contemporary international relations. In 2010, in the face of the revolutions in Arab countries, the disruptive economic-social thrusts that the same technology has accelerated and unveiled in recent years, together with the use of the web by some 2 billion users,[4] the United States spoke of a triple paradigm shift that has occurred for the first time in history, since the transition from telegraph to telephone, and for the mass media, from print media to radio to television. To such dynamism, Washington decided to respond and had to intercept its positive and negative developments, even revolutionising its diplomatic methods and work within embassies. With Rex Tillerson and especially Mike Pompeo, secretaries of state in Donald Trump's administration, very active with his Twitter diplomacy, eDiplomacy encounters further challenges, culminating certainly with the coronavirus pandemic. The pandemic further and radically altered diplomatic tools and dialogues, particularly due to travel restrictions.

The British experience, as described by the former chief information officer (CIO) of the Commonwealth Foreign Office, Nicholas Westcott,[5] bears many similarities to its US neighbour, however much the UK has chosen the term digital diplomacy, which is very close to the world of public diplomacy. As Westcott wrote, a more targeted and ingenious approach is needed to achieve a dynamic presence in online media, enhancing a comparative advantage in providing authoritative and trusted information. On the other hand, digital diplomacy carries weight because the British Foreign Office can communicate faster with other offices (Westcott, 2008) and needs to leverage internet technology to manage information flows more systematically and efficiently. However, as with US foreign policy and eDiplomacy, there are limitations. For example, physical presence and assistance to vulnerable compatriots remain the mainstay of the FCO's work.

The notion of virtual diplomacy is also used in Canada, as described by the author and diplomacy expert Daryl Copeland (Copeland, 2008). Copeland's definition is not far from Hanson's idea: it is the application of the internet and the use of computers and technology in the Foreign Office, but Copeland goes beyond what Fergus Hanson and Nicholas Westcott describe. While for Copeland, the use of websites is certainly one of the first steps in defining the presence of diplomatic institutions on the web, the creation of virtual embassies (as implemented by Sweden, the Republic of Maldives, the Philippines, Estonia, Serbia, Macedonia, and Albania) represents a more mature development through the virtual world of the so-called Second Life (computer platforms that simulate reality, and integrate synchronous and asynchronous communication tools, where users can act using their online identity) (Canestrari & Romeo, 2008). At the same time, pleading the cause of the virtual world, Copeland emphasises the benefits already noted by Hanson and Westcott concerning the efficiency of the medium and possible greater transparency but adds additional insights.

The central point related to the choice of different terminology that clarifies diplomacy's approach and familiarity with the technology remains the multiple possibilities that the web world can offer in the work and practices of ministries. Moreover, virtual (or digital) diplomacy might appear in contrast with traditional diplomacy, where individuals conduct the latter. At the same time, the former relies on technology to the point of prompting us to imagine a future in which new information systems will come to replace practices established over centuries. However, ICTs, in this sense, enable and amplify diplomacy but do not alternate and substitute its basis and functions.

COVID-19 and the UN: A Case Study

With the arrival of the coronavirus in 2020, virtual diplomacy has become a useful tool to avoid the pandemic-induced hibernation of relations between ministers, representations, and embassies. The 75th UN General Assembly, whose plenary debate opened with the United States and Brazil on September 22 and ended with North Korea on September 29, was attended by as many as 170 speakers. Attendees participated in a major exercise in remote Zoom diplomacy (when, under normal circumstances, each UN member state has six reserved seats in the Assembly), as the speeches of heads of state and government had been recorded beforehand, sent, and then projected in sequence from the famous green marble stage of the United Nations Secretariat Building. However, UN Secretary-General Antonio Guterres and the new president of the General Assembly, Türkiye's Volkan Bozkir, were present. Representatives of the five permanent members of the Security Council also delivered speeches. It took persistent work for the member countries in this format to confront each other on major international policy dossiers.[6] However, the president of the Russian Federation, Vladimir Putin, together with the former president of the United States of America, Donald Trump,[7] strongly criticised the importance of multilateralism and global governance in contrast with the UN's fundamental principles.

The 75th UN General Assembly was conducted unprecedentedly, with the lack of the usual bilateral exchanges between diplomats, usually held in the corridors of the UN Secretariat building. Moreover, during the 75th UN General Assembly, there was no shortage of technical problems, mostly related to the use of technology. Several diplomats admitted to feeling like fishes out of the water, a situation that had already occurred in previous months as they moved between empty embassies or during remote calls during which colleagues were asked to turn off audio or video to avoid confusion. In addition, Hreinn Pàlsson, deputy head of the Irish representation to the UN, followed by other diplomats, highlighted how diplomacy conducted on Zoom is difficult, fraught with obstacles, without real interaction, less direct and confidential than negotiations conducted in person (Wintour, 2020).

However, one must recognise the great improvements innovative technology has introduced and opened the door to a global audience. Diplomats are thus being pushed to re-evaluate the use of their available time: as it happened, since March 2020, G-20 meetings, including those dedicated to Sherpas, have been conducted entirely online.

During the summer of 2020, diplomacy retraced its steps, resuming in-person visits and missions. Among other meetings, one may recall the trip of US Secretary of State Mike Pompeo for the signing of the agreement between Israel and the United Arab Emirates; Chinese Foreign Minister Wang Yi's visit (which lasted a week) to Europe and included five capitals of the continent; the mission of the UK Secretary of State for Foreign Affairs, Dominic Raab, to Israel and Washington; and the talks held among some of the European ministers from September 7 to 9 in Montreux, Switzerland, under the auspices of UNSMIL. Yet, with the pandemic still ongoing, it isn't easy to imagine when diplomacy will be able to resume the ceremony and practice that has identified it for centuries. Instead, it would be easier to take for granted how the habits shaped by technology in recent months remain altered due to the increasing use of tools and the use of the web. If the Rubicon has yet to be crossed, we can say that we are well along the journey.

Conclusion: Challenges and Trends in the Digital Disruption Era

The COVID-19 pandemic represents one of the highest disruptive events in the world's recent history. Modelling the crisis management and impacts of the pandemic, virtual diplomacy addressed this challenge using technology to fulfil the gap created by the obstacles related to COVID-19: virtual diplomatic meetings and offices organised by the web have to be effective in creating links between experts and specialised officials. With the end of the emergence, this can help future generations of diplomats to be active in the virtual world, thanks, for example, attitude can help the use of 3D graphics, real-time voice communications, or the study of cyberspace. In addition, these technological experiments can be replicated in the field and provide an appropriate response to high-risk negotiation strategies, an alternative to even the most complex conflict resolution scenarios. Copeland, in this regard, cites the case of possible negotiations with the Taliban (Copeland, 2008).

The relationship between diplomacy and communication remains strong and has been reinvigorated in recent decades. The role of communication looms critically over the part of contemporary and future diplomacy, as described by some definitions such as "techno-diplomacy," "media-diplomacy," and "digital diplomacy" (Dizard, 2001). Several scholars tend to emphasise the new face, and simultaneously the decline, of diplomacy in the front of new transportation and communication technologies.

It is certain that diplomacy is interfacing in important ways with the digital age and that its virtual version has partly updated some of the traditional diplomatic functions of representation, negotiation, reporting, facilitation, and coordination. However, virtual diplomacy remains highly unlikely to replace practices established over centuries, making them redundant gradually.

Analytically, it is important to remember how diplomacy has survived every historical change, such as a pandemic. Technology (as well as the telegraph, among other discoveries and innovations) represents a tool or medium useful to it. Moreover, the very openness of the VVPs and the effort of countries such as the United States towards eDiplomacy constitute only a part of the possible initiatives that diplomacy can and will be able through future developments to deploy thanks to ICT.

Notes

1 The Lascaux caves show that long before the beginning of urban civilization, humans were creating imitations of reality, in which they used components of the real world, reshaped them, and recombined them, following fantasies and imagination. The comparison between today's films and virtual realities, with the cinematic images we often encounter, is inevitable. Both express our desire to escape into seemingly human worlds, made realistic through applying art and technology, where the landscape is that of the imagination.
2 In 2002, US Ambassador James Holmes created the eDiplomacy Task Force. Since October 2003, the office has been an integral and permanent part of the Bureau of Information Resource Management. It is responsible for, among other functions, keeping the link between diplomats of different states alive by technology and making usable documents, reports, analyses, databases, and other information.
3 Among the US VVPs, we can mention the Western Sahara embassy created in 2020 and the other embassies: San Marino, Seychelles, and Comoros Island. In 2007, the VVPs were 42.
4 According to the ITU (International Telecommunication Unit), in 2019 the number of internet users was 4 billion, which represented 51% of the world population.
5 Westcott was in charge from 2002 to 2007.
6 The Assembly focused particularly on the UN response to the COVID-19 pandemic, albeit taking action on other aspects. On that occasion, it decided to provide 50% of vaccines for children worldwide, investing $28.8 billion as coordinated funds for

humanitarian needs and assisting 50 nations in holding elections. 196 nations also announced their plans to counter the rise in global temperature.
7 During the 75th session of the General Assembly, Donald Trump was the second speaker to speak. As on other occasions, he pointed his finger at the "Chinese virus" and the World Health Organization (WHO), which has been called into question particularly for its handling of the pandemic. He then focused on the role of the United States as an international peacemaker, highlighting the signing of the Abraham Agreement (between Israel, Bahrain, and the United Arab Emirates) and between Kosovo and Serbia in September 2020.

References

US Department of State. *21st Century Statecraft*, US Department of State, Diplomacy in Action. 2017.
Arquilla, J & Ronfeldt D. *The Emergence of Noopolitik*, RAND Corporation, Santa Monica. 1999a.
Arquilla, J & Ronfeldt D. *What if there is a Revolution in Diplomatic Affairs?*, Institute of Peace, Washington D.C. 1999b.
Canestrari, P & Romeo A. *Second Life, oltre la realtà virtuale*, Lupetti, Milano. 2008.
Cooper, J R. 'Diplomacy in the Information Age: Implications for Content and Conduct', in B Fulton (ed.), *Net Diplomacy I: Beyond Foreign Ministries*, pp. 3–6. Washington D.C. 2000.
Copeland, D. 'Connectivity and Networks Rule: Virtuality, Public Diplomacy and the Foreign Ministry', *USC Center on Public Diplomacy Blog*. 2008. https://uscpublicdiplomacy.org/blog/connectivity-and-networks-rule-virtuality-public-diplomacy-and-foreign-ministry (Accessed 26 November 2018).
Dizard, W. *Digital Diplomacy: U.S. Foreign Policy in the Information Age*, Praeger, Westport. 2001.
Eckstein, R. 'Ping-Pong Diplomacy: A View from behind the Scenes', *The Journal of American-East Asian Relations*, vol. 2, no. 3, pp. 327–342. 1993.
Feichtmeir, K. 'The On-line Information Revolution in California', *California History*, vol. 58, no. 2, pp. 78–81. 1979.
Hanson, F. *Revolution @State: The Spread of EDiplomacy*, Lowy Institute for International Peace, Sydney. 2012.
Keohane, R O & Nye J. *Power and Interdependence*, Little, Brown & Co, Boston. 1977.
Metzl, J F. 'Network Diplomacy', *Georgetown Journal of International Affairs*, vol. 2, no. 1, pp. 78–87. 2001.
Rice, C. *Presentation of Final Report of the Secretary's Advisory Committee on Transformational Diplomacy*, Archive of U.S. Department of State. 2008.
Salomon, R. *The Information Revolution and International Conflict Management*, University of Michigan Library, Ann Arbor. 1997.
Smith, G. *Reinventing Diplomacy: A Virtual Necessity*, United States Institute of Peace, Washington. 2001.
Westcott, N. *Digital Diplomacy: The Impact of the Internet of International Relations*, Oxford Internet Institute, Oxford. 2008.
Wintour, P. 'Bye bilaterals: UN general assembly to embrace Zoom diplomacy', *The Guardian*. https://www.theguardian.com/world/2020/sep/19/bye-bye-bilaterals-un-general-assembly-embrace-zoom-diplomacy. 2020 (Accessed August 19, 2022).

5 Diplomacy 3.0 in the Pandemic
Digital Diplomacy and Beyond

Erman Akıllı and Gülnihan Cihanoğlu Gülen

Introduction

Developments in information and communication technologies (ICT) profoundly transformed the traditional environment where international relations are conducted. The digitalisation of almost all spheres of life and the replacement of traditional media sources with social media altered the realm of diplomacy as well. Especially the digitalisation of communication brought new opportunities and challenges in diplomacy that can be associated with speed, transparency, and trust. Some scholars even argue that states are capable of tracking and monitoring individuals much easily thanks to ICT, but they are losing their ability to control and influence the perceptions of the public because they cannot control the flow of information (Ronald, 1997: 167). Since billions of people across the world are linked by satellites and fibre optics, the importance of public diplomacy increased more than ever before. The process of traditional foreign policy formulation by the Ministries of Foreign Affairs and their fait accompli policy lost credibility in the eyes of the public and non-state actors involved in international relations (Tuncer, 2006: 68).

In the Digital Age, public diplomacy has also transformed because new online media offers a two-way communication where multiple actors take part and public diplomacy practitioners have to listen to the public. This online process is called digital diplomacy. However, digital diplomacy has acquired different names in the literature such as "Public Diplomacy 2.0," "virtual diplomacy," "electronic diplomacy (e-diplomacy)," or "Diplomacy 3.0." These concepts can be used as synonyms for digital diplomacy. However, other concepts in the literature cannot be regarded as synonyms such as "cyber diplomacy." Thus, there is conceptual confusion in the literature. The first section of this study tries to define digital diplomacy and elaborates on existing literature in the discipline of international relations regarding this concept. While the second part investigates the evolution of digital diplomacy, the third part examines significant practices during and after the COVID-19 pandemic. The final part covers anticipations regarding digital diplomacy practices in the future.

DOI: 10.4324/9781003377597-6

Digital Diplomacy and International Relations Theories

Although there are several different definitions for digital diplomacy and no consensus has been reached among scholars, the concept can broadly be understood as the conduct of public diplomacy via digital tools (McClory, 2021: 24). For sure, these digital tools are not limited to social media, but digital diplomacy usually takes place on social media. Thus, broad definitions regarding digital diplomacy seem more suitable for making sense of this concept. For instance, Bjola defines digital diplomacy as a strategy for managing change through digital tools and virtual collaboration (Bjola, 2015: 15).

Since the concept can be considered quite new, there is much room to contribute to the literature. In fact, the theoretical aspect of public diplomacy has been neglected in the existing literature. Therefore, the theoretical framework for digital diplomacy, which can be regarded as a tool of public diplomacy, has also not been extensively researched. Even though the key theories in the discipline of international relations help researchers make sense of public diplomacy, the only relevant theoretical concept associated with public diplomacy can be considered soft power. For this reason, public diplomacy studies are often influenced by Joseph S. Nye Jr., who coined the concept of soft power. Although the relationship between soft power and public diplomacy is considered inexplicit by some scholars (Szondi, 2008), only soft power can provide a valuable theoretical framework for analysing public diplomacy in international relations. According to Nye Jr., the soft power of a country rests primarily on three resources. These resources are identified as culture, political values, and foreign policies (Nye Jr., 2008). Thus, conducting successful cultural diplomacy, which is an essential part of public diplomacy, enables states to accumulate soft power. It can be argued that soft power basically lies in the capability to manipulate the preferences of others. But if a country's culture, values, and policies are not attractive enough to have an influence, the public diplomacy that broadcasts them cannot produce soft power. Therefore, making a culture popular and attractive to other countries lies at the heart of public diplomacy. But Nye himself underlines that soft power is only an analytical concept, not a theory (Nye Jr., 2010: 219). Consequently, it can be argued that there is a big gap in the literature regarding a theoretical framework to explain digital diplomacy.

The Evolution of Digital Diplomacy

Although the first online participation session in multilateral diplomacy was held by the International Telecommunication Union (ITU) in 1963 (Digital Diplomacy in 2021, 2021), Digital Diplomacy became popular in the 21st century. The United States (US) pioneered digital diplomacy by establishing a task force on e-diplomacy in 2002, which transformed into the Office of eDiplomacy within the State Department in 2003 (Hanson, 2012: 3). The US even opened a virtual presence post in Russia's Yekaterinburg. It is argued that this virtual presence post was an indicator of fundamental change in diplomacy, particularly public diplomacy (Bronk, 2016: 94).

Other than those developments in the US State Department, the first activities of digital diplomacy began in 2006, when the University of Southern California's Center on Public Diplomacy launched the Virtual Worlds Project. To discover the possibilities for public diplomacy in virtual worlds, researchers at the mentioned centre purchased an island in a 3D virtual world called Second Life, developed and run by a San Francisco-based technology company in 2003 (Public Diplomacy and Virtual Worlds, 2018). In May 2007, the Maldives became the first country to open a virtual embassy in Second Life (Page, 2007). Shortly after that, the second country that opened a virtual embassy in Second Life was Sweden (Manor, 2014). Led by the Swedish Institute, the Swedish virtual embassy did not offer any consular services but only provided information to promote Sweden's image and culture in the popular virtual world of Second Life. The virtual world of Second Life continues to exist today; however, the diplomacy island in Second Life no longer exists after the funding for the Virtual Worlds Project ended. Although the project was not sustainable, the project can be regarded as one of the first examples of digital diplomacy initiatives.

Other than those virtual embassies, individual social media activities of some politicians involved in foreign policymaking marked digital diplomacy efforts. Popular opinion about digital diplomacy is that the Arab Spring in 2010 motivated the Ministries of Foreign Affairs to be more active on digital platforms. This opinion is supported by the fact that the revolts organised via social media against the governments during the Arab Spring helped states realise the importance of social media in shaping public opinion. As social media became so crucial in mass movements and enabled the spread of information, leaders also got interested in actively using social media accounts.

But although there have been digital diplomacy initiatives since the early 2000s, there is still no proper framework to assess their success. The only index measuring the efficiency of digital diplomacy is the Digital Diplomacy Index (DDI) developed by a Paris-based global public communication agency. Moreover, the DDI only uses limited data based on the Twitter presence and activity of G20 countries to make a cross-national comparison. There is no comprehensive evaluation model for measuring the efficiency of digital diplomacy in the international relations literature either. Thus, it is beyond dispute that substantial gaps exist in the literature. For this reason, digital diplomacy presents a great field of study as an emerging topic.

Nevertheless, it should be accepted that digital diplomacy is part of the reality of today's diplomacy and public diplomacy. Therefore, the benefits and risks of digital diplomacy should be assessed as well. First of all, the opportunities created by digital media enable leaders or politicians involved in foreign policymaking to instantly and more actively engage with foreign publics. In this way, they can reach beyond the limited audience and get the chance to interact in formal visits and events. Through the control of information flow on social media, government agencies, especially foreign ministries, can correct misinformation quickly without causing great escalation abroad. Moreover, conducting digital diplomacy is cost and time efficient due to less travel and the avoidance of expenses related to the organisation of physical events. It can also be argued that digital diplomacy is indirectly environmentally friendly because it involves less travel and fewer printed materials, thus contributing to the protection of the environment.

On the other hand, several issues can be pointed out regarding digital diplomacy, as well. Primarily the spread of fake news and disinformation on digital platforms can endanger security and perception. There is the risk of official social media accounts getting hacked or encountering imposter accounts on social media. In addition, videos produced by using deepfake technology shared on social media platforms can be dangerous because the masses will tend to believe what they see without knowing that it was created with the help of artificial intelligence. Until it is proven that the published videos are fake, enough damage can already be caused to the national image of the concerned country or lead to widespread public reactions and protests. For example, the video of a public address allegedly belonging to Ukrainian President Volodymyr Zelenskyy asking Ukrainian soldiers to lay down their weapons had a great impact on social media. However, it was stated that the video was a provocative deepfake product created by Russia and was removed from social media platforms immediately after (Akıllı, 2022). Therefore, the lack of trust in digital platforms often undermines the importance of digital diplomacy.

Besides all these risks on social media, cybersecurity poses to most important risk regarding digital diplomacy. For instance, WikiLeaks disclosures are considered the largest unauthorised release of contemporary classified information in history (Calabresi, 2010). Consequently, states may neglect or avoid the digital transformation of diplomacy. Moreover, conveying the right message on digital platforms is not an easy task. Being active on social media makes leaders and diplomats approachable and open to public criticism on digital platforms. Comments on published posts on social media may be disabled but misunderstandings or provocations may also occur between leaders and diplomats. Tensions on social media may result in a diplomatic crisis, which can also have major consequences. One example of such a diplomatic crisis may be the tweet sent by Chrystia Freeland in 2018, who was the Canadian foreign minister at that time. Freeland fuelled a diplomatic crisis with Riyadh because she tweeted demanding the release of human rights activists imprisoned in Saudi Arabia. A similar tweet about the immediate release of the mentioned human rights activists was sent from the official account of the Canadian Foreign Ministry the following day. After another tweet by the Embassy of Canada in Saudi Arabia, which was the translation of those tweets into the Arabic language, the Saudi government took drastic action against Canada. The Saudi government expelled Canada's ambassador, declared him persona non grata, and also recalled Saudi Arabia's ambassador to Canada. Moreover, the Saudi Foreign Ministry announced that all new trade and investment deals were frozen (Ljunggren et al., 2018). In addition, 17,000 students studying in Canada with scholarships were also withdrawn and accommodated in other countries. In the end, the relations got so tense that even Saudi Arabia's state airline Saudi Arabia suspended flights to and from Toronto shortly after these decisions (Berlinger, 2018). Therefore, this incident also had economic consequences. It was estimated that this tension has cost Canada more than $20 billion, according to initial reports

(Aydoğan, 2018). Based upon this example, it is evident that social media is more than just gaining many followers and being popular among domestic and foreign publics. It is serious business and requires exceptional carefulness. In conclusion, it can be argued that digital diplomacy should be conducted strategically; otherwise, the emergent challenges and risks might outweigh its benefits.

The COVID-19 Pandemic and Digital Diplomacy

The COVID-19 pandemic has altered how we communicate, perform our jobs, and handle international affairs. Diplomats have had to adapt to a new reality of remote work and virtual communication since the disruption of diplomatic activities that previously relied on in-person communication. Thus, the COVID-19 pandemic can be deemed another turning point for digital diplomacy because restrictions on travel, borders, and gatherings transformed the conduct of not only public diplomacy but also traditional diplomacy. Virtual meetings due to quarantine measures and lockdowns have been a key catalyst for the digitalisation of traditional diplomacy. During the COVID-19 pandemic, diplomats increasingly turned to digital technologies to address the challenges. Social media platforms such as Twitter, Facebook, and LinkedIn were utilised to share information and engage with other nations. Additionally, video conferencing tools like Zoom, Skype, and Microsoft Teams were employed to conduct virtual meetings and negotiations. Digital technologies played a significant role in coordinating international responses to the pandemic. Even the ceremonies for the presentation and handing over of the letter of credence by the ambassadors were done via videoconference, like in the example of the first Lithuanian ambassador to Bahrain to the foreign minister of Bahrain in 2022 (Ministry of Foreign Affairs of the Republic of Lithuania, 2022).

Nonetheless, there are benefits and drawbacks to using digital technologies in diplomacy. Digital diplomacy can, on the one hand, improve accessibility, effectiveness, and cost-effectiveness while also enabling diplomats to reach a wider audience. However, there are worries about the security, privacy, and risk of misunderstanding that comes with digital communication. Examples abound that show how COVID-19 responses have made use of digital diplomacy. While various countries have used digital tools to share information and coordinate their efforts, the World Health Organization has used them to organise the global response to the pandemic. The annual General Assembly and other UN meetings have all been conducted virtually thanks to the usage of digital technologies. Thus, for wielding digital diplomacy effectively, Bjola and Manor have identified three major tasks that foreign ministries had to handle during the COVID-19 pandemic. The first task was identified as offering consular assistance to citizens who were stranded abroad; the second was supplying medical and personal protective equipment from other nations; and the third was promoting international partnerships for the development of a vaccine against the coronavirus. To offer consular assistance, artificial intelligence (AI) assisted chatbots on the websites of the ministries were used to provide health advice regarding COVID-19, information on travel restrictions, consular services, and quarantine measures (Bjola and Manor, 2020).

In addition to the change in the nature of traditional tasks performed by the diplomats, politicians, and ministries of foreign affairs, the national images of the states were influenced by the COVID-19 pandemic as well. It is argued that the COVID-19 pandemic influenced the public image of states profoundly because some states struggled to maintain their positive image (Pop, 2021: 255). According to research elaborating on the effects of the pandemic on the soft power and public diplomacy of states, conducted by the Sanctuary Counsel and the USC Center on Public Diplomacy, the COVID-19 pandemic changed public opinion about foreign states. The research was conducted based on seven online round table sessions, organised according to several regions in the world with 121 participants from foreign ministries, NGOs, academia, media, cultural institutions, and relevant private sector organisations. Across all groups, 91% stated that the pandemic had changed the way they form an opinion on a given country. The research also revealed that China's reputation had suffered throughout the pandemic (McClory, 2021: 17). This study proves that the pandemic affected not only the way diplomacy and public diplomacy are conducted but also the countries' images in general, depending on how they managed the challenges of the pandemic. Beyond any doubt, the change in the reputation and national image of the countries was also affecting their soft power.

Irrespective of how successfully the challenges for conducting diplomacy during the pandemic were overcome, having fewer face-to-face meetings and being obliged to organise major international events online left states no other choice but to begin showing interest in digital diplomacy. Therefore, it can be argued that states that were previously not actively involved in digital diplomacy were obligated to accelerate the digitalisation of diplomatic practices. Thus, the need for adapting strategies and new approaches regarding digital diplomacy emerged.

The Future of Digital Diplomacy: Diplomacy 4.0

Despite new opportunities arising from information and communication technologies, the essential structure of diplomacy has remained unchanged. However, it can be argued that digital diplomacy became an important component of public diplomacy for achieving foreign policy goals. Considering that digital diplomacy influences people to have empathy or sympathy for countries, including those who don't have an idea on which continent that respective country is located, the importance of digital diplomacy is indisputable. After all, the latest Twiplomacy Study conducted in 2020 indicates that 98% of the 193 UN member states have an official presence on Twitter. This means that the governments and leaders of 189 countries used social media, minus only four countries that did not have a Twitter presence as of 2020, namely Laos, North Korea, Sao Tome and Principe, and Turkmenistan (Twiplomacy Study 2020, 2020).

Disregarding technical obstacles to digital transformation, it can be observed that digitalisation continues in every sphere of life at an incredible speed. Before the importance of digital diplomacy is substantially understood, discourses about Diplomacy 4.0 emerged. It is argued that Diplomacy 4.0 will become the diplomatic paradigm of an era that we can call post-digital or post-internet. Insomuch that a digital world referred to as the Metaverse is being created. The Metaverse can be described as a virtual universe where people can interact with each other by creating virtual characters that represent themselves online, known as avatars. In the Metaverse, people can shop, socialise, and even attend virtual meetings, including business meetings. Although the Metaverse is currently in its early stages and its evolution will take time, people have shown great interest in it. In fact, serious events such as defence industry fairs have begun to take place in the Metaverse.

Besides the Metaverse, new digital technologies such as AI, deepfake technologies, etc. are going to accelerate the digital transformation in diplomacy. Even now AI is already being used for diplomatic purposes. Not only in the form of AI-assisted chatbots but also in decision-making processes for foreign policy. It is known that the US and China pioneer AI research. But China is trying to take the lead by revealing an AI system used for foreign policy suggestions. Thus, it can be argued that AI has also become an element of competition between great powers, as well.

Moreover, big data will be a game changer in digital diplomacy considering the fact that data is knowledge and knowledge is power in the Digital Age. Kim et al. assert that governments expect big data to enhance their ability to serve their citizens and address major national challenges regarding the economy, health care, job creation, natural disasters, and terrorism (Kim et al., 2014). But it should not be forgotten that there is also a dark side of big data. With the help of AI, data analysts can use some algorithms for uncovering the vulnerabilities of people. This information about vulnerabilities can be used for manipulating people and to conduct better public diplomacy in order to accumulate more soft power. In fact, even the decisions of voters can be manipulated by using the appropriate algorithms strategically (DeBrabander, 2021). Thus, big data introduces great dangers as well as great opportunities. The potential abuse of big data by data analysts should be prevented by law, which necessitates states to take action immediately. The COVID-19 pandemic has led to an increase in the adoption of digital technologies in diplomacy, and this is expected to have lasting implications for international relations. Future developments in digital diplomacy are likely to include the wider use of tools like artificial intelligence and virtual reality. It is essential to ensure that digital diplomacy is utilised in a manner that promotes global peace, security, and equity while also acknowledging and addressing any potential threats or challenges. Nonetheless, in the near future, states that do not use algorithmic diplomacy and artificial intelligence, tackle bots, or detect fake news will not be successful at conducting digital diplomacy and will fall behind great powers (The 10 Commandments for Successful Digital Diplomacy, 2018). For this reason, studies about digital diplomacy should become more prevalent and create awareness.

Conclusion

Digital diplomacy presents a great field of study as an emerging topic. Not only conceptual clearance is needed but also substantial gaps exist in the international relations literature regarding the theoretical aspect of the concept of digital diplomacy.

Moreover, there is a need to develop a proper framework to assess the success of digital diplomacy initiatives because the only index measuring their efficiency is the DDI, which is very limited. Therefore, this study tries to create awareness about the fact that more studies are needed to underline the importance of digital diplomacy regarding public diplomacy and the achievement of foreign policy objectives. Moreover, the study sheds light on the benefits and risks of digital diplomacy, proving that its use requires exceptional caution. Otherwise, it is foreseen that the emergent challenges and risks might outweigh the benefits of digital diplomacy. Regarding its evolution, it is argued that digital diplomacy became prevalent in the 21st century. To be more specific, it is claimed that the Arab Spring in 2010 aroused the interest of states to be more actively involved on digital platforms, but the COVID-19 pandemic was a turning point for digital diplomacy. Research showed that the COVID-19 pandemic mandatorily accelerated the digital transformation of diplomacy and the public images of states were also influenced during this period. The pandemic demonstrated the importance of digital diplomacy. Moreover, the Metaverse as well as new digital technologies such as AI and deepfake technologies demonstrated that there is a need for adapting strategies and new approaches to digital diplomacy. It is envisaged that these recent developments will determine the power relations in the future because those topics became fields of competition between states, as well. Thus, it is underlined that states should master digital diplomacy to avoid falling behind. Moreover, potential risks regarding big data and artificial intelligence should be mitigated through new policies and legislation. In conclusion, digital diplomacy has been crucial in addressing the challenges posed by COVID-19, and it has provided new avenues for international cooperation and communication. However, it is crucial to exercise caution regarding the potential challenges and risks associated with digital diplomacy and ensure that it is utilised in a manner that advances global peace, security, and equity.

References

Akıllı, E. (26 March 2022). *Diplomaside Dijital Dönüşüm: Deepfake, Dezenformasyon ve 'Hakikat Ötesi' Üzerine*. Sabah. https://www.sabah.com.tr/yazarlar/perspektif/erman-akilli/2022/03/26/diplomaside-dijital-donusum-deepfake-dezenformasyon-ve-hakikat-otesi-uzerine

Aydoğan, S. (8 August 2018). *Kanada Dışişleri Bakanı'ndan '20 milyar dolarlık tweet'*. Anadolu Ajansi. https://www.aa.com.tr/tr/dunya/kanada-disisleri-bakanindan-20-milyar-dolarlik-tweet/1225246

Berlinger, J. (6 August 2018). *Saudis expel Canadian envoy, vow to relocate students over tweets about rights activist*. CNN. https://edition.cnn.com/2018/08/06/middleeast/saudi-arabia-canada-intl/index.html

Bjola, C. (2015). Introduction – Making Sense of Digital Diplomacy. In C. Bjola, M. Holmes, C. Bjola & M. Holmes (Eds.), *Digital Diplomacy – Theory and Practice* (pp. 1–9). Abingdon, New York: Routledge.

Bjola, C. and Manor, I. (31 March 2020). *Digital diplomacy in the time of the coronavirus pandemic*. USC Center on Public Diplomacy. https://uscpublicdiplomacy.org/blog/digital-diplomacy-time-coronavirus-pandemic

Bronk, C. (2016). *Cyber Threat: The Rise of Information Geopolitics in U.S. National Security.* Santa Barbara: Preager.

Calabresi, M. (2 December 2010). WikiLeaks' war on secrecy: Truth's consequences. *Time.* https://time.com/5568727/wikileaks-war-on-secrecy/

DeBrabander, F. (2021). The political risks of Big Data dominance. *The New Statesman.* https://www.newstatesman.com/ideas/agora/2021/11/the-political-risks-of-big-data-dominance

Hanson, F. (2012). *Baked in and Wired: ediplomacy@State.* Foreign Policy at Brookings. https://www.brookings.edu/wp-content/uploads/2016/06/baked-in-hansonf-5.pdf

Kim, G., Trimi S. & Chung J. (2014). Big-data applications in the government sector, *Communications of the ACM*, Vol. 57, No. 3, pp. 78–85. https://doi.org/10.1145/2500873

Ljunggren, D., El Yaakoubi, A. & Paul, K. (11 August 2018). A Canadian tweet in a Saudi king's court crosses a red line. Reuters. https://www.reuters.com/article/us-saudi-canada-tweet-idUSKBN1KV2FC

Manor, I. (25 June 2014). *On virtual embassies in the age of digital diplomacy.* Exploring Digital Diplomacy. https://digdipblog.com/2014/06/25/on-virtual-embassies-in-the-age-of-digital-diplomacy/

McClory, J. (2021). *Socially Distanced Diplomacy.* South Carolina: Sanctuary Counsel & USC Center on Public Diplomacy.

Ministry of Foreign Affairs of the Republic of Lithuania (14 December 2022). *Ambassador Davidonis presents copies of his letters of credence to Bahrain's Foreign Minister.* https://urm.lt/default/en/news/ambassador-davidonis-presents-copies-of-his-letters-of-credence-to-bahrains-foreign-minister

Nye, J. S. (2008). Public diplomacy and soft power, *The ANNALS of the American Academy of Political and Social Science*, Vol. 616, No. 1, pp. 94–109. https://doi.org/10.1177/0002716207311699

Nye, Jr. J. S. (2010). Responding to My Critics and Concluding Thoughts. In I. Parmar & M. Cox (Eds.), *Soft Power and US Foreign Policy: Theoretical, Historical and Contemporary Perspectives.* London: Routledge. pp. 4–11.

Page J. (24 May 2007). Tiny island nation opens the first real embassy in virtual world. *The Times.* https://www.thetimes.co.uk/article/tiny-island-nation-opens-the-first-real-embassy-in-virtual-world-c3phsx2n2r0

Pop, A. (2021). Digital diplomacy approached as a subtype of public diplomacy. *Proceedings of the 17th International Scientific Conference Strategies XXI*, Vol. 17, No. 1, pp. 251–257. https://doi.org/10.53477/2668-2001-21-31

Public Diplomacy and Virtual Worlds. (2018.) USC Center on Public Diplomacy. https://uscpublicdiplomacy.org/research_project/public-diplomacy-and-virtual-worlds (Accessed January 18, 2023).

Ronald, J. D. (1997). *Parchment, Printing, and Hypermedia: Communication in World Order Transformation.* New York: Columbia University Press

Szondi, G. (2008). *Public Diplomacy and Nation Branding: Conceptual Similarities and Differences.* The Hague: Netherlands Institution of International Relations 'Clingendael'.

Tuncer, H. (2006). *Küresel Diplomasi.* Ankara: Ümit Yayıncılık

The 10 Commandments for Successful Digital Diplomacy (19 March 2018). Twiplomacy. https://www.twiplomacy.com/the-10-commandments/the-10-commandments

Twiplomacy Study 2020 (20 July 2020). Twiplomacy. https://www.twiplomacy.com/twiplomacy-study-2020

6 Science Diplomacy and COVID-19 Politics

Ebru Canan-Sokullu and Atakan Yılmaz

Introduction

The 21st century has witnessed an expansion of types and frequencies of security challenges such as pandemics, climate change, ever-deepening poverty, and wider technological disruption. These new challenges are called "wicked problems," as coined by Stone (2019: 8). Solutions to these problems have predominantly been through scientific explorations or collaborations across members of a global society. Technocrats and experts have become more addressed as solution providers (Turchetti and Lalli, 2020: 1). However, it has also been acknowledged that fighting emerging global challenges requires collaborations at multiple levels through science-diplomatic tools and strategies developed and adopted at individual, institutional, and governmental levels.

By fostering a constructive interaction and exchange of information/experience between the scientific and foreign policy communities, "science diplomacy" seeks to address global challenges and promote peaceful and productive relations among nations. It provides a novel and vital venue for collaboration that extends beyond the scientific community's scope to encompass governmental and academic processes (Buyuktanir Karacan, 2021: 9). Scholars of science diplomacy (Hormats, 2012; Royal Society/AAAS, 2010; Turekian and Neureiter, 2012) emphasise that science diplomacy offers a public good that can support efforts to manage global challenges, advance understanding, and enhance prosperity. They also assume that science diplomacy is a win-win formula that all parties of science diplomacy benefit from. Due to this faith, even if science diplomacy was conceived as a tool to promote national interests in its original formulation (Kaltofen and Acuto, 2018: 9), science diplomacy has gained more importance as the field prioritised normative concerns as well as dedication to meet demands of the governmental sector in the last decades.

The COVID-19 pandemic, which began as a health crisis and yet turned out to have severe implications on a great range of societal, economic, and political sectors, has urged a comprehensive examination of the role of and need for science diplomacy due to the simple fact that such a global crisis could be overcome through the guidance of scientific and diplomatic collaboration across the nations. Based on the COVID-19 case, this chapter addresses the importance and role of science diplomacy in facing global challenges in the post-COVID-19 era.

DOI: 10.4324/9781003377597-7

To this end, firstly, this study examines the concept of science diplomacy and its three pillars. The second part will discuss how national interest has played an essential role in science diplomacy from a critical perspective. Thirdly, the role of science diplomacy during the COVID-19 pandemic will be examined through international scientific cooperation between developed and underdeveloped countries. Finally, through the lenses of the COVID-19 case study, how science diplomacy would be advanced and improved to construct more resilient policies in the post-COVID-19 era will be discussed.

Triangular Conceptualisation of Science Diplomacy

Science diplomacy aims to build a constructive interaction between the scientific and foreign policy communities by bringing them together to address global issues and promote cooperation (Stone, 2019: 55). Science diplomacy provides a novel and vital venue for collaboration that goes beyond the scope of the scientific community to include the academic and government sectors (Buyuktanir Karacan, 2021: 9). To tackle global issues, it promotes scientific exchanges and collaborations across borders, enables innovative research capabilities, and establishes formative ties between countries (Fedoroff, 2009: 9; Turchetti and Lalli, 2020: 2). Science diplomacy combines scientific processes embedded in diplomatic relations among states. It is commonly interpreted as the use of science by integrating it into the field of foreign policy under the umbrella of international relations (IR) (Flink and Schreiterer, 2010). However, as a tool for foreign policy, science diplomacy goes beyond traditional diplomacy channels and constraints and operates beyond the ministries of foreign affairs.

Science diplomacy is an umbrella concept that is discussed regarding three domains, that is, "Science in diplomacy," "diplomacy for science," and "science for diplomacy" (Royal Society/AAAS, 2010). Firstly, "science in diplomacy" (SinD) implies using scientific knowledge and expertise to inform and strengthen diplomatic efforts. This pillar recognises science as an integral part of the diplomatic process. Scientific knowledge and guidance assist foreign policymakers when addressing global challenges. "Science in diplomacy" requires foreign policymakers to have basic scientific knowledge and responsibility to engage scientific foundations in policymaking (Bint El Hassan, 2012: 5; Özkaragöz Doğan, 2015: 48). The "Paris Climate Agreement," the "Agreement on Enhancing International Arctic Scientific Cooperation," and the Anti-Ballistic Missile Treaties can be examples of the SinD approach.

The second approach to science diplomacy is "Diplomacy for Science" (D4S), which incorporates achieving or pursuing technical and scientific international cooperation through trans-governmental diplomatic efforts and resources. Diplomatic tools and approaches are being utilised to establish and advance international scientific research and collaborations. A multi-partnered project such as the European Organization for Nuclear Research (CERN) is a prime example of D4S. Teamwork is essential for D4S as scientific initiatives and processes have extensive costs and require substantive infrastructure investments. States cannot bear economic and structural burdens individually (Royal Society/AAAS, 2010: 9).

Last, "Science for Diplomacy" (S4D) refers to utilising international scientific knowledge and collaborations to enhance or build diplomatic dialogue between states. While science has been primarily used as a hard power tool (i.e., in the military sector), the core idea of S4D is to ensure that states can continue communicating on scientific matters even during political stagnation among nations. Therefore, science not only does pave the way for impactful channels of political dialogue but can also contribute to expanding or preserving inter-state talks (Özkaragöz Doğan, 2015: 61). For example, the water issue has been a deadlock between Kyrgyzstan, Tajikistan, Kazakhstan, Uzbekistan, and Turkmenistan for years, and it has been posing a great obstacle to a better level of relations between them. By establishing the "European Union-Central Asia Water Science Diplomacy Platform," the European Commission seeks to use scientific cooperation as a tool to enhance regional coordination and strengthen dialogue between the EU and regional states (European Union External Action, 2018; Young et al., 2020: 52).

Forgotten Part of Science Diplomacy: National Interest

Some scholars have challenged the triangular conceptualisation of "Science Diplomacy." According to Fagerstein (2022: 5), such a triad taxonomy is useful when presenting various scientific practices; however, it explains little about the motivation, goals, or interests of actors involved in the process. Feuerstein (p. 6) offers a more straightforward definition of "science diplomacy" as "the use of science for foreign policy purposes," yet he does not exclude the possibility that this may incorporate practices of the triad if they are intentional efforts to link science to the pursuit of foreign policy goals. Even if practitioners have positively portrayed scientific diplomacy as a tool that may bring them closer to tackling global issues, it should always be kept in mind that science diplomacy is considered a means to promote national interests for most governments (Gluckman et al., 2017; Kaltofen and Acuto, 2018: 9).

Proponents of science diplomacy (Hormats, 2012; Royal Society/AAAS, 2010; Turekian and Neureiter, 2012) usually emphasise the utility of science diplomacy regarding its relevance to its capacity to manage global challenges, boost understanding, and increase influence and prosperity. This approach assumes that all parties of science diplomacy benefit from it; countries construct more positive ties, and through that development, societies benefit as well. Science diplomacy is portrayed as a magic win-win formula in which all societies benefit (Turchetti and Lalli, 2020: 2–3). However, the concept is still uncertain as it fails to provide a clear framework for how science diplomacy brings policymakers and scientists into collaborative relations (Fähnrich, 2015) and how it produces policy actions (Flink and Schreiterer, 2010).

Moreover, since science diplomacy practices are constructed by policymakers who constantly sacrifice science for political ends, scientists regard science diplomacy with prejudice (Stone, 2019: 63). In particular, the concern that politicians will interfere with the work of scientists and the possibility of political concerns' impact on scientific studies led to researchers' hesitation to engage in diplomacy. A caveat has been addressed by the "EU Strategic Forum for International Science and Technology Cooperation (SFIC) Task Force on Science Diplomacy" that "there was an urgent need to get out of the naive mainstream discourse on science diplomacy, driven by the idealism and internationalism of science" (European Research Area and Innovation Committee Strategic Forum for International S&T Cooperation, 2020: 8). In that respect, even if the concept of science diplomacy has expanded to include normative and global aspirations in the last decades, the core aspects of science diplomacy, which is to provide for the needs of states, have always remained the central part of the concept.

Indeed, in its original formulation, science diplomacy was conceived as a tool to advance national interests (Kaltofen and Acuto, 2018: 9). According to Scott Burchill (2005: 9–30), national interest is a dynamic concept that can be changed according to time and different factors such as domestic politics and international developments. Despite its dynamic nature, national interest is often equated with the realist tradition. It is considered a part of hard power politics rather than soft power in this context, when science is used to develop military technologies, as, during the Cold War, it is often considered as serving national interests. However, when science is regarded as a soft power tool, as in the case of science diplomacy, the role of national interest is mostly forgotten.

On the contrary, science serves as the normative aspect of diplomacy. As Nye (2004) underlines, states utilise scientific exchange and technical collaboration as soft power. In this way, they might use science to influence foreign policymakers and promote their research environments overseas that they might not otherwise reach. In other words, national interests and power politics pose significant obstacles to the normative aspects of science diplomacy. Power politics determine how states instrumentalise science diplomacy as a means of militarisation. For instance, due to the trade war between China and the United States (US) in 2020, the US either rejected or tightened Chinese graduate students' and researchers' visas to block Beijing from obtaining US technology with possible military uses (CNBC, 2021). Even Chinese students and researchers who are not related to military schools experience visa barriers, showing the usage of the visa as a political tool (Jeyaretnam, 2022). Power politics is also observed in deterrence. Due to the stagnation in relations between Türkiye and the EU over the last decade, EU visa procedures for scientists and researchers deteriorate scientific collaboration and the exchange of scientific diplomatic knowledge.[1] Even in a global health crisis like COVID-19, that developed countries were so unwilling and slow in implementing facilitation regulations to ease the restrictions over the patent of COVID-19 vaccines appears as another clear evidence of how power politics come into play.

The utility and conduct of science diplomacy are linked with states' development and industrial capabilities (Masters, 2016: 170). The emerging economies and underdeveloped/developing countries are considered "consumers," while the developed countries are the "producers" of scientific knowledge (Flink and Schreiterer, 2010: 665–677; Masters, 2016). For this reason, even if there is strong collaboration between states, unequal information sharing casts a shadow over cooperation. This has even led to criticisms as science diplomacy is a new kind of colonialism between the developed Western states, especially the sub-Saharan states (Stone, 2019: 63).

Science Diplomacy amid COVID-19: Medical Response Capabilities and Vaccine Nationalism

COVID-19 has served as a laboratory for science diplomacy and a testing ground for scientific cooperation between the Global South and the Global North. The international scientific community also serves as goodwill ambassadors that foster the global common good. The recent evidence for this understanding has been observed during the COVID-19 pandemic. Scientific community members collaborated primarily to develop a cure and response to the pandemic by relentlessly pioneering research, and World Health Organization (WHO) encouraged transnational scientific communities for enhanced cooperation without limiting their pandemic response research to national interests.[2] COVID-19 primarily emerged as a health crisis and spilt over into other security sectors. While states tried to restrict the movements of individuals through lockdowns and closing borders to prevent the spread of the virus, each strategy has led to disastrous impacts on other sectors. COVID-19 resulted in tremendous destructive consequences, including the deaths of almost 7 million people (WHO, 2022). Nearly all countries suffered from the collapse of healthcare systems in rapid and effective treatment capacities, and economies went into dire straits, which would linger in the long term. Trust in political systems collapsed as consequent restrictive measures were implied by governments in the framework of pandemic governance. However, scientific R&D achieved an unprecedentedly speedy discovery of COVID-19 vaccines and effective treatment methods, which emerged as a beacon of hope for individuals, societies, institutions, and governments at bleak times. So, what role did science diplomacy play?

Science diplomacy served as an important catalyst to respond to a global crisis – a pandemic – for two reasons concerning medical response capabilities. Firstly, science has played a substantial and impactful role in coping with the pandemic, which urged governments to allocate critical supplies for medical collaboration and dealing with humanitarian assistance (Pisupati, 2019: 13). Although COVID-19 is a member of the coronavirus family whose genome and structure have been studied for years, scientists developed a vaccine that would take 10–15 years to create under normal conditions in less than a year without compromising safety (Solis-Moreira, 2021). There are various reasons for this fast-paced vaccine development: The limited time amid a worldwide pandemic, increasing funding from governments, private firms, and multilateral organisations, technological development, and international scientific cooperation (Klobucista, 2022). At national and international levels, scientists mobilised quickly and initiated collaborations across different organisations and institutions. As a result, the pace of scientific progress in terms of the diagnosis, treatment, and development of vaccine has been unprecedented in scientific history.

Secondly, the role of diplomacy, especially in terms of cooperation for the distribution of the vaccine and protective equipment, has provided a significant foundation for governments' emergency response behaviour – mostly driven by self-interests. At the outset of the pandemic, states were short of protective equipment such as masks, gloves, and disinfectants. Their emergency survival response was to import these materials rather than producing at home. For instance, France seized 6 million masks in the stock of Swedish producer Mölnlycke headed to Spain and Italy (France 24, 2020). Moreover, Germany banned exporting protective medical equipment to Switzerland and Austria (Dahinten and Wabl, 2020). What is more, even among the EU members, instead of diplomatic cooperation and the principle of solidarity, states rushed to meet their citizens' safety needs, locking down the territorial borders to each other for collaboration. This was a moment of hard-core survival behaviour which egoistically lasted until the discovery and mass production of COVID-19 vaccines. Following the immediate aftermath of the discovery, global vaccine production was inevitably insufficient, yet the global demand was too high. Indispensably this process led to the so-called vaccine nationalism.

Vaccine nationalism had two implications. Firstly, major COVID-19 vaccine-producer countries exploited COVID-19 vaccines to advance their national diplomatic interests. For instance, Russia and China donated vaccines to other countries as aid or leveraged the distribution of vaccines to gain political influence (Connolly, 2021; Zhang and Jamali, 2022). Moreover, in some cases, the COVID-19 vaccine was weaponised against recipient countries to intervene in their domestic politics. For instance, China leveraged Sinovac vaccines to pressure Türkiye to deport Uighur Muslims (Gehrke, 2020). Secondly, shortages and inequities occurred during the distribution of vaccines. Even before the development of the COVID-19 vaccines, high-income countries had already signed purchase agreements that guaranteed them quicker and prior access to vaccines. Inevitably, this led the front runners with supplies of vaccines, where underdeveloped countries were left without any (Cansever, 2022). Accordingly, 72.8% of the people in high-income countries have been vaccinated with at least one dose, while only 28.31% of the population has been vaccinated with at least one dose in low-income countries (as of November 30, 2022; Data Futures Platform, n.d.).

As WHO Director-General Tedros Adhanom Ghebreyesus underlined, "Unless an unequal distribution of COVID-19 vaccines between rich and poor countries ends, the COVID-19 pandemic will not end" (Schlein, 2021). In this context, high-income countries have preferred to donate vaccines to overcome the inequity of COVID-19 vaccine distribution. So far, developed states have donated almost 2.5 billion doses of the COVID-19 vaccine to low-income countries (Our World in Data, 2022). Furthermore, dozens of countries at the World Trade Organization (WTO) have supported a patent waiver for COVID-19 vaccines to increase global production. However, some developed countries, such as Germany, oppose the idea because they believe patents motivate companies to continue pushing forward with new research (Klobucista, 2022; Reuters, 2022). Nonetheless, the WTO agreed to a deal to ease intellectual property constraints for producing the COVID-19 vaccine after a nearly two-year effort. Although this was a crucial step for science diplomacy, it should be noted that this decision came only after the pharmaceutical manufacturers were eventually able to produce an overstock of vaccines (Baschuk, 2022). The following remark of Piyush Vedprakash Goyal, who is the Minister of Commerce & Industry of India, depicts the issue quite well:

> What we are getting is completely half baked, and it will not allow us to make any vaccines ... Vaccines have already lost relevance ... It's just too late ... There is no demand for vaccines anymore ...
> (Ministry of Commerce & Industry of India, 2022)

In short, vaccine nationalism undermined science diplomacy. It fostered an atmosphere of deep mistrust and competition among states rather than collaboration. Inevitably, these developments hampered the sharing of resources and information vital for addressing a cross-border crisis like the COVID-19 pandemic.

Conclusion: Need for Revisiting Science Diplomacy

The COVID-19 pandemic reveals two important implications for science diplomacy. Firstly, it once again demonstrated how science diplomacy is critical for addressing global challenges. Since science diplomacy brings together scientific research communities, policymakers, and other stakeholders from different sectors and countries, it has a great potential to facilitate the share of information and cooperation in the event of a crisis. On the other hand, although the normative aspect of science diplomacy has come to the fore more in recent years, COVID-19 explicitly demonstrated the continued role of national interests in times of crisis. While some states prioritised sharing scientific knowledge and resources during the early phase of the pandemic, they primarily focused on securing their national interest and seriously neglected international collaboration. For instance, let alone not sharing personal protective equipment with other states, some countries seized the protective gear that would have been imported to other states. They have also acquired more vaccines than their own population needed, which caused the delay in accessing vaccines for other countries, especially underdeveloped countries. Hence, the lack of transparency and cooperation hampers global efforts to understand and address the pandemic and decreases trust among nations during globalisation.

This study argued that a mechanism that balances international scientific cooperation and national interest must be built for science diplomacy to achieve practical functionality. After all, it will not be a prophecy to predict that states will act in a way that prioritises themselves in a possible crisis in the post-COVID era. There is no method to reverse this situation in the foreseeable future. This study reiterated the nationalist assumption that science diplomacy is limited by national interests during the crisis. Moreover, science diplomacy should prioritise a structure in which states have a resilient mechanism for crises. Without a resilient mechanism, it is impossible to maintain a system that sustains scientific diplomatic dialogue and cooperation, at least in the early phase of the crisis. As for the post-pandemic era, crises will continue to exist. Therefore, it would be more realistic to argue that science diplomacy does not eradicate crises but serves to implement effective preventive or recovery mechanisms. To boost resilience, states need to invest in research and development and strengthen their infrastructure and the capacity of professionals. In cases where states are insufficient, international organisations need to lend assistance.

If each state has resilience against global problems, states can fight independently, and international collaboration can be more easily attained. This way, support can be more easily provided to countries needing assistance. To this end, this study emphasised the increasing responsibility of international organisations and cooperative initiatives to support science diplomacy.

Notes

1 Due to deteriorating relations between the EU and Türkiye, the percentage of Schengen visa refusals for Turks significantly increased. While it was 4% in 2014, it will grow to 19% in 2021 (SchengenVisaInfo, 2022).
2 For instance, "COVID-19 Clinical Research Coalition" is a forefront international scientific network coordinating clinical research to develop new treatments and vaccines and understanding the long-term impacts of COVID-19 on health (COVID-19 Clinical Research Coalition, 2022). Also, with the coordination of the WHO, there have been significant international scientific initiatives such as "*The WHO Solidarity PLUS Trial*" and "*The Covid-19 Vaccine Global Access (COVAX) Facility.*" "The WHO Solidarity PLUS Trial" involves researchers from more than 100 countries testing the efficacy of potential treatments for COVID-19 (WHO, 2021). On the other hand, "The COVID-19 Vaccine Global Access (COVAX) Facility" is a global partnership led by the WHO, vaccine alliance GAVI, the Coalition for Epidemic Preparedness Innovations (CEPI), and UNICEF to ensure that COVID-19 vaccines are developed and distributed equitably around the world (WHO, 2020).

References

Baschuk, B. (2022) 'WTO approves vaccine-patent waiver to help combat Covid pandemic', *Bloomberg*, June 17. Available at: https://www.bloomberg.com/news/articles/2022-06-17/wto-approves-vaccine-patent-waiver-to-help-combat-covid-pandemic (Accessed: November 19, 2022).

Bint El Hassan, S. (2012) 'New partnerships to sustain the Middle East and the world', *Science & Diplomacy*, 1(3). Available at: https://www.sciencediplomacy.org/sites/default/files/new_partnerships_to_sustain_the_middle_east_and_the_world_science__diplomacy.pdf (Accessed: September 18, 2022).

Burchill, S. (2005) *The national interest in international relations theory*. New York, NY: Palgrave Macmillan.

Buyuktanir Karacan, D. (2021) 'Science diplomacy as a foreign policy tool for Türkiye and the ramifications of collaboration with the EU', *Humanities and Social Sciences Communications*, 8(1), pp. 1–12.

Cansever, İ. H. (2022) 'We first! Vaccine nationalism in the Covid-19 process', *Turkish Journal of Public Health*, 20(2), pp. 244–258.

CNBC (2021) 'Chinese students hit by US visa rejections amid tension', Available at: https://www.cnbc.com/2021/09/14/chinese-students-hit-by-us-visa-rejections-amid-tension.html (Accessed: November 14, 2022).

Connolly, K. (2021) 'Sputnik V: How Russia's Covid vaccine is dividing Europe', *BBC News*, April 17. Available at: https://www.bbc.com/news/world-europe-56735931 (Accessed: September 28, 2022).

COVID-19 Clinical Research Coalition (2022) 'Global coalition to accelerate COVİD-19 clinical research in resource-limited settings', *The Lancet*, 395(10233), pp. 1322–1325.

Dahinten, Jan, & Wabl, M. (2020) 'Germany faces backlash from neighbors over mask export ban', *Bloomberg*, March 09. Available at: https://www.bloomberg.com/news/articles/2020-03-09/germany-faces-backlash-from-neighbors-over-mask-export-ban (Accessed: September 13, 2022).

Data Futures Platform (n.d.) 'Global dashboard for vaccine equity', Available at: https://data.undp.org/vaccine-equity/ (Accessed: November 30, 2022).

European Research Area and Innovation Committee Strategic Forum for International S&T Cooperation (2020) 'Fic Task Force on science diplomacy working paper', September. Available at: https://data.consilium.europa.eu/doc/document/ST-1357-2020-INIT/en/pdf (Accessed: November 17, 2022).

European Union External Action (2018) 'Regional coordination and support for the EU-Central Asia enhanced regional cooperation on Environment, Climate Change and Water (WECOOP Phase 2)', June 26. Available at: https://www.eeas.europa.eu/node/47276_en (Accessed: December 05, 2022).

Fähnrich B. (2015) 'Science diplomacy: Investigating the perspective of scholars on politics-science collaboration in international affairs', *Public Understanding of Science*, 26(6), pp. 688–703.

Fedoroff, N. V. (2009) 'Science diplomacy in the 21st century', *Cell*, 136(1), pp. 9–11.

Flink, T., & Schreiterer, U. (2010) 'Science diplomacy at the intersection of S&T policies and foreign affairs: Toward a typology of national approaches', *Science and Public Policy*, 37(9), pp. 665–677.

France 24 (2020) 'Solidarity? Regarding masks, it's every nation for itself', April 03. Available at: https://www.france24.com/en/20200403-solidarity-when-it-comes-to-masks-it-s-every-nation-for-itself (Accessed: September 14, 2022).

Gehrke, J. (2020) 'China "leveraging" coronavirus vaccine to pressure Türkiye to deport Uighur Muslims back to repression', *Washington Examiner*, December 30. Available at: https://www.washingtonexaminer.com/policy/defense-national-security/china-coronavirus-vaccine-uighur-deportations-Türkiye (Accessed: October 4, 2022).

Gluckman, P. D., Turekian, V., Grimes, R. W., & Kishi, T. (2017) 'Science diplomacy: A pragmatic perspective from the inside', *Science & Diplomacy*, 6(4). Available at: https://www.sciencediplomacy.org/article/2018/pragmatic-perspective (Accessed: November 19, 2022).

Hormats, R. D. (2012) 'Science diplomacy and twenty-first century statecraft', *Science & Diplomacy*, 1(1). Available at: http://www.sciencediplomacy.org/perspective/2012/science-diplomacy-and-twenty-first-century-statecraft (Accessed: November 9, 2022).

Jeyaretnam, M. (2022). 'Chinese students at Yale continue to face challenges getting visas', *Yale Daily News*, September 7. Available at: https://yaledailynews.com/blog/2022/09/07/chinese-students-at-yale-continue-to-face-challenges-getting-visas/ (Accessed: November 19, 2022).

Kaltofen, C., & Acuto, M. (2018) 'Rebalancing the encounter between science diplomacy and international relations theory', *Global Policy*, 9(3), pp. 15–22.

Klobucista, C. (2022) 'A guide to global Covid-19 vaccine efforts', Council of Foreign Relations. Available at: https://www.cfr.org/backgrounder/guide-global-Covid-19-vaccine-efforts (Accessed: November 5, 2022).

Masters, L. (2016) 'South Africa's two track approach to science diplomacy', *Journal for Contemporary History*, 41(1), pp. 169–186.

Ministry of Commerce & Industry of India (2022) 'Statement by Shri Piyush Goyal during the WTO 12th Ministerial Conference at the meeting with co-sponsors of TRIPS waiver', June 14. Available at: https://pib.gov.in/PressReleasePage.aspx?PRID=1834066 (Accessed: November 19, 2022).

Nye, J. (2004) *Soft power: The means to success in world politics*. New York: Public Affairs.

Our World in Data (2022) 'Covid-19 vaccine doses donated to COVAX', March 23. Available at: https://ourworldindata.org/grapher/covax-donations (Accessed: November 24, 2022).

Özkaragöz Doğan, E. (2015) 'Science Diplomacy in the Global Age: Examples from Türkiye and the World', PhD Thesis, Middle East Technical University, Ankara.

Pisupati, B. (2019) 'Science diplomacy: COVİD-19 and beyond', *RIS Diary Third Special Issue on Covid*. Available at: https://ris.org.in/newsletter/diary/2020/Covid%2019%20III/pdf/Balakrishna%20Pisupati.pdf (Accessed: September 26, 2022).

Reuters. (2022) 'Germany speaks out against COVİD-19 vaccine patent waiver', March 28. Available at: https://www.reuters.com/world/europe/germany-speaks-out-against-Covid-19-vaccine-patent-waiver-2022-03-28/ (Accessed: November 05, 2022).

Royal Society/AAAS (2010) *New frontiers in science diplomacy*. London: Royal Society.

SchengenVisaInfo (2022) 'Turkish nationals face problems due to Schengen visa delays & refusals,' August 26. Available at: https://www.schengenvisainfo.com/news/turkish-nationals-face-problems-due-to-schengen-visa-delays-refusals/ (Accessed: November 4, 2022).

Schlein, L. (2021) 'Pandemic will end when vaccine inequity ends, WHO chief says', *VOA*, December 20. Available at: https://www.voanews.com/a/pandemic-will-end-when-vaccine-inequity-ends-who-chief-says-teaser-who-says-boosters-should-be-given-to-the-elderly-and-people-who-are-immunocompromised-and-not-to-those-at-low-risk-such-as-children-/6362485.html (Accessed: November 30, 2022).

Solis-Moreira, J. (2021). 'How did we develop a COVID-19 vaccine so quickly?', *Medical News Today*, November 13. Available at: https://www.medicalnewstoday.com/articles/how-did-we-develop-a-Covid-19-vaccine-so-quickly (Accessed: November 19, 2022).

Stone, D. (2019) *Making global policy*. Cambridge University Press.

Turchetti, S., & Lalli, R. (2020) 'Envisioning a "science diplomacy 2.0": On data, global challenges, and multi-layered networks', *Humanities and Social Sciences Communications*, 7(1), pp. 1–9.

Turekian, V.C., & Neureiter, N. P. (2012) 'Science and diplomacy: The past as prologue', *Science & Diplomacy*, 1(1). Available at: https://www.sciencediplomacy.org/sites/default/files/science_and_diplomacy.pdf (Accessed: December 10, 2022).

World Health Organization (WHO) (2020) 'More than 150 countries engaged in COVİD-19 vaccine global access facility', July 15. Available at: https://www.who.int/news/item/15-07-2020-more-than-150-countries-engaged-in-Covid-19-vaccine-global-access-facility (Accessed: November 20, 2022).

———. (2021). 'Solidarity Trial Plus Protocol'. Available at: https://cdn.who.int/media/docs/default-source/documents/r-d-blueprint-meetings/who_covid19_solidarityplus_prtcl_v1.0_en_2021.04.05.pdf?sfvrsn=393190e1_5&download=true (Accessed: November 20, 2022).

———. (2022). WHO Coronavirus (COVİD-19) Dashboard. Available at: https://covid19.who.int/ (Accessed: December 4, 2022).

Young, M., Flink, T., & Dall, E. (2020) *Science diplomacy in the making: Case-based insights from the S4D4C project*. Vienna: S4D4C.

Zhang, D., & Jamali, A. B. (2022) 'China's "weaponized" vaccine: Intertwining between international and domestic politics', *East Asia*, 39, pp. 279–296.

Part II

National and Regional Responses to COVID-19

7 Global Health Diplomacy and Türkiye[1]

İdris Demir

Introduction

Problems such as chronic diseases, infectious diseases, armed conflicts, and deaths of newborns and young children are humanitarian crises. These humanitarian crises can lead to conflict, displaced communities, food shortages, political instability, deterioration of the social structure of society, and permanent damage to countries' infrastructure. Durable solutions to such problems require international cooperation, even if they occur within the borders of nation-states. Developing multilateral collaboration, ensuring the equitable distribution of resources, and emphasising diplomacy require an interdisciplinary approach. Global health diplomacy is becoming a sui generis field of study that struggles to overcome such problems (Barber et al., 2011: 481).

In this context, the World Health Organization (WHO) defines global health diplomacy as "concentrating on the negotiations that shape and govern global health-related policy, bringing together the disciplines of public health, international relations, management, law and economics" (WHO, 2018). Global health also includes basic needs necessary to ensure human security, such as universal respect for human rights, personal protection, the rule of law, access to food and drink, health care, education, basic infrastructure, and safety (Nang and Martin, 2017: 1457).

International efforts to control infectious diseases date back to the implementation of quarantine in Dubrovnik in the 14th century. In 1851, an "International Health Conference" was convened in Europe to prevent the spread of epidemic diseases such as cholera and the plague and establish multilateral and multidimensional cooperation. These efforts paved the way for international health agreements and pioneered the studies for establishing organisations such as the Pan American Health Organization and the WHO in the future (Hotez, 2014: 1).

Global health diplomacy opens a new window for International Relations and public health studies. In terms of the level of development in the health sector, Türkiye has great potential to increase its effectiveness and develop new areas of cooperation within the framework of global health diplomacy in geographies where it has historically developed close relations, such as the Middle East, Central Asia, the Balkans, and Africa. Successfully putting this potential into practice and

DOI: 10.4324/9781003377597-9

achieving various gains in the field of international relations can be possible with the coordination of public and non-governmental organisations (NGOs) operating in the health sector.

In this context, the first part of this study describes the theory of global health diplomacy. The second part examines the interaction between health diplomacy and international relations theories. The third part covers examples regarding health diplomacy practices from various countries and some activities of Türkiye in this new diplomacy branch.

Global Health Diplomacy

Global health diplomacy is defined as political work that aims to strengthen international relations studies in problem areas such as conflict zones and resource-scarce regions while raising the level of global health (Novotny and Adams, 2007: 1). International health diplomacy can be considered as a new concept in foreign policy studies, expressed as the efforts of state and non-governmental actors to integrate health into foreign policy negotiations and the creation of new forms for global health governance (Kickbusch et al., 2007: 230). In this context, health issues can be discussed under six policy frameworks in foreign policy studies. These frameworks are security, development, being a global public product, trade, human rights, and moral/ethical reasons (Labonte and Gagnon, 2010: 15). Global health diplomacy focuses on international negotiation processes on health or health-related issues (Smith and Irwin, 2016: 1).

In 2007, the Ministers of Foreign Affairs of Brazil, France, Indonesia, Norway, Senegal, South Africa, and Thailand came together and announced the Oslo Ministerial Declaration. In this declaration, the ministers defined topics and problems regarding health as "the dominant and challenging foreign policy events of our time." It is noteworthy that this study, which examines foreign policy and development strategies from the perspective of global health, was carried out with the participation of the foreign ministers of the signatory countries rather than by the ministers of health.

In November 2008, 55 UN member states initiated a United Nations General Assembly Resolution on global health and foreign policy, which warned member states to "take into account health issues while formulating foreign policy" (Labonte et al., 2012: 163). This was followed by some states' government decisions, policies, and commentary reports. Sweden's development policy, Switzerland's health foreign policy approach, Norway's policy adaptation commission, and the UK's Health is Global strategy can be evaluated within this framework. In addition, in 2009, the United States (US) created a report on foreign policy regarding global health, and the United Nations Economic and Social Council emphasised global public health.

In this context, the US launched the US Global Health Initiative in 2009. A $63 billion fund has been allocated for studies related to HIV/AIDS, tuberculosis, malaria, prevention of infant and child mortality, etc. In addition, the Global Fund was established to solve global health problems and comprised representatives of various states, the private sector, non-governmental organisations, and non-state actors. The scope and budget of the Global Fund, which contributed to global health studies with a budget of $21.7 billion in 2011, continued to increase over the years (Balcius and Novotny, 2011: 234–235).

There is a multi-stakeholder structure in the field of global health diplomacy. International organisations, various international non-governmental organisations, some foundations, and nation-states carry out their studies in global health diplomacy at different scales and geographies and contexts. Actors like the Melinda-Bill Gates Foundation, a wide range of nation-states from Türkiye to Cuba, and some international organisations such as the WHO can carry out multilateral and unilateral studies in different geographies of the globe, at other times and with different contents.

The Millennium Development Goals, announced by the UN, form the basis and infrastructure of the coordination and financing of many global health efforts today. In this context, some UN agencies such as UNICEF, the Joint United Nations Programme on HIV and AIDS (UNAIDS), the United Nations Population Fund (UNFPA), the United Nations Development Programme (UNDP), the World Food Programme (WFP), the United Nations Environment Programme (UNEP), the Food and Agriculture Organization (FAO), and the International Fund for Agricultural Development (IFAD) and with institutions corporate identities like the World Bank and the International Monetary Fund (IMF) undertake the responsibility of carrying out studies on the financing and social dimensions of the activities related to global health (Mackey and Liang, 2013: 13).

Global health diplomacy enables the balancing of concrete national interests and the common intangible concerns of the international community about health in a broader sense and brings them together. It also seeks to reduce and eliminate unequal access to health services internationally. It helps to secure global human rights. It paves the way for international health interventions to be sensitive to historical, economic, social, cultural, and political differences. In this context, foreign policymakers have also realised the importance of global health issues in the international economy, global health security, and regional political stability (Mackey and Strathdee, 2015: 5–6).

The main concerns of foreign policy and diplomacy have traditionally been trade, economy, energy, politics, sanctions, and defence. After global health diplomacy studies became popular, policymakers, diplomats, decision-makers, public officials, and other stakeholders have become more aware of the importance and priority of health issues within the foreign policy framework. Topics such as infectious diseases crossing borders and increasing epidemics have begun to be considered problem areas that require urgent action in the diplomatic negotiation processes.

Considering that health is a common value shared by all people, it should be remembered that international health programmes can form the basis of diplomacy and negotiation processes which will bring together countries that do not have a common ground and agenda. It should be kept in mind that cooperation and aid processes while combating global health problems will improve diplomatic relations and pave the way for pursuing common foreign policies (Katz and Singer, 2007: 234). In this sense, it is evident that global health diplomacy has features that will contribute to international peace and stability.

Health Diplomacy and International Relations Theory

Health is an issue that requires the keen attention of every nation-state. Infectious diseases, epidemics, and natural disasters that easily cross borders necessitate international intervention. In this context, the transfer of scientific knowledge, diplomatic studies, and joint projects developed against common threats can form the basis for the development of strong ties between nation-states; moreover, they can lead to the establishment of new communication channels and reduce tensions (Rao et al., 2017: 143). Thus, diplomacy and foreign policy have increasing importance in global health studies.

The relationship between global health and the theory and practice of international relations is such as it will make significant contributions to the efforts for ensuring world peace (Kevany, 2014a: 2). In today's international relations, where concepts such as integration, interdependence, and globalisation come into prominence, the importance of health issues (Frist, 2007: 210) that go beyond political and cultural boundaries in foreign policy studies is increasing.

In global health interventions, it is stated that appropriate diplomacy and foreign policy sensitivities can be applied in harmony with each other. International health programmes can be implemented to ensure global security, conflict resolution, and stability in unsafe areas. In addition, international health programmes can also be carried out to be closely acquainted with the cultures and preferences of local communities to analyse them better (Kevany, 2015c: 833).

When properly selected, shaped, and implemented, global health interventions and studies pave the way for significant diplomatic advantages for donor and recipient countries. But it should be kept in mind that overlooking the principles and objectives of foreign policy and international relations while designing, selecting, and shaping global health programmes may result in tension and turmoil (Kevany, 2015a: 2).

There are approaches stating that the relationship between global health and foreign policy is generally handled within the framework of the realist tradition of International Relations theory. The relationship between the economic interests and national security perceptions of nation-states is perceived as a high policy issue. The attitudes and priorities of nation-states in case of international health events are evaluated within this framework. Global health diplomacy enables nation-states to use their diplomatic skills and practices in multilateral or bilateral negotiation processes to achieve goals in these areas (Jones et al., 2017: 69).

However, it is worth noting that time has passed since the emergence of global health diplomacy has made progress at both theoretical and practical levels within the scope of international relations studies, considering its evolution.

It is known that the execution of bilateral medical aid programmes by states within the scope of global health diplomacy contributes to their international image and increases their recognition and prestige. As a result, it is accepted that the soft power of those states also grows, and their area of influence expands.

States, the basic building blocks of the discipline of International Relations, can use their soft power capacities through global health policy practices and increase and strengthen their influence on other states and the public. In this sense, the fact that health has become a foreign policy issue is generally associated with the constructivism theory of International Relations (Ruckert et al., 2016: 63).

If the concept of global health diplomacy is addressed as an umbrella term, interactions related to international public health can be examined under three different categories. These can be categorised as core diplomacy, multi-stakeholder diplomacy, and informal diplomacy (Katz et al., 2011: 506).

Core diplomacy includes formal interaction, communication, and contacts between governments or nation-states. These contacts include policy implementation, new policy development, negotiation, intelligence, and issue-based diplomatic activities. When examined from the perspective of 1648 Westphalia, one of the main building blocks of international relations studies, core global health diplomacy is defined as negotiations aiming to solve the problems between nation-states and creating official agreements (Katz et al., 2011: 506).

Bilateral negotiations between two countries are the most common traditional form of core diplomacy. Negotiation processes can be evaluated within this framework, in which high-ranked representatives of nations come together and sign formal agreements until the results are binding. Another dimension of core diplomacy includes international multilateral agreements. Multilateral/multinational agreements that enable multilateral international organisations regulating global health practices and norms, such as the WHO, to come to life and become operational can be evaluated within this framework. Studies such as the World Health Assembly (WHA), the Framework Agreement on Tobacco Control, and international health regulations can be assessed within this framework (Katz et al., 2011: 506–507).

Multi-stakeholder diplomacy in global health studies encompasses international negotiation processes in which various states, non-states, and multilateral actors interact to solve common problems. Institutions of states, non-state organisations, and representatives of the private sector can distribute health services, capacity-building projects, and research and development studies in cooperation. Public and private sector institutions can carry out global health collaborations. Organisations such as the Global Fund to Fight AIDS, Tuberculosis and Malaria, the GAVI Alliance and the Global Polio Eradication Initiative can be interpreted within this framework (Katz et al., 2011: 508).

On the other hand, informal global health diplomacy includes interaction, communication, and work with public health actors and their colleagues in different geographies of the globe. These include the work of civil servants of host countries, healthcare professionals and representatives of non-state organisations, and private and public sector entrepreneurs (Katz et al., 2011: 510).

The health aspects linked with a foreign policy are examined from a classical International Relations theory perspective; many states consider them "high politics" issues by affiliating them with national security and economic interests. It can be stated that issues such as development, human rights, and moral/ethical reasons, which are among the reasons for global health aid, are considered "low policy" issues of International Relations; however, in practice, they do not find a common place (Labonte and Gagnon, 2010: 1). However, it is worth noting that there is no unity in the literature on this issue. Even though all health issues are elaborated within low-policy topics, with the development of global health diplomacy, health issues are considered high political problems today.

Securitisation of health has now become an enduring element of health governance. A healthy society is one of the fundamentals of security, stability, and prosperity. It is stated that diseases cause conflict; as a result, they harm social life and threaten political power and political structure.

Security is vital for the nation-state and is considered among the most important components of international relations studies. In this context, it should be noted that even military security interventions are made with health concerns in mind. There are three main reasons for interventions in foreign states due to epidemics. First, it should be remembered that epidemic-based, health-centred national problems will likely expand and spread onto the regional plane. The effects of regional expansion, on the other hand, have the potential to cause regional instability by disturbing the balanced regional foreign policy. The second reason is the approach that health-related poverty, misery, and unfavourable living conditions lead to an increase in terrorist activities, which in turn poses a threat to national security. These terrorist activities within the country's borders may cross borders and threaten neighbouring states and regional security. Thirdly, it is stated that epidemics, health-based national and regional conflicts, and peacekeeping efforts can slow down the economic development of other neighbouring countries that are not a party to the problem, reduce their exports, and as a result harm their financial security (Labonte and Gagnon, 2010: 3–4).

In addition to security, it is known that investments in global health issues and activities in this field also contribute to the international reputation of countries. To see health as a human right norm by providing solidarity at the international level can also provide an opportunity to develop cooperation between different stakeholders as a platform (Gagnon and Labonte, 2013: 17). In this aspect, normative, ethical, and moral motives can explain the interaction between International Relations theory and global health diplomacy practices. Whether with security concerns or normative considerations, nation-states nowadays can be observed trying to open up a wide area for themselves in international politics by using tools and practices of global health diplomacy.

Various Health Diplomacy Practices

Although health problems are defined and perceived as transnational, it is useful to remember that nation-states are at the centre of diplomatic practices. Nation-states must develop health and foreign policy practices that can contribute to their national interests in harmony with the diplomatic, epidemiological, and ethical realities of today's globalised world (Drager and Fidler, 2007: 162).

For instance, the COVID-19 pandemic was not limited to the city of Wuhan, China, where it emerged. The virus has spread to all countries of the globalised world in a very short time. According to the estimates of the WHO, approximately 14.9 million deaths were associated with the COVID-19 pandemic in 2020 and 2021 (WHO, 2022). As of February 2023, it is still needed to be clarified how long the deadly effects of this epidemic will continue and when it will be brought under control. Efforts to contain the pandemic and eliminate its negative effects require national and global cooperation. To prevent this pandemic, nation-states, international organizations, NGOs, and other health stakeholders must act together and make joint contributions to global health diplomacy studies.

Cuba is one of the leading countries within the scope of global health diplomacy studies. Considering economic parameters, geographical location, military capacity, and political power, Cuba seems far from maintaining a prominent position in international politics; however, it is one of the leading countries in the world in the field of global health diplomacy studies. Cuba's health diplomacy has been described as "quiet and effective." Cuba has given importance to soft power elements in international politics. In this context, Cuba used health diplomacy for purposes such as winning over friendly nations for the regime and being effective on the public opinion of the countries with which it interacts. Health diplomacy has been one of the cornerstones of Cuban foreign policy. Despite being a developing country, Cuba has periodically provided medical support to many developing countries, offered humanitarian aid through health diplomacy, displayed ideological solidarity, and endeavoured to serve the purpose of ensuring its national interests (Erman, 2016: 84). Cuba started its health diplomacy studies in the 1960s. The new government established in Cuba sent medical teams to Algeria, which was waging a civil war against France, and Chile, which was trying to heal the wounds of a devastating earthquake. In this way, it has sought to develop various levels of cooperation with these countries and the peoples of these countries. It is stated that between the years 1961 and 2008, 270.743 Cuban health workers and doctors operated in health diplomacy in 154 countries (Werlau, 2013: 58).

Within the framework of south-south cooperation, Brazil also seeks to develop structural collaboration with African countries on health issues. As one of the signatories of the Oslo Ministerial Declaration signed in 2007, Brazil carries out capacity-building activities in the health sector of African countries and attaches importance to long-term health investments and cooperation according to the country's needs. Health diplomacy activities, which progress simultaneously with Brazil's investments in mining and construction projects in Africa, undoubtedly open new market areas for export products of Brazilian origin (Ramirez et al., 2018: 10).

It is worth mentioning that China is also conducting health diplomacy, especially in the African region. Chinese medical aid in Africa dates to 1963 when a Chinese medical team began operating in Algeria. With the Forum on China-Africa Cooperation (FOCAC) held in 2000, China's contribution to Africa's health sector increased even more. In 2009, China provided an estimated $1.4 billion in development aid to 48 African countries (McLaughlin et al., 2014: 583). China's health diplomacy in Africa also includes building health institutions, training health employees, and granting scholarships to African students to study medicine at Chinese universities. China's health investments in Africa have improved its health conditions and diplomatic relations. The development of China-Africa diplomatic relations has provided alliances in international organisations such as the United Nations and contributed to various trade and business opportunities (McLaughlin et al., 2014: 584).

Türkiye's Health Diplomacy Profile

It is accepted that the international system-level interaction of global health diplomacy is the WHO. WHO's global health policies and practices include the WHA, one of the most effective decision-making mechanisms of global health governance, where representatives of member countries present their approaches, exchange ideas, and interact. As a country that has been trying to be effective in global health diplomacy studies in recent years, Türkiye took the floor 65 times in WHA meetings between 2000 and 2012 and informed the international public about its perspectives. It is worth noting that Türkiye ranks 18th among 194 member countries with this performance (Rijt and Pang, 2015: 397).

In addition to these efforts at the level of international organisations, some Turkish NGOs also carry out useful and effective work within the framework of global health diplomacy. Organisations such as the Red Crescent, Doctors Worldwide, Doctors Without Borders, the International Doctors Association, and the Disaster and Emergency Management Authority (AFAD) (Hayran, 2017: 21) carry out health activities outside the borders of Türkiye and try to make significant contributions to the elimination of health problems in various geographies.

The Republic of Türkiye has been involved in various humanitarian aid activities, especially regarding health issues, in geographies with which it has interacted closely in the past, such as the Middle East, Central Asia, the Balkans, and Africa, via state institutions and NGOs. However, what matters most is to make grounded analyses to provide permanent solutions to problems and leave positive effects on global and bilateral relations rather than helping a lot (Hayran, 2017: 21).

Academic programmes in global health have recognised the key importance of practical experience. Moreover, today's students will be tomorrow's policymakers and practitioners. Thus, global health diplomacy practices and research should raise students' awareness regarding the realities of international policymaking and implementation processes (Wipfli and Kotlewski, 2014: 839). Every level of education programme that includes this approach in its academic structure will establish long-term constructive relations between the parties in the field of health diplomacy at the institutional level.

It is worth noting that the University of Health Sciences (Sağlık Bilimleri Üniversitesi) in Türkiye has opened various academic programmes in the African continent as part of the institutional training pillar of Türkiye's health diplomacy studies. Although there are programmes that have already started education by recruiting students, there are also departments that are in the establishment process and will begin admitting students soon. Vocational schools of the University of Health Sciences abroad, namely Bamgsomoro Sultan Kudarat Vocational School of Health Services, Somali Mogadishu Recep Tayyip Erdoğan Vocational School of Health Services, Sudan Nyala Vocational School of Health Services, Uzbekistan Bukhara Ibni Sina Vocational School of Health Services, and institutes such as the Sudan Khartoum Institute of Health Sciences (University of Health Sciences, 2022) contribute to training activities. These institutions can be evaluated as permanent elements of Türkiye's health diplomacy.

Türkiye has actively contributed to the cooperation initiatives against the COVID-19 outbreak. Based on the data provided by the Ministry of Foreign Affairs of the Republic of Türkiye, Türkiye has received assistance requests in different categories (material grants, cash assistance, purchase/export permits) from 161 countries and has provided aid to 160 countries during the COVID-19 pandemic. Among the regions from which Türkiye received aid requests were mostly from the African continent with 49 countries. Europe followed Africa with 41 countries, Asia with 35 countries, America with 21 countries, and Oceania with 15 countries. The Ministry also stated that in addition to these countries, 20 international organisations/its affiliated organisations have also requested assistance from Türkiye. The requests of 12 organisations, namely the United Nations Office for the Coordination of Humanitarian Affairs (OCHA), UNICEF, the Pakistani Air Force (PAF), the Central American Integration System (SICA), the Caribbean Community and Common Market (CARICOM), NATO, the Intergovernmental Authority on Development (IGAD), the WHO, the OSCE, the International Federation of Red Cross and Red Crescent Societies (IFRC), the UN Relief and Works Agency for Palestine Refugees in the Near East (UNRWA), and the Africa Centres for Disease Control and Prevention (Africa CDC), have been met by Türkiye, in part or entirely. The aid mostly consisted of medical equipment, particularly personal protective equipment such as masks, but respiratory devices produced in Türkiye were also granted to the countries in need. As of April 20, 2022, more than 6.3 million vaccine doses have been donated to Bosnia and Herzegovina, Montenegro, the Turkish Republic of Northern Cyprus (TRNC), Kyrgyzstan, North Macedonia, Libya, Moldova, Uzbekistan, Senegal, Tunisia, Turkmenistan and Burkina Faso, Democratic Republic of Congo, Benin, Niger, Somalia, Tanzania, Mali, and Sierra Leone (Republic of Türkiye Ministry of Foreign Affairs, 2022).

Moreover, Türkiye was also involved in the vaccine development efforts for COVID-19 and declared that Türkiye would offer the Turkovac vaccine, which has been authorised for emergency use at the national level, to the service of all humanity (Presidency of the Republic of Türkiye, 2021).

Conclusion

Traditional diplomacy perspectives and studies expanded on economy and trade in the 1950s and developed further in the 1980s to include environmental issues. On the other hand, it is claimed that the focus of 21st century diplomacy studies is on "health" issues (Kickbusch et al., 2007: 232).

Efforts to blend and harmonise public health and foreign policy practices are increasingly continuing. Nation-states, the main actors of International Relations, have tended to make global health activities an institutional element of their foreign policies.

Different nation-states have begun to employ "Health Attachés" within the structures of their foreign ministries and their representations in other nation-states with which they have relations. Emphasis is placed on the efforts of health attachés to gain competence in matters such as diplomacy, negotiation, and intercultural harmony. In this context, it is worth noting that there are diplomats accredited with the title of "Health" in the Capital, Washington, among the foreign delegations operating in the US. A health advisor from Canada, a Health and Business Attaché from Denmark, a Minister-Consultant for Food Safety from the European Union, a Health and Consumer Relations Attaché from France, a Health Attaché from Kuwait, and a Health Counsellor each from Saudi Arabia and South Africa are represented in the US to carry out diplomatic activities (Brown et al., 2018: 3).

Global health diplomacy brings together the art of diplomacy and the science of public health on common ground (Hunter et al., 2013: 87). Diplomatic negotiations, in which global health and the foreign policy objectives of nation-states are blended ethically and coordinated in harmony with each other, can alleviate political and military conflicts and differences. It should not be forgotten that such an approach, while creating a common ground for achieving a concept such as "world peace," also contributes to attaining international health goals (Kevany, 2015b: 613). However, time will tell whether Türkiye, as a developing country, is getting stronger and has come a long way in making its weight and influence felt more and more in international politics, or if it will be successful in taking a leading role by realising its existing potential in health diplomacy.

Notes

1 Material in the chapter has been reused from the article published in Turkish in the *Iğdır Üniversity Journal of Social Sciences* "Küresel Sağlık Diplomasisi ve Türkiye", 2021 Special Issue, pp. 131–149. The author is grateful for permission to reuse this.

References

Balcius, J. and Novotny, T. (2011). "New Approaches to Global Health Governance: The Evolution to Public-Private Partnerships", *Journal of Commercial Biotechnology*, Volume 17, No. 3, pp. 233–240.

Barber, J., Rockswold, P., and Cohen, B. (2011). "Global Health Diplomacy: A Call to Action", *Military Medicine*, Volume 176, May 2011, pp. 481–483.

Brown, M., Bergmann, J., Novotny, T., and Mackey, T. (2018). "Applied Global Health Diplomacy: Profile of Health Diplomats Accredited to the United States and Foreign Governments", *Globalization and Health*, Volume 14, No. 2, pp. 1–11. DOI: 10.1186/s12992-017-0316-7

Drager, N. and Fidler, D. (2007). "Foreign Policy, Trade and Health: At the Cutting Edge of Global Health Diplomacy", *Bulletin of the World Health Organization*, Volume 85, March 2007, 162–162.

Erman, K. (2016). "Quiet and Effective: Cuba's Medical Diplomacy", *International Relations*, Volume 12, No. 48, pp. 77–94.

Frist, W. (2007). "Medicine as a Currency for Peace through Global Health Diplomacy", *Yale Law and Policy Review*, Volume 26, No. 1, pp. 209–229.

Gagnon, M. and Labonte, R. (2013). "Understanding How and Why Health Is Integrated into Foreign Policy – A Case Study of Health Is Global, a UK Government Strategy 2008-2013", *Globalization and Health*, Volume 9, pp. 1–19. http://www.globalizationandhealth.com/content/9/1/24 (Accessed: January 2, 2019).

Hayran, O. (2017). "Health Diplomacy and Its Impact on Global Health". In O. Özen (Ed.), *Health Diplomacy: Health Policy System Analyst Training* (pp. 13–22). Istanbul: Istanbul Medipol University Press.

Hotez, P. (2014). "'Vaccine Diplomacy': Historical Perspectives and Future Directions", *PLOS Neglected Tropical Diseases*, Volume 8, No. 6, pp. 1–7. DOI: 10.1371/journal.pntd.0002808 (Accessed: January 2, 2019).

Hunter, A., Wilson, L., Stanhope, M., and Hatcher, B. (2013). "Global Health Diplomacy: An Integrative Review of the Literature and Implications for Nursing", *Nursing Outlook*, pp. 85–92. DOI: 10.1016/j.outlook.2012.07.013 (Accessed: February 14, 2019).

Jones, C., Clavier, C., and Potvin, L. (2017). "Adapting Public Policy Theory for Public Health Research: A Framework to Understand the Development of National Policies on Global Health", *Social Science and Medicine*, Volume 177, pp. 69–77. DOI: 10.1016/j.socscimed.2017.01.048 (Accessed: January 1, 2019).

Katz, R. and Singer, D. (2007). "Health and Security in Foreign Policy", *Bulletin of the World Health Organization*, Volume 85, No. 3, March 2007, pp. 233–234.

Katz, R., Arnold, G., Kornblet, S., and Lief, E. (2011). "Defining Health Diplomacy: Changing Demands in the Era of Globalization", *The Milbank Quarterly*, Volume 89, No. 3, pp. 503–523.

Kevany, S. (2014a). "Global Health Diplomacy: A 'Deus ex Maxhina' for International Development and Relations", *International Journal of Health Policy and Management*, Volume 3, No. 2, pp. 1–2. DOI: 10.15171/ijhpm.2014.67 (Accessed: January 2, 2019).

Kevany, S. (2015a). "Diplomatic Advantages and the Threats in Global Health Program Selection, Design, Delivery and Implementation: Development and Application of the Kevany Riposte", *Globalization and Health*, Volume 11, pp. 1–10. DOI: 10.1186/s12992-015-0108-x (Accessed: February 1, 2019).

Kevany, S. (2015b). "Global Health Diplomacy, 'San Francisco Vlues,' and HIV/AIDS: From Local to the Global", *Annals of Global Health*, Volume 81, No. 5, pp. 611–617.

Kevany, S. (2015c). "James Bond and Global Health Diplomacy", *International Journal of Health Policy and Management*, Volume 4, No. 12, pp. 831–834.

Kickbusch, I., Silberschmidt, G., and Buss, P. (2007). "Global Health Diplomacy: The Need for New Perspectives, Strategic Approaches and Skills in Global Health", *Bulletin of the World Health Organization*, Volume 85, March 2007, pp. 230–232.

Labonte, R. and Gagnon, M. (2010). "Framing Health and Foreign Policy: Lessons for Global Health Diplomacy", *Globalizaton and Health*, Volume 6, pp. 1–19. http://www.globalizationandhealth.com/content/6/1/14 (Accessed: January 2, 2019).

Labonte, R., Runnels, V. and Gagnon, M. (2012). "Past Fame, Present Frames and Future Flagship? An Exploration of How Health Is Positioned in Canadian Foreign Policy", *Administrative Sciences*, Volume 2, pp. 162–185. DOI: 10.3390/admsci2020162 (Accessed: January 2, 2019).

Mackey, T. and Liang, B. (2013). "A United Nations Global Health Panel for Global Health Governance", *Social Science and Medicine*, Volume 76, pp. 12–15. http://dx.doi.org/10.1016/j.socscimed.2012.09.038 (Accessed: January 2, 2019).

Mackey, T. and Strathdee, S. (2015). "Responding to the Public Health Consequences of the Ukraine Crisis: An Opportunity for Global Health Diplomacy", *Journal of the International AIDS Society*, Volume 18, pp. 1–7. DOI: 10.7448/IAS.18.1.19410 (Accessed: February 14, 2019).

McLaughlin, M., Lee, M., Hall, B., Bulterys, M., Ling, L., and Tucker, J. (2014). "Improving Health Service for African Migrants in China: A Health Diplomacy Perspective", *Global Public Health*, Volume 9, No. 5, pp. 579–589.

Nang, R. and Martin, K. (2017). "Global Health Diplomacy: A New Strategic Defense Pillar", *Military Medicine*, Volume 182, January/February 2017, pp. 1456–1460.

Novotny, T. and Adams, V. (2007). "Global Health Diplomacy: A Global Health Sciences Working Paper". University of California San Francisco Global Health Sciences. http://igcc.ucsd.edu/pdf/GH_Diplomacy.pdf

Presidency of the Republic of Türkiye (2021). "TURKOVAC aşımızı tüm insanlıkla paylaşmaktan memnuniyet duyacağız". https://www.tccb.gov.tr/haberler/410/134067/-turkovac-asimizi-tum-insanlikla-paylasmaktan-memnuniyet-duyacagiz- (Accessed: December 26, 2022).

Ramirez, J., Valdivia, L., Rivera, E., Santos, M., Sepulveda, D., Labonte, R., and Ruckert, A. (2018). "Chile's Role in Global Health Diplomacy: A Narrative Literature Review", *Globalization and Health*, Volume 14, pp. 1–13. https://doi.org/10.1186.s12992-018-0428-8 (Accessed: January 2, 2019).

Rao, C., Henao, O., Goryoka, G., and Clarke, K. (2017). "Global Disease Detection-Achievements in Applied Public Health Research, Capacity Building and Public Health Diplomacy, 2001-20016", *Emerging Infectious Diseases*, Volume 23, December 2017, pp. 138–146. DOI: https://doi.org/10.3201/eid2313.170859 (Accessed: February 14, 2019).

Republic of Türkiye Ministry of Foreign Affairs. (2022). "Our Role and Vision during the Coronavirus Pandemic". https://www.mfa.gov.tr/koronavirus-salginindaki-rol-ve-vizyonumuz-20-04-2022.en.mfa (Accessed: December 26, 2022).

Rijt, T. and Pang, T. (2015). "Governance within the World Health Assembly: A 13 Year Analysis of WHO Member States' Contribution to Global Health Governance", *Health Policy*, Volume 119, pp. 395–404. DOI: 10.1016/j.healthpol.2014.12.008 (Accessed: January 2, 2019).

Ruckert, A., Labonte, R., Lencucha, R., Runnels, V., and Gagnon, M. (2016). "Global Health Diplomacy: A Critical Review of the Literature", *Social Science and Medicine*, Volume 155, pp. 61–72.

Smith, R. and Irwin, R. (2016). "Measuring Success in Global Health Diplomacy: Lessons from Marketing Food to Children in India", *Globalization and Health*, Volume 12, No. 28, pp. 1–4. DOI: 10.1186/s12992-016-0169-5

University of Health Sciences. (2022). "Vocational Schools". https://www.uhs.edu.tr/academics/vocational-schools (Accessed: December 26, 2022).

Werlau, M. (2013). "Cuba's Health Care Diplomacy: The Business of Humanitarianism", *World Affairs*, Volume 175, No. 6, March-April 2013, pp. 57–67.

Wipfli, H. and Kotlewski, J. (2014). "Into the Deep End: Incorporating a Global Health Governance and Diplomacy Experience in Graduate Public Health Training", *Global Public Health*, Volume 9, No. 7, pp. 827–840.

WHO. (2018). "Global Health Diplomacy". http://www.who.int/trade/globalhealthdiplomacy/en/index.html (Accessed: October 20, 2018).

WHO. (2022). "14.9 million excess deaths associated with the COVID-19 pandemic in 2020 and 2021". https://www.who.int/news/item/05-05-2022-14.9-million-excess-deaths-were-associated-with-the-covid-19-pandemic-in-2020-and-2021 (Accessed: December 26, 2022).

8 Government Responses to the COVID-19 Pandemic

Comparative Health Policies in the US and Canada

Çağrı Erhan and Efe Sıvış

Introduction

While the COVID-19 pandemic has claimed the lives of over 6.3 million people worldwide, it has had several far-reaching socio-economic and governmental implications worldwide. Many countries coped remarkably well in the face of the pandemic. According to Bloomberg's COVID Resilience Rankings, Norway and Ireland handled the pandemic very well since both countries made great efforts to impose lockdowns and vaccinate their public (Bloomberg, 2020). While the United States (US) now conducted effective vaccination drives in the direction of the present government of Biden, the previous Trump government's mismanagement of the pandemic turned it into a full-fledged catastrophic event during the early phases from its very inception. Donald Trump specifically referred to the virus as the "Chinese Virus" (Kurtzman, 2021). This not only fuelled anti-Asian racism but also depicted his insensitive reaction to a pandemic that might kill almost 385,000 Americans in only 2020 (Crist, 2021). Moreover, the Trump administration's earlier neglect of the virus outbreak resulted in a massive death toll and startled the social and geopolitical dynamic of the North American region and the global community. As the 2020 US elections had seen the maximum voter participation, experts attributed this to enhanced disunity, political interference, deliberate misinformation, and an overall absence of integrity and liability about the COVID-19 pandemic under Trump's presidency. In contrast, Trump's isolationist and right-wing approaches, in particular, forced Canada into an isolated situation in its fight against the virus. Canada still handled the virus more efficiently than the USA. Canada implemented strong lockdown policies and financial assistance programmes. The government of Canada heavily contributed to and endorsed healthcare programmes, specifically investigations and studies related to COVID-19. All the initiatives helped Canada recover from this crisis effectively. Furthermore, a contrast between the 2020 US and the 2021 Canadian elections showed that, while most Americans were highly sceptical of Trump's COVID action plan, most Canadians opted to re-elect Trudeau due to his competent management of the pandemic. In this review, we aim to examine how the United States and Canada handled the COVID-19 crisis and the implications for both countries' internal political affairs and international geopolitics.

DOI: 10.4324/9781003377597-10

Background

COVID-19 started first in Wuhan, China. The first case in the United States was confirmed on January 21, 2020, in Snohomish County, Washington State (History.com, 2021). Soon after that, Seattle was turned into the COVID-19 hub, with 39 inhabitants dying of COVID comorbidities in just four weeks. Though the pandemic gave international leaders a clear chance to demonstrate their management expertise, US President Trump failed to employ the crisis as a disguised option to quiet his opponents through efficient strategic leadership and management. After the virus spread, Trump asserted that it had risen from a lab in Wuhan and dubbed it the "Chinese Virus" (Rogers et al., 2020). His response to the virus conveyed his contemptuous behaviour towards a significant threat and fuelled concerns of ethnocentric intolerance throughout the United States. As Trump proceeded to trivialise the virus's risk, declaring in the Oval Office that the danger for "the vast majority of Americans" is "very, very low," Dr. Anthony Fauci, a representative of the White House coronavirus response team, stated "on the very day that 'bottom line, it's going to get worse'" (Summers, 2020). Accordingly, whereas most health authorities stressed the importance of facial masks to prevent virus transmission, Trump was reported as mentioning, *You can do it. You don't have to do it. I'm choosing not to do it, but some people may want to do it, and that's OK (Ibid)*. Considering President Trump's constant downplaying of the virus, an eminent news portal claimed, *If U.S. President Donald Trump gets his way, North America may soon embark on a massive, life-and-death medical experiment with hundreds of millions of people as guinea pigs, including you and me and our American friends and relatives* (Ibbitson, 2020).

Till March 29, 2020, just a few months after the cases began to rise, New York City had emerged as among the worst affected regions of the USA, with 30,000 cases reported and over 2000 lives lost. This prompted the demand for comprehensive national lockdowns and the closure of markets and educational institutions. The steep rise in the overall cases forced Trump to set aside $8.3 billion to combat the emergence and spread and announce the situation as a national emergency. His administration bought a significant quantity of healthcare equipment under the Defence Production Act of 1950.

Due to the Trump Administration's deferred and mixed handling of the situation, local and state governments failed to contain the virus's dispersion amidst mask restrictions and certain other standard operating procedures (SOPs). There was an unusually high percentage of cases among the Black and Latino populations, decreased vaccination rates, and the prevalence of xenophobia against Blacks and Asian Americans. The assassination of George Floyd was a notable tragedy that depicted not only systemic racism but also the evolving racial intolerance in the immediate wake of the Trump administration's biased perspective on COVID-19 (Toure et al., 2021).

Comparison of Trump's and Trudeau's Viewpoints on the Pandemic

Since the discovery of the COVID-19 virus in January 2020, the Trump presidency's intervention has been signified by carelessness, insufficiency of resource management, and the deliberate disperse of rumours and fabrications. Trump insisted on

January 22nd at the World Economic Forum in Davos, "*We have it totally under control. It's one person coming in from China. It's going to be just fine.*" While Trump initially voiced contentment with China's "efficiency and transparency" in containing the virus, he appeared perplexed by its deadliness (Lambert, 2020). The preceding remarks left Americans confused in determining whether the virus posed a serious threat to them or not. Trump also asserted that "*I think the virus is going to be—it's going to be fine,*" "*it's also more deadly than even your strenuous flu ... This is deadly stuff,*" he went on (Ibid). The preceding remarks definitely left Americans perplexed in determining whether COVID-19 posed a serious threat to them or not.

Furthermore, in addition to expressing his ambiguity, President Trump's dismissive comments about the roots of the virus revealed his discriminatory attitude towards the virus. A few months after the spread, Trump referred to coronavirus as "China-Virus" during official events and press conferences. Likewise, at a campaign in Tulsa, Oklahoma, Trump addressed the virus as "*Kung-Flu,*" adding, "*I can name 19 different versions of names*" (Zhou, 2020). Harvey Dong, a professor of American and Asian diaspora research at the University of California, Berkley, criticised the racially biased viewpoint, claiming that "*it's racist and it creates xenophobia*" (Chiu, 2020). Due to discriminatory declarations by Trump government representatives, many Asian American citizens across the state have indicated ethnic physical and verbal threats linked to coronavirus concerns.

While Mr. Trump repeatedly used racist words about the virus, Canadian president Trudeau's stance was distinct and communitarian. Trudeau said at a Lunar New Year meeting at a Chinese banquet hall in Toronto on February 1, 2020, "*There is no place in our country for discrimination driven by fear or misinformation*" (Jones, 2020). He persuaded Canadians to join hands and alerted against the propagation of any racist misconceptions about the pandemic roots.

As a result, one could notice a huge distinction between the general approach evident in Trump's and Trudeau's remarks. While President Trump's statements and discussions revealed his discriminatory attitude and unpreparedness for the COVID-19 pandemic, Prime Minister Trudeau's disposition was notably different. In contrast to Trump's "China-virus" racist remarks, Trudeau not only publicly denounced "*hateful rhetoric*" but also stressed the importance of a coordinated attempt to fight the virus's dispersion (Tasker, 2022). His remark well demonstrated this, "*My focus is standing with Canadians and getting through this pandemic*" (BBC News, 2022).

Assessment of the COVID Initiatives of the United States and Canada

On February 2, 2020, US President Trump and Canadian President Trudeau spoke by a call about the virus's increasing prevalence and measures taken to contain and lessen its dispersion (Holland & Harte, 2020). This came just two days after the Trump government decided to enact emergency travel bans and mandatory quarantine for Chinese citizens (Leslie, 2020). Taking cognisance of the conversation, one might expect the two presidents to put aside their disagreements to devise mutual tactics to contain the virus from spreading further.

But this ray of hope was short-lived because both figureheads had drastically distinct approaches to leadership. For example, while President Trump commemorated the Fourth of July at Mount Rushmore by making racist statements about the coronavirus, Trudeau observed Canada's national day by planting at an Ottawa land (Leyland, 2020). Likely, while Trump and his followers decided against wearing masks in public, it became SOP in Canada from the start (Ibid).

The differing opinions of both presidents caused a marked contradiction in the percentage of cases in both countries during the year 2020. Since July, the United States had recorded over 3 million cases, whereas Canada's total cases remained markedly over time and were 60 times lower than the USA. Dr. Isaac Bogoch, an infectious disease specialist, referred to the distinction as *"it's like night and day: From coast to coast, we have the epidemic in Canada under excellent control. We've been able to suppress cases at the community level. Of course, we're still seeing some small outbreaks, but we've been able to suppress the vast majority of the infection and rapidly identify small outbreaks"* (Leyland, 2020).

The drastic contrasts in cumulative COVID occurrence rates between the United States and Canada were due to variations in both countries' general policy initiatives. When the first coronavirus incidents were revealed in March 2020, all Canadian regions and provinces announced a state of emergency. They imposed lockdowns on educational institutes, restricted gatherings, closed non-essential organisations, and severely controlled and monitored border entry. Since the outbreak of 2004 SARS, the Ministry of Health exercised the Quarantine Act, mandating all tourists visiting the state to undertake a requisitive 14-day self-quarantine (McQuigge, 2022). Resultantly, Canada saw a significant decrease in the overall incidence rate until the second wave that occurred in September 2020.

In the United States, on the contrary, the Trump government proceeded to understate the possible risks posed by the virus, even though it had recently terminated and dissolved the group in charge of dealing with a pandemic in 2018 (Lopez, 2020). The successive major cuts in general public finance exacerbated the Trump government's failure to manage an emergency of the magnitude of COVID-19 efficiently. Major postponements characterised the Trump government's mishandled reaction in successfully closing the influx of tourists into the US. Furthermore, the government could not promptly deliver testing kits and preventative medical equipment to public health personnel. These factors were critical in mobilising a coordinated reaction to the emergency. Trump's repeated claims that wearing a mask was unnecessary to contain the virus only fuelled the emergency.

It should be recognised that President Trump quickly understood the pandemic's significant risk, especially in the months following the crisis in New York City. He started wearing a mask in the community and appearing on television from the Oval Office more frequently, requesting people to adhere to socially isolating SOPs and highlighting his government's COVID-19 regulations. However, this belated realisation came at the expense of several lives lost throughout the United States due to the administration's public health failures, lack of adequate testing kits, effective lockdowns, and SOPs.

Canada, in contrast, managed to stay more assertive and productive in its response to the pandemic, as said before. Observers such as David Frum claimed that the country levied urgent 14-day self-isolation initiatives for tourists and visitors (Frum, 2020). Upon entrance, visitors were asked, "What will they do with the grocery shopping?" Whether or not they were aware of their country's masking prerequisites? What contact information might be employed to contact them while they are isolated? Upon entrance, Canadian healthcare institutions maintained direct contact with all visitors subjected to the requisite self-quarantine. They would indeed take calls, voice messages, and texts from the health systems regularly, commending them for being law-abiding citizens, notifying them of the rest of the days, and focusing on their physical and psychological health.

Geopolitical Implications of Trump's COVID Reaction for the US and Canada

The pandemic appeared to be a significant health threat worldwide, killing many people and transforming into a significant global problem across country boundaries. Due to continuous border shutdowns, limitations on mobility, and other lockdown provisions, global movements of individuals and world trade reached all-time declines. Admittedly, it was internationalisation that allowed the virus to transmit from Wuhan to the world at large quickly. As a result, its dispersion posed various risks to the geopolitics of nations all over the globe.

The geopolitical implications of COVID-19 were far-reaching for the USA. Previously in March 2020, US Vice President Mike Pence directed the nation's disease control authority to efficiently lock all borders of the state, amidst authorities' suggestions that there was no indication that such an action would be successful in preventing the distribution of the virus (Dearen, 2020). Due to these initiatives, nearly 150,000 children and adults were deported from the state. The United States' borders with Canada and Mexico were closed, impacting thousands of refugees attempting to enter the United States. As a result, many people and children, who were normally afforded special constitutional protections through federal law, were deported back to the country. Numerous people returned to nations with highly unstable situations, including Afghanistan, Honduras, and El Salvador. Critics denounced the Trump government for simply waiting for an opportunity to penalise immigrants, as it did before taking office in 2016. Lee Gelernt, an official with the American Civil Liberties Union's Immigrants' Rights Project, claimed: *"That is what the Trump administration has been trying to do for four years and they finally saw a window"* (Ibid). Only a few months after the borders were closed, Trump used the actions as propaganda in his campaign for the upcoming presidential election. He stated this at a gathering in Arizona: *"It's a great — it's a great feeling to have closed up the border."*

The Trump government's decision to haphazardly close all of the national borders had many consequences for the state, its neighbourhood, and worldwide geopolitics. The pandemic raised the competitiveness between the United States and China, having detrimental consequences on providing worldwide health-related products while enhancing the total destabilisation of the world order (Bahi, 2021). Instead of focusing on the virus's risks, the two countries' attitudes showed a zero-sum mentality predicated on the demand to enhance their worldwide financial interests at the expense of others. As a result, the overall confidence in worldwide state collaboration dropped drastically. This scenario was aggravated by the absence of international or regional governance during a worldwide emergency, which jeopardised world peace. Because of the obvious US-China fierce competition during the pandemic, Europe and Canada identified themselves as secluded in their efforts to address the disaster adequately. In the post-Cold War situation, Europeans thought they were creating a global order governed by rules, with their landmass at the centre. But, in the after-effects of the pandemic, influential international organisations like the World Health Organization (WHO) had seen themselves being utilised by the potential global superpowers – the United States and China – in their rivalry. Instead of efficiently addressing the issues that humans experience globally, the institutions become a focal point for global competition. As a result, Europe found itself isolated in terms of developing workarounds for the pandemic (IWM, 2022). This abandonment was compounded by Europe's allied powers acting unilaterally: Trump proceeded to irritate the European Union by enforcing travel restrictions on people of 26 Schengen countries, a move denounced by most European Union leaders as pre-emptive and unjustifiable (The Parliament Magazine, 2020). While Trump initially underestimated the virus's perceived risk, he struck the European Union in a video statement for failing to handle the "foreign virus" successfully while accusing European visitors of "seeding" the virus's transmission in the United States (KFF, 2020).

Similarly, Canada became detached due to President Trump's inconsistent strategies, geopolitical confrontation with China, border limitations, and inability to properly deal with the virus in the United States. Trudeau's administration attempted to tread a fine line between China, its second largest bilateral trade and investment associate, and the United States, its biggest trading partner, natural associate, and neighbour.

Trump decided to close the borders while arming it shortly after the pandemic started. This had already been putting a strain on both countries' economic cooperation, Trump's plan to suspend N-95 mask exports to Canada while afterwards restoring the border only heightened conflicts between the neighbours, abandoning Canada isolated (Blatchford, 2022). But this can be interpreted as a follow-up to Trump's preliminary provocations to rip up the NAFTA trade agreement. Therefore, Trudeau must have been prepared for violent calls by the Trump presidency during the pandemic.

To better cope with Trump's risks of undefined practices, Trudeau's administration utilised comprehensive conciliatory and regulatory measures to mitigate the virus's risks. In the case of N-95 masks, for example, the Canadian administration and its lower levels teamed up with the lower wings of the USA government to maintain consistent supply. When it became clear that his province might not have enough N-95 mask stockpiles, Ontario Premier Doug Ford negotiated with US Trade Representative Robert Lighthizer. Likewise, in response to Trump's declaration that military units would be sent to the borders, Canada vigorously opposed it while maintaining direct relationships with US Homeland Security to prevent such a step. Shortly after knowing of such strategies, Canada's Deputy Prime Minister Chrystia Freeland quickly called US Vice President Mike Pence and Homeland Security officials, voicing her apprehensions about any more prospective movements of soldiers at the borders. She informed them emphatically that additional militarisation at the borders would be "damaging" to both nations' relationships. Furthermore, Canadian authorities proceeded to warn their American counterparts of how interconnected their distribution channels were and how devastating it would be to both nations if commerce were to have been halted in this way – particularly when it came to the transfer of basic healthcare infrastructure and supplies. As a result of this approach at multiple levels of the Canadian authorities, the country successfully overcame President Trump's potential danger to its attempts to curb the transmission of the infection successfully.

Economic Risks of the COVID-19 Pandemic for the United States and China

The International Monetary Fund's (IMF) annual World Economic Outlook disclosed that the total economic outcome in the United States reduced by 4.7% in 2020, the initial phase of the pandemic. Canada, on the other hand, performed far worse, with a 5.4% decline in volume. This might be interpreted as a consequence of Canada's strict lockdowns and closures of unnecessary educational institutes and markets. These measures aided in uplifting its economic growth and limiting the transmission of the virus more effectively than in the United States. In a broad sense, the COVID-19 pandemic had hindered markets around the globe in a variety of forms: it caused demand distress, and it also caused supply chain disruptions and a budgetary startle (Bauer et al., 2022).

The pandemic had a geographically distinct pattern, as it typically started in heavily populated regions and then distributed to semi-urban and rural areas of states (Triggs and Kharas, 2020). Most COVID-19 cases detected in the USA were reported from densely inhabited urban metropolitan areas, especially on the East Coast, like New York City, New Jersey, and Boston. Furthermore, distinct social and ethnic communities were impacted by the pandemic in a divergent manner. Because of historic and pervasive disparities and exclusion in academics, health services, management, and work opportunities, definite racial minorities, especially Blacks, were at a higher risk of contracting the virus. The deferring, taken together, only contributed to the nation's significant financial crisis.

The National Bureau of Economic Research (NBER) revealed that February 2020 signified the end of the USA's apex in monthly business growth that also began in 2009 in the wake of the global economic recession (NBER, 2020). The pandemic's crucial devastating economic impacts on the US economic system included a steep drop in GDP and a swift spike in inflation accompanied by joblessness. In April 2020, employment in the United States tumbled by more than 20.5 million. The drop in GDP and joblessness resulted from the huge instability in worldwide supply chain operations. The current trade wars between the United States and China weakened the risks by depriving the United States of huge volumes of import stuff required to maintain its market and combat the virus by itself during the pandemic.

Since some sectors of the economy, including grocery shops, dispensaries, and e-commerce firms, benefited from the pandemic, the vast largest portion of retail revenues fell due to huge fluctuations in household consumption. The rise in joblessness, combined with rising inflationary pressures, only exacerbated the problem for retail companies all over the state. Smaller companies were particularly hard hit. A survey showed that small company profitability dropped by more than 20% with the virus's emergence in January 2020 (Engidaw, 2022). Smaller companies in travel and hospitality were adversely affected due to the restrictions imposed by authorities during the pandemic.

The unemployment rate in the United States had exceeded 14.7% in April 2020, the biggest increase after the Great Depression (Center for American Progress, 2021). Nearly 37.6 million Americans applied for unemployment benefits, reflecting the country's tragic economic situation (FRED, 2022). The Trump government's broad, failed policies, which began long before the actual COVID-19 pandemic, amplified the financial collapse. His decisions hampered the nation's capacity to deal with an actual public health emergency like the pandemic.

The United States' economic crisis may also be compared to its many global contemporaries, such as China, European Union nations, and Canada. According to multiple references, economically sound policies in the United States might have possibly assisted the nation in avoiding drastic joblessness and other financial implications. South Korea, for example, was successful in maintaining a low unemployment rate of 3.8%, just a little higher than the average 3.3% rate before the emergence of the COVID-19 pandemic. This was due to the government's important interventions like lockdowns that also contributed in saving the country economically from crippling in the subsequent phases. Correspondingly, Germany's unemployment rate increased relatively from 5.0% to 5.8%, compared to 14.7% in the USA.

The scenario of Canada appeared differently in relation to the United States. The Canadian administration implemented several quick and efficient measures as an aspect of its "COVID-19 Economic Response Plan" to safeguard its people from the prospective financial consequences of COVID-19 (Government of Canada, 2020). In the initial pandemic phases, Canada had a sound financial position, a minimal GDP-to-debt ratio, and relatively low debt levels. All these factors aided the authorities in dealing with COVID-19 effectively. While the administration's first primary concern was to actively stop the virus's transmission by strengthening public health care facilities, its choice to place lockdowns on inessential markets and educational institutions caused substantial employment and revenue losses, as well as disproportionate effects on many sections of the population. Provided the preceding considerations, the Canadian state chose to stimulate its economic growth through mitigation actions. These constituted around $212 billion in assistance to Canadian people and companies. Furthermore, it offered about $14 billion in finance to provinces to help them gradually expand their economic systems. Accordingly, the Canadian administration had set aside $600 billion in funds for impacted companies across the state through Canadian banks and financial organisations. Resultantly, through these appropriate approaches as a component of the "Response Plan," Canada has been inclined to confront the likely negative economic consequences of the pandemic productively and dynamically, ensuring the balance of its economy in times of crisis. This strategy was implemented when Canada was pretty deserted due to the unexpected and unjustifiable decisions of US President Donald Trump, including the border restrictions that also negatively affected Canada's trade balance revenue.

It is also important to recognise that Canada's economic strategy arose due to the country's early efforts to halt the transmission of the pandemic. Shortly after the virus's emergence, the Canadian authorities made significant investments in health facilities and public health agencies throughout all Canadian provinces to provide them with the greatest available processes to deal with a prospective public health emergency. The financial assistance provided by the government was also in favour of the advancement and enhancement of successful virtual care and mental health instruments. Furthermore, the national healthcare's immediate reaction involved quick and easy COVID-19 testing services. As a result, during the early period of the pandemic, the nation's COVID testing per head of population was greater than in most other states (Samson, 2022). This resulted from the government's huge $210 million financing in COVID-19 R&D programmes in March 2020. Given the United States' growing geo-political and geo-economic competition with Canada, as well as the closing of its borders with the United States, the Canadian authorities were capable of successfully obtaining personal protective equipment (PPE) through various channels (Ibid). This was accomplished, in phase, by engaging domestic industries and financing domestically made healthcare items and tools. Similarly, after the pandemic began, the administration invested approximately $1.4 billion to fund vaccine innovation and education and approximately $3.4 billion in humanitarian support against the COVID-19 virus (Ibid).

Canada's economy profited immensely from efficacious lockdowns and strong financial stimulus packages, rebounding twice as quickly as the United States, its principal trading partner, in the third period (Smith, 2020). In August 2020, the nation's economy expanded at an annual rate of 36%, compared to 20% in the United States. Likewise, Canada's rate of daily COVID cases fell dramatically in the third year, to below 400 from 1800 in May. In contrast, the huge increase in cases that occurred simultaneously in different states across the United States caused them to reconsider their intentions to restart their markets.

The COVID-19 pandemic situation has had a considerable effect on Canada, leading to fundamental changes in social, economic, and political sphere. The Canadian response to COVID-19 had been many-sided, including measures to decrease the spread rate of the virus, preserve vulnerable groups, backing the healthcare system, and tackle the economic consequences of the pandemic. One of the first steps that had been taken against the pandemic was the foundation of the COVID-19 Immunity Task Force (CITF), which aimed at using serology, that is, the scientific study of serum and other body fluids to struggle with the virus in Canada. CITF has been covered in various research articles so far, including the one that argued that the number of people who had been infected with COVID-19 was bigger than announced figures, indicating the need for continued readiness in struggling the virus (Statistics Canada, 2020).

Besides the establishment of CITF, the Canadian government applied various measures to decrease the rate of spread, including lockdowns and restrictions on travel and gatherings. These measures were useful in decreasing the number of cases in Canada, although there were some difficulties in enforcing the rules and managing compliance (Urrutia et al., 2021).

The Canadian government had given priority to its healthcare system in this period. The funding for scientific research and development of treatments and vaccines is sufficient enough. Canada has been one of the top countries in vaccine development, with several corporations located in Canada contributing to the global effort to produce effective vaccines (Government Canada, 2022). Another significant dimension of the Canadian measures to the pandemic was the support provided to citizens and commercial units affected by the economic impact of the pandemic.

Several programmes were implemented by the government for the purpose of providing financial assistance to those who lost incomes or were forced to close their businesses, including the Canada Emergency Response Benefit (CERB) and the Canada Emergency Wage Subsidy (CEWS). Canadian response to the COVID-19 pandemic was comprehensive, with a particular focus on slowing the spread of the virus, hence supporting the healthcare system and addressing the economic impact of the pandemic as well. Whilst challenges appeared and there was still room for improvement, Canada is still honoured for its response to the pandemic.

The Canadian economy was affected severely because of the COVID-19 pandemic. The pandemic resulted in closing of particular businesses, job losses, and a particular decrease in consumer choices. The Canadian economy shrank by 5.4% in 2020, which marked as the worst annual decline since the Great Depression (Government of Canada, 2020). The pandemic's impact on the Canadian labour market was severe as well. In April 2020, the Canadian unemployment rate rose to 13%, the highest record-keeping level since 1976 (Statistics Canada, 2020). Despite the decrease in the unemployment rate, it still remains above prepandemic leverage. Certain sectors, such as hospitality and tourism, were affected badly and still have long-term unemployment rates that are higher than the others (CBC, 2021).

The pandemic affected the Canadian government's finances as well. The federal government introduced several programmes for the purpose of supporting individuals and businesses during the pandemic, including the Canada Emergency Response Benefit (CERB) and the Canada Emergency Wage Subsidy (CEWS). These programmes resulted in a significant increase in government spending, which led to a federal deficit amounting to USD 354.2 billion approximately in between the years 2020 and 2021, being the largest debt in Canadian history (Statistics Canada A and B, 2022). It can be concluded undoubtedly that the pandemic had a significant negative impact on the Canadian economy, with long-term effects that are expected to continue in upcoming years. In addition, the COVID-19 pandemic situation had a wide-ranging social impact on Canadian society. One of the most significant impacts, amongst others, was the increase in social isolation, loneliness experienced by many Canadians due to lockdowns and social distancing measures (Mo et al., 2020). Hence, this situation had a particular impact on elders and individuals with pre-existing mental health conditions. There was also a major increase in domestic violence and child abuse cases due to increase in the number of people who were forced to stay home and spend more time in close proximity with their abusers (Abramson, 2020).

The pandemic situation also highlighted the existing inequalities within the Canadian society, particularly the ones relating to the healthcare access and employment. People from marginalised communities, such as low-income individuals and racialised groups, were disproportionately impacted by the pandemic due to pre-existing systemic inequalities and, as a result, making them more vulnerable to the virus (Kemei et al., 2023). Moreover, the pandemic highlighted the precarity of many jobs in the gig economy and other low-wage sectors wherein workers often lacked paid sick leave and a variety of other employment protections. On the other hand, it also resulted in an increase in community solidarity and activism since Canadians cooperated for supporting each other and advocating for policy changes with the aim of addressing the challenges of the pandemic (Statistics Canada, 2020).

The COVID-19 pandemic had a significant impact on both Canada and the United States. While both countries faced similar challenges, there were some notable differences in their approaches to managing the crisis. One key difference was the timing of the response. Canada began implementing public health measures, such as social distancing and mask mandates, earlier than the United States, which was slower to respond due to a lack of federal leadership and politicisation of the pandemic. The delay in the US response likely contributed to the higher number of cases and deaths in the country compared to Canada. Another difference was the level of coordination between the federal government and provinces/states. In Canada, the federal government worked closely with the provinces and territories to coordinate a unified response to the pandemic, while in the US, there was a lack of coordination between the federal government and states, with some states implementing their own measures while others did not.

The two countries also differed in terms of financial support for citizens and businesses affected by the pandemic. Canada provided more comprehensive financial assistance programmes, such as the Canada Emergency Response Benefit (CERB), which provided income support to millions of Canadians who lost their jobs due to the pandemic. In contrast, the US response was more fragmented, with different states implementing their own financial assistance programmes and the federal government providing limited support. The differences between the Canadian and American responses to the pandemic can be attributed to a combination of factors, including differences in political leadership, federal-state/provincial relations, and financial support programmes.

Examining Trump's Inability and Trudeau's Victory in the 2020/2021 Elections

Many researchers regarded the 2020 US elections as a plebiscite on whether Trump had dealt successfully with the COVID-19 pandemic. The electoral outcomes show that most Americans voted for the opposite. Amidst Trump's electoral victory in 2016, even after his inconsistent statements about females and non-natives, Americans largely denounced his identical arguments regarding the COVID-19 emergency. Furthermore, Trump's negative rhetoric coincided with the state's large financial recession, reducing his possibility of re-election. A Cambridge study revealed that data about the economic recession reduced his endorsement across all sections of society, especially middle- and low-income families (Neundorf and Pardos-Prado, 2021). On either side, his government's ineffectual management of the public health emergency weakened his approval among older people aged 55–77. A further study found that if the COVID-19 cases were already 5–10% lesser, Trump could have been elected president (Brodeur and Baccini, 2021). It was especially the case in states like Arizona, Georgia, and Washington, where Joe Biden won by a sharp edge. Even so, it is a generalisation to recommend that the 2020 election results reflected the general trend of Americans regarding Trump's gross incompetence of the pandemic, as evidenced by his preliminary trivialising of the virus, the huge sharp rise in cases in urban metropolitan areas including New York City, and his persistent disinclination to highlight COVID SOPs like the wearing of masks in the crowd.

In Canada, on the contrary, Justin Trudeau successfully secured his third win in the 2021 Canadian election campaign (Leyland, 2021). Even though Trudeau's choice to convene an election soon during the pandemic was criticised by his opposition, Trudeau's party was capable of effectively justifying its policy initiatives, as evidenced by its electoral victory, though somewhat narrower than ever before. The election findings demonstrated that most Canadians were pleased with how Trudeau and his administration reacted to the pandemic and managed to save the nation from significant public health and financial crisis. Furthermore, this may be interpreted as the achievement of a political leader with pluralism and a liberal electoral mission statement versus the defeat of one who had a polarising one.

Conclusion

The initial findings show that Donald Trump's improper disposal of the COVID-19 pandemic had dire effects on the United States and international geopolitics. While his immediate dismissal of the virus contributed to many deaths and peaks in cases in major cities such as New York City, the shortage of swift COVID testing, combined with the inability to enforce efficient lockdowns, had a negative impact on the US economy, as evidenced by rising inflation and joblessness. Furthermore, Trump's discretionary decisions, including closing the US-Canada border and announcing the deployment of forces to the border, weakened its diplomatic cooperation with Canada, abandoning Canada detached. But, through policies including fiscal stimulus packages for public health agencies, R&D, and acquisition and local production of PPE and other health supplements, Canada was capable of successfully controlling the pandemic. As an outcome of these immediate initiatives, Canada fared comparatively well during the pandemic, as evidenced by its fast-improving economy and a decreasing trend in total cases compared to the United States. Furthermore, Trump's mismanagement of the COVID pandemic effectively killed his re-election chances in the 2020 US elections. On the contrary, the majority of Canadians re-elected Trudeau for the third time in 2021, demonstrating their faith in his COVID policy initiatives.

References

Abramson, Ashley. "How COVID-19 May Increase Domestic Violence and Child Abuse." American Psychological Association, April 8, 2020. https://www.apa.org/topics/covid-19/domestic-violence-child-abuse

Bahi, Riham. "The Geopolitics of COVID-19: US-China Rivalry and the Imminent Kindleberger Trap", *Review of Economics and Political Science*. 2021 June. 6(1): 76–94.

Bauer, Lauren, Kristen E. Broady, Wendy Edelberg, & Jimmy O'Donnell. "Ten Facts about Covid-19 and the U.S. Economy." Brookings, March 9, 2022. https://www.brookings.edu/research/ten-facts-about-covid-19-and-the-u-s-economy/

BBC News. "Freedom Convoy: Trudeau Calls Trucker Protest an 'Insult to Truth'." BBC News, January 31, 2022. https://www.bbc.com/news/world-us-canada-60202050

Blatchford, Andy. "Trudeau Waits out Trump's Coronavirus Provocations." POLITICO. Accessed June 19, 2022. https://www.politico.com/news/2020/04/21/trudeau-canada-trumpcoronavirus-provocations-197014

Bloomberg. The Best and Worst Places to Be as Covid Flareups Break Records." Bloomberg.com. Bloomberg. https://www.bloomberg.com/graphics/2020-coronavirus-cases-world-map/. Accessed June 19, 2022.

Brodeur, Abel, & Leonardo Baccini. "How Covid-19 Led to Donald Trump's Defeat." The Conversation, October 14, 2021. https://theconversation.com/how-covid-19-led-to-donald-trumps-defeat-150110

CBC. "2020 Was the Worst Year on Record for Canada's Economy. It Shrank by 5.4%." CBC, March 2, 2021. https://www.cbc.ca/news/business/statscan-economy-2020-1.5933072

Center for American Progress. "5 Ways the Trump Administration's Policy Failures Compounded the Coronavirus-Induced Economic Crisis." Center for American Progress, November 7, 2021. https://www.americanprogress.org/article/5-ways-trump-administrations-policy-failures-compounded-coronavirus-induced-economic-crisis/

Chiu, Allyson. "Trump Has No Qualms about Calling Coronavirus the 'Chinese Virus.' That's a Dangerous Attitude, Experts Say." The Washington Post. WP Company, March 20, 2020. https://www.washingtonpost.com/nation/2020/03/20/coronavirus-trump-chinese-virus/

Crist, Carolyn. "U.S. Covid-19 Deaths in 2021 Surpass 2020 Total." WebMD, November 22, 2021. https://www.webmd.com/lung/news/20211122/us-covid-deaths-2021-surpass-2020-total

Dearen, Jason. "Pence Ordered Borders Closed after CDC Experts Refused." AP NEWS. Associated Press, October 3, 2020. https://apnews.com/article/virus-outbreak-pandemics-public-health-new-york-health-4ef0c6c5263815a26f8aa17f6ea490ae

Engidaw, Abriham Ebabu. "Small Businesses and Their Challenges during COVID-19 Pandemic in Developing Countries: In the Case of Ethiopia." *Journal of Innovation and Entrepreneurship*. 2022 January. 11(1): 1.

FRED. "Initial Claims." FRED. Accessed June 19, 2022. https://fred.stlouisfed.org/graph/?g=r5p2

Frum, David. "Canada Got Better. The United States Got Trump." The Atlantic, July 24, 2020. https://www.theatlantic.com/ideas/archive/2020/07/i-moved-canada-during-pandemic/614569/

Government Canada. "Backgrounder – Government of Canada investments in the biomanufacturing, vaccine and therapeuties ecosystem." Government of Canada, May 30, 2022. https://www.covid19immunitytaskforce.ca/

Government of Canada, Department of Finance. "Overview of Canada's COVID-19 Economic Response Plan - Canada.ca." Government of Canada, March 16, 2020. https://www.canada.ca/en/department-finance/services/publications/economic-fiscal-snapshot/overview-economic-response-plan.html

History.com. "First Confirmed Case of COVID-19 Found in U.S." History.com. A&E Television Networks, January 19, 2021. https://www.history.com/this-day-in-history/first-confirmed-case-of-coronavirus-found-in-us-washington-state

Holland, Steve, & Julia Harte. "Trump and Trudeau Discussed Coronavirus in Friday Phone Call." Reuters, February 2, 2020. https://www.reuters.com/article/us-china-health-usa-canada-idUSKBN1ZW02J

Ibbitson, John. "Trump and Trudeau Are on a Collision Course over Covid-19 Isolation." The Globe and Mail, March 27, 2020. https://www.theglobeandmail.com/politics/article-trump-and-trudeau-are-on-a-collision-course-over-covid-19-isolation/

IWM. "Geopolitical Europe in Times of Covid-19." IWM. Accessed June 19, 2022. https://www.iwm.at/blog/geopolitical-europe-in-times-of-covid-19

Jones, Ryan Patrick. "PM Warns against Discrimination at Lunar New Year Event as Fears of Coronavirus Spread." CBCnews. Radio Canada, February 1, 2020. https://www.cbc.ca/news/politics/coronavirus-canada-trudeau-february-1-1.5448834

Kemei, Janet, Mia Tulli, Adedoyin Olanlesi-Aliu, Modupe Tunde-Byass, & Bukola Salami. "Impact of the COVID-19 Pandemic on Black Communities in Canada", *International Journal of Environmental Research and Public Health*. 2023 January; 20(2): 1580.

KFF. "U.S. Government's Mixed Messages on, Politicization of COVID-19 Complicating Outbreak Response, Preparedness, Media Outlets Report." KFF, March 2, 2020. https://www.kff.org/news-summary/u-s-governments-mixed-messages-on-politicization-of-covid-19-complicating-outbreak-response-preparedness/

Lambert, Lisa. "Trump: U.S. Appreciates China's 'Efforts and Transparency' on Coronavirus." Reuters, January 24, 2020. https://www.reuters.com/article/us-china-health-usa-trump-idUSKBN1ZN2IK

Laura, Kurtzman. "Trump's 'Chinese Virus' Tweet Linked to Rise of Anti-Asian Hashtags on Twitter." UC San Francisco, 2021. https://www.ucsf.edu/news/2021/03/420081/trumps-chinese-virus-tweet-linked-rise-anti-asian-hashtags-twitter

Leslie, Josephs, & Breuninger, Kevin. "Trump Imposes Travel Restrictions, Mandatory Quarantines over Coronavirus Outbreak." CNBC, February 5, 2020. https://www.cnbc.com/2020/01/31/white-house-to-hold-briefing-on-coronavirus-friday-afternoon.html

Leyland, Cecco. "'It's like Night and Day': Trudeau's and Trump's COVID-19 Responses Fuel Wildly Different Outcomes." The Guardian. Guardian News and Media, July 9, 2020. https://www.theguardian.com/world/2020/jul/09/canada-coronavirus-us-justin-trudeau-donald-trump

Leyland, Cecco. "Justin Trudeau Secures a Third Victory in an Election 'Nobody Wanted'." The Guardian. Guardian News and Media, September 21, 2021. https://www.theguardian.com/world/2021/sep/21/justin-trudeau-wins-third-election-victory

Lopez, German. "The Trump Administration's Botched Coronavirus Response, Explained." Vox, March 14, 2020. https://www.vox.com/policy-and-politics/2020/3/14/21177509/coronavirus-trump-covid-19-pandemic-response

McQuigge, Michelle. "The Quarantine Act Explained, as Isolation Becomes Mandatory for Some." Coronavirus. CTV News, March 27, 2020. https://www.ctvnews.ca/health/coronavirus/the-quarantine-act-explained-as-isolation-becomes-mandatory-for-some-1.4868457

Mo, Guangying, Wendy Cukier, Akalya Atputharajah, Miki Itano Boase, & Henrique Hon. (2020). "Differential Impacts during COVID-19 in Canada: A Look at Diverse Individuals and Their Businesses", *Canadian Public Policy*. 2020 October; 46(S3): S261–S271.

NBER. "Business Cycle Dating Committee Announcement June 8, 2020." NBER. Accessed June 19, 2022. https://www.nber.org/news/business-cycle-dating-committee-announcement-june-8-2020

Neundorf, Anja, & Sergi Pardos-Prado. "The Impact of Covid-19 on Trump's Electoral Demise: The Role of Economic and Democratic Accountability", *Perspectives on Politics*, 2021 August; 20(1): 170–186.

Rogers, Katie, Lara Jakes, & Ana Swanson. "Trump Defends Using 'Chinese Virus' Label, Ignoring Growing Criticism." The New York Times, March 18, 2020. https://www.nytimes.com/2020/03/18/us/politics/china-virus.html

Samson, Alyson. "N.B. Has Highest COVID-19 Test-Positivity Rate in the Country: Public Health Agency of Canada." Atlantic. CTV News, May 14, 2022. https://atlantic.ctvnews.ca/n-b-has-highest-covid-19-test-positivity-rate-in-the-country-public-health-agency-of-canada-1.5903533

Smith, Fergal. "Canada's Economic Growth Seen Outpacing U.S. as Virus Containment Pays Off." Reuters, August 19, 2020. https://www.reuters.com/article/us-health-coronavirus-canada-economy-idCAKCN25F29V

Statistics Canada. "The Impact of COVID-19 on the Gig Economy: Short- and Long-Term Concerns." Statistics Canada, May 20, 2020. https://www150.statcan.gc.ca/n1/pub/45-28-0001/2020001/article/00021-eng.htm

Statistics Canada A. "COVID-19 in Canada: A Two-year Update on Social and Economic Impacts." Statistics Canada, March 10, 2022. https://www150.statcan.gc.ca/n1/pub/11-631-x/11-631-x2022001-eng.htm

Statistics Canada B. "Consolidated Canadian Government Finance Statistics, 2021." Statistics Canada, November 22, 2022. https://www150.statcan.gc.ca/n1/daily-quotidien/221122/dq221122b-eng.htm

Summers, Juana. "Timeline: How Trump Has Downplayed the Coronavirus Pandemic." NPR, October 2, 2020. https://www.npr.org/sections/latest-updates-trump-covid-19-results/2020/10/02/919432383/how-trump-has-downplayed-the-coronavirus-pandemic

Tasker, John Paul. "Trudeau Tests Positive for Covid-19, Condemns 'Hateful' Rhetoric." CBCnews. Radio Canada, February 1, 2022. https://www.cbc.ca/news/politics/trudeau-protest-ottawa-1.6333316

The Parliament Magazine "EU Leaders Criticise Trump's Coronavirus Travel Ban." The Parliament Magazine, June 29, 2020. https://www.theparliamentmagazine.eu/news/article/eu-leaders-criticise-trumps-coronavirus-travel-ban

Toure, Kadi, Etienne V. Langlois, Mehr Shah, Lori McDougall, and Helga Fogstad. "How George Floyd and Covid-19 Are Highlighting Structural Inequities for Vulnerable

Women, Children and Adolescents - International Journal for Equity in Health." BioMed Central, August 28, 2021. https://equityhealthj.biomedcentral.com/articles/10.1186/s12939-021-01540-0

Triggs, Adam, and Homi Kharas. "The Triple Economic Shock of Covid-19 and Priorities for an Emergency G-20 Leaders Meeting." Brookings, March 17, 2020. https://www.brookings.edu/blog/future-development/2020/03/17/the-triple-economic-shock-of-covid-19-and-priorities-for-an-emergency-g-20-leaders-meeting/

Urrutia, Deborah, Elisa Manetti, Megan Williamson, & Emeline Lequy. "Overview of Canada's Answer to the COVID-19 Pandemic's First Wave (January–April 2020)", *International Journal of Environmental Research and Public Health*. 2021 July; 18(13): 7131.

Zhou, Li. "Trump's Racist References to the Coronavirus Are His Latest Effort to Stoke Xenophobia." Vox, June 23, 2020. https://www.vox.com/2020/6/23/21300332/trump-coronavirus-racism-asian-americans

9 China's Global Health Diplomacy in the Post-Pandemic Era

Implications for Southeast Asian Countries

Cemre Pekcan

Introduction

The People's Republic of China (PRC) was established in 1949 and has faced numerous challenges over the years. One of the key factors contributing to China's status as the second largest economy in the world is Deng Xiaoping's reform and opening-up strategy from 1978, as well as China's admission to the World Trade Organization (WTO) in 2001. Xi Jinping, who was elected general secretary of the Communist Party of China (CCP) in 2012 and became president of China in 2013, is widely regarded as one of the most powerful leaders in the country's history. Under Xi Jinping's assertive policies and the Belt and Road Initiative (BRI), he initiated, China has begun to exert a greater influence on regional and global affairs.

The COVID-19 pandemic, which originated in Wuhan, China, in 2019, had a devastating impact on health systems worldwide. Despite criticisms of China for notifying the World Health Organization (WHO) late, it rapidly rebounded and gained recognition for fulfilling other nations' medical supply needs. China has taken advantage of the situation to reintroduce the Health Silk Road (HSR) as an agenda for international health cooperation. The West, particularly the United States (US), sees China's emergence as a threat and has made it a top priority to impede China's progress.

This chapter examines China's COVID-19 response and its impact on health diplomacy in Southeast Asia. It begins by assessing how Xi's foreign policy has affected the world through initiatives such as the China Dream and the BRI. The second part summarises the HSR, China's COVID-19 response, and China's efforts to become a global leader in health through vaccination and mask diplomacy, especially in the midst of the pandemic. The third part focuses on China's health policies towards Southeast Asian nations and their effects on relations. Surveys conducted by Singapore's Yusof Ishak Institute compare China's image in Southeast Asian countries with that of the US. This chapter argues that while China's COVID-19 response has allowed it to showcase its capabilities in health diplomacy, it has not been effective enough to strengthen its ties with nations in Southeast Asia, particularly in light of concerns over vaccine efficacy and transparency.

DOI: 10.4324/9781003377597-11

China's Foreign Policy under Xi Jinping

Under Deng Xiaoping's reform and opening-up programme in the late 1970s, China adopted a capitalist economic growth model. In the late 1980s, China also adopted the "keeping a low profile" (TGYH) strategy in foreign affairs, emphasising internal concerns, calm handling of difficulties, and avoidance of a leadership role. This ambiguous strategy led to the perception in the West that China was hiding its true power and intentions and might reveal them unexpectedly, resulting in the concept of the "China threat." To counter this perception, President Hu Jintao, who took office in 2003, stated that China's development did not threaten the world and established foreign policy principles such as a harmonious world, harmonious society, peaceful rise, and peaceful development. The US responded by shifting its focus to the Asia-Pacific region with its "pivot to Asia" strategy, as China became the second largest economy after the US in 2010. Under President Obama, the US sought to "rebalance" China by strengthening ties with allies in the region, deepening partnerships with Southeast Asian countries, and adopting a balanced and pragmatic approach to China. However, with the election of Xi Jinping in China in 2013 and Donald Trump in the US, the US strategy towards the Asia-Pacific and Sino-US relations changed.

Under Xi, China has adopted a new discourse, the "China Dream," which aims to improve the welfare of the Chinese people and strengthen reforms and economic growth (Xi, 2017). Xi's "striving for achievement" strategy also indicates that China is moving away from its previous "keeping a low profile" strategy in foreign affairs. Xi Jinping introduced the concept of a "China Dream" to emphasise the improvement of the welfare of the Chinese people, the efforts to realise socialism with Chinese characteristics, and the strengthening of reforms and economic growth. Xi also proposed a "new model of great power relations" for China-US relations, which emphasised "no conflicts or confrontations, mutual respect, and win-win cooperation" (Qi, 2015: 350). This has brought the concept of a "community of common destiny" (CCD) to the forefront, focusing on world peace, collaboration, understanding, and shared development for all nations. China's BRI is the largest infrastructural development project in the world, and the concept of a community of common destiny has become an important goal of the BRI.

BRI, announced in 2013, connects the Asian, European, and African continents with various corridors. It is a project to revive the old silk and spice road, which aims to connect countries and contribute to global economic growth through trade routes starting from China and reaching Europe through Asia, Africa, and the Middle East (Pekcan and Uygun, 2021: 1154). BRI consists of two roads: the 21st Century Maritime Silk Road and Silk Road Economic Belt. By building relationships, investments, and a variety of opportunities for cooperation, the initiative opens the door for China to become a regional and global power (Engin Güder and Pekcan, 2020: 187). As of March 2022, 147 countries joined BRI (Nedopil, 2022).

With the COVID-19 outbreak, China rhetorically expanded the BRI with the HSR, Digital Silk Road (DSR), and Space Silk Road (SSR) and built physical infrastructure links to Europe. The next part will examine China's health diplomacy efforts through the HSR and how those efforts have affected its relations with Southeast Asian nations.

Health Silk Road, China's COVID-19 Response, and Efforts for the Global Health Leadership

China pursued its health diplomacy by sending medical personnel, including doctors, nurses, and medical aid, to developing African nations in the 1960s. The emergence of severe acute respiratory syndrome (SARS) in 2003 hastened China's transition to a modern healthcare system (Calabrese, 2022). The 2013 announcement of the BRI catalysed the development of the HSR and China's ambitions to take the lead in global health. As mentioned earlier, with the aim of the CCD, HSR became a significant component of the BRI.

The HSR is a comprehensive and flexible structure for international collaboration in the health sector on both bilateral and multilateral levels. It was first mentioned in 2015 in the "Three-Year Plan for the Implementation of the Belt and Road Initiative Health Exchange and Cooperation (2015-2017)" (Brînză, 2020). Chinese President Xi Jinping officially coined it during a visit to Geneva in 2017. The Beijing Communiqué on BRI Health Cooperation and the HSR was signed in August 2017 by representatives from various nations, international organisations, and NGOs (Moritz, 2021: 3) and lists the following goals: enhancing North-South, South-South, and trilateral cooperation; promoting people's health and well-being; encouraging health development and innovation; and fostering friendship, mutual understanding, and trust (Beijing Communiqué of The Belt and Road Health Co-operation & Health Silk Road, 2017). Health China 2030 is another programme related to the HSR that aims to improve the health of Chinese citizens by implementing over 20 policy measures, including health education and public healthcare facilities (Ngeow, 2020: 11).

Before the pandemic, China had already begun to work with numerous nations in health initiatives. Thousands of medical personnel were sent to Africa to build hospitals and laboratories and fight the Ebola virus, strengthening ties with African and Arab nations (Wu, 2018). The China-Arab States Health Cooperation Forum was held in 2015 and resulted in the signing of the Yinchuan Declaration (Feng, 2015). The China-ASEAN Health Cooperation Forum was undertaken in 2016, and the first Forum of Health Ministers between China and Central and Eastern European countries was held in 2015 (First China-CEEC Health Ministers' Forum Held in the Czech Republic, 2015). The importance of these initiatives increased with the outbreak of COVID-19, and the HSR became the key element.

The virus was first detected in China. On December 27, 2019, China reported pneumonia infections from unknown sources in Wuhan. China notified the WHO on January 3, 2020, and declared the coronavirus outbreak on January 9, 2020. The WHO officially named the virus COVID-19 on February 11, 2020 (National Health Commission of the People's Republic of China, 2021). The virus rapidly spread worldwide and was declared a pandemic by the WHO in March 2020. As of August 3, 2022, the WHO had confirmed 577,018,226 cases and 6,401,046 deaths worldwide (World Health Organization, 2022a).

The Chinese government was charged with concealing the epidemic and downplaying its severity, and the government's tardy and ambiguous response to COVID-19 attracted initial criticism (Reuters, 2020; Wadhams and Jacobs, 2020).

However, as soon as the problem was recognised, the Chinese government put strong controls in place to contain the virus. These procedures included a large lockdown of Wuhan and the other cities, thorough testing, contact tracking, and hospital construction (Burki, 2020). China also shared its expertise and knowledge with the world, sending teams of medical professionals and medical supplies to underdeveloped nations. In addition, as soon as China managed to contain the pandemic within its borders, it began providing medical assistance to several countries by donating masks and vaccines.

Vaccine and Mask Diplomacy

The COVID-19 pandemic has changed daily routines globally. Face masks and vaccines have become essential items. China quickly took action to address the global mask and vaccine shortage. Sinopharm, developed by the Beijing Institute of Biological Products, was the first non-Western vaccine to receive emergency approval from the WHO (BBC News, 2021). Sinovac Biotech Ltd. also developed CoronaVac using inactivated viral technology.

Upon the rapid increase in cases in Europe, China sent millions of masks and supplies to several countries. According to the WTO, in 2019, face mask exports from China comprised approximately 25% of global exports (WTO, 2020). Even though some Western nations view China's assistance as "political manipulation," Brian Wong (2020) contends that it can boost China's reputation in countries like Italy, where the EU has failed to assist. According to Uygun (2021), the pandemic has highlighted the fragility of EU solidarity and raised concerns about EU integration. The EU was unable to respond to Italy's needs during the pandemic, but China was able to respond to requests before EU countries (Uygun, 2021: 77).

Not just Europe but also a large number of developing nations worldwide have received aid from China. Especially BRI and HSR were crucial in ensuring access to vaccines and medical supplies in Latin America, the Middle East, and sub-Saharan Africa before the Western nations. For instance, Egypt was the first nation in Africa to produce the Sinovac vaccine from China and become both the Middle East's and Africa's primary vaccine producer (Ridwan, 2022).

In addition to offering health assistance to developing nations, China has worked closely with international organisations, including the WHO, the UN, and African Union, to increase its involvement in global governance, take the lead in global health, and enhance its reputation as a responsible power. At the opening ceremony of the WHO's 73rd World Health Assembly, Xi announced humanitarian and development support to the least developed countries and other gravely affected countries. He also took part in the G20 special conference on the pandemic (Song, 2020). China also collaborated with United Nations Relief and Works Agency (UNRWA) for Palestinian refugees in the Middle East and donated 200,000 doses of Sinopharm vaccines to the UNRWA (UNRWA, 2022). Moreover, to expedite the development and production of COVID-19 vaccines and ensure fair and equal access for every nation in the world, China joined COVAX in October 2020 (World Health Organization, 2022b).

China was the world's leading supplier of COVID-19 vaccines, but demand for its vaccines is dropping due to the superior efficacy of Pfizer-Moderna vaccines. By August 14, 2022, China had sold 1.9 billion doses of vaccines and donated 272 million doses (Bridge Beijing, 2022). China claims that its vaccines and medical supplies donations are meant "to make Chinese-made vaccines a worldwide public benefit and help build a community with a shared future for mankind" (Hu, 2021). Still, there are differing perspectives on the motivations behind China's health diplomacy. Some argue that domestic policy is more effective than external factors in China's efforts to prevent the pandemic (Kowalski, 2021: 213). In contrast, others claim that China's health diplomacy gives it a geopolitical advantage to strengthen its hegemonic position (Gauttam et al., 2020).

With this premise, this study focuses on whether China's global health diplomacy has improved China's image as a leading power in Southeast Asia compared to the US by analysing China's relations with Southeast Asian countries in the post-pandemic era. In this context, the next part will compare China's relations with Southeast Asian countries regarding health diplomacy before and after the COVID-19 pandemic.

China's Relations with Southeast Asian Countries in Terms of Health Diplomacy

Southeast Asia is becoming increasingly important due to its geography and strategic location for international trade. The Strait of Malacca, a crucial shipping lane between East Asia and the Middle East, is between Indonesia and Malaysia. The Strait of Malacca transports 40% of global trade and more than 70% of China's LNG and petroleum exports (Krishnan, 2020).

Southeast Asia comprises 11 nations: Brunei, Cambodia, East Timor, Indonesia, Laos, Malaysia, Myanmar, Philippines, Singapore, Thailand, and Vietnam. Ten of these countries are members of the Association of Southeast Asian Nations (ASEAN). The region's countries have diverse economic, ethnic, cultural, geographic, and religious characteristics and have faced challenges since gaining independence.

ASEAN is a regional organisation promoting economic growth, peace, and stability in Southeast Asia (ASEAN, 2022). Its member countries have experienced strong economic growth and have a combined economy ranking as the fifth largest in the world. China and the US are competing for influence in the region, with China using BRI and health diplomacy to strengthen its presence.

Before the COVID-19 Outbreak

COVID-19 has brought attention to the infrastructure and service needs of emerging nations. Southeast Asian countries are important to China economically and geopolitically. After the Cold War, the US was the only superpower, but China has risen and challenged the US. China has less power than the US but has a lot of influence, particularly in Southeast Asia. China gained strength in the region due to the US focusing on the Middle East and the war on terrorism, China's admission to the WTO in 2001, and its faster recovery from the 2008 financial crisis compared to Western nations.

Throughout the 1990s, China and Southeast Asian nations had positive relations and China became a Dialogue Partner with ASEAN in 1996. In 1999, China, India, Myanmar, and Bangladesh organised the Kunming Initiative (KI) to promote economic cooperation and connectivity in the region (The Kunming Initiative for a Growth Quadrangle between China, India, Myanmar and Bangladesh, 2000). The Bangladesh, China, India and Myanmar (BCIM) Regional Cooperation Forum replaced KI in 2011 and aimed to revitalise the "Old Burma Road" (Michael, 2013: 174). The BCIM was added to the BRI as the BCIM economic corridor (BCIM-EC) in 2015 to connect Kolkata and Kunming and industrialising areas along the way (Tao, 2022: 146). However, due to India's opposition to BCIM-EC being included in the BRI and its lack of progress on infrastructure projects, it was not included in the 2019 list of BRI corridors (Chaudhury, 2019).

China and ASEAN signed a free trade agreement (FTA) and Declaration on the Conduct of Parties in the South China Sea in 2002. The FTA aimed to foster economic, trade, and investment cooperation and liberalise and promote trade in goods and services (Framework Agreement on Comprehensive Economic Co-Operation Between the Association of South East Asian Nations and The People's Republic of China, 2002). The declaration emphasised dialogue and consultation to settle disputes based on equality and mutual respect within the framework of international law. The objectives were to maintain the status quo, resolve issues amicably, and prevent conflict in the South China Sea (Pekcan, 2017: 63). The South China Sea is a hotspot for potential conflict due to overlapping territorial claims by countries with a coastline. China claims almost all of the South China Sea and calls this area the nine-dash line. Despite the 2002 declaration, there are still frequent disputes over the South China Sea, particularly between China, Vietnam, and the Philippines.

The 2003 SARS outbreak made China aware of the value of international collaboration in healthcare. China contributed 10 million RMB to the Sino-ASEAN Foundation on Public Health Cooperation, established in April 2003 by the health ministers of ASEAN+3 (ASEAN members plus China, Japan, and South Korea). That same year, ASEAN and China established their strategic partnership (Baruah, 2021: 4).

The US under President Obama implemented a "pivot to Asia" strategy, which prioritised the Asia-Pacific region and asserted US interests in the South China Sea. This caused divisions among ASEAN governments in their response to China's ambitions. In 2016, ASEAN and the US upgraded their relations to a strategic partnership, and the US strengthened its defence and military ties with Indonesia, Malaysia, the Philippines, and Singapore. The US also improved relations with Vietnam by lifting the weapons embargo and mended relations with Brunei and Myanmar (Shambaugh, 2018: 104–105).

In contrast to Obama, President Donald Trump did not prioritise Southeast Asia and withdrew from the Trans-Pacific Partnership Agreement (TPP), a key aspect of Obama's "pivot to Asia" strategy. The TPP was a trade agreement signed in 2016 between 12 countries, including the US, in the Asia-Pacific region. Trump's

"America First" policy and withdrawal from the TPP have damaged the US' credibility in the area (Shambaugh, 2018: 108).

China has increased its influence in Southeast Asia through social, cultural, economic, and security measures. It has established comprehensive strategic cooperative partnerships, the highest level of diplomatic ties, with Vietnam, Laos, Cambodia, Myanmar, and Thailand. In 2013, China prioritised its relations with neighbouring nations through its periphery diplomacy. The BRI has also led to the acceleration of infrastructure projects in the region, including the creation of a Pan-Asian Railway Network with three lines connecting China and Southeast Asia (Zhao, 2018: 6). Before the BRI was established, health played a significant role in China's relations with ASEAN nations, as evidenced by a memorandum of understanding on health cooperation signed in 2012 and the Nanning Declaration in 2016, which aimed to promote information sharing, illness prevention and control, the education of health sector personnel, the promotion of Traditional Chinese Medicine, and the deployment of Chinese physicians (Moritz, 2021: 2).

After the COVID-19 Outbreak

China's health diplomacy in Southeast Asia has been shaped by the pandemic in several ways. The pandemic has presented both opportunities and challenges for China's health diplomacy in the region. For example, after the COVID-19 outbreak, China utilised its health capabilities to aid Southeast Asian nations by dispatching medical experts and material aid from the government and private sector and sharing medical knowledge and expertise through video conferencing (Gauttam et al., 2020: 325). China also became the first country to ship vaccinations to Southeast Asia and promised to provide 50 million vaccines to the region by the end of 2021, with 40 million already distributed. During the November 2021 ASEAN-China Special Summit, Chinese President Xi promised an additional 150 million vaccines to ASEAN member nations (Maude and Fraser, 2022).

In 2020 and 2021, ASEAN replaced the EU as China's largest trading partner, with Vietnam, Malaysia, and Thailand as its top three economic partners in the region (Maude and Fraser, 2022). China has also increased its influence on diaspora communities in Southeast Asian countries, such as through the donation of medical supplies by Filipino Chinese cultural and commercial organisations in the Philippines (A. Wong, 2020). At the beginning of the COVID-19 pandemic, China's assistance was appreciated by some Southeast Asian leaders (Baruah, 2021: 5). On the other hand, as it became apparent that the Chinese vaccine provided less protection than others, nations began to favour vaccines from Pfizer or Moderna. The US also increased its presence in the region through the US-ASEAN Health Futures programme, introduced in April 2020 (Ngeow, 2020: 18). By the end of 2021, the US had surpassed China as the main vaccine donor in Southeast Asia, with 87 million doses promised and 74 million already given (Maude and Fraser, 2022).

China has relied on Laos and Cambodia as allies in Southeast Asia, with some scholars referring to them as client or vassal states. While Laos follows a slightly more neutral policy, Cambodia has more closely embraced China and supports its position in the South China Sea dispute (Pang, 2017). More than 80% of Cambodians have been vaccinated with Chinese vaccines.

Vietnam and the Philippines are the Southeast Asian nations with the most issues with China, largely due to conflicting interests in the South China Sea and the Philippines being a key ally of the US in the region. On the other hand, Indonesia follows an "independent and active" foreign policy and tries to maintain a balance between China and the US. Despite this, it remained friendly with China during the COVID-19 pandemic and imported many Chinese vaccines (Radio Free Asia, 2021). Thailand also follows a pragmatic foreign policy, seeking to maintain alliances with China and the US.

At the beginning of the COVID-19 pandemic, relations between Malaysia and China were based on mutual trust and aid, as both countries provided medical assistance to each other. However, the South China Sea issue and pressure from the US for Malaysia to adopt its Indo-Pacific strategy could erode the long-standing mutual trust, according to Lee and Akhir (2021).

According to a survey conducted in 2021 by the ISEAS-Yusof Ishak Institute in Singapore, 44.2% of respondents in ASEAN countries viewed China as having provided the most help to the region during the COVID-19 pandemic. The highest ratings for China were in Brunei (87.9%), Thailand (65.6%), and Malaysia (64.1%), while Japan received the most votes in Myanmar (41.0%), and the US was the top choice in Vietnam (29.7%). Indonesia, Cambodia, and Singapore's top choices were China (Seah et al., 2021). In a survey conducted in 2022, China was seen as the country providing the most vaccine aid to the region, followed by the US and Australia. However, when examining vaccine preferences, 54.8% of participants preferred Pfizer and Moderna, with the highest preference in Singapore (90.1%), followed by Myanmar (68.6%), Laos (65.9%), and Brunei (62.3%) (Seah et al., 2022). This preference may be due to a decrease in the reliability of Chinese vaccines in 2022.

According to the survey, 76.3% of respondents viewed China as the most important economic force in Southeast Asia, a trend that has persisted since 2019. The highest levels of recognition of China's economic influence were in Laos (87.5%), Thailand (84.7%), Singapore (83.5%), Myanmar (83.3%), and Cambodia (80.8%). In 2020, Vietnam (90.4%), Thailand (79.3%), and the Philippines (77.5%) expressed concerns about China's growing economic influence, and this sentiment remained unchanged in 2022, with Myanmar, the Philippines, and Singapore being the most concerned. However, there was a significant shift in how Vietnam and Thailand viewed China, with both nations appearing less concerned than the previous year. Thailand's reduced concern may be due to the BRI it initiated with China, which has enhanced relations between the two countries through a high-speed train link between China, Thailand, and Laos. However, the project was delayed due to the pandemic and other factors, and efforts to accelerate it in 2022 (Tanakasempipat, 2022) may have relieved Thailand's concerns.

According to a different survey, seven ASEAN countries (excluding Singapore, Vietnam, and the Philippines) preferred China in 2020. However, in 2021, the percentage of respondents in Myanmar who chose China decreased from 61.5% to 51.9%, dropping from 57.7% to 46.2% in Cambodia. The greatest decrease was in

Indonesia, where the percentage of people who favoured China dropped from 52% in 2020 to 35.7% in 2021. In 2022, while other nations preferred the US, Brunei, Cambodia, and Laos preferred China, with the percentage of people in Cambodia who chose China rising to 81.5%, an increase of almost 100%. In Myanmar, the rate of respondents who preferred China sharply decreased to 8% in 2022, possibly due to the coup that occurred in the country in 2021. China's desire to maintain its relations with the military regime in Myanmar to protect its investments and interests (Kurlantzick, 2022) may have contributed to the negative public reaction.

According to the survey, more people in Southeast Asia now view the US as a trustworthy strategic partner than they did in 2020. This increase in support for the US, which rose from 34.9% in 2020 to 55.4% in 2021 (Seah et al., 2021), may be due to the Biden administration. However, this percentage dropped to 42.6% in 2022. At the same time, China's credibility has also increased, with 26.8% of respondents viewing it as reliable in 2022, compared to 16.5% in 2021 (Seah et al., 2022).

Conclusion

As a powerful and responsible state with ambitious programmes and projects under President Xi Jinping, China has come to the forefront of the international system. In demonstrating its status as a reliable and benevolent nation, the COVID-19 pandemic has been a significant turning point. The COVID-19 pandemic has shed light on China's role in global health governance and its approach to international relations in general. Leveraging the BRI, China has brought the HSR to the forefront in this context. Adopting the rhetoric of a "community of shared destiny," China began providing health assistance to the entire world after quickly bringing the pandemic under control within its borders. By donating health equipment, particularly masks and vaccines, to numerous countries, China's actions were widely viewed as admirable and positively impacted its image.

Throughout the pandemic, China has been actively engaging with Southeast Asian countries through its global health diplomacy initiatives. China's early efforts to provide aid and medical supplies to Southeast Asian countries helped to alleviate the initial burden of the pandemic, and its ongoing efforts to share knowledge and resources have helped to mitigate the long-term impact of the pandemic. However, China's approach to global health diplomacy has also been criticised for being self-serving and lacking transparency. The lack of transparency in the early stages of the pandemic and China's initial response to the outbreak have raised questions about its commitment to global health governance and its willingness to cooperate with other countries.

This chapter assessed the perspective of Southeast Asian nations towards China and the diplomatic and economic ties between the two. To examine public perception of China, the chapter utilised a survey conducted by Singapore's ISEAS-Yusof Ishak Institute. Findings from the intergovernmental relationships indicate that most Southeast Asian nations have appreciated Chinese assistance. Except for Cambodia and, to a lesser extent, Laos, it can be argued that other nations have adopted a pragmatic approach or hedging strategy rather than aligning with either China or the US. Despite the declining efficacy of Chinese vaccines during the later stages of the pandemic, it can be argued that China's health diplomacy efforts have improved ties with Southeast Asian governments.

However, when examining public perception, some noteworthy findings emerged. According to the survey, China is viewed as the nation that has provided the most assistance to the region during the pandemic. This is particularly true for Thailand, Malaysia, and Brunei. However, when considering the results from 2022, it is notable that Brunei has chosen Pfizer and Moderna as its preferred vaccine suppliers. All nations in the region view China as the most significant economic force, and the 2020 survey indicates that Vietnam, Thailand, and the Philippines are the nations most concerned about this. This concern is likely due to conflicts of interest in the South China Sea, and, unsurprisingly, Vietnam and the Philippines view China as a potential threat. While Thailand views China as the most helpful nation, and there are no major issues between the two countries, the Thai people are concerned about China's influence in the region. In 2022, there is an increase in concerns among Myanmar and Singapore, while problems among Vietnam and Thailand will decrease.

It is clear from the analysis presented in this chapter that China's efforts to utilise health diplomacy to strengthen its relationships with Southeast Asian nations have had some success, particularly in terms of improving relations with governments in the region. However, these efforts have not impacted public perceptions of China as much. The survey results show that, while some countries see China as the most helpful nation during the pandemic, there are still concerns about its economic influence and reliability as a strategic partner.

This chapter reveals that the pandemic has presented both opportunities and challenges for China's health diplomacy in Southeast Asia. While China has provided significant medical assistance to the region, it has also faced challenges related to vaccine diplomacy and criticism of its initial handling of the pandemic. In conclusion, China's health diplomacy efforts have played a significant role in improving its relations with Southeast Asian nations. By providing assistance during the COVID-19 pandemic, China has demonstrated its reliability as a strategic partner and improved its image in the region. While the effectiveness of these efforts has varied among different countries and has not had a significant impact on public perception of China, they have had a positive impact on intergovernmental relationships. To continue building on this success, China may need to address the concerns of the countries and adopt more transparent and open policies and make better use of its soft power.

References

ASEAN. (2022) 'ASEAN Aims'. Available at: https://asean.org/what-we-do#asean-aims (Accessed: August 12, 2022).

Baruah, A. G. (2021) 'China's Health Diplomacy: Taking Forward the Health Silk Road in Southeast Asia', Focus Asia: Perspective and Analysis, Institute for Security and Development Policy, pp. 1–11. Available at: https://www.isdp.eu/publication/chinas-health-diplomacy-taking-forward-the-health-silk-road-in-southeast-asia/

BBC News. (2021) 'Sinopharm: Chinese Covid Vaccine Gets WHO Emergency Approval', May 7. Available at: https://www.bbc.com/news/world-asia-china-56967973 (Accessed: August 4, 2022).

Beijing Communiqué of The Belt and Road Health Cooperation & Health Silk Road. (2017), *National Health Commission of the People's Republic of China*, August 18. Available at: http://en.nhc.gov.cn/2017-08/18/c_72257.htm (Accessed: August 3, 2022).

Bridge Beijing. (2022) 'China COVID-19 Vaccine Tracker', August 14. Available at: https://bridgebeijing.com/our-publications/our-publications-1/china-covid-19-vaccines-tracker/ (Accessed: August 15, 2022).

Brînză, A. (2020) 'Some Say China's Belt and Road Helped Create This Pandemic. Can It Prevent the Next One?', *The Diplomat*, April 2. Available at: https://thediplomat.com/2020/04/some-say-chinas-belt-and-road-helped-create-this-pandemic-can-it-prevent-the-next-one/ (Accessed: August 1, 2022).

Burki, T. (2020) 'China's Successful Control of COVID-19', *Lancet Infectious Diseases*, 20(11), pp. 1240–1241. doi: 10.1016/S1473-3099(20)30800-8

Calabrese, J. (2022) 'China's Health Silk Road and the BRI Agenda in the Middle East', *Middle East Institute*, January 11. Available at: https://www.mei.edu/publications/chinas-health-silk-road-and-bri-agenda-middle-east (Accessed: July 20, 2022).

Chaudhury, D. R. (2019) 'Kunming Meet Revives BCIM Link Plan', *The Economic Times*, June 24. Available at: https://economictimes.indiatimes.com/news/politics-and-nation/kunming-meet-revives-bcim-link-plan/articleshow/69921135.cms (Accessed: August 12, 2022).

Engin Güder, B. and Pekcan, C. (2020) 'Bir Kuşak Bir Yol Projesi Çerçevesinde Çin'in Afrika Politikası Ve Çatışma Çözümü Yaklaşımı', *International Journal of Politics and Security*, 2, pp. 173–196.

Feng, H. (2015) 'China-Arab States Health Cooperation Forum Declaration', *National Health Commission of the People's Republic of China*, September 18. Available at: http://en.nhc.gov.cn/2015-09/18/c_45733.htm (Accessed: August 3, 2022).

First China-CEEC Health Ministers' Forum Held in the Czech Republic. (2015) *Ministry of Foreign Affairs of the People's Republic of China*, June 16. Available at: https://www.mfa.gov.cn/ce/cegv//eng/wjyw/t1274345.htm (Accessed: August 3, 2022).

Framework Agreement on Comprehensive Economic Co-Operation Between the Association of South East Asian Nations and The People's Republic of China. (2002) Available at: https://asean.org/wp-content/uploads/2021/08/Framework-Agreement-on-Comprehensive-Economic-Co-Operation_ASEAN-Rep-of-China.pdf (Accessed: August 12, 2022).

Gauttam, P., Singh, B., and Kaur, J. (2020) 'COVID-19 and Chinese Global Health Diplomacy: Geopolitical Opportunity for China's Hegemony?', *Millennial Asia*, 11(3), pp. 318–340. doi: 10.1177/0976399620959771

Hu, Y. (2021) 'China's Vaccines Are Global Public Goods', *China Daily*, April 28. Available at: https://global.chinadaily.com.cn/a/202104/28/WS60889a0ba31024ad0babad4d.html (Accessed: August 17, 2022).

Kowalski, B. (2021) 'China's Mask Diplomacy in Europe: Seeking Foreign Gratitude and Domestic Stability', *Journal of Current Chinese Affairs*, 50(2), pp. 209–226. doi: 10.1177/18681026211007147

Krishnan, S. (2020) 'The Malacca Dilemma: No Panacea But Multiple Possibilities', *The Institute of Chinese Studies*, May 22. Available at: https://icsin.org/blogs/2020/05/22/the-malacca-dilemma-no-panacea-but-multiple-possibilities/ (Accessed: August 7, 2022).

Kurlantzick, J. (2022) 'China's Support for Myanmar Further Shows the World Dividing into Autocracy versus Democracy', *Council on Foreign Relations*, April 4. Available at: https://www.cfr.org/blog/chinas-support-myanmar-further-shows-world-dividing-autocracy-versus-democracy (Accessed: August 20, 2022).

Lee, C. L. and Akhir, M. N. Md. (2021) 'Malaysia–China Relations during the Movement Control Order Period and Beyond: Assessment from the Mutual Trust Variable'. In Peng, N. (ed.), *The Reshaping of China-Southeast Asia Relations in Light of the COVID-19 Pandemic*, pp. 69–93. Singapore: Springer.

Maude, R., & Fraser, D. (2022). *Chinese diplomacy in Southeast Asia during the Covid-19 pandemic*. New York: Asia Society.

Michael, A. (2013) *India's Foreign Policy and Regional Multilateralism*. Basingstoke: Palgrave Macmillan.

Moritz, R. (2021) 'China's Health Diplomacy during Covid-19: The Belt and Road Initiative (BRI) in Action', *German Institute for International and Security Affairs*, No. 9, SWP Comment.

National Health Commission of the People's Republic of China. (2021) 'Timeline: China's Transparency in the Fight against COVID-19', September 6. Available at: http://en.nhc.gov.cn/2021-09/06/c_84547.htm (Accessed: July 28, 2022).

Nedopil, C. (2022) 'Countries of the Belt and Road Initiative', Shanghai, Green Finance & Development Center, FISF Fudan University. Available at: www.greenfdc.org (Accessed: August 2, 2022).

Ngeow, C. B. (2020) 'COVID-19, Belt and Road Initiative and the Health Silk Road: Implications for Southeast Asia', Frederick-Ebert-Stiftung, Indonesia.

Pang, E. (2017) '"Same-Same but Different": Laos and Cambodia's Political Embrace of China', *Perspective*, No. 66, pp. 1–7.

Pekcan, C. (2017) 'Uluslararası Hukuk Çerçevesinde Güney Çin Denizi Krizinin Değerlendirilmesi', *Uluslararası Kriz ve Siyaset Araştırmaları Dergisi*, 1(3), pp. 54–80.

Pekcan, C. and Uygun, A. G. (2021) 'Çin'in Akdeniz Politikaları Kapsamında Avrupa Birliği-Çin Stratejik Ortaklığı', *Atatürk Üniversitesi İktisadi ve İdari Bilimler Dergisi*, 35(3), pp. 1145–1164.

Qi, H. (2015) 'China Debates the 'New Type of Great Power Relations', *The Chinese Journal of International Politics*, 8(4), pp. 349–370. https://www.jstor.org/stable/48615943

Radio Free Asia. (2021) 'More Than 80 Percent of Indonesia's Vaccine Supply Comes From China', September 24. Available at: https://www.rfa.org/english/news/china/vaccine-09242021173110.html (Accessed: August 15, 2022).

Reuters. (2020) 'China Concealed the Early Coronavirus Outbreak, Former MI6 Spymaster Says', April 15. Available at: https://www.reuters.com/article/us-health-coronavirus-britain-china-idUSKCN21X0VY (Accessed: April 22, 2023).

Ridwan, P. M. (2022) 'China's Health Silk Road in the Middle East', *East Asia Forum*, July 29. Available at: https://www.eastasiaforum.org/2022/07/29/chinas-health-silk-road-in-the-middle-east/ (Accessed: August 2, 2022).

Seah, S. et al. (2022) 'The State of Southeast Asia: 2022 Survey Report', *ISEAS-Yusof Ishak Institute*. Available at: https://www.iseas.edu.sg/wp-content/uploads/2022/02/The-State-of-SEA-2022_FA_Digital_FINAL.pdf (Accessed: August 2, 2022).

Seah, S., Ha, H. T., Martinus, M., and Thao, P. T. P. (2021) 'The State of Southeast Asia: 2021 Survey Report', *ISEAS-Yusof Ishak Institute*. Available at: https://www.iseas.edu.sg/wp-content/uploads/2021/01/The-State-of-SEA-2021-v2.pdf (Accessed: August 2, 2022).

Shambaugh, D. (2018) 'US-China Rivalry in Southeast Asia: Power Shift or Competitive Coexistence', *International Security*, 42(4), pp. 85–127.

Song, W. (2020) 'China's Global Engagement to Fight the Novel Coronavirus Pandemic', *Global Health Research and Policy*, 5(44), 1–4.

Tanakasempipat, P. (2022) 'Thailand Pledges to Finish High-Speed Rail Link to China by 2028', *Bloomberg*, July 6. Available at: https://www.bloomberg.com/news/articles/2022-07-06/thailand-pledges-to-finish-high-speed-rail-link-to-china-by-2028 (Accessed: August 20, 2022).

Tao, S. (2022) 'Yunnan Connecting China and Southeast Asia'. In Ploberger, C., Ngampamuan, S., and Tao, S. (eds.) *China's Belt and Road Initiative: The Impact on Sub-Regional Southeast Asia*, pp. 129–148. New York, NY: Routledge.

The Kunming Initiative for a Growth Quadrangle between China, India, Myanmar and Bangladesh. (2000) *China Report*, 36(3), pp. 417–424.

UNRWA. (2022) 'The Government of The People's Republic of China Provides Covid-19 Vaccines to Help Protect Palestine Refugees', United Nations Relief and Works Agency for Palestine Refugees in the Near East. Available at: https://www.unrwa.org/newsroom/press-releases/government-people%E2%80%99s-republic-china-provides-covid-19-vaccines-help-protect (Accessed: July 25, 2022).

Uygun, A. G. (2021) 'Avrupa Birliği Dayanışması: Kriz Dönemlerinde Normatif Ve Kavramsal Bir Değerlendirme', *Uluslararası İlişkiler ve Diplomasi Dergisi*, 4(2), pp. 68–85.

Wadhams, N. and Jacobs, J. (2020) 'China Concealed Extent of Virus Outbreak, U.S. Intelligence Says', *Bloomberg*, April 1. Available at: https://www.bloomberg.com/news/articles/2020-04-01/china-concealed-extent-of-virus-outbreak-u-s-intelligence-says#xj4y7vzkg (Accessed: April 22, 2023).

Wong, A. (2020) 'COVID-19 and China's Information Diplomacy in Southeast Asia', *Brookings*, September 3. Available at: https://www.brookings.edu/blog/order-from-chaos/2020/09/03/covid-19-and-chinas-information-diplomacy-in-southeast-asia/ (Accessed: August 13, 2022).

Wong, B. (2020) 'China's Mask Diplomacy', *The Diplomat*, March 25. Available at: https://thediplomat.com/2020/03/chinas-mask-diplomacy/ (Accessed: August 13, 2022).

World Health Organization. (2022a) 'Coronavirus Disease (COVID-19)'. Available at: https://www.who.int/emergencies/diseases/novel-coronavirus-2019 (Accessed: August 4, 2022).

World Health Organization. (2022b). 'COVAX'. Available at: https://www.who.int/initiatives/act-accelerator/covax (Accessed: August 13, 2022).

WTO. (2020) 'Trade in Medical Goods in the Context of Tackling COVID-19', April 3. Available at: https://www.wto.org/english/news_e/news20_e/rese_03apr20_e.pdf (Accessed: August 15, 2022).

Wu, G. (2018) 'Building the Silk Road with Health', *GGTN News*, June 28. Available at: https://news.cgtn.com/news/7a556a4d35457a6333566d54/index.html (Accessed: August 2, 2022).

Xi, J. (2017) 'Secure a Decisive Victory in Building a Moderately Prosperous Society in All Respects and Strive for the Great Success of Socialism with Chinese Characteristics for a New Era', *China Daily*. Available at: https://www.chinadaily.com.cn/china/19thcpcnationalcongress/2017-11/04/content_34115212.htm

Zhao, H. (2019) 'China–Japan Compete for Infrastructure Investment in Southeast Asia: Geopolitical Rivalry or Healthy Competition?', *Journal of Contemporary China*, 28(118), 558–574.

10 COVID-19 and South Korea

Focusing on Cultural Public Diplomacy with *Hallyu*

Yunhee Kim and Erman Akıllı

Introduction

In March 2020, the World Health Organization (WHO) officially declared the COVID-19 outbreak a pandemic. The world abruptly changed and struggled to adjust to the numerous shifts in everyday life in the aftermath of the virus spreading worldwide. As of January 2023, globally there had been 665,078,673 COVID-19 cases reported to the WHO, including 6,725,248 deaths, although 13,156,047,747 were vaccinated (WHO, 2023). All countries around the globe laid out a new set of rules to stop the virus from spreading further. The most common rules were social distancing, wearing a mask, overseas and domestic travel restrictions, mandatory vaccination, and working from home. However, the effect of COVID-19 around the world demonstrated a large gap according to countries' ability to take care of the health crisis's after-effects.

The pandemic has transmuted the international situation, including the sealing of borders with neighbouring countries. Powerful nations were only concentrating on their nationals and national interests, and all diplomatic discussions were held online due to social distancing. Whole nations could not continue enjoying their leisure cultural activities and moved to online platforms instead. Therefore, over-the-counter (OTT) media streaming consumption during the COVID-19 lockdown soared compared to the pre-pandemic period. In other words, the world changed our social life and foreign policies by shifting interactions to virtual space through video conferences online. The pandemic also accelerated utilising smartphones, computers, and TVs to contact people amid social distancing. After that, numerous people worldwide gained more chances to come across *Hallyu* than in the pre-COVID-19 era.

Considering the situation, the South Korean government attempted to introduce Korea through *Hallyu* and promote it to the world. Under the Moon Jae-in administration, South Korea established the Hallyu Content Cooperation Division for the first time. It raised its interagency promotion plan to enhance the spillover effect of K-culture diffusion. The organisation is designed to cope with non-face-to-face events and support *Hallyu*-related industries suitable for the pandemic era; consequently, it expanded to spread the popularity of the Korean language and K-foods after people worldwide experienced K-movies and K-music. The copyright trade balance also recorded a surplus in 2020 (Lee, 2022).

DOI: 10.4324/9781003377597-12

According to a South Korea's Ministry of Culture, Sports, and Tourism survey, in 2021, the competitive power of *Hallyu* content increased, meaning the consumption and scale proportion of K-content grew (KOCCA, 2022). K-movies and K-music, such as *Parasite, Squid Game*, BTS, and Black Pink, started to create *Hallyu* fandom worldwide and set the stage for the expansion of Korean soft power, boosted by the growing international audience. Thus, the focal point of this chapter is to re-examine the role and the effect of *Hallyu* in the COVID-19 pandemic in Korea. The first section begins by posing a discussion of soft power, culture, and public diplomacy. The next part examines the meaning of *Hallyu* broadly and specifically from the perspective of the Korean government. The last part analyses the effect of *Hallyu* in Korea during the COVID-19 pandemic.

"Cultural" Public Diplomacy: What Do States Make of It?

In the globalised world, states are competing through many different assets; from culture to tourism, from gastronomy to democracy, every country uses various values to climb to the top in this competition for promoting their positive image. Why is it important? This question needs to be answered through a couple of different aspects. First and foremost, a country's positive image perception in international society can directly boost the legitimacy of its implemented foreign policy. Second, this positive image can also attract foreign investors, tourists, students, and academicians to the country. Joseph S. Nye has argued this competition and coined the term that explains this competition in a broad sense: soft power. Nye coined the soft power concept in international relations literature in his famous book *Bound to Lead: The Changing Nature of American Power* (Nye, 1990). Nye explains the concept of Soft Power as, "The ability to persuade through culture, values, and ideas, as opposed to 'hard power,' which conquers or coerces through military might" (Nye, 1990: 34).

Today, soft power is used to promote a positive image worldwide. Considering the soft power concept as a tree's body, the tree's branches should be cultural diplomacy, public diplomacy, foreign aid, nation branding, and digital diplomacy (Akıllı, 2016: 152). All these alt concepts are related to soft power. In this chapter, we aimed to examine Korea's cultural public diplomacy through the COVID-19 pandemic, crowned by *Hallyu*. Since cultural elements heavily influence Korean public diplomacy, as this chapter mainly emphasises the concept of *Hallyu*, we prefer to use cultural public diplomacy to explain Korea's practice and implementation, especially in the dire times of the COVID-19 pandemic. Thus, to explain cultural public diplomacy, it's vital to shed light on two equally far and close concepts: cultural diplomacy and public diplomacy.

Cultural diplomacy can be described as a course of action based on and utilising the exchange of ideas, values, traditions, and other aspects of culture or identity. Through this exchange, relationships between states could be strengthened, sociocultural cooperation between states may be enhanced, or mutual national interests could be promoted. Cultural diplomacy can be practised by the public sector, private sector, or civil society (Akıllı, 2016: 153–154). Another description of cultural diplomacy is as follows, "Cultural diplomacy represents a facet of diplomacy that has not been utilised completely in building better relationships and although it could serve as a linking bridge toward better relations" (Kitsou, 2011: 21). It is said that cultural diplomacy is one the most important instruments for positive advertising image facilitating diplomatic affairs (Chartrand, 1992: 134). According to another definition, cultural diplomacy is the strategy of developing mutual understanding between states through human communication and exchange as a concept of international relations (Purtaş, 2013). More precisely, it is easier to convince a country you have influenced with your cultural values to accept the legitimacy of your foreign policy decisions. Moreover, as Zhang suggests, institutions, principles, or initiatives to influence international politics and the global conversation more significantly are less important than culture (Zhang, 2017: 44). Nonetheless, thanks to globalisation, cultural diplomacy is a must for countries as well. Since the trust of investors, tourists, consumers, donors, immigrants, the media, and the governments of other nations is directly related to the positive image of a country, those tools are vital armaments in the arsenal of diplomacy for countries (Nye, 2002: 34). Nonetheless, a positive image delivered through cultural diplomacy may facilitate diplomatic affairs (Nye, 2004: 15–21). Furthermore, cultural diplomacy establishes two-way communication and trust with other countries. In this context, cultural diplomacy has the potential to make a lasting impression on other countries and peoples if it is managed well (Akıllı, 2016: 153) and as mentioned above, Korea's soft power, in general, shines on the cultural assets that Korea has and provides through *Hallyu*.

Regarding public diplomacy, its impact on international relations dates further back compared to soft power. Edmund Gullion, director of the Edward Murrow Centre at the Fletcher School of Law and Diplomacy at Tuft University, introduced the idea of public diplomacy in 1965. Gullion noted that the concept encompasses a wide range of relationships, including the impact of public opinion in other nations, the exchange of information and ideas, and the interaction of interest groups in various countries, as opposed to the "effect of public behaviour in the formation and execution of policies" (Akıllı, 2016: 166).

According to Eytan Gilboa, public diplomacy is conducted through various channels and techniques. In fact, among the tools and techniques of public diplomacy are international publishing, scientific and cultural student exchange programmes, scholarships, participation of artists and intellectuals in conferences, festivals, and exhibitions, commercial cooperation, the establishment of joint associations, establishment of cultural centres, and learning foreign languages. Gilboa emphasises that whereas cultural channels are used to influence the public indirectly, mass media channels affect the public directly. As a result, while cultural channels focus on long-term attitudes, mass media focuses on current issues (Gilboa, 2006: 716–717).

Nye explains public diplomacy in three different dimensions: (i) daily communication, (ii) strategic communication, and (iii) long-term communication (Nye, 2008: 101–102). When governments make decisions about their domestic and foreign policies, Nye discusses the "daily communication" aspect and how they share those decisions with their national media. Nye emphasises that governments typically ignore the external media when making these announcements during this process. The second factor, "strategic communication," that Nye addresses encompasses the consistency and continuity of the message the government conveys to the entire globe or a particular target. Nye discusses the third dimension, "long-term communication," which focuses on public diplomacy and the development of long-term relationships, two essential components of the soft power idea.

Today, with the new developments in mass communication technologies, György Szondi refers to public diplomacy as "new public diplomacy" and explains that it encompasses two-way communication, information management, and image construction over the internet (interactive websites, popular YouTube videos, and social media platforms like Twitter and Facebook) as top soft power components (Szondi, 2009: 303–305). Szondi contrasts classical and new public diplomacy, highlighting differences in elements such as circumstances, objectives, strategy, communication, R&D, message content, target audience, tools, and budget (Szondi, 2009: 305).

As seen above, cultural diplomacy and public diplomacy are intertwined yet distinct concepts, and Korea's public diplomacy is a sum of both. In the next section, "The meaning of *Hallyu*," we will give details about the concept of *Hallyu* and how Korean (pop) culture relates.

The Meaning of *Hallyu*

The meaning of *Hallyu*, also called "the Korean Wave" in English, varies according to the Korean government's and scholars' understanding. The *Encyclopaedia of Korean Culture*, operated by the Academy of Korean Studies under the umbrella of the Ministry of Education, defines *Hallyu* as "a cultural phenomenon that Korean mass culture elements are disseminated to foreign countries centring on Asia and garnered great popularity" (Encyclopaedia of Korean Culture, n.d.). Scholars comprehended the meaning of *Hallyu* as "a collective term that encompasses a wide range of Korean popular culture" (Park, 2021: 17) and "the widespread consumption of Korean popular culture overseas" (Choe, 2016: 3). Lee also argued that *Hallyu* is "the varied and uneven reception process of South Korean culture/media products and images in Asia as well as particular forms of media and cultural representations in the transborder flows of South Korean popular culture in South Korea" (Lee, 2008: 175). By extension, Lee and Kim (2018) claimed that *Hallyu* was a means of cultural exchange through the media at the early stage, and now it represents all activities based on Korean culture. It furthermore developed to pave the way for leading the new trends of fostering cultural brands as a nation or industrial branding of Korea.

The different understandings of *Hallyu* are explicable by reviewing its origin. The predominant definition of *Hallyu* began with the popularity of the K-drama titled "What is Love?" (*Sarangi Mogilrae*) in 1997 in China. The K-drama "Jealousy" (*Jiltu*) had already been broadcast in 1993 and exported to Hong Kong and

114 *Yunhee Kim and Erman Akıllı*

Taiwan, but it failed to garner the same attention from the local people (Jin, 2016). Since K-music was officially launched in Taiwan and China in 1998, *Hallyu* has spread out earnestly in Chinese-speaking countries, Japan, Vietnam, and Asia. The phenomena were affected by domestic and international environment changes; for instance, Korea promoted international exchanges in the aftermath of the 1996 Asian Games, and around the same time, J-pop, J-drama, and Hong Kong movies stole the show in Asia (Jang, 2011). With this backdrop, the term *Hallyu* was called 韓迷 or 哈韓族, meaning that Chinese people exuberate in Korean popular music; it was later used mixed with 韓朝 and 韓風 in China during the mid of 1990s (Lee and An, 2004). The popularity of Korean popular culture spread rapidly with the term 韓流 (*Hallyu*) combined with the Japanese word 流 (*ryu*) in the late 1990s. Then, *Hallyu* was adopted by the Ministry of Culture and Tourism of Korea when they distributed a publicity compact disc (CD) to China under the name of 韓流, "Song from Korea," in 1999 (Lee, 2012).

It has been around 20 years since *Hallyu* was introduced to the world. The transition of Hallyu has moved from *Hallyu 1.0* to *New Hallyu* (*shinhallyu*). As Table 10.1 notes, Hallyu began with *Hallyu 1.0* based on K-drama. Still, it advanced gradually through *Hallyu 2.0* centred on a few idol stars, and *Hallyu 3.0* carried out *Hallyu* globalisation in earnest. Finally, the Korean government designated the year 2020 as the first year of the *New Hallyu* (K-culture) to manage *Hallyu* comprehensively and suggested the "Strategy for Boosting New *Hallyu* Promotion Policy" as long-range plans with the objectives of diversification of *Hallyu* content, leading *Hallyu*-related industries, and establishing the groundwork for sustainable *Hallyu* diffusion. Drawing on it, the meaning of *New Hallyu*, unlike the previous

Table 10.1 The Classification of *Hallyu* through the Years

	Hallyu 1.0	*Hallyu 2.0*	*Hallyu 3.0*	*New Hallyu (K-culture)*
Period	1997–mid-2000s	mid-2000s–early 2010s	early 2010s–2019	2020 onwards
Character	The beginning of Hallyu, centring on media content	Diffusion of Hallyu Centring on idol stars	Hallyu globalisation	Hallyu diversification and globalisation through online communication
The field of K-contents	K-drama	K-pop	K-culture	K-culture and its related industry
Target country	Asia	Asia, Central and South America, the Middle East, some parts of the Americas	The whole world	The whole world with diffusion strategically
Consumer	A few Hallyu lovers	In teens and twenty-somethings	Cosmopolitan	Cosmopolitan with a customised approach

Source: The Ministry of Culture, Sports, and Tourism (2020)

Hallyu approach, is to seek long-lasting and high-spread effects of Hallyu standing based on discovering *Hallyu* contents in all areas of Korean culture, reinforcement of *Hallyu*-related industries such as service and consumer goods, and pursuing intercultural exchange.

Hallyu's Impact on South Korea under the Prolonged COVID-19 Pandemic

From the Economic Perspective

After BTS's popularity exploded in 2017, K-movies and K-dramas recorded the highest viewing rate and gained cinematic quality and popularity in the global movie world. For instance, the K-dramas *Hell Bound* and *Squid Game* and K-movies *Parasite* and *Train to Busan* became great hits on Netflix in 2021. *Squid Game* and *Parasite* portrayed personal desire and social contradictions in modern society by lampooning life in Korea. They evoked sympathy, all-pervading absurd structures, including disparity in wealth, social hierarchy, and racial discrimination. They led to K-content gaining stature; thereby, *Hallyu* has a considerable amount of economic value with its social and cultural value (KOFICE, 2021). Consumers worldwide purchased Korean products after being exposed to *Hallyu* content, appreciating its cultural value and images (Cho and Yoon, 2013). In the same vein, the meaning of the increase in Korean consumer goods abroad in the aftermath of the Korean Wave is a favourable Korean image under the influence of Korean culture.

As a result, the Korean government under the Moon Jae-in administration established the "Strategy for Boosting New *Hallyu* Promotion Policy" to constantly diffuse *Hallyu* and maximise its spin-off effects. Therefore, the government carried out the strategy under New *Hallyu* (K-Culture). It focused on discovering creative and diverse *Hallyu* content from the whole Korean culture and connecting it to *Hallyu*-related industries. It did this by using its economic ripple effects for sharpening the competitiveness of consumer goods and service industries in Korea, which lead to encouraging mutual growth. The trend also expects to encourage an increase in Korean culture consumers that are amicable to Korea and pave the way for Korea's higher status in international society. Thus, under the Yoon Suk-yeol administration of 2022, the MCST supported more in the area of K-content in conjunction with Korean companies that stimulate private initiatives. The projects concentrated on the support for K-movies, K-pop, and video service systems on OTT as a pivot of Korea's economic growth, attracting companies that have global intellectual property rights (IPRs) with expanding political finances, combining artificial intelligence (AI) technology with *Hallyu* to move to a virtual world, and other steps (Policy briefing, 2022).

From the economic perspective, the expansion of *Hallyu* leads to increased profits for Korean companies that produce *Hallyu*-related products and offers employment opportunities. As a result, *Hallyu*'s economic effect is divided into two parts: *Hallyu* content and its related service exports, and *Hallyu* derivative product exports, such as consumer goods and tour packages. Thus, the effect of export

Figure 10.1 Associated image of Korea.
Source: KOFICE (2022)

enlargement through *Hallyu* is directly related to Korea's general *Hallyu*-related industries, including production, added value, and employment (KOFICE, 2021). According to the research from the Oversea Economy Research Institute, an organisation affiliated with the Export-Import Bank of Korea, the export of Korean consumer goods increased by $1.8 billion when the export of K-content rose by $1 billion based on the analysis of the number of consumer goods exported, such as clothing, cosmetic products, IT devises, and processed food from 2006 to 2020. The research team found that an increase in the favourability of Korean products in sync with the proliferation of K-content directly led to the rise of exports. More specifically, the phenomenon occurred more strongly outside Chinese-speaking countries. Foreigners showered attention on K-pop and K-movies among K-content, affecting Korea's export items, especially cosmetics and processed foods (EXIM Bank of Korea, 2022).

Despite the prolonged COVID-19, the amount of K-content export was $12.4 billion in 2021, which rose 4.4% compared to 2020. The total sales of K-content increased by 7.1% as well. The number of content industry-related businesses in Korea was 109,000, which also grew by 9.1%. The *Hallyu* club members spent over $15 million, an all-time high. Not only that, but the competitiveness of *Hallyu* content was also rising (KOCCA, 2022). The Brand Power Index of Hallyu was introduced in 2020 by the Korean government to assess the value of *Hallyu* now and in the future. The index increased by 3.1 points in 2021 compared to 2020, and it showed a high index in the field of K-foods (67.6 points), K-beauty (65.3 points), and K-movies (64.3 points) (KOFICE, 2022). It is also connected to the associated image of Korea, as Figure 10.1 shows. It implies that K-content and its related industry are commended according to the Korean government's new *Hallyu* (K-Culture) strategy.

From the Societal Perspective

Drawing on the efforts of the Korean government's cultural public diplomacy with *Hallyu*, foreigners grew more interested in Korea after becoming familiar with Korean culture (especially modern culture, including K-pop, K-movies, and K-beauty) through online platforms and broadcasting, according to the Korean Culture and Information Service's (KOCIS) research on the country's international image in 2021 (KOCIS, 2021). Moreover, Korea earned positive reviews, 80.5%, rising by 2.4 points compared to the results of 2021, from the participants[1] (KOCIS, 2021). The role of culture as an element of soft power has grown in international society.

Hallyu is now a reception phenomenon, not propagation. Although *Hallyu* content preferences are varied and different according to each country's trend, the common ground of *Hallyu* consumers' reaction to why they like Korean content is linked to Korea's cultural identity and sentiments such as affection (*jeong*, 情), consideration for others, and Confucian values (Hong and Jing, 2021). The charm is not deduced from an objective experience and does not exist alone. Instead, it results from intersubjective social activities and is made by communication and interchange (Son, 2020). Like the perspective of Constructivism (Wendt, 1999), people from diverse cultures all over the world share a mutual interest in *Hallyu* through communication in person or online platforms; thereby, it leads to the collective identity that affects nations' behaviour or action later. Thus, the Korean government attempts to spread universal values and lead international norms via K-culture, as a recent official speech of the Minister of MCST, Park Bo-gyun, pointed out. While delivering his speech at the G20 cultural ministers' meeting, he stressed that K-culture connotes a message of hope, human rights, protection of the environment, and peace; the Korean government seeks a culture for a sustainable life, which is one of the aims for realising a charming culture country (KOCIS, 2022).

Such efforts come from the *Hallyu* fandom (the so-called ARMY) that connects global online networks. A representative example is BTS, which positively impacted Korea's image in 2021 (KOCIS, 2021). The strategy of BTS is the continuous construction of a bond of sympathy with lyrics that BTS members write for their songs based on their own experiences, thereby steering favourable influence on society that casts away prejudice, discrimination, and violence. Thus, BTS reflected its message, including diversity, solidarity, environment, consideration, positivity, love, and speaking up for yourself and others. BTS members also share their daily life with fans on online platforms. The daily life of BTS's members, such as having Korean foods, showing Korean cities, and speaking the Korean language, is exposed to SNS (social networking services) so that BTS fans naturally become accustomed to Korean soft power, in other words, Korea's cultural public diplomacy.

The BTS activities cause ripple effects not only to introduce Korea to the world but also to provide a place for BTS fans from all over the world to connect and share their common interest, which could lead to ties between Korea and foreign countries through ARMY. The ARMY is BTS's official fan club name and the abbreviation of "Adorable Representative M.C. for Youth," which includes the meaning of always being together (US BTS ARMY, n.d.). As of 2023, there are 73.2 million subscribers of the BTS channel and more than 48 million and 71 million followers on the group's Twitter and Instagram official accounts, respectively. The members of the ARMY vary in age, occupation, and academic background. The number of people who joined the ARMY also steadily increased and soared 1.5 times in 2020, despite the COVID-19 pandemic (BTS ARMY Census, 2022). Now the ARMY speaks with one voice, growing as a grassroots network that does not have borders. The ARMY from all over the world not only translates BTS's lyrics into English and other languages but also adds additional clarification about the Korean history and cultural background mentioned in BTS's songs. For example, the ARMY explained the democratic movement that had happened in Kwangju on May 18, 1980, due to the lyrics "062-518" on the song of "Ma City" in the album 화양연화 Young Forever in 2015. Also, the ARMY has a voice in the alienated field in our society. A couple of famous stories regarding the ARMY are as follows. Big Hit Entertainment, an affiliate of BTS, donated $1 million to the Black Lives Matter Movement in 2020. The ARMY joined it and raised funds of over $1 million within a day by spreading the hashtag "We Love Black ARMY." The ARMY in Brazil stopped the severe devastation of the Amazon tropical rainforest by a large conflagration in 2019 under the name of ARMY Help the Planet (AHTP). Since then, the AHTP has carried out different types of environmental protection activities, such as an antifire campaign, raising funds for planting native species of trees in the Amazon and raising funds in response to COVID-19.

Conclusion

COVID-19 has changed the world, and the aftermath of the pandemic is reflected in many different dimensions. Many countries had to make dire decisions to protect their citizens from the virus, such as forced curfews, closing borders, and the obligation to wear masks in public. In other words, starting from late 2019, the last couple of years have been hard for everyone. Many countries' image was damaged due to politics and actions during the pandemic, especially in Europe; the ghost of the "every man for himself" principle haunted the continent (Reuters, 2020; Daily Sabah, 2020; France 24, 2020). Besides the medical supplies, vaccination inequality among the countries also led to an image and perception crisis for many (Sidibé, 2022; WHO, 2023). Furthermore, COVID-19 also wreaked havoc on many countries' economies (The World Bank, 2022) and devastated some industries like leisure and hospitality (Klein and Smith, 2021).

Thanks to *Hallyu* content, Korea rose as a winner among nations during the COVID-19 pandemic, both in terms of image and economy. As millions of people stayed indoors during the curfews, the consumption of the *Hallyu* content skyrocketed (YouTube subscriber numbers for BTS and Black Pink attest to this) compared to the pre-pandemic years. Nonetheless, since *Hallyu* is a *de facto* tool for the South Korean government, it boosted the positive image and directly promoted interest in the country. After opening the borders and easing the restrictions, huge waves of tourists poured into the country (Globaldata, 2022), thanks to *Hallyu* content's appeal. Furthermore, as mentioned above, exported *Hallyu* content generated economic income that protected the Korean economy from the pandemic's negative effects, contrary to many countries during the pandemic. From Netflix to

YouTube, platforms used as facilitators for exporting *Hallyu* boosted Korean cultural public diplomacy and promoted the Korean image. Public diplomacy policies shine on cooperation and solidarity, centring on values and norms that are required of the international society. During the COVID-19 pandemic, solidarity became a vital aspect for countries. Henceforth, Korea's cultural public diplomacy is a vital tool for South Korea. The country endured the pandemic and rose whereas many other countries saw a drastic drop in their soft power.

Note

1 The survey participants were 102,500 people over 16 years old and living in 24 countries. The survey was conducted from September 1 to September 29, 2021, by the Korean Culture and Information Service under the umbrella of the Ministry of Culture, Sports, and Tourism.

References

"Accelerating COVID-19 vaccine deployment". *World Health Organisation*, April 20, 2022. https://www.who.int/publications/m/item/accelerating-covid-19-vaccine-deployment

Akıllı, E. (2016) *Türkiye'de Devlet Kimliği ve Dış Politika*, 2nd ed. Ankara: Nobel Yayınevi.

BTS ARMY Census (2022) 2022 Census Results. Available at: https://twitter.com/armycensus (Accessed: August 22, 2022).

"Macron says France is there for Italy, Europe must not be 'selfish'", *Reuters*, March 28, 2020, https://www.reuters.com/article/us-health-coronavirus-france-italy-idUSKBN21F001 (Accessed: August 22, 2022).

Chartrand, H. H. (1992). "International Cultural Affairs: A Fourteen Country Survey". *Journal of Arts Management, Law and Society*. 22 (2). http://www.compilerpress.ca/Cultural%20Economics/Works/ICR%201992.htm

Cho, I. and Yoon, Y. K. (2013) "A Study on the YouTube Far-Reaching Effects Having Impact on Korean Wave: Focused on Singer PSY Syndrome". *Journal of Korea Entertainment Industry Association*. 7 (2), pp. 9–18.

Choe, Y. (2016) *Tourist Distractions: Traveling and Feeling in Translation Hallyu Cinema*. Durham: Duke University.

Encyclopaedia of Korean Culture (n.d.) Hallyu. Available at: http://encykorea.aks.ac.kr/Contents/Item/E0066892 (Accessed: August 2, 2022).

EXIM Bank of Korea (2022) "The economic effect of K-content's exports". Seoul: Institute of the overseas economy. https://keri.koreaexim.go.kr/HPHFOE052M01/101017?curPage=1 (Accessed: August 22, 2022).

"France seizes millions of masks, gloves intended for Spain and Italy". *Daily Sabah*, April 03, 2020. https://www.dailysabah.com/world/europe/france-seizes-millions-of-masks-gloves-intended-for-spain-and-italy (Accessed: August 22, 2022).

Gilboa, E. (2006) "Public Diplomacy: The Missing Component in Israel's Foreign Policy". *Israel Affairs*. 12 (4). http://uscpublicdiplomacy.org/pdfs/gilboa_israel_publicdiplomacy_Oct06.pdf

Gilboa, E. (2006) "Public Diplomacy: The Missing Component in Israel's Foreign Policy". *Israel Affairs*. 12 (4), pp. 715–747.

Hong, S-K and Jing, D. Y. (eds) (2021) *Transnational Convergence of East Asian Pop Culture*. London: Routledge.

Jang, G. (2011) "Study of Korean Wave's the Origin and the Usage". *Journal of the Korean Contents Association.* 11 (9), pp. 166–173. Available at: http://dx.doi.org/10.5392/JKCA.2011.11.9.166

Jin, D. Y. (2016) *New Korean Wave: Transnational Cultural Power in the Age of Social Media.* Chicago: University of Illinois Press.

Kitsou, S. (2011) "The power of culture in diplomacy: The case of U.S. cultural diplomacy in France and Germany". Ionian University. https://surface.syr.edu/exchange/vol2/iss1/3/ (Accessed: August 22, 2022).

Klein, A. and Smith, E. (2021) "Explaining the economic impact of COVID-19". *Brookings*, February 5. https://www.brookings.edu/research/explaining-the-economic-impact-of-covid-19-core-industries-and-the-hispanic-workforce/

KOCCA (2022) "The analysis of K-content industry annual trend". Korea Creative Content Agency, Naju.

KOCIS (2021) "Research on country image". Korean Culture and Information Service, Sejong.

KOCIS (2022) "The Minister speeches Korea's culture that includes hope, human rights, and peace message". Available at: https://www.kocis.go.kr/koreanet/view.do?seq=1042584 (Accessed: August 21, 2022).

KOFICE (2021) "Study on the ripple effect of Hallyu". Korean Foundation for International Cultural Exchange, Seoul.

KOFICE (2022) "Research on the actual condition of Hallyu abroad". Korean Foundation for International Cultural Exchange, Seoul.

Lee, D and An, M (2004) "Diffusion and Problems of the Korean Wave in East Asia: Focusing on Culture and Nationalism". *The Korean Journal of Area Studies.* 25 (1), pp. 99–126.

Lee, J and Kim, Y (2018) "A Study on the Relationship between Korean Wave and National Brand Attitude". *Journal of Practical Research in Advertising and Public Relations.* 11 (2), pp. 123–148.

Lee, K. (2008) "Mapping Out the Cultural Politics of 'the Korean Wave' in Contemporary South Korea". In H. C. Beng and K. Iwabuchi (eds) *East Asia Pop Culture: Analyzing the Korean Wave,* pp. 175–189. Hong Kong: Hong Kong University Press.

Lee, S. (2012) "Characteristics and Comparative Power of Korean Wave Dramas". *Comparative Korean Studies.* 20 (1), pp. 59–84.

Lee, S. E. (2022). "The exports of Hallyu content increased 16 per cent". YTN, January, 24. Available at: https://www.ytn.co.kr/_ln/0106_202201241345323856 (Accessed: August 24, 2022).

Sidibé, M. (2022) "Vaccine inequity: Ensuring Africa is not left out". *Brookings*, January 24, 2022, https://www.brookings.edu/blog/africa-in-focus/2022/01/24/vaccine-inequity-ensuring-africa-is-not-left-out/(Accessed: August 22, 2022).

Nye, J. S. (1990) *Bound to Lead: The Changing Nature of American Power.* New York: Basic Books.

Nye, J. S. (2008) "Public Diplomacy and Soft Power". *The Annals of American Academy of Political and Social Science.* 616 (94). http://courses.essex.ac.uk/gv/gv905/W07%20Readings/nye_soft_power_08.pdf

Nye, J. S. (2002) *The Paradox of American Power.* New York: Oxford University Press.

Nye, J. S. (2004) *Soft Power the Means to Success in World Politics.* New York: Public Affairs.

"Outbound tourism from South Korea set to boom with COVID-19 travel restrictions easing up, observes Global Data". *Global Data*, April 29, 2022. https://www.globaldata.com/media/travel-tourism/outbound-tourism-south-korea-set-boom-covid-19-travel-restrictions-easing-observes-globaldata/

Park, H. (2021) *Understanding Hallyu: The Korean Wave through Literature, Webtoon, and Mukbang*. Abingdon: Routledge.

Policy briefing. (2022) "We lead our economy with K-Content". Available at: https://www.korea.kr/news/policyNewsView.do?newsId=148904804 (Accessed: August 18, 2022).

Purtaş, F. (2013) "Türk Dış Politikasının Yükselen Değeri: Kültürel Diplomasi". *Gazi Akademik Bakış*. 7 (13), pp. 1–14.

Son, Y. (2020) "Korea's charming diplomacy learning from BTS". EAI, December 29. Available at: http://www.eai.or.kr/new/ko/pub/view.asp?intSeq=20274&board=kor_workingpaper (Accessed: August 21, 2022).

Szondi, György (2009) "Central and Eastern European Public Diplomacy: A Transitional Perspective on National Reputation Management", P. Taylor and N. Snow (eds.) *Routledge Handbook of Public Diplomacy*. New York: Routledge.

"Solidarity? When it comes to masks, it's every nation for itself". *France 24*, 03/04/2020, https://www.france24.com/en/20200403-solidarity-when-it-comes-to-masks-it-s-every-nation-for-itself (Accessed: August 22, 2022).

"The economic impacts of the COVID-19 crisis". *The World Bank*, 2022. https://www.worldbank.org/en/publication/wdr2022/brief/chapter-1-introduction-the-economic-impacts-of-the-covid-19-crisis (Accessed: August 22, 2022).

The Ministry of Culture, Sports, and Tourism. (2020) "Hallyu will continue to keep popularity around the world with New Hallyu (K-Culture)." Available at https://www.mcst.go.kr/kor/s_notice/press/pressView.jsp?pSeq=18151 (Accessed: August 10, 2022).

US BTS ARMY. (n.d.) ARMY Dictionary. Available at: https://www.usbtsarmy.com/army-dictionary/#a (Accessed: 21 August 2022).

Wendt, A. (1999) *Social Theory of International Politics*. Cambridge: Cambridge University Press.

WHO. (2023) WHO Coronavirus (COVID-19) Dashboard. Available at: https://covid19.who.int (Accessed: January 25, 2023).

Zhang, Guozuo (2017) *Research Outline for China's Cultural Soft Power*. Singapore: Springer.

11 ASEAN's COVID-19 Pandemic Response

Regional and Global Reflections

Hatice Çelik

ASEAN and COVID-19: A General Overview

Southeast Asia, one of the most populous sub-regions of the globe, was hit hard by the COVID-19 pandemic starting around the first months of 2020. Compared to many other regions, Southeast Asia also has another crucial peculiarity: It is home to a well-known regional organisation, ASEAN. The organisation now consists of 11 nation-states, as Timor-Leste's application[1] was recently accepted in principle. It should be remembered that in the first months of the pandemic, there were intensive discussions about whether European countries, mainly the European Union (EU), were capable of showing solidarity among themselves against this pandemic crisis.

Considering these developments, this chapter aims to understand how ASEAN first reacted to the COVID-19 pandemic in its region. Later, the institution's steps and presence at the global level are discussed. Based on the institution's different mechanisms, it will be examined whether ASEAN can be considered successful enough to meet the expectations of its member states and a more global community. However, at this point, it is significant to keep in mind that although ASEAN is a regional organisation and seems to have limits/borders, it represents more than just its member states. In other words, its vision and goals have the potential to produce wider repercussions for the global community. To better understand how ASEAN reacted to the pandemic crisis, two levels will be examined: the first one is how ASEAN dealt with the pandemic at the regional level; the second one is the global one. This analysis examines how ASEAN performed at the global level and how its regional issues were reflected at the international level.

ASEAN's Reactions and Reflections on the Regional Level

While leaving behind almost three years of the COVID-19 pandemic, it is believed that assessing the measures and reactions of ASEAN to the pandemic might be a more grounded analysis. At the beginning of the pandemic, one could expect various responses and different results at the member level since there are considerable differences in economic, political, and sociocultural aspects among the members of ASEAN. For example, while Singapore is one of the most developed nations in

DOI: 10.4324/9781003377597-13

ASEAN and at the global level, having a gross domestic product (GDP) per capita of $65.83 in 2019, Laos had $2.61 in the same year (The World Bank, 2019). However, an institutional perspective may better evaluate the struggle against the pandemic. By late March, all 10 member states of ASEAN had been affected by the pandemic, according to data released by the World Health Organization (WHO) on March 11, 2020 (Fernando et al., 2020: 32).

Since the beginning of the crisis, high-level official meetings and ASEAN summits have spent a lot of time and effort launching agreements intended to lessen the crisis's effects. These include, among others, the ASEAN Travel Corridor Arrangement Framework, the ASEAN Response Fund, the Strategic Framework for Public Health Emergencies, and the ASEAN Comprehensive Recovery Framework (Randhawa, 2022: 6). The first reactions of ASEAN can be grouped under different mechanisms of the organisation itself. To exemplify, in a statement on February 15, 2020, Vietnam, then ASEAN's chair, emphasised the need to address COVID-19 as soon as possible and collaborate closely with allies and the world community to lessen its negative effects (Fernando et al., 2020: 32). One of the earliest steps of ASEAN was to cooperate with the WHO. On February 3, 2020, the ASEAN Plus Three Senior Officials Meeting for Health Development (APT SOMHD) was held and attended by all ASEAN Plus Three (APT) countries, as well as representatives from the WHO. Officials gathered via video conference to discuss the current state of affairs in each country, the technical know-how, lessons learnt in the detection of COVID-19, and the preparedness measures taken by each nation.

One of the critical intra-institutional mechanisms was the ASEAN Emergency Operations Centre (EOC) Network for public health. Led by Malaysia's Ministry of Health, the ASEAN EOC Network for Public Health gave officials from the ASEAN member states working in the respective crisis centres and/or disease prevention and control a forum to exchange information quickly through various communication channels. The WhatsApp mobile app was used for frequent and everyday contact among the members, including information exchange on new confirmed instances and any national-level actions taken. To exchange updates provided by the APT on any new confirmed instances and press releases made by the member states, daily and regular email communication was also conducted. For COVID-19, the ASEAN EOC Network created a list of national and local hotlines and call centres in the ASEAN member states, which was then shared with the public via ASEAN's social media platform. Additionally, each Ministry of Health in ASEAN members has set up a webpage to disseminate any updates on COVID-19 (ASEAN Emergency Operations Centre (EOC) Network for Public Health, 2022).

Another supportive mechanism was the ASEAN BioDiaspora Regional Virtual Centre (ABVC). The national risk assessments, preparation, and response planning activities are supplemented by the ABVC for big data analytics and visualisation. Recent reports on the risk assessment for the international dissemination of COVID-19 across the ASEAN region were generated by the ABVC, which is led by the Philippines (ASEAN Emergency Operations Centre (EOC) Network for Public Health, 2022). These steps and mechanisms are fundamental to prove that ASEAN had taken the issue seriously and reacted promptly. However, this successful first institutional response doesn't change the fact that all member states have encountered diverse challenges throughout the pandemic. In one of the earliest studies on ASEAN's reaction to COVID-19, the authors claimed that "One Vision, One Identity, One Community" looks like a utopia because each ASEAN member state treats its borders as absolute sovereignty and lacks a collective vision of the "greater good" for all (Djalante et al., 2020: 11). This necessitates an individual state-level analysis and Djalante et al. explored this discussion in detail (2020). For this reason, this chapter will be more of an institutional-level approach and will try to contribute to the existing literature by doing so.

Regional organisations like ASEAN faced one of the most challenging dichotomies of the pandemic. On the one hand, acting together in solidarity might be a better option to ease the impact of the crisis. Still, on the other hand, the national borders and the nation-states gained importance since the national leaders prioritised their citizens acquiring medicine and vaccines first. On Tuesday, March 2, 2021, the first 324,000 AstraZeneca COVID-19 vaccinations from the COVAX Facility were shipped to Cambodia. Through this programme, Cambodia becomes the first nation in the Western Pacific and ASEAN to receive immunisations (EU External Action, 2021). In addition, ASEAN worked to overcome the different national-level applications for the registration of vaccines and developed one system for the region. On May 14, 2022, the 15th ASEAN Health Ministers' Meeting was held in Bali. It was stated that member states would cooperate on the mutual recognition of COVID-19 vaccination certificates and the ASEAN universal verification mechanism would be voluntarily applied (ASEAN Health Ministers' Meeting, 2022). It is one of the great steps to show the togetherness and functionality-based approach that ASEAN adopted during the crisis.

Another negative effect of the pandemic faced by ASEAN was the manner in which diplomacy was conducted within the ASEAN circle. The "ASEAN Way," which is the operation of diplomatic relations at a more informal level, was seriously affected by the pandemic since most meetings had to be held online (Dalpino, 2020: 53). The other impact of this situation on the external powers' relations with ASEAN will be touched upon in the coming section.

ASEAN's Reactions and Reflections on the Global Level

One of the first studies that analyse ASEAN's pandemic struggle from a diplomatic relations perspective is Katsumata's article. The author argued that by engaging in "equidistant diplomacy" with both China and the United States (US), ASEAN has been able to maintain good ties and gain their support (Katsumata, 2022: 117). As has been the case for many regions and countries, the COVID-19 pandemic has been one of ASEAN's most critical non-traditional security issues. At this point, ASEAN has been supported by external powers in various ways, such as masks, vaccines, and health diplomacy in general. Among these supporters were China, the US, South Korea, and Japan as part of the APT initiative. A special summit of the APT countries on COVID-19 was organised on April 14, 2020. Chinese Premier Li Keqiang emphasised the notion that "we are in a community with a shared future" and added that China would provide an additional 100 million face masks, 10 million protective suits, and other urgently needed medical supplies to ASEAN countries (China.org.cn, 2020). This supportive stance deserves appreciation; however, another issue that cannot be ignored between ASEAN and China is the South China Sea dispute.

While China carries a significant advantage as a major trading country for most ASEAN member states, with Vietnam on top with the trade of $98 billion, followed by Singapore and Malaysia at $55 billion and $52.5 billion, respectively, China's decision to provide a $2 billion COVID-19 aid package has arguably made the situation more complicated (Kamdar, 2020).

Yet another issue that is difficult to categorise as only an "intra-ASEAN issue" is the Rohingya case. The 36th ASEAN summit was held under the slogan of cohesive and responsive ASEAN. On the same day as the summit, Indonesian fishermen rescued nearly 100 Rohingya refugees, including 79 women and children, in Aceh province after officials told them they were considering pushing them back out to sea (Tahjuddin, 2020). It was an excellent example of ASEAN citizens demonstrating unity and solidarity, but leaders' claims of its effectiveness remained hollow (Santiago, 2020). Besides the Rohingya people trying to migrate, the ones living in the refugee camps in Cox's Bazar have been seriously affected by the pandemic. According to a previous World Food Program assessment, 86% of Rohingya refugees would be at high risk of poverty and hunger by the end of 2020, up from 70% in 2019 (Yeasmine and Donovan, 2021). In addition to these challenges, the vaccination of the Rohingya people in the refugee camps also became an essential step of the pandemic management. One can easily remember that vaccine supply, just as the mask supply, became one of the vital priorities of many countries in the first months following the results of the different vaccines such as BioNTech, Sinovac, Moderna, etc. Later it turned out to be a competition point for the countries aiming to be the first to acquire vaccine supplies for their respective citizens. Unsurprisingly, refugees were among the most vulnerable communities since they were hardly accepted as equal individuals in the societies in which they lived.

At this point, the Bangladesh government did not ignore the Rohingya people. With the support of the UN Refugee Agency (UNHCR), the WHO, Gavi, and other national and international organisations, Rohingya people were also included in Bangladesh's national vaccination campaign. Dr. Md. Shamsul Haque, National Vaccine Deployment Committee member secretary and line director at the Directorate General of Health Services (DGHS), mentioned that forcibly displaced Myanmar nationals (FDMN) were included in the vaccination programme thanks to the COVAX Facility (Al Amin, 2022). In that regard, it can be argued that the Rohingya crisis, similar to any other migration/forcibly displaced people issues, encompasses a border-crossing character, and in times of crisis, should be dealt with through a multi-layered approach.

Santiago also criticises some ASEAN governments' COVID-19 stances as contradictory to human rights. He continued his argument by giving the example of the Malaysian government, which has used the crisis as a justification to suppress and arrest migrants and refugees (Santiago, 2020). He also added Cambodia, the

Philippines, and Thailand as other ASEAN member states that have performed authoritarian approaches during the pandemic. Virgil and Lie (2020) shed light on the humanitarian side of the pandemic in the ASEAN region. To begin with, it is remarkable that the International Convention on the Protection of the Rights of All Migrant Workers and Members of Their Families was ratified by only two ASEAN members, Indonesia and the Philippines, while Cambodia once signed but never acceded to the convention (Tobing, 2017). Although the ASEAN Declaration on the Protection and Promotion of the Rights of Migrant Workers seemed to be drawing a promising framework for the migrant workers living in ASEAN member countries, according to Paragraph 3 (ASEAN Declaration on the Protection and Promotion of the Rights of Migrant Workers, 2007), they must be safeguarded without weakening state laws, which are argued to be undoubtedly written to support the member states' sovereign authority over their national legislation under the non-interference policy (Virgil and Lie, 2020: 111–112). As one of the fundamental principles of ASEAN, the policy of non-interference in domestic politics becomes clear concerning the migrant workers' conditions throughout the pandemic. One clear example within ASEAN is Singapore. On April 5, 2020, Minister Lawrence Wong, co-chair of the Multi-Ministry Taskforce on COVID-19, at a press conference on the pandemic, mentioned that there were imported (originating in people returning from abroad) and local transmission cases. The second category again consisted of two groups: workers in the dormitories and locally transmitted cases within their community in Singapore (Wong, 2020). As the ministry drew the line, migrant workers in the dormitories were seen as a separate category to be dealt with within Singaporean society.

During the first months of the pandemic, all migrant workers across Singapore were banned from leaving their dormitories until May 4, 2020 (Han, 2020). Almost two years later, the situation still requires a closer look. It is primarily because the migrant workers still lack some of the primary liftings of pandemic restrictions. Although more than 98% of the workers living in dorms are fully vaccinated, Singaporean authorities insisted on preserving tough limitations applied to migrant workers (Hancock, 2022). However, the Ministry of Health announced on June 10, 2022, that starting on June 24, migrant workers residing in dormitories would not need an exit card to visit public spaces, except for four busy areas: Chinatown, Geylang Serai, Jurong East, and Little India (Kurohi, 2022). Within this regard, although there is a growing enhancement of the migrant workers' living conditions, they have become a controversial issue in Singapore's pandemic management.

Another significant connection revealed by the pandemic is the relations between ASEAN members and China. Grundy-Warr and Lin (2020) argued that existing and ongoing links between politics and business are shaping the major response to COVID-19, pointing to Cambodia and Myanmar and their relationship with China as cases within the Southeast Asia region. When Vietnam and Singapore, both ASEAN members, decided to ban flights from China following the pandemic outbreak, Cambodian Prime Minister Hun Se chose not to do so by declaring that the Kingdom of Cambodia shows solidarity with China in turbulent times (Bong, 2020). The prime minister expressed that banning flights from China would destroy

Cambodia's economy and affect the good relationship between China and Cambodia (Cambodian PM, 2020). This solidarity was demonstrated during an official visit of Cambodian Prime Minister Hun Sen to China on February 5, 2020. Bong argued that Hun Sen used the pandemic as a political move to enhance his national and international image by playing a dangerous game by showing Cambodians that they need not worry because he is in command (2020). Following the visit of the prime minister to Beijing in early February 2020, there was a flow of aid from China to Cambodia. China's Ministry of Defence donated 16 tonnes of medical supplies to Cambodia's Ministry of Defence, a value of some $1 million and including 11 items (Chhen, 2020). Neak and Sok (2021) argued that Cambodia strengthened its relationship with China politically and economically through the pandemic; however, amid the emerging US-China confrontation, it must be careful and keep its neutral foreign policy in relations with China and the US. Concerning Myanmar, Grundy-Warr and Lin mentioned that China emphasises Myanmar not only for its contiguous northern border link, which Cambodia lacks in direct geographic proximity, but also for its strategic resource, trade, and energy link across the Bay of Bengal and beyond (2020: 503). This, in return, is a significant sign that the pandemic is a very concrete example of non-traditional security and diplomatic conditions. To consider the overall outlook of the external powers' relations with ASEAN, a survey conducted in 2021 by the ISEAS-Yusof Ishak Institute says noteworthy things. China is viewed as having helped the area the most out of ASEAN's 10 dialogue partners; 44.2% of respondents chose China, followed by Japan (18.2%) and the EU (10.3%) (Seah et al., 2021: 13). However, considering the relations of ASEAN with China, it is emphasised that if it isn't evaluated carefully, it carries the risk of impacting ASEAN's future cohesion (Rüland, 2021: 85).

It is also impossible to think that the pandemic has no negative impact on the conduct of diplomatic relations in the traditional sense. For instance, because the ASEAN-China joint working group on the South China Sea Code of Conduct could not meet, antagonism and mistrust between the two countries have persisted over the disputed maritime area all year (Vatikiotis, 2020). This applies to situations like a Malaysian coast guard vessel firing on Vietnamese fishing boats, which resulted in casualties and China's naval operations (Vatikiotis, 2020). Although many organisations and institutions have begun to use online platforms for the continuation of the exchanges, it might be said that they couldn't provide the same environment as face-to-face ones.

Conclusion: What Lessons Has the Pandemic Taught ASEAN?

Looking back at the whole picture regarding ASEAN's performance during the pandemic, it can be argued that there are two basic scenarios for ASEAN's future, considering what they have learnt from the pandemic. The first one is that the COVID-19 pandemic was a disaster that forced ASEAN to face its fragile issues and structural problems ignored for a considerable time. Among them, migrant workers' conditions, human rights, and the risk of authoritarian regimes' using such crises to consolidate their power particularly come to the fore. ASEAN member states can turn this crisis into an opportunity and, by taking necessary precautions, can see positive results in the medium and long term. The second scenario includes the external powers and their policies' reflections on ASEAN. As mentioned above, China has been one of the external powers that provided the most help to the region during the pandemic. However, it also carries the risk that China's relations with the member states might potentially disturb the solidarity of ASEAN members among themselves. This is mainly seen in conflictual issues such as the South China Sea dispute. Although the pandemic started as a health crisis, it evolved into a non-traditional security challenge. It might even be a direct security challenge depending on the conditions in which those states reacted and managed it. In this regard, ASEAN should better evaluate the crisis from a multidimensional perspective and design its policies accordingly for a smoother functioning institution in the future.

Notes

1 The application of Timor-Leste was accepted in principle by ASEAN and the country was given an observer status. For the full statement of ASEAN, refer to "ASEAN Leaders' Statement on The Application of Timor-Leste for ASEAN Membership," which is available at https://asean.org/wp-content/uploads/2022/11/05-ASEAN-Leaders-Statement-on-the-Application-of-Timor-Leste-for-ASEAN-Membership.pdf.

References

Al Amin, M. (August 25, 2022) "Quelling the pandemic in the world's largest refugee camp", GAVI, https://www.gavi.org/vaccineswork/quelling-pandemic-worlds-largest-refugee-camp (Accessed: December 10, 2022).

ASEAN Declaration on the Protection and Promotion of the Rights of Migrant Workers (2007) https://www.ilo.org/dyn/migpractice/docs/117/Declaration.pdf (Accessed: 15 December 2022)

ASEAN Health Ministers' Meeting (2022) "ASEAN Health Ministers' Meeting Joint Statement on Mutual Recognition of Covid-19 Vaccination Certificates", https://asean.org/wp-content/uploads/2022/05/4.-15th-AHMM-Joint-Statement-on-Mutual-Recognition-of-COVID-19-Vaccination-Certificates.pdf (Accessed: December 21, 2022).

ASEAN Emergency Operations Center (EOC) Network for Public Health (2022) https://asean.org/asean-health-sector-efforts-in-the-prevention-detection-and-response-to-coronavirus-disease-2019-covid-19-3/ (Accessed: December 10, 2022).

Bong, C. (February 24, 2020) "Hun Sen's political gamble: The COVID-19 epidemic", The Japan Times, https://www.japantimes.co.jp/opinion/2020/02/24/commentary/world-commentary/hun-sens-political-gamble-covid-19-epidemic (Accessed: December 7, 2022).

Cambodian PM: "Ban of China flights to destroy Cambodian economy" (January 30, 2020) Office of the Council of the Ministers, https://pressocm.gov.kh/en/archives/62685 (Accessed: December 9, 2022).

Chhen, N. (April 26, 2020) "China delivers plane-load of aid", The Phnom Penh Post, https://www.phnompenhpost.com/national/china-delivers-plane-load-aid (Accessed: December 9, 2022).

China.org.cn (April 15, 2020) "China calls on ASEAN Plus Three countries to work for early victory against COVID-19 in East Asia", http://www.china.org.cn/world/2020-04/15/content_75933851.htm (Accessed: December 9, 2022).

Dalpino, C. (2020) "Diplomatic Doldrums: ASEAN Loses Momentum in the Pandemic as Security Tensions rise". *Comparative Connections*. 22 (2), pp. 51–60.

Djalante, R., Nurhidayah, L., Van Minh, H., Phuong, N. T. N., Mahendradhata, Y., Trias, A. ... & Miller, M. A. (2020) "COVID-19 and ASEAN Responses: Comparative Policy analysis". *Progress in Disaster Science*. 8, p. 100129.

EU External Action (March 3, 2021) "Cambodia becomes the first country in ASEAN to receive COVID19 vaccines through the COVAX scheme", https://www.eeas.europa.eu/eeas/cambodia-becomes-first-country-asean-receive-covid19-vaccines-through-covax-scheme_en (Accessed: December 21, 2022).

Fernando, M. F. et al. (2020) "COVID-19: A Collective Response in ASEAN". *The ASEAN*. (1), May, pp. 30–35.

Grundy-Warr, C. and Lin, S. (2020) "COVID-19 Geopolitics: Silence and Erasure in Cambodia and Myanmar in Times of Pandemic". *Eurasian Geography and Economics*. 61 (4–5), pp. 493–510.

Han, K. (April 8, 2020) "Singapore's migrant workers on front line of coronavirus shutdown", Al-Jazeera, https://www.aljazeera.com/news/2020/4/8/singapores-migrant-workers-on-front-line-of-coronavirus-shutdown (Accessed: December 20, 2022).

Hancock, A. (January 30, 2022) "Singapore migrant workers labour under COVID curbs", https://www.aljazeera.com/news/2022/1/30/singapore-migrant-workers-covid-curbs (Accessed: December 19, 2022).

Kamdar, D. (2020) "ASEAN's COVID-19 conundrum", The ORF, July 15, 2020, https://www.orfonline.org/expert-speak/aseans-covid19-conundrum/

Katsumata, H. (2022) "ASEAN's Diplomatic Tasks during the Pandemic". *East Asia*. 39 (2), pp. 117–126.

Kurohi, R. (June 10, 2022), "Capacity limits for nightclubs, exit pass requirement for migrant workers to be eased", The Straits Times, https://www.straitstimes.com/singapore/health/capacity-limits-for-nightclubs-exit-pass-requirement-for-migrant-workers-to-be-eased (Accessed: December 18, 2022).

Neak, C. and Sok, S. (2021) "Cambodia's Response to COVID-19 and Its Impacts on Cambodia–China Relations". *The Reshaping of China-Southeast Asia Relations in Light of the COVID-19 Pandemic*, pp. 51–67. Singapore: Springer.

Randhawa, D. S. (2022) "Lessons from the Covid-19 pandemic for developing a resilient ASEAN". https://www.rsis.edu.sg/wp-content/uploads/2022/02/PR220215_Lessons_from_the_COVID19_Pandemic_for_Developing_a_Resilient_ASEAN.pdf (Accessed: December 18, 2022).

Rüland, J. (2021) "COVID-19 and ASEAN: Strengthening State-Centrism, Eroding Inclusiveness, Testing Cohesion". *The International Spectator*. 56 (2), pp. 72–92.

Santiago, C. (September 28, 2020). "The COVID New (Ab)Normal: Post-COVID-19 ASEAN and the Centrality of Human Rights", Asia Society Policy Institute, https://asiasociety.org/policy-institute/covid-new-abnormal-post-covid-19-asean-and-centrality-human-rights (Accessed: December 8, 2022).

Seah, S. et al. (2021) *The State of Southeast Asia: 2021*. Singapore: ISEAS-Yusof Ishak Institute.

Tahjuddin, H. (2020, 26 June) "Indonesian fishermen rescue nearly 100 Rohingya refugees in Aceh", Reuters, https://www.reuters.com/article/us-indonesia-rohingya/indonesian-fishermen-rescue-nearly-100-rohingya-refugees-in-aceh-idUSKBN23X0TG (Accessed: December 9, 2022).

The World Bank (2019) "GDP per capita for Singapore and Laos". https://data.worldbank.org/indicator/NY.GDP.PCAP.CD?locations=SG and https://data.worldbank.org/indicator/NY.GDP.PCAP.CD?locations=LA (Accessed: December 10, 2022).

Tobing, D. H. (November 16, 2017) "The problem with ASEAN's new migrant workers pact", The Jakarta Post, https://www.thejakartapost.com/academia/2017/11/16/the-problem-with-aseans-new-migrant-workers-pact.html (Accessed: December 16, 2022).

Vatikiotis, M. (November 11, 2020) "COVID-19 exposes ASEAN's fragility", Nikkei Asia, https://asia.nikkei.com/Opinion/COVID-19-exposes-ASEAN-s-fragility (Accessed: December 17, 2022).

Virgil, D. and Lie, R. (2020) "ASEAN's Covid-19 Response: Why Minorities and the Most Vulnerable Matter". *Global Asia*. 15 (2), pp. 110–115.

Wong, L. (April 5, 2020) "Remarks by Minister Lawrence Wong, Co-chair of the Multi-Ministry Taskforce on COVID-19, at Press Conference on COVID-19 at National Press Centre on 5 April 2020", https://www.sgpc.gov.sg/sgpcmedia/media_releases/mnd/speech/S-20200405-1/attachment/Remarks%20by%20Minister%20Lawrence%20Wong%20at%205%20Apr%20Press%20Conference%20on%20COVID-19.pdf (Accessed: December 15, 2022).

Yeasmine, I. and Donovan, L. (2021) "Pandemic-hit Rohingya refugees and local Bangladeshis get help to grow food", UNCHR, https://www.unhcr.org/news/stories/2021/5/60a26da14/pandemic-hit-rohingya-refugees-local-bangladeshis-help-grow-food.html (Accessed December 8, 2022).

12 Beyond Central Asia's Chessboard

Human Movement, Policies, and COVID-19[1]

Olga R. Gulina

Central Asia and the Caucasus' COVID-19 Migratory Landscape

Gaining independence in the 1990s and suddenly transforming borders forced a colossal amount of migration and proclaimed sovereignty within Eurasia, even if most Central Asian and Caucasian countries had long been dreaming of becoming more self-sufficient (Souleimanov, 2013). Three decades later, the spread of COVID-19 and Russia's invasion of Ukraine have again had a multidimensional and multifaceted impact in Central Asian and Caucasian countries. Caucasian and Central Asian states have prioritised their anti-coronavirus strategies differently while trying to balance the population's health and the provision of economic assistance (or the absence thereof) with the state's security (OECD, 2022).

Looking at the initial responses over the first year of the COVID-19 outbreak, the steps taken by newly independent states can be placed into four broad categories: early responders (Armenia, Georgia, Moldova, Kazakhstan, and Russia), late responders (Azerbaijan, Kyrgyzstan, and Uzbekistan), laggards (Belarus), and deniers (Tajikistan and Turkmenistan) (Gulina, 2020; Laruelle and McCann, 2020). Another classification suggested the division of the newly independent countries into four groups, depending on their pandemic reactions:

i States that restricted freedom of movement. By the end of March 2020, all Central Asian and Caucasian states had restricted border crossings (except cargo). The borders of Azerbaijan, Turkmenistan, Tajikistan, and Uzbekistan were completely closed. Kyrgyzstan's borders remained partly open for nationals of Kyrgyzstan and Russia and transit crossings via Kazakhstan (Ryazantsev et al., 2020). Kyrgyzstan also clamped down on Kyrgyz labour migrants entering the country from Eurasia to ensure they observe the quarantine guidelines.
ii States that declared a quarantine. Azerbaijan, Kazakhstan, and some regions of Kyrgyzstan ordered quarantines. Later Azerbaijan further narrowed its list of businesses and employees allowed to work during the quarantine. Kazakhstan, Kyrgyzstan, and Armenia placed targeted restrictions on certain groups of countries' inhabitants, restricting the movement of people (Armenia) over the age of 65 (Kazakhstan) or in some cities (Kyrgyzstan).

DOI: 10.4324/9781003377597-14

iii States that announced special measures. The president of Azerbaijan created a COVID-19 containment fund consisting of contributions made by state agencies and institutions employees, who were required to do so irrespectively of their wishes. Uzbekistan announced the establishment of an anti-crisis fund worth 10 trillion sums (about $1 million), as well as tax and customs relief measures for businesses and the population. According to some scholars, such an outstanding initiative indicated national-level changes in priorities, strategies, and personalities among leaders of the Eurasian regions and highlighted Uzbekistan's role as a regional leader (Ibbotson, 2020; McGraw Olive, 2021).
iv States that rejected any measures to stop the spread of COVID-19. Tajikistan[2] and Turkmenistan[3] officially eschewed introducing anti-coronavirus containment measures. The leadership of both countries stated that no cases of COVID-19 had been registered in the countries and chose not to share preventive information with the population. However, Tajikistan, like Turkmenistan, banned international flights. Turkmenistan redirected all flights from outside the country to the Lebap airport, where authorities built a quarantine zone to keep those who arrived separate (Pannier, 2020).

To sum up, Azerbaijan, Kazakhstan, and Uzbekistan were able to respond promptly to the crisis by implementing strict confinement, sanitary, and fiscal measures and closing borders. These countries adopted special regulations and took steps to combat the spread of the coronavirus, albeit with a slower implementation (Jones and King, 2021; OECD, 2022). In contrast to these countries, Kyrgyzstan's and Armenia's responses were limited. Tajikistan and Turkmenistan reported few or no cases of COVID-19 (ESCAP, 2020) and were reluctant even to acknowledge the existence of COVID-19 in their countries.

The Plight of Stranded Migrants

The coronavirus was an enormous challenge for Caucasian and Central Asian states (UN Women Regional Office for Europe and Central Asia, 2020). The pandemic severely strained national healthcare systems and hard-pressed fiscal and bureaucratic states' capacities (UNDP, 2020) and seriously restricted human movement across the region (Murzakulova et al., 2021; Ryazantsev et al., 2020). The pandemic froze the migration corridors between Russia as a migrant-receiving country and Central Asian and Caucasian states as migrant-sending countries.

Border closures and lockdowns in Russia resulted in widespread job losses and reduced remittances while growing inflation, poverty and food insecurity affected migrant families left behind, and movement restrictions stranded many migrant workers in Russia with no possibility of returning home. Those who managed to return home have had no jobs and employment perspectives in their countries of origin. Based on Uzbekistan's official statistics, about 498,000 migrant workers returned to Uzbekistan and had no fixed income after their return (Sibagatulina, 2021). A lack of transport connectivity prevented migrant workers from leaving countries, causing an abundance of labour supply and growing unemployment in the region. The United Nations Development Programme (UNDP) and the Asian Development Bank (ADB) estimated that the unemployment ratio in Kyrgyzstan had reached 21% by the end of the pandemic, while over 20% of the country's population was already living in poverty in 2019 (UNDP and ADB, 2020). Amid the pandemic, the unemployment working-age population rose from 9.1% in 2019 to 13.2% in 2020 in Uzbekistan (Sibagatulina 2021) and from 17.7% to 19% in Armenia (World Bank, 2021).

Vaccine Politics amid Rising Tensions

Considerable financial and human resources have been thrown into the fight against the pandemic, and vaccine diplomacy has become a key factor in the region. As of February 2021, the Russia-made vaccine Sputnik V was registered in 32 countries, including six newly independent states: Armenia, Kazakhstan, Kyrgyzstan, Belarus, Turkmenistan, and Uzbekistan. These countries unconditionally accepted the Russian vaccine and certified it for mass use (Gulina, 2021). Over the months, Azerbaijan and Tajikistan negotiated the purchase of vaccines with Russia and other countries. Finally, Azerbaijan got assistance and support in the fight against the pandemic from Türkiye (Azernews, 2022). Tajikistan purchased a Russia-made vaccine supported by international donors like the World Bank and United Nations Children's Fund (UNICEF) (Fazylova, 2021). Kazakhstan, along with Russia, has been much more fortunate. Kazakhstan developed the national vaccine, Qaz Covid-in, created by the Research Institute for Biological Safety Problems in Kazakhstan (WHO, 2021). The fight against the pandemic in Kazakhstan deserves our special attention. The country began vaccinating its population almost two weeks before Sputnik's official registration in Kazakhstan (Zhunusova, 2021). Kazakhstan produced the Russian vaccine in its territory while developing a national vaccine.

Political Landscape in a Post-Pandemic World

It was reasonable to expect that the impact of the COVID-19 outbreak, the antipandemic and vaccine measures, and national recovery strategies would be the main factors that could specify regional fiscal and political indicators and determine migratory dynamics as well as the future in the region for upcoming years. However, such an understanding was only justified before Russia invaded Ukraine and the war broke out in Eurasia in February 2022. Both the pandemic and the Russo-Ukrainian war became two emergency events that Eurasian policymakers had to face (IMF Annual Report, 2022). These crises have triggered large-scale humanitarian, institutional, and economic challenges and caused migration and refugee emergencies in the countries that were still dealing with the impact of the COVID pandemic. The war in Ukraine exacerbates threats of food insecurity and rising poverty, generates inflationary tension, and hampers security, growth, and prosperity in the Eurasian region. It also triggers many dimensional challenges for geopolitical and financial safety, human mobility, conflict potential, integration dynamics, food availability, and energy and water supply within Eurasia (Dilip & Eung 2022).

The tremors from the war in Ukraine are rocking established interests in Central Asia and the Caucasus. Most countries of Central Asia and the Caucasus still cannot clearly and openly state their stance on the military actions of the Kremlin in Ukraine. The vote on the United Nations (UN) resolutions against Russia's invasion of Ukraine (UNGA, 2022a) and the UN resolution on humanitarian consequences of the aggression against Ukraine (UNGA, 2022b) were very indicative: only Georgia joined in condemning Russia's invasion of Ukraine. Representatives of Armenia and several Central Asian states – Kazakhstan, Kyrgyzstan, and Tajikistan – abstained, while representatives of Azerbaijan, Uzbekistan, and Turkmenistan did not vote at all.

The positions of the countries of the region on Russia's invasion of Ukraine are split into four groups: (i) the position of relative neutrality seen from Azerbaijan, Kazakhstan, and Uzbekistan; (ii) the position of Armenia, Tajikistan, and Turkmenistan can be classified as "silence is golden"; (iii) Georgia is between and betwixt, keeping a foot in both flanks; and (iv) the position of open and repeatedly support of a conflict party made by Kyrgyzstan.

Position of Relative Neutrality

Two days before Russia's invasion of Ukraine, the president of Azerbaijan and his wife were on an official visit to Moscow, which, according to Ilham Aliyev, brought the relationship between Russia and Azerbaijan to the level of an "alliance" (AZERTAG, 2022). Azerbaijan views Russia as "the main partner in finding a way to normalize relations between Azerbaijan and Armenia" (Aliyev, 2022a). At the official level, Azerbaijan called on both sides for a ceasefire, although it delivered medicine, humanitarian aid, and fuel to Ukraine (Aliyev, 2022b).

Kazakhstan has also distanced itself from both sides of the war. On March 2, 2022, a week after the outbreak of hostilities in Ukraine, Kazakh President Kassym-Jomart Kemeluly Tokayev called on both conflict parties to "find ways for dialogue and conflict resolution" (Tokayev, 2022b). Officially, representatives of Kazakhstan did not express their condemnation of Russia or support for Ukraine. However, the head of the country's Foreign Ministry, Mukhtar Tleuberdi, stated that recognition of the Luhansk and Donetsk People's Republics is not in Kazakhstan's plans (E-Government of Kazakhstan, 2022). Kazakhstan refused to support the Russian military, and President Tokayev, after a telephone conversation with German President Frank-Walter Steinmeier, ordered that medicines and humanitarian aid be sent to the people of Ukraine.

Uzbekistan maintains a balanced, neutral position on the military actions carried out by Russia on the territory of Ukraine. It believes that all disputes and disagreements "should be resolved solely based on international law" (Press Secretary of the President of Uzbekistan, 2022). The recognition of the Luhansk and Donetsk republics is not on the country's agenda either.

Silence Is Golden

The official representatives of Armenia, Tajikistan, and Turkmenistan do not comment on Russia's invasion of Ukraine. While maintaining silence on the part of

Tajik officials about the events in Ukraine, the country's Foreign Ministry back in February 2022 called on Tajiks residing in Ukraine to comply with the requirements of the wartime regime imposed by Ukrainian President Volodymyr Zelenskyy (MFA of Tajikistan, 2022a). In March 2022, citizens of Tajikistan were evacuated from Ukraine due to a "tense situation within the country" in a joint operation of Tajikistan's Ministry of Foreign Affairs and Frontex (MFA of Tajikistan, 2022b). Turkmenistan officially adheres to the policy of permanent neutrality. Interestingly, the web page of the country's embassy in Ukraine doesn't contain any information at all about the war and the attitude of representatives of Turkmenistan regarding the events taking place in the territory of Ukraine.

Another curious point is that Armenia remains the only country from the bloc of newly independent states that President Zelenskyy has not mentioned in his tweets. Neither newly elected Armenian President Vahagn Khachaturian nor other high-ranking politicians have commented on the situation in Ukraine. Only the press secretary of the Armenian Ministry of Foreign Affairs, Vahan Hunanyan, once mentioned that Armenia has no intentions to recognise the self-proclaimed Donetsk and Luhansk People's Republics following their recognition by Russia (Armenpress, 2022).

Position of Two Fronts

Georgian President Salome Zourabichvili considered Russia's attack on Ukraine "deliberate, unprovoked and unjustified" and supported Ukraine in this "unjust war" (Bloomberg, 2022). At the same time, Georgia did not join the financial and economic sanctions against Russia, as it is and remains to be against Georgia's national interests (Garibashvili, 2022). Georgia continues supplying agricultural products to the Russian market.

Kyrgyzstan: The Region's Only Country Openly Supporting One Side

Kyrgyz President Sadyr Japarov has been the only Central Asian head of state to voice his support for Russia's actions. He stated that this invasion "was necessary to protect the civilian population of the territories of Donbas, where a large number of Russian citizens live" (Japarov, 2022). The telephone conversation between the Russian and Kyrgyz presidents confirmed the leader of Kyrgyzstan's approval of Russia's actions and his support for the Russian side's decisive actions to protect Donbas' civilian population and Kyiv's responsibility for the failure of the Minsk agreements (Kremlin, 2022).

The War's Impact on Eurasia's Power Balance and Mobility

Maintaining political neutrality in Central Asia and the Caucasus, with the actual non-recognition of Russia's position in Ukraine and the sanctions imposed on Russia, has already had an impact on the economic and political agenda of the region, as well as its integration initiatives. Turbulence across the region has brought big changes and challenges for newly independent states. Even countries outside the

Eurasian Union (Uzbekistan, Tajikistan, Georgia, Azerbaijan, and to a lesser extent Turkmenistan) face economic, political, and social constraints. Therefore, the vision and the future of Eurasian integration and the development of events in the regions become very relevant.

Three scenarios are currently possible: (i) the idea of Eurasian integration will be revised with a change in the role of a key player; (ii) frozen integration of the EAEU with(out) strengthening a bilateral and/or inter-states integration, and (iii) the collapse of the EAEU and the withdrawal of member countries from the EAEU.

The First Scenario

Given the de facto exclusion of Russia from international business, the countries of Central Asia and the Caucasus members of the EAEU leverage their geographical positioning. They create new logistics corridors and businesses for the development of their countries. In line with this trend, Kazakh President Kassym-Jomart Tokayev confirmed, "Unfolding events in the post-Soviet space are challenging, but they will not derail (Kazakhstan's) march forward" (Tokayev, 2022a).

Kazakhstan is most likely to become a key figure in the integration of the countries of the region. Tokayev also pointed out that "Partnership is still the only way to build a better common future of peace and prosperity" (Tokayev, 2022a).

Second Scenario

The processes of political integration in the EAEU have stalled for a long time (Vinokurov et al., 2017). It seems that economic integration within the EAEU became less relevant for the member countries of the Eurasian Union. Each new day of the war in Ukraine undermines the existence and capacities of the Eurasian Union.

Over the last decades, Russia has played an exceptionally important role in ensuring economic and political stability and security in Eurasia. The war in Ukraine and its consequences will lead to a revision of the role and involvement of Russia in any emergencies in the region. Moreover, Russia will face internal challenges for years to come. After the war broke out, the confrontation between Armenia and Azerbaijan and the violent clashes in the Gorno-Badakhshan Autonomous oblast of Tajikistan are shifting quickly, and no one knew how to mediate such tensions and how to respond to them. Therefore, this scenario seems to be the most realistic one for years to come.

Third Scenario

Nowadays many factors – encompassing the diversification of migration corridors and flows, the search and introduction of new transport routes, bypassing Russia, and the ongoing devaluation of the Russian ruble – can become factors contributing to the collapse of the EAEU.

In 2021 Russia was the largest trading partner of many newly independent states and is the country that hosted, among others, 4.5 million citizens of Uzbekistan,

2.4 million citizens from Tajikistan, 884,000 citizens of Kyrgyzstan, 163,000 citizens of Kazakhstan, and 7,000 citizens of Turkmenistan (Ministry of Internal Affairs of RF, 2020). Remittances from migrant workers remained an important source of external financing in the Caucasus and Central Asia countries, reaching a significant share of their gross domestic product (GDP): 10.5% in Armenia, 11.6% in Uzbekistan, 13.3% in Georgia, 26.7% in Tajikistan, and 31.3% in Kyrgyzstan (Ratha & Kim, 2022).

By May 2022, there were 1.262.695 million Tajiks; 1.626.308 Uzbekistan's citizens; 681.165 Kyrgyz nationals; 428.239 Belarusians; 228.142 Kazakhs; 215.481 Azerbaijani; 280.520 Armenians; 76.645 Moldavans; and 59.7051 Ukrainians on the territory of Russia (Florinskaya, 2022). It shows that 91% of all foreign nationals registered in Russia were nationals of CIS/NIS countries compared to 86% in 2019. As Florinskaya pointed out, from March to May 2022, the number of labour migrants from Ukraine, Kazakhstan, Moldova, and Kyrgyzstan on the territory of Russia slightly decreased by 10%, 9%, 6%, and 3%, respectively, contrary to the number of migrants from other CIS/NIS countries, which is slightly increased by 3–5% (Ibid).

With the existing development of events and growing conflict potential in the region, Russia will cease to be a migrant-receiving country and the Russian ruble will cease to be a liquid currency for trade within Eurasia. Unemployment and demographic pressure in the region, especially in Kyrgyzstan, Uzbekistan, and Tajikistan, will increase incredibly, which could lead to increased discontent, social protests, and political instability within Eurasia. Such internal challenges in the countries of the region, along with the weakening of Russia, will lead to major transformation processes and a drop in interest in any form of integration, including the EAEU.

In sum, it is unrealistic to expect any scenarios in line with the pre-pandemic past when Russia was involved in all inter-state tensions, played the role of a key player and mediator in the region, and reinforced its declining labour force while Central Asian and Caucasian countries received sizeable sums in remittances.

Migration Landscape in Reverse

Over the decades, Russia remained a major migrant-receiving country (Ivakhnyuk, 2009; Malkhov, 2014; Poletaev, 2019). The war in Ukraine brought extensive changes in migration trends in Eurasia, and as a result Russia became a migrant-sending country, with nationals leaving the country en masse to settle outside of Russia. Given the lack of air service and bureaucratic difficulties in obtaining legal residency in Western countries, modern émigré have rushed to newly independent states that accept holders of Russian passports. Uzbekistan, Kyrgyzstan, Kazakhstan, Armenia, and Georgia faced an influx of Russian nationals entering their territories.

These Eurasian countries are an ideal option for modern Russia's emigre. Firstly, the countries of Central Asia and the Caucasus, apart from Georgia, are officially neutral on the issue of the war in Ukraine and abstained from voting on the UN resolutions (UNGA, 2022a, 2022b). Secondly, the countries of Central Asia and the Caucasus are not on the list of unfriendly countries for the Russian Federation, which is approved by the Russian government (Ordinance of the Government of the RF of March 5, 2022). This is a very important point, which makes it possible to return to Russia (if necessary) and does not impose restrictions on the use of property in Russia. According to the Decrees of the President of the Russian Federation, the presence of dual citizenship or a residence permit in countries classified by the Russian government as "unfriendly" automatically leads to a ban on the sale, purchase, or turnover of property on the territory of the Russian Federation. Thirdly, the countries of Central Asia and the Caucasus have liberal admittance for citizens of the Russian Federation.

According to the current rules, citizens of the Russian Federation can stay on the territory of the EAEU countries without registration for 30 days and can then register in the territory of the EAEU country. Georgia allows Russians to stay in the country with a Russian passport for up to one year, after which a Russian citizen must leave Georgia or obtain a temporary or permanent residence permit from the Georgian Civil Registry Agency. Uzbekistan has re-launched the electronic portal for issuing e-visas for foreign citizens and stateless persons, which suspended its work due to the coronavirus pandemic. Furthermore, moving to the countries of Central Asia and the Caucasus does not require special cultural or linguistic adaptation for Russian citizens. In most countries of the region, Russian remains the language of everyday communication, and the rules and laws of residence are similar to those enforced in Russia.

Most of the people leaving today's Russia are emigres and expats, not refugees. Departure from Russia is, on the one hand, a forced measure and, on the other, their free choice. People leave their homeland to pursue their own businesses and live in a way that seems to them the most satisfying and free, or at least less restrictive. These people have no desire to return to today's Russia, although, crucially, they can do so legally if they wish. The countries of Central Asia and the Caucasus can profit from migration outflows from Russia and the acquisition of highly qualified specialists. However, to what extent those choosing to leave will be able to use the opportunity of these unexpected advantages amid the war depends largely on themselves (Halbach, 2007).

Conclusion

The COVID-19 pandemic has posed challenges to security, mobility, and travel connectivity and raised tensions in the countries of the region. The war in Ukraine destabilised regional mobility regimes across the borders of Eurasia. It affected labour market regulations and capacities and EAEU regulations, damaged migration corridors, and changed the dynamics and characteristics of migration flows. It also weakened regional and global security, the security of each newly independent state, and the security of its inhabitants (Allison, 2008; Lewis, 2008).

Today's tensions in Central Asia and the Caucasus, such as an unending territorial confrontation between Armenia and Azerbaijan followed by inhumane blockade of Artsakh, water and energy disputes between energy-deprived Tajikistan and water-starved Uzbekistan, and conflicting claims over the unmarked border between Kyrgyzstan and Tajikistan, remain to be at an alarming rate and fulfilled political agendas across Eurasia. Both the COVID-19 pandemic and Russia's invasion of Ukraine cautiously have had two side effects.

On the one hand, leaders of some Central Asian countries, i.e. Kyrgyzstan, Kazakhstan, and Uzbekistan, were starting making cautious steps towards each other, having held consultative meetings and signed an agreement on friendship, good neighborliness, and cooperation for the development of Central Asia in the 21st century. On the other hand, many interstate agreements and alliances, to the creation of which a lot of effort was put in, are losing their significance and influence. As a result, tensions and confrontations across Eurasia are growing and some other frozen conflicts are threatening to become a field of new confrontations (Bichsel, 2009).

By the end of 2022, it remained uncertain as to whether any solutions to these challenges would be available and how and to what extent these hardships and uncertainties would apply to each country of Central Asia and the Caucasus in the nearest future.

Notes

1 This chapter uses material which was published in "Migration in reverse: How today's Russia has become a supplier of migrants to the countries of Eurasia" on the Central Asian Bureau for Analytical Reporting (CABAR.asia) website: https://cabar.asia/en/migration-in-reverse-how-today-s-russia-has-become-a-supplier-of-migrants-to-the-countries-of-eurasia; and in "How the Ukraine war could disrupt Eurasia's power balance" (https://ridl.io/how-the-ukraine-war-could-disrupt-eurasia-s-power-balance/) and "COVID-19 vaccine: Lifeline, or geopolitical loyalty?" (https://ridl.io/covid-19-vaccine-lifeline-or-geopolitical-loyalty/) on the Riddle website. The author is grateful for permission to reuse these.
2 Tajik authorities did not acknowledge the spread of COVID-19 infections until late April 2020.
3 Since January 31, 2020, Turkmenistan has not officially confirmed any cases of COVID-19; however, it has experienced a surge in pneumonia cases.

References

"Azerbaijan to hold TURKOVAC vaccine trials next week". *Azernews*, March 3, 2022. https://www.azernews.az/healthcare/190073.html (Accessed: December 8, 2022).
Aliyev, I. [@presidentaz]. (2022a) [Twitter] February 23, 2022. Available at https://twitter.com/presidentaz/status/1496438945550323713 (Accessed: December 8, 2022).
Aliyev, I. [@presidentaz]. (2022b) [Twitter] February 26, 2022. Available https://twitter.com/presidentaz/status/1497614100884561922 (Accessed: December 8, 2022).
Allison, R. (2008) "Virtual Regionalism, Regional Structures and Regime Security in Central Asia". *Central Asian Survey*. 27 (2), pp. 185–202.
AZERTAG. (2022) "President Ilham Aliyev: This declaration brings Azerbaijan-Russia relations to the level of an alliance". *Azertag-news*, February 23. Available at https://azertag.az/en/xeber/2025989 (Accessed: December 8, 2022).

Bichsel, C. (2009) *Conflict Transformation in Central Asia: Irrigation Disputes in the Ferghana Valley*. London: Routledge.

Bloomberg [@BloombergTV]. (2022) "President Salome Zourabichvili discusses war in Ukraine". [Twitter] March 4, 2022. Available at https://twitter.com/BloombergTV/status/1499859936062451717 (Accessed: December 8, 2022).

Ratha, D. and Kim, E. J. (2022) "Russia-Ukraine conflict: Implications for remittance flows to Ukraine and Central Asia". *World Bank Blog*, March 4. Available at https://blogs.worldbank.org/peoplemove/russia-ukraine-conflict-implications-remittance-flows-ukraine-and-central-asia (Accessed: August 15, 2022).

E-Government of Kazakhstan. (2022) 'Reply of Mr. Mukhtar Tleuberdi, a Minister of Foreign Affairs'. Available at https://dialog.egov.kz/blogs/all-questions/728248 (Accessed: June 9, 2022).

ESCAP. (2020) "COVID-19 in North and Central Asia: Impacts, responses & strategies to build back better". Policy Brief. No. ESCAP/8.3-WP/1. December 1. Available at https://www.unescap.org/sites/default/d8files/knowledge-products/NCA%20Covid19%20Policy%20Brief_final.pdf (Accessed: August 15, 2022).

Fazylova, U. (2021) "COVID-19 vaccination campaign started in Tajikistan [V Tadzhikistane startovala kampaniya po vaktsinatsii protiv COVID-19]". https://www.unicef.org/tajikistan/covid-19-vaccination-campaign-started-tajikistan (Accessed: May 19, 2022).

Florinskaya, Y. (2022) "The monitoring of economic situation in Russia". Policy Brief. Nr 7/160. June, pp. 24–27. Available at https://www.iep.ru/ru/publikatcii/publication/monitoring-ekonomicheskoy-situatsii-v-rossii-7-160-iyun-2022-g.html (Accessed: January 20, 2023).

Garibashvili, I. (2022) "Interview of the PM Gharibashvili for TV-news". 1tv.ge. February 25. Available at https://1tv.ge/news/irakli-gharibashvili-saqartvelo-chveni-erovnuli-da-khalkhis-interesebis-gatvaliswinebit-ar-apirebs-monawileoba-miighos-finansur-da-ekonomikur-sanqciebshi-aghnishnuli-mkholod-daazianebs-gacilebit/ (Accessed: February 25, 2022).

Gulina, O. (2020) "(Re)categorizing Post-Soviet State COVID-19 containment strategies". *PONARS Eurasia*. Available at https://www.ponarseurasia.org/re-categorizing-post-soviet-state-covid-19-containment-strategies/ (Accessed: May 19, 2022).

Gulina, O. (2021) "COVID-19 vaccine: lifeline, or geopolitical loyalty?" *Riddle*. February 25. Available at https://ridl.io/en/covid-19-vaccine-lifeline-or-geopolitical-loyalty/ (Accessed: May 19, 2022).

Halbach, U. (2007) "Russlands 'Ohnmachtszone': Gewalt und Instabilität in Nordkaukasus". In S. Weiss and J. Schmierer (eds.) *Prekäre Staatlichkeit und Internationale Ordnung*, pp. 135–153. Wiesbaden: Springer Verlag.

Ibbotson, S. (2020) "COVID-19: Approaches, Outlooks, and Power Dynamics in Central Asia". *Asian Affairs*. 51 (3), pp. 528–541. doi: 10.1080/03068374.2020.1805891 (Accessed: December 8, 2022).

IMF Annual Report. (2022) "Crisis upon crisis. COVID-19 and the war in Ukraine". Available at https://www.imf.org/external/pubs/ft/ar/2022/in-focus/covid-19/ (Accessed: April 24, 2023)

Ivakhnyuk, I. (2009) "Russian migration policy and its impact on human development". UNDP Human Development Research Paper. 14. Available at https://mpra.ub.uni-muenchen.de/19196/1/MPRA_paper_19196.pdf (Accessed: December 8, 2022).

Japarov, S. (@SadyrJaparov) Account of the Kyrgyzstan's President [Facebook]. (2022). Available at https://www.facebook.com/100004948146129/posts/2071368826371369/?d=n (Accessed: February 22, 2022).

Jones, P. and King, Elizabeth J. (2021) "COVID-19 Response in Central Asia: A Cautionary Tale". In Scott L. Greer, Elizabeth J. King, Elize Massard da Fonseca, and André Peralta-Santos (eds.) *Coronavirus Politics: The Comparative Politics and Policy of COVID-19*, pp. 196–212. University of Michigan Press. Available at http://www.jstor.org/stable/10.3998/mpub.11927713.13 (Accessed: December 8, 2022).

Souleimanov, E. (2013). *Understanding Ethnopolitical Conflict: Karabakh, South Ossetia, and Abkhazia Wars Reconsidered*, London: Palgrave MacMillan.

Kremlin, R. U. (2022) "Telephone conversation between the President of Russia and the President of Kyrgyzstan". Available at http://www.kremlin.ru/events/president/news/67869 (Accessed: February 26, 2022).

Laruelle, M. and McCann, M. (2020) "Post-Soviet state responses to COVID-19: Making or breaking authoritarianism?". PONARS Eurasia, Policy Memo 641. Available at http://www.ponarseurasia.org/memo/post-soviet-state-responses-covid-19-making-or-breaking-authoritarianism (Accessed: December 8, 2022).

Lewis, D. (2008) "The Dynamics of Regime Change: Domestic and International Factors in the 'Tulip Revolution". *Central Asian Survey*. 27 (3), pp. 265–277.

Malkhov, V. (2014) "Russia as a New Immigration Country: Policy Response and Public Debate". *Europe-Asia Studies*. 66 (7), pp. 1062–1079. doi: 10.1080/09668136.2014.934140

McGraw Olive, M. (2021) "Post-COVID-19: Can Central Asia be central to Eurasian integration?". *CAP Paper*, No. 239. Available at https://www.centralasiaprogram.org/wp-content/uploads/2020/09/CAP-Paper-239-by-Marsha-McCraw-1.pdf (Accessed: February 22, 2022).

MFA of Tajikistan. (2022) "Official call for Tajik nationals residing in Ukraine". February 24. Available at https://www.mfa.tj/ru/main/view/9714/obrashchenie-k-grazhdanam-respubliki-tadzhikistan-nakhodyashchimsya-v-ukraine (Accessed: February 24, 2022).

MFA of Tajikistan. (2022) "Official call for Tajik nationals residing in Ukraine. Return of Tajik nationals residing in Ukraine through Poland's borders". March 11. Available at https://www.mfa.tj/ru/main/view/9844/vozvrashchenie-grazhdan-tadzhikistana-cherez-polshu (Accessed: March 11, 2022).

Ministry of Internal Affairs of RF. (2020) "Migration Statistics from January to December 2020". Available at https://tinyurl.com/mrxrct72 (Accessed: November 15, 2021).

Murzakulova, A., Dessalegn, M. and Phalkey, N. (2021) "Examining Migration Governance: Evidence of Rising Insecurities Due to COVID-19 in China, Ethiopia, Kyrgyzstan, Moldova, Morocco, Nepal and Thailand." *Comparative Migration Studies*. 9, p. 44. https://doi.org/10.1186/s40878-021-00254-0 (Accessed: December 8, 2022).

OECD. (2022) "COVID-19 crisis response in Central Asia". *OECD Library*. November 16. Available at https://read.oecd-ilibrary.org/view/?ref=129_129634-ujyjsqu30i&title=COVID-19-crisis-response-in-central-asia (Accessed: May 30, 2022).

Ordinance of the Government of the RF of March 5, 2022, No. 430-r. "On approval of the list of foreign states and territories committing unfriendly actions against the RF". Russian legal entities and individuals. *Garant.Ru*. Available at https://base.garant.ru/403615676/ (Accessed: June 10, 2022).

Pannier, B. (2020) "Central Asian countries use different strategies to deal with Coronavirus crisis". *RFE/RL's Central Asian services*. March 18. Available at https://www.rferl.org/a/central-asian-countries-use-different-strategies-to-deal-with-coronavirus-crisis/30495792.html (Accessed: March 18, 2020).

Poletaev, D. (2019) "From Mistrust to Solidarity or More Mistrust? Russia's Migration Experience in the International Context". *Russia in Global Affairs*. 17 (1). doi: 10.31278/1810-6374-2019-17-1-171-200 (Accessed: December 8, 2022).

Press Secretary of the President of Uzbekistan. (2022) [@Telegram] February 26. Available at https://t.me/Press_Secretary_Uz/1321 (Accessed: March 3, 2022).

Armenpress. (2022) "Recognition of Donetsk and Lugansk People's Republics is not on agenda of Armenia [V povestke Armenii net voprosa o priznanii nezavisimosti Donetskoy I Luganskoy Respublik]". *Armenpress*, February 23, 2022. https://armenpress.am/rus/news/1076234.html (Accessed December 8, 2022).

Ryazantsev, S., Molodikova, I. and Bragin, A. (2020) "The Effect of COVID-19 on Labour Migration in the CIS". *Baltic Region*. 12 (4), pp. 10–38. https://doi.org/10.5922/2079-8555-2020-4-2 (Accessed: December 8, 2022).

Sibagatulina, Z. (2021) "Embracing a dynamic future: Monumental shifts in Uzbek labour migration policy". *IMCPD Prague Process*. July 23. Available at https://www.pragueprocess.eu/en/migrationobservatory/publications/document?id=284 (Accessed: December 8, 2022).

Tokayev, K.-J. (2022a) "Turbulence across Eurasia will not slow Kazakhstan's progress". *The National Interest*. April 4. Available at https://nationalinterest.org/feature/turbulence-across-eurasia-will-not-slow-kazakhstan%E2%80%99s-progress-2015912022 (Accessed: December 8, 2022).

Tokayev, K-J. [@TokayevKZ] (2022b) [Twitter] March 1. Available at https://twitter.com/TokayevKZ/status/1498667029301239809 (Accessed: December 8, 2022).

UNGA. (2022a) UN Resolution. "Aggression against Ukraine." UN General Assembly. Available at https://s3.documentcloud.org/documents/21314169/unga-resolution.pdf (Accessed: February 28, 2022).

UNGA. (2022b) UN Women Regional Office for Europe and Central Asia. "The impact of Covid-19 on women's and men's lives and livelihoods in Europe and Central Asia". *Report*. July 17. Available at (https://data.unwomen.org/publications/impact-covid-19-womens-and-mens-lives-and-livelihoods-europe-and-central-asia (Accessed: December 8, 2022).

UNDP. (2020) "COVID-19 and Central Asia: Socio-economic impacts and key policy considerations for recovery". *UNDP Report*. Available at https://www.undp.org/eurasia/publications/covid-19-and-central-asia-socio-economic-impacts-and-key-policy-considerations-recovery (Accessed: April 16, 2022).

UNDP and ADB. (2020) "COVID-19 in the Kyrgyz Republic: Socioeconomic and vulnerability impact assessment and policy response". Available at https://www.kg.undp.org/content/kyrgyzstan/en/home/library/poverty/socio-economic-impact-covid-19.html (Accessed: August 15, 2020).

Vinokurov, E., Korshunov, D., Pereboev, V., and Tsukarev, T. (2017) *Eurasian Economic Union*. St. Petersburg: Eurasian Development Bank.

WHO. (2021) "COVID-19 vaccine tracker and landscape". January 20, 2021. Available at https://cdn.who.int/media/docs/default-source/blue-print/20january2021-novel-covid-19-vaccine-tracker.zip?sfvrsn=c0e106b_3&download=true (Accessed: January 20, 2022).

World Bank. (2021) "Armenia: Citizens' perceptions on COVID-19 pandemic". Available at https://www.worldbank.org/en/country/armenia/publication/armenia-citizens-perceptions-on-covid-19-pandemic (Accessed: April 7, 2021).

Zhunusova, A. (2021) "Vaccination against coronavirus began in Kazakhstan: What everyone should know [Vaktsinatsiya ot koronavirusa nachalas' v Kazakhstane: chto nuzhno znat']." *Tengriznews*, February 1. Available at https://tengrinews.kz/kazakhstan_news/vaktsinatsiya-koronavirusa-nachalas-kazahstane-nujno-znat-427018/ (Accessed: May 23, 2022).

13 The COVID-19 Pandemic and the Middle East

Changing Policies and Mindset of Regional States

Muhittin Ataman and Mehmet Rakipoğlu

Introduction

Considering that the Middle East is one of the most penetrated regions in the world, it is no secret that COVID-19 has significant political, military, and economic implications for Middle Eastern countries. The first confirmed cases of COVID-19 in the region were seen in Iran and quickly spread to the neighboring states. Therefore, it can be argued that after the so-called Arab Spring,[1] the coronavirus pandemic is the second most important development that has changed the political and economic climate in the Middle East. However, unlike the Arab insurgencies, it is an unconventional threat to regional stability. COVID-19 showed that the regional countries might face new threats that would cause new social, economic, and political challenges. To tackle these problems and combat the spread of COVID-19, many countries took strict measures during the first phases of the pandemic, such as quarantine, compulsory curfews, closure of schools, declaration of a state of emergency, and disabling the mobility of people by restrictions in or beyond the borders (Gomes et al., 2020). The Middle East region, which consists of more than two dozen countries, depending on the definition of the region, experienced different challenges and opportunities because of the pandemic.

Due to its complexity, an academic consensus has yet to be reached on the political impact of the pandemic in the Middle East. In this context, we acknowledge the difficulty in assessing how COVID-19 affected the region; however, this study attempts to understand the geopolitical effects and results of the pandemic in the region. This chapter argues that the new geopolitical atmosphere that emerged after COVID-19 is more akin to cooperation than competition. If not directly due to COVID-19, at least by its effects, the geopolitics in the Middle East has shifted in a more positive direction. We collected data and information from the Armed Conflict Location (The Armed Conflict Location & Event Data Project, 2022) and Event Data Project and the Uppsala Conflict Data Program (Uppsala Conflict Data Program, 2022) to prove our argument. Since it is the period when the effects of the pandemic are felt most clearly, we have considered 2020 and 2021 years as the main focus of our research. Since examining 28 countries independently would be too comprehensive for a book chapter, we have examined the overall impact of COVID-19 on the regional countries. We have accordingly focused the study

DOI: 10.4324/9781003377597-15

on three main issues. Firstly, we go deeper into regional crises such as Libya, Yemen, and Syria, where armed conflicts exist. In this sense, we try to measure how COVID-19 affects civil wars or regional conflicts. Have conflicts decreased or increased due to COVID-19? Secondly, we determine how COVID-19 affected Middle Eastern security architecture and foreign policymaking processes. Thirdly, we try to comprehend how COVID-19 affected the economy and society of the regional countries, especially those in the Gulf.

The Impact of COVID-19 on the Middle Eastern Security Architecture

COVID-19 has influenced different aspects of Middle Eastern security architecture. On the one hand, the pandemic has increased the state power in the region, leading to further authoritarianism (Ardovini, 2020: 58). The struggle against the pandemic has required a robust centralised administration, which ended up in increased intervention in the political system (Aydınlı, 2020). On the other hand, it has increased political instability and vulnerability in domestic politics. With their limited state capacities, the Middle Eastern countries have mobilised much of their economic resources for the pandemic-related sectors, including health and food. This has led to the undermining of the traditional security sector (Ataman, 2020).

Compared to the others, the countries affected by conflicts had to carry more burden during the pandemic since their infrastructure and health system had already been destroyed. For example, since the outbreak of the Syrian war, the most destructive conflict in the region since the 1980s (Rivlin, 2021: 2), the public and private health systems have nearly shattered. WHO's reports indicate that only 41% of Syria's hospitals and 46% of Syria's primary healthcare facilities are operated (Asi, 2022). In this sense, it can be argued that the regimes have gained from COVID-19 against their rivals. For example, the Assad regime has securitised the COVID-19 measures to smash the opposition groups (Hoffman, 2020: 10). The regime bombed the hospitals, blocked convoys transporting babies, and shut down the electricity and other necessary infrastructure (Sahloul, 2021). Therefore, COVID-19 helped the Assad regime and its allies weaponise healthcare, enabling attacks, militarising health facilities, besieging medicines, and targeting health workers (Jabbour and Fardousi, 2022: 403).

The fact that the Assad regime is the "legitimate government" in the eyes of the United Nations (UN) also affects the dynamic of the conflict. In this sense, with the support of Russia, Assad began to instrumentalise humanitarian aid and use it against the opposition. For example, Russia caused tension at the UN over the humanitarian aid going to Idlib and other opposition regions, which needs humanitarian aid at a rate of 75%, according to reports from the United Nations Office for the Coordination of Humanitarian Affairs (Yarar, 2021). Even though COVID-19 helped the Assad regime consolidate power and hegemony, we found that the conflicts and battles lessened, and the number of deaths decreased. Even though Syria became home to the bloodiest conflicts of the 21st century, the conflicts and violence de-escalated in 2020 compared to 2019 because of COVID-19, among other

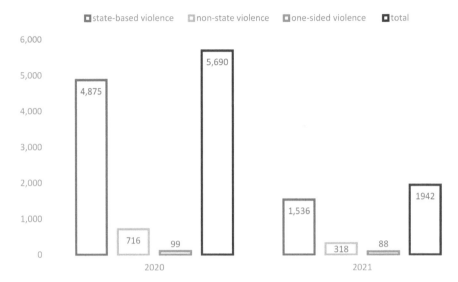

Figure 13.1 Number of deaths in Syria (2020–2021).
Source: Uppsala Conflict Data Program

factors. A group of academicians at the Uppsala Conflict Data Program found that conflicts in Syria have decreased by around 40% (Pettersson et al., 2021: 812) (Figure 13.1).

Yemen is another country that has been affected by armed conflicts for the last decade. Having been described as the world's worst humanitarian disaster, Yemen has been suffering from civil war since 2015. Houthis, a tribe engaged deeply with Iran, seized the capital, Sanaa, and then the Saudi-led coalition launched military operations to bring the status quo back. However, after nearly a decade of conflict, Yemen became an area of regional competition between Saudi Arabia and Iran. The already collapsed health system in Yemen only worsened after the war. But the developments, especially after COVID-19, have revealed the positive impacts of the pandemic on the civil war in Yemen (Figure 13.2).

For example, in 2019, the United Arab Emirates (UAE) announced the withdrawal of its troops from Yemen, which enabled more local dialogue. Similarly, Saudi Arabia took a more constructive stance in Yemen. Within this context, two critical developments took place in April 2022. Firstly, an UN-brokered ceasefire was announced between the Saudi-led coalition and the Houthis. This ceasefire contributed to the reduction of conflicts. Secondly, Saudi Arabia formed a presidential council to activate local groups. Therefore, the two most important parties in the war, the UAE and Saudi Arabia, transferred their powers to the local actors. Eventually, death, violence, and conflicts decreased throughout the country.

Like Syria and Yemen (see Figure 13.3), the number of deaths and the level of violence decreased in Libya between 2020 and 2021. The current economic difficulties in Libya have increased due to COVID-19. This situation affected the already fragile

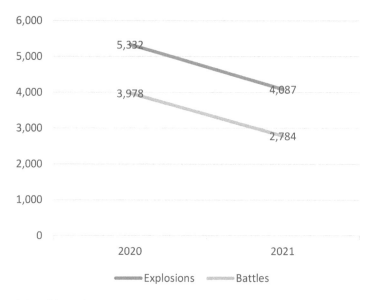

Figure 13.2 Fall in violence in Yemen (2020–2021).
Source: The Armed Conflict Location & Event Data Project

internal political balances, state authority was shaken, and authoritarian figures got stronger. In this sense, putschist General Khalifa Haftar got stronger. European actors are showing more tolerance for Haftar because of their fear of immigration and his control of oil (Özcan, 2020: 129). In addition, the fighting capacity of the parties has been diminished due to the COVID-19 outbreak. Data from the Uppsala Conflict Data Program proves that the number of deaths in Libya has decreased. The total number of deaths was 689 in 2020, whereas this figure sharply dropped to 12 in 2021. Therefore, it can be argued that since COVID-19 obstructed international transportation, including weapons, warring parties had to take the initiative in the war, resulting in a decrease in deaths. In Libya, an UN-brokered ceasefire

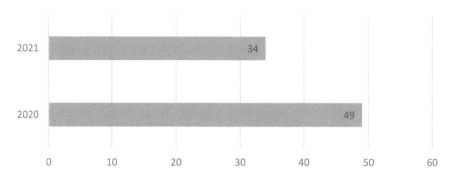

Figure 13.3 Civil deaths in Yemen (2020–2021).
Source: Uppsala Conflict Data Program

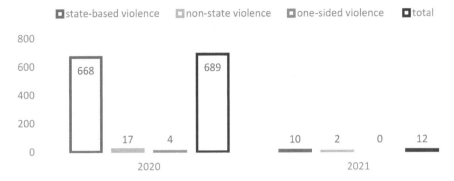

Figure 13.4 Number of deaths in Libya (2020–2021).
Source: Uppsala Conflict Data Program

announced in 2020 de-escalated conflicts, halting the war between the warring parties (Pettersson et al., 2021, p. 812) (Figure 13.4).

All these figures prove that the war and conflicts slowed in the Middle East during the COVID-19 outbreak. Moreover, there has been a noticeable decrease in conflicts in the hot regions, such as Libya, Syria, and Yemen. Therefore, the pandemic alleviated conflict-related deaths to some extent and contributed positively to the region's politics. Moreover, the COVID-19-related difficulties experienced by the regional countries contributed to the process of normalisation and cooperation between different regional actors. In this sense, almost all regional actors in the Middle East, including non-state actors, have restructured and recalibrated their foreign policies. It can be easily inferred that the Middle East has been more cooperative after the COVID-19 pandemic.

Restructuring of Foreign Policies of the Middle Eastern Countries

With the rise of coronavirus-related problems in the region, Middle Eastern countries have been trying to increase their autonomy in their foreign policies. Especially after the increasing interdependence and interconnectedness on the regional and global scales, they have been looking for ways to become influential regional players. Since then, all countries, small or large, have to consider globalisation and interdependence in their foreign relations. Middle Eastern countries have realised that they cannot overcome the prolonged regional crises and regional threats unless they comply with the principles of international cooperation and solidarity. This has led the Middle Eastern states to prioritise cooperation over tension and conflict in their relations with other regional states. As a result, the COVID-19 pandemic can be seen as one of the main driving forces of the Middle Eastern normalisation process (Norell, 2020).

This has led to the restructuring of foreign policies. First, although regional countries have learnt the significance of self-help and self-survival, they have initiated regional reconciliation processes after COVID-19 as well as new economic

(Zarifoğlu, 2020) and political processes to increase the capacity and capability of their state institutions. In this sense, the Gulf countries, in particular, strengthened their structures by repairing the intra-Gulf feuds. The Gulf Cooperation Council (GCC) crisis, or the blockade against Qatar, ended in January 2021 after Qatar was invited to the summit meeting of the GCC held in Saudi Arabia. Other Gulf states also joined Doha and Riyadh and began following similar flexible agendas (Bakır, 2022: 59). Since then, we have witnessed more intra-regional cooperation between GCC members. Therefore, within the Gulf, a subregion of the Middle East, COVID-19 has provided an opportunity for unlocking the GCC consensus by which cooperation flourished among regional countries (Kleim, 2020).

Second, Middle Eastern countries have lost trust in global powers and decided not to remain dependent on them. Accordingly, they have decided to diversify their foreign relations. In this regard, almost all regional actors in the Middle East boosted engagement policies with rising powers such as China and Russia (Singh, 2022). Within this context, some Gulf states, such as Qatar and Saudi Arabia, have chosen to become dialogue partners of the Shanghai Cooperation Organization (SCO).

Third, they have initiated normalisation processes with other regional actors to support regional stability. Since regional countries do not have the luxury to otherize one another, they began diversifying their foreign policies (Bakır, 2022). As mentioned by Bakır (2022), after the outbreak of COVID-19 in the Middle East, most regional countries began "to follow pragmatic behaviour and prioritize the economy business, trade, and interest-based agendas rather than ideological ones" (p. 60). In other words, the pandemic has provided a suitable atmosphere for the regional players such as Türkiye, Egypt, Israel, Qatar, the UAE, and Saudi Arabia "to approach each other with a pragmatic mindset that aimed to compensate for the devastating economic and financial losses caused by the pandemic" (p. 60).

As discussed above, the GCC crisis ended after the UAE and Saudi Arabia took the initiative to normalise ties with Qatar. In addition to the Gulf states, other regional states have followed multidimensional and comprehensive normalisation processes since 2020. In this regard, negotiations between the Gulf states and Iran are still ongoing. In addition to this dimension, the region has also witnessed a Türkiye-centred normalisation process. Türkiye has normalised its relations with the UAE, Israel, and Saudi Arabia as well as engaged in efforts to fix its ties with Egypt. COVID-19 has pushed regional countries to reconsider their foreign policy; hence, almost all regional states prioritised cooperation rather than competition (Kleim, 2021).

Since the multilateral and regional organisations failed to deal with the pandemic effectively, a positive atmosphere emerged in the region where cooperation to combat the pandemic flourished. This resulted in collective action or an increase in regional cooperation (Fawcett, 2021: 1–9). In this regard, violence and conflicts in the Middle East decreased, especially in Libya, Yemen, and Syria (Pettersson et al., 2021: 809). For example, the UAE became a hub for sending aid missions to several countries, such as Iran and Syria, even though its relations with these states have been complicated. By collaborating with the World Health Organization

(WHO), the UAE attempted to achieve at least two objectives. First, the UAE wanted to maintain engagement channels with Iran since its trade volume with Tehran cannot be neglected. Similarly, the UAE wanted to change the balance of power in Syria by extending a helping hand to the Assad regime, which normalised its relations in 2018 in the fight against the pandemic (Rakipoğlu, 2020). Second, the UAE's humanitarian aid to Iran positively affected the prestige and position of the regime in international public opinion (Diwan, 2020: 30); it paved the way for deepening cooperation with Western countries. Therefore, though some countries have been using foreign aid as a tool or instrument in foreign policy, COVID-19 helped some regional governments increase their engagement, accelerated the regional normalisation process, and boosted regional cooperation.

The Impact on the Economic Structure of the Middle East

During the pandemic, Middle Eastern countries have faced a wide range of economic hardships. One major issue was the loss of tourism revenue, including visitors to sacred places. The decrease in tourism revenues due to the COVID-19 affected the stabilisation and democratisation in the Middle East. Many states, Egypt in particular, became more authoritarian due to economic and financial hardships, i.e., the decrease in tourism revenues. Similarly, due to the decrease in tourism revenues and the rise of economic problems in Tunisia after COVID-19, the country turned away from democracy. It became autocratic with the moves of the Tunisia President, Kais Saied.

On the one hand, oil and natural gas producing countries such as the Gulf states, Iran, Iraq, Libya, and Algeria, which get their income mainly from exporting natural resources, have experienced severe economic difficulties. They were negatively influenced by the shrinking oil market in which the oil prices fell to their lowest level in the last two decades. On the other hand, countries such as Egypt, Tunisia, Jordan, and Palestine that do not have natural resources such as oil and natural gas and obtain their foreign exchange needs through tourism, employee remittances, loans from international organisations, etc., experienced much more challenging conditions. Therefore, COVID-19 brought economic challenges that forced the regional countries to cooperate.

Although the Gulf countries are financially more potent than other actors in the Arab world, they are adversely affected by the coronavirus in a multidimensional way. The fact that the Gulf is economically dependent on the outside world in terms of imports and exports and labour and capital shows that the crisis caused by the coronavirus will reflect on the Gulf in social, economic, and political terms. The Gulf countries are badly affected by COVID-19 since they differ from the rest of the region in various dimensions (Baycar, 2020a). The following paragraphs will provide a detailed analysis of the Gulf states.

The GCC countries faced significant geopolitical challenges for different reasons. Firstly, the workforce in the Gulf is highly dependent on foreign workers. With the stagnation effect of COVID-19, the flow of foreign workers to the Gulf markets stalled since many foreign workers come from countries such as the

Philippines, India, and Pakistan. The spread of COVID-19 created great concern regarding the mobilisation of foreign workers.

Secondly, tourism remains an important sector for the Gulf economies. Since COVID-19 originated in China, the Gulf countries naturally prevented Chinese tourists from visiting their countries. In other words, as part of the measures taken within the context of international tourism, the Gulf countries were deprived of Chinese tourists, who frequently visit the Gulf and are expected to continue to do so. Almost every year, around 1.5 million Chinese tourists visit the GCC countries. The GCC countries are competing to attract more Chinese tourists. It is alleged that GCC countries aim to attract more Chinese tourists and increase the number to 2.2 million next year. In this context, Dubai is heavily exposed to the negative impact of COVID-19 as the Emirates has been receiving more than a million Chinese tourists annually since 2019 (Kerr & England, 2020). This figure makes Dubai the Chinese tourists' favourite destination within the Gulf. Therefore, along with Dubai, all GCC members and their cities have been adversely impacted by COVID-19 in terms of economy and tourism due to the implementation of the virus-related travel restrictions. Dubai Expo 2020 was set to host 25 million visitors (Augustine, 2020) and earn $33 billion (Baycar, 2020b), but it failed to attract these tourists because of the travel ban. In this sense, Saudi Arabia and the UAE, which earn significant income from tourism, also experienced great losses. While the UAE's postponement of the 2020 Expo Dubai festival hurts its economy, it is also expected to see a 2% decrease in annual revenue after Saudi Arabia suspended its Hajj and Umrah activities.

The fact that the virus originated in China has reduced the contribution of Chinese tourists going to the Gulf. The Gulf countries, expected to reach 2.2 million by 2023 and host approximately 1.4 million Chinese tourists annually, are losing these gains due to the coronavirus. Hotels in Dubai, which hosted 1 million Chinese tourists in 2019, declined to their lowest level due to the cancellation of international events.

On the other hand, China's decline in international trade also negatively affected the Gulf economies. China mainly exports services and industrial products to the Gulf while importing gas and oil from the Gulf countries. In this sense, the trade balance in favour of the Gulf has led these countries to support China's fight against the virus. Similarly, China has increased its soft power in the region by sending health aid to the Gulf in the context of medical support during the pandemic (Zhang and Jamali, 2022: 279–296).

The golden age of oil ended when oil prices began to decline with the outbreak of COVID-19. The GCC countries have adopted strategies and visions to transform the economic structure to deal with being dependent on the export of natural sources. In this regard, COVID-19 offered an alternative or opportunity to transform their economies and prepare their economic system for the post-oil structure. Due to COVID-19 hindering international trade, including energy flow, diversification policies and implications became more apparent and obligatory for the GCC members. IMF reports proved that the GCC members began prioritising non-oil trade activities after COVID-19 spread worldwide.

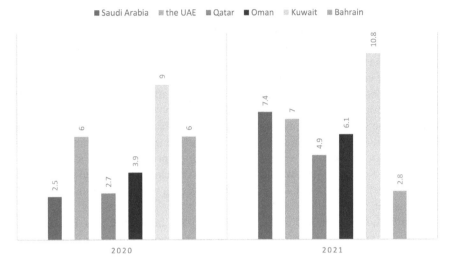

Figure 13.5 Rise of non-oil trade in GCC countries' GDP.
Source: IMF

As seen in Figure 13.5, COVID-19 accelerated the non-oil trade development process. Cooperation areas are preferred instead of competition to transform the oil-dependent economy and increase non-oil commercial revenues. In this regard, all GCC countries are aiming to seize investment opportunities. China is one of the most prominent investors in the Middle East and the Gulf. COVID-19 shattered trade, complicating investments and opportunities. For example, due to health and security concerns arising from COVID-19, transporting goods and people has become much more difficult.

Thirdly, the Gulf economies rely on trade and investment, which deteriorated after COVID-19. A report published by *S&P Global Ratings* (2020) reveals that the GCC economies and their growth are on the edge of risk due to the outbreak and spread of COVID-19. Lowering the oil prices hurt the fiscal balances of the GCC countries. In this regard, it is noted that Brent crude oil prices have fallen over 10% since the outbreak. The fact that the epidemic has almost frozen global trade shook the oil supply-demand balance, prices, and, therefore, the economies of the Gulf countries.

It is widely known and proven that China is the biggest customer of Gulf oil and natural gas. Similarly, the GCC countries, especially Oman, buy various goods and services from China's companies. China's exports to the GCC countries neither exceed 50% nor are below 50%. Therefore, there has been growing harmony in terms of trade. Since the capacity of China's manufacturing sector declined after COVID-19, the pandemic decreased the Gulf-China bilateral trade volume. The Chinese production in the Gulf countries fell, creating a supply shortage. This circle caused an increase in prices and made it challenging to reach goods. Moreover, since COVID-19 increased national expenditure, Chinese investors have delayed buying property in the GCC, severely influencing the trade volume between China and the GCC. China, which has an important position in Oman's export market with a rate of 45%, was also very effective in other Gulf countries' export and import markets (Augustine, 2020).

The Gulf countries, which have not yet been able to diversify their economies within the scope of vision projects, are adversely affected by the reductions in China's imports and exports due to the security problems caused by the coronavirus. On the other hand, the outbreak negatively affected the stock market of the Gulf. According to a report published by Bloomberg, the Gulf stock market, which experienced a "twin crisis" with the decrease in oil prices, suffered a total loss of $77 billion (Nereim, 2020). With the decline of Aramco shares offered to the public in December 2019 to their lowest levels, Saudi Arabia suffered the most in the Gulf stock market.

Fourth, the total amount of exports and imports between China and the Gulf countries is much higher than the trade of other regional countries with Beijing. Therefore, any trade rupture or contraction from China directly affects the Gulf economies since China and the GCC countries established strategic partnerships or cooperation (Cheng, 2016: 35–64). Even though China is not a direct neighbour to the GCC countries, the outbreak and spread of COVID-19 concerned the Gulf economies. The outbreak severely impacted sectors such as oil, tourism, production, construction, and trade that the Gulf economies depend on. For instance, many Gulf-based airline companies, especially Abu Dhabi-based Etihad and Dubai-based Emirates airlines, stopped most of their flights due to the restrictions, resulting in severe financial losses. In this sense, the Riyadh administration has announced that it will reduce budget expenditures and take financial measures. Amid the pandemic, the international credit rating agency Moody's changed its outlook from "stable" to "negative" while maintaining Saudi Arabia's credit rating at "A1" (Abdullah and Karabacak, 2020).

Pandemic's Effect on the Gulf's Social Tension

COVID-19 left an impact on the Gulf's social base since the pandemic is recorded as one of the most severe socio-economic challenges ever faced by the region (Hoogeveen and Lopez-Acevedo, 2021: 11). From a social perspective, it can be easily observed that COVID-19 revealed the abuse of migrant workers in the regional states. There has been growing social unease within the Gulf societies. The Gulf countries have a special demographic status due to the millions of foreign workers in these states. For example, 35% of the population of Saudi Arabia, 80% of the Saudi private sector, and 80% of the labour sector in the UAE rely on foreign workers.

The presence of foreign workers has many negative consequences in the Gulf's fight against the coronavirus. In this sense, another problem faced by the Gulf states in struggling against the coronavirus is that the health system is mainly dependent on foreign workers and is not yet fully developed. For instance, the UAE and Saudi Arabia employ 85% and 70% of foreign health personnel, respectively, many of them from Pakistan, Egypt, Jordan, and Palestine (Albejaidi and Nair, 2021: 481–497; Hanieh, 2013: 128). It is aimed to increase these rates within the scope of the UAE's 2021 Vision, Saudi Arabia and Qatar's 2030 Vision, Kuwait's 2035, and Oman's 2040 Vision. Therefore, it is expected that foreign health personnel and workers contracting the virus will directly affect the health system of the Gulf states.

On the other hand, due to the high number of workers, the financial dimension of the fight against the virus is among the most critical concerns of the Gulf states. Most of the workers in the Gulf come from countries neighbouring China. As an interesting case, the nearly 180,000 Chinese employed in the UAE have caused the country's security alarms to sound. The second issue related to foreign workers in the Gulf states is closely related to the continuation of the stagnation caused by the epidemic. The slowdown or even a halt in economic activity due to the crisis may result in businesses employing foreign workers and their owners terminating their contracts to reduce their financial losses. In this case, workers may have to return to their home countries. Therefore, as in the UAE-India relations, a "worker migration crisis" may occur in the Gulf (Aarthi and Sahu, 2021: 427). The situation may result in the halt of the economies in the Gulf.

It is estimated that foreign workers are influential in spreading the virus because they live in crowded environments and are constantly mobilised. This situation has been an essential factor in the increase of anti-migration sentiments in the region. In this sense, the Kafala system is called modern slavery in many Gulf countries, and the ill-treatment of foreign workers has been reflected in the press. As the coronavirus cases increase, anti-migration attitudes also increase in many Gulf countries, especially in Kuwait, where 70% of the population is foreign workers. Therefore, it can be claimed that the virus has also increased social tension in the Gulf. In addition, nationalisation projects such as "Saudization" and "Omanization," in which the Gulf countries aimed to add their citizens to the workforce, also froze the oil prices, and therefore the Gulf economies, due to the profound impact of the virus (Alsahi, 2020: 9).

Conclusion: Future Implications

The Middle East has been going through dramatic changes since the eruption of the Arab uprisings and revolutions in 2011, which led to the collapse of the political Arab world. While many Arab governments, such as Tunisia and Egypt, were overthrown by the widespread protests, some states, such as Syria, Yemen, and Libya, have fallen into protracted civil wars (Baycar, 2022). After the so-called Arab Spring, the coronavirus pandemic is the second most important development that has changed the political and economic climate in the region.

This study found that during this period, the conflicts were mitigated. Since COVID-19 brought out new costs to the states, the intensification of conflicts declined. Therefore, as the epidemic's impact diminishes, conflicts in the Middle East are expected to increase. Hence, agreeing with the argument that COVID-19 challenged the traditional system in the region, we propound that COVID-19 also opened new doors of opportunity for countries whose population mainly consists of young people, such as the Middle Eastern countries (Asi, 2021). Therefore, the young portion of the Arab houses protected states or regimes from the worst scenarios of COVID-19 (Asi, 2022). In other words, this study highlighted many points, such as the rise of cooperation, normalisation, authoritarianism, and structural change in economies and societies, which haven't been underlined acutely. As an international crisis, COVID-19 provided a window of opportunity for leaders to implement long-waited obligatory reforms. Under the status quo, these reforms were hard to pursue (Bechri, 2022). Therefore, challenged by COVID-19 and its repercussions, the Middle Eastern countries adopted more cooperative policies.

While Perthes claimed that UN Secretary-General António Guterres' call for warring parties to stop the armed conflicts and focus instead on fighting COVID-19 has not found a positive response in Libya, Yemen, and Syria (Perthes, 2020: 114), this chapter found that the intensity of the conflicts lessened. We do not mean that there are no more conflicts in the region; instead, we put forward that COVID-19 facilitated cooperation among the regional states. In other words, COVID-19 revealed the importance of regional cooperation in the Middle East and building platforms for coordination in many fields.

Many impacts of COVID-19 were/are temporary since the expectations and targets – geopolitical and geo-economic objectives – of regional and global powers towards the region did not change. Regional states and global powers renewed their positions in the frozen conflicts after the end of the pandemic. Regional blocs such as pro-American, pro-Russian, or independent coalitions will continue to dominate regional politics. If the regional states' national interests and identity politics continue, the region's conflictual character will remain intact.

Middle Eastern countries have learnt essential lessons from the COVID-19 pandemic and reoriented their domestic and foreign policies accordingly. First, they have learnt that they must take necessary measures to consolidate their state structures for survival. Second, they have decided to diversify their economies to decrease their dependence on one product, such as oil or natural gas. Diversification of regional economies will require diversification of their overall foreign policies, and thus it will decrease their dependence on traditional colonial powers, namely the Western countries.

Third, the increased interdependence among the regional countries requires the Middle Eastern countries to normalise their relations with other regional states. As a result, since the outbreak of COVID-19, many Middle Eastern states have de-escalated their tensions. For example, the Gulf countries sent humanitarian aid to Iran, which has been considered a rival and a threat in the past.

Fourth, they have understood that they cannot trust global powers to solve their national or regional problems. During COVID-19, all global powers have focused on domestic political and economic agendas and mainly followed autarkic policies. In line with the self-survival strategies, they have largely remained indifferent to humanitarian and health crises in other countries.

Note

1 The Arab uprisings in 2011 and the revolutions that followed were/are described as the Arab Spring, a misleading concept first coined by Western academic and political circles and later generally used by the world public opinion.

References

Aarthi. S. V. and Sahu, M. (2021) Migration policy in the Gulf Cooperation Council (GCC) states: A critical analysis, *Contemporary Review of the Middle East*, Vol. 8, No. 4, pp. 410–434.

Abdullah, M. F. M. and Karabacak, S. (2020) 'Suudi Arabistan Ekonomik Krizle Mücadele İçin Kemer Sıkma Önlemlerini Artırdı', *Anadolu Ajansı*, https://www.aa.com.tr/tr/ekonomi/suudi-arabistan-ekonomik-krizle-mucadele-icin-kemer-sikma-onlemlerini-artirdi/1836681 (accessed May 11, 2021).

Albejaidi, F. and Nair, K. S. (2021) Nationalisation of health workforce in Saudi Arabia's public and private sectors: A review of issues and challenges, *Journal of Health Management*, Vol. 23, No. 3, pp. 482–497.

Alsahi, H. (2020) 'COVID-19 and the Intensification of the GCC Workforce Nationalization Policies', *Arab Reform Initiative*, https://www.arab-reform.net/pdf/?pid=14948&plang=en (accessed December 18, 2022).

Ardovini, L. (2020) 'Resilient Authoritarianism and Global Pandemics: Challenges in Egypt at the Time of COVID-19', in the *COVID-19 Pandemic in the Middle East and North Africa*, POMED Studies, No. 39.

Asi, Y. M. (2021) 'What Future Exists for the Arab Youth of Today?', *Arab Center Washington DC*, https://arabcenterdc.org/resource/what-future-exists-for-the-arab-youth-of-today/ (accessed April 15, 2022).

Asi, Y. M. (2022) 'Two Years of COVID-19 in the Arab World: Social, Economic, and Political Effects', *Arab Center Washington DC*, https://arabcenterdc.org/resource/two-years-of-COVID-19-in-the-arab-world-social-economic-and-political-effects/ (accessed January 8, 2022).

Ataman, M. (2020) 'Lack of Global Safety Is Tragedy of the Commons', *Daily Sabah*, https://www.dailysabah.com/opinion/columns/lack-of-global-safety-is-tragedy-of-the-commons (accessed March 16, 2022).

Augustine, B. D. (2020) 'How Coronavirus Will Hurt UAE, Gulf Economies If Not Contained Soon', *Gulf News*, https://gulfnews.com/business/how-coronavirus-will-hurt-uae-gulf-economies-if-not-contained-soon-1.69763830 (accessed May 9, 2022).

Bakır, A. (2022) The 2021-2022 'de-escalation moment' in the Middle East: A net assessment, *Insight Turkey*, Vol. 24, No. 2, pp. 55–66.

Baycar, H. (2020a) 'Coronavirus and Its Impact in the Gulf', *E-International Relations*, https://www.e-ir.info/2020/02/28/opinion-the-coronavirus-pandemic-and-its-impact-in-the-gulf/ (accessed August 27, 2022).

Baycar, H. (2020b) 'The Sudden Cost of Unexpected Threats: The Novel Coronavirus and Dubai', *Gulf Insights Series*, No. 18.

Baycar, H. (2022) Civil war and pandemic: Syrian's response to the COVID-19, *Syrian Studies Association Bulletin*, Vol. 26, No. 1, pp. 33–43.

Bechri, M. (2022) 'The COVID-19 Crisis: An Opportunity to Transition to a Post-Oil Economy', *Washington Institute*, https://www.washingtoninstitute.org/policy-analysis/COVID-19-crisis-opportunity-transition-post-oil-economy (accessed September 30, 2022).

Cheng, J. Y. S. (2016) China's relations with the Gulf Cooperation Council states: Multilevel diplomacy in a divided Arab World, *China Review*, Vol. 16, No. 1, pp. 35–64.

Diwan, K. (2020) 'Coronavirus in the Gulf Imperils National Ambitions and Tests National Unity', in *the COVID-19 Pandemic in the Middle East and North Africa*, POMED Studies, No. 39.

Aydınlı, E. (2020) Pandemics and the Resilience of the International System. In U. Ulutaş (Ed.), *The Post-COVID-19 Global System: Old Problems, New Trends*. Ankara: MATSA Printing House.

Fawcett, L. (2021) The Middle East and COVID-19: Time for collective action, *Globalization and Health*, Vol. 17, No. 1, 133. https://doi.org/10.1186/s12992-021-00786-1

Kleim, F. (2020) 'Realism and the Coronavirus Crisis', *E-International Relations*, https://www.e-ir.info/pdf/82712 (accessed November 24, 2022).

Kleim, F. (2021) ASEAN and the EU amidst COVID-19: Overcoming the self-fulfilling prophecy of realism, *Asia Europe Journal*, Vol. 19, pp. 371–389.

Gomes, A., Al-Ragam, A. and Alshalfan, S. (2020) 'Reflections on COVID-19 and Public Space Use in Kuwait: The Potential of a New "Normal"', *Blog LSE*, https://blogs.lse.ac.uk/mec/2020/05/06/reflections-on-COVID-19-and-public-space-use-in-kuwait-the-potential-of-a-new-normal/ (accessed October 15, 2022).

Hanieh, A. (2013) *Lineages of Revolt: Issues of Contemporary Capitalism in the Middle East*. Chicago: Haymarket Books.

Hoffman, A. (2020) 'The Securitization of the Coronavirus Crisis in the Middle East', in the *COVID-19 Pandemic in the Middle East and North Africa*, POMED Studies, No. 39.

Hoogeveen, J. G. and Lopez-Acevedo, G. (2021) Introduction. In Distributional Impacts of COVID-19 in the Middle East and North Africa Region. MENA Development Report. Washington, DC: World Bank Group.

Jabbour, S. and Fardousi, N. (2022) Violence against health care in Syria: Patterns, meanings, implications, *British Journal of Middle Eastern Studies*, Vol. 49, No. 3, pp. 403–417.

Kerr, S. and England, A. (2020) 'Gulf Economies Rocked by Coronavirus and Oil Price War', *Financial Times*. https://www.ft.com/content/b7a7902a-68ff-11ea-800d-da70cff6e4d3 (accessed October 15, 2022).

Nereim, V. (2020) 'Back to Square One:' Saudi Arabia's Double Crisis Hits Home', *Bloomberg*, https://www.bloomberg.com/news/articles/2020-05-21/the-month-that-shook-saudi-economy-just-the-start-of-a-long-slog#xj4y7vzkg (accessed July 19, 2022).

Norell, M. (2020) The coronavirus in the MENA region: Enhancing turbulence or mitigating conflicts? *European View*, Vol. 19, No. 2, pp. 206–211.

Özcan, M. (2020) The Coronavirus Pandemic's Potential Impact on the Middle East. In *The World After COVID-19: Cooperation or Competition?* Ankara: SAM Publications.

Pettersson T., Davies S., Deniz A., Engström G., Hawach N., Högbladh S., Sollenberg M. and Öberg M. (2021) "Organized violence 1989–2020, with a special emphasis on Syria." *Journal of Peace Research*, Vol. 58, No. 4, pp. 809–825.

Perthes, V. (2020) The Corona Crisis and the International Relations: Open Questions, Tentative Assumptions. In *The World After COVID-19: Cooperation or Competition?* Ankara: SAM Publications.

Rakipoğlu, M. (2020) 'BAE İnsani Yardımlarla Salgını Fırsata Çevirme Uğraşında', *Anadolu Ajansı*, https://www.aa.com.tr/tr/analiz/bae-insani-yardimlarla-salgini-firsata-cevirme-ugrasinda/1824286 (accessed March 19, 2022).

Rivlin, P. (2021) The impact of COVID-19 and conflict on Middle Eastern economies, *Middle East Economy*, Vol. 11, No. 1, pp.1–10.

Saadi, D. (2020) 'GCC Economies at Risk from Coronavirus, OPEC+ Cuts: S&P Global Ratings', *S&P Global.com*, https://www.spglobal.com/commodityinsights/en/market-insights/latest-news/oil/021720-gcc-economies-at-risk-from-coronavirus-opec-cuts-sampp-global-ratings (accessed June 11, 2022).

Sahloul, Z. (2021) 'Why Was Syria Just Elected to the WHO's Executive Board?', *Foreign Policy*. https://foreignpolicy.com/2021/07/06/syria-assad-who-executive-board-covid-pandemic-civil-war/ (accessed June 11, 2022).

Singh, M. (2022) 'The Middle East in a Multipolar Era: Why America's Allies Are Flirting with Russia and China?', *Foreign Affairs*. https://www.foreignaffairs.com/middle-east/middle-east-multipolar-era (accessed June 11, 2022).

'The Armed Conflict Location & Event Data Project', https://acleddata.com/#/dashboard, (accessed October 2022)

'Uppsala Conflict Data Program', https://ucdp.uu.se/ (accessed October 2022)

Yarar, E. (2021) 'Over 3M People in Idlib Depend on Aid to Meet Basic Needs: OCHA', *Daily Sabah*, https://www.dailysabah.com/world/syrian-crisis/over-3m-people-in-idlib-depend-on-aid-to-meet-basic-needs-ocha (accessed May 28, 2022)

Zarifoğlu, E. (2020) Post-COVID-19 Global Economic Trends. In U. Ulutaş (ed.), *The Post-COVID-19 Global System: Old Problems, New Trends*. Ankara: MATSA Printing House.

Zhang, D. and Jamali, A. B. (2022) China's 'weaponized' vaccine: Intertwining between international and domestic Politics, *East Asia*, Vol. 39, pp. 279–296.

14 The UK's New Migration Policy

Post-Brexit and Post-COVID Implications

Ayşe Gülce Uygun

Introduction

2020 was a challenging year for the UK for two main reasons, among others. First, in January 2020, the UK left the EU, and four decades of EU membership ended following extended negotiations on how the new rules of the game would be settled. Second, in March 2020, the World Health Organization (WHO) declared the coronavirus outbreak a pandemic, which would later affect every level of society. Alongside the health, social, political, economic, and migratory concerns, the exit process itself was influenced by difficulties caused by the COVID-19 pandemic. While dealing with the multifaceted damage caused by the global crisis, Brexit meant "taking back control" for Prime Minister Boris Johnson with the opportunity "to make (their) own laws and manage (their) own money," which translated to "keeping what works" and "changing what doesn't" (Cabinet Office, 2022a: 3). Within this context, a new migration policy has been framed as an ambitious means to regain "control of borders" to "build back better" during the post-Brexit and post-COVID era.

This chapter builds on a theoretical framework of the international migration-pandemic-security nexus to discuss the UK's post-Brexit migration policy during the COVID-19 era. Based on the existing literature, official statistics, government reports, as well as policy papers and media coverage, the theoretical framework is used to have a better understanding of how the coronavirus as well as migratory flows may be seen as security threats that enable extraordinary state measures. In light of this theoretical background, this chapter aims to reveal how the "borders" are instrumentalised and secured through government policy. The "borders" of the UK are used to connect three interrelated and simultaneous post-Brexit policies during the pandemic: first, under the restrictions and measures introduced by lockdowns and border closures to slow the spread of the coronavirus; second, the new point-based migration framework to take control of who passes through the borders; and third, the Rwanda Asylum Settlement to not allow asylum seekers through the borders. All three border control policies are discussed in the context of the UK's *Global Britain* approach. Considering that transnational migration is not the only challenge in the post-COVID international order, the main claim of this chapter is that *Global Britain*'s migration vision needs to be reviewed based

DOI: 10.4324/9781003377597-16

on a long-run comprehensive approach rather than focusing on the cost-benefits in the short run.

The first part of this chapter, therefore, focuses on the migration-pandemic-security nexus to further discuss how the borders are instrumentalised to gain control over a "threat." The second part is devoted to the UK's COVID-19 response post-Brexit. The third part analyses the main assumptions of the *Global Britain* approach within the framework of migration and aims to show why the UK has formulated a new migration policy. The fourth part focuses on the point-based system and the UK-Rwanda asylum partnership as two cases of the new migration policy of the UK. The final part reveals the concerns and risks of the new migration policy while discussing its (in)consistencies with the *Global Britain Vision*.

Theoretical Framework: International Migration, the Pandemic, the Security Nexus

The transnational movement of people, including legal permanent immigration, legal temporary migration, irregular or undocumented immigration, refugee and asylum flows, and whether voluntary or forced, has long been on the agenda of international affairs (Teitelbaum, 1984). "If everybody moves, when does movement become migration? Whose movement counts as migration, and why?" Anderson (2019: 2) asks. While answering those questions, she distinguishes between three types of migrants: "the 'migrant' in law and policy; the 'migrant' in data; and the 'migrant' in public debate." Moreover, she emphasises that what becomes important concerning the political debates is the fact that "a migrant is a person whose movement, or whose presence, is considered a problem" (Anderson, 2019: 2). As a problematic issue of political debates and related to these different forms of movement, the migration policy of an actor is, therefore, an interdisciplinary subject that deals with "the admission and selection of immigrants, temporary migrant workers, and refugees as well as attempts to restrict illegal immigration" (Meyers, 2000: 1–246). How, by whom, and through what means, under what circumstances (individual, national, global), at what cost, and with what likely consequences an actor's migration policy is formulated thus become critical questions to address.

The migration policy of an actor may be analysed via the insights of several theoretical approaches. Yet, since the last years of the Cold War period, both the phenomenon of migration and the concept of security have been transformed, and the connection between migration and security has been discussed at different levels. Critical security studies that emerged in this period questioned military-oriented and mostly realistic traditional security understandings of the actors. The analyses "broadened" and "deepened" the meaning as well as the actors of the security phenomenon by emphasising the social construction of threats and dangers. The level of analysis of the state-oriented approach that focuses on national security has been the target of first-wave critical security approaches, and therefore societies, communities, groups, and individuals have also begun to be seen as subjects of security. During this period, when military threats began to decrease, many different issues, such as economic, political, social, and environmental problems, ethnic conflicts, diseases, epidemics, famine, migration, and international smuggling associated with migration, began to be a part of the security agenda of actors as well as subject to several academic studies (e.g., Akgül Açıkmeşe, 2014; Booth 1991; Buzan 1983; Buzan et al., 1998; Mathews 1989; Rumelili and Karadağ, 2017; Wæver et al., 1993).

Furthermore, the security-migration nexus may also be studied under the externalisation of migration and the politicisation of migration frameworks. The externalisation of migration management may be described as "extraterritorial state actions to prevent migrants, including asylum seekers, from entering the legal jurisdictions or territories of destination countries or regions or making them legally inadmissible without individually considering the merits of their protection claims" (Frelick et al., 2016: 193). With the externalisation of migration, the border control mechanisms, practices, and responsibilities are "outsourced" to a third country (Palm, 2020: 11–12), which may be described as "borders' control by proxy" (Panebianco, 2020: 14). When it comes to the politicisation of migration, Benson et al. (2022) argue that the "creation of an exclusionary politics of belonging" based on "racial nationalism" may become possible. As in the case of the UK, the emergence of a new immigration policy could occur because of the politicisation of migration since taking back control of the UK's borders has been the main political theme that preceded the country's EU exit. No longer required to comply with EU law, Brexit appears to have allowed the UK to restructure its migration governance regime in ways that push the boundaries of these commitments even further, even though it is still bound by other international frameworks (including the global refugee protection regime) (Benson et al., 2022).

Since the spread of critical security studies among scholars, besides international migration, the disease, as one of the non-military threats to security, has been a concern for both academic circles and policymakers (Kirk and McDonald, 2021). First, because of global health crises since the 1980s such as HIV/AIDS, SARS, Ebola, and Zika and, second, due to the shifted and broadened understanding of the concept of "security" under the influence of critical security studies, health-related issues have been brought into the agenda of "high politics" (Kirk and McDonald, 2021). On the other hand, the securitisation theory, building on the "existential threats" that enable extraordinary and exceptional practices, enables actors to take emergency measures such as "expanded police powers, national lockdowns, and border closures." This has also been the case during the COVID-19 outbreak, with the rhetoric that "we are at war with the coronavirus" (Kirk and McDonald, 2021: 1).

Moreover, a discussion regarding the capacity of developed democracies to respond successfully to emergencies affecting their populations has been sparked by the public health crisis of COVID-19 and underlined once more pre-existing crises of governance and democratic stability. These crises are joined by the migration crisis, exacerbating and strengthening them. Since the largest and quickest drop in global human mobility in modern history was caused by pervasive travel and immigration restrictions, COVID-19 may profoundly change migration patterns in the long run (Boucher et al., 2021).

According to Boucher et al. (2021), the importance of visa policy, the legal status of migrants without access to public support, and the connection between migration and the labour market are three fundamental and pre-existing concerns multiplied by the migration crisis. Furthermore, the post-Brexit migration approach of the UK may have implications for rising nationalism and anti-immigrant sentiments and promote protectionist attitudes within the labour market (Boucher et al., 2021), debates on the sovereignty of the UK, and compliance with international norms and institutions as well as human rights considerations. The new migration policy, together with the *Global Britain* vision, appears therefore vital for the UK's domestic as well as international politics of post-COVID.

The UK's Pandemic Response: Living with COVID-19 Post-Brexit

The pandemic, seen as an existential threat, has enabled extraordinary measures. Multiplied with the influence of post-Brexit conditions, the UK introduced policies such as border security measures, travel restrictions, and nationwide lockdowns. To slow the spread of COVID-19, the UK started taking socially and economically disruptive actions in March 2020, just like other countries across the world. Johnson declared a nationwide lockdown on March 23, 2020, making a tactical U-turn in response to accusations that the government had delayed action for too long. The government relaxed the rules as the number of cases decreased during the summer, but in November 2020, the government reinstated a four-week nationwide lockdown in response to a rise in cases (Mix, 2021). Strong criticism of the second lockdown came from a variety of sources, with some claiming that the government once again disregarded expert recommendations to act sooner. Others denounced the lockdown as being detrimental to the economy and a violation of civil freedoms, and critics on both sides insisted that the government still lacked a well-coordinated, coherent strategy for dealing with the virus (Landler and Castle, 2020; Mix, 2021;).

Johnson declared a third nationwide lockdown for January 2021. The government further activated a four-step plan to eliminate all restrictions by June 2021. The condition was that England meet vaccination and case rate requirements. Based on the *COVID-19 Response- Spring 2021 Roadmap*, the government removed most restrictions in England during the fourth step and opened earlier than many other comparable countries (Cabinet Office, 2022b). In the UK, there had been around 4.4 million COVID-19 cases as of April 2021, leading to around 150,000 fatalities. Initially discovered in the UK in September, the so-called UK variant of the virus proved to be considerably more contagious than the original version (Mix, 2021). Yet, observers consider the UK's vaccination programme to be a success. As of April 2021, approximately 40 million vaccinations, more than half of the adult population, had been delivered. This gave the UK one of the highest immunisation rates in the world (Mix, 2021).

Despite the high immunisation rate and multiple lockdowns, especially because of the omicron variant that spread rapidly across the country earlier in 2022, the UK "has seen one of the highest numbers of deaths from COVID-19 in the world"

(CNN, 2022). However, as of August 2022, there are currently no COVID-related restrictions on international travel to the UK since the government's *Living with COVID-19 Plan* was announced in February 2022. According to the Living with COVID-19 plan, although the global pandemic is not yet over, the government admits that "border measures have carried very high personal, economic, and international costs." Therefore, it "will only consider implementing new public health measures at the border in extreme circumstances where it is necessary to protect public health" (Cabinet Office 2022b: 35).

To reduce the worst effects of the pandemic, the White Paper, namely, *Levelling Up the United Kingdom*, highlighted the importance of new measures in February 2022. One of the important steps, within the context of this chapter, has been presented as strengthening the new migration policy via controlling the "immigration system by ending free movement and introducing a new points-based immigration system, giving the UK the freedom to decide who comes to the country based on the skills people have to offer" (Department for Levelling Up, Housing and Communities, 2022: 2).

The Global Britain Vision and the New Migration Policy

The Integrated Review *Global Britain in a Competitive Age*, published by the UK government in March 2021, outlines the government's vision for the country to become a "global leader" in various areas (Home Office, 2021). It emphasises the importance of a new migration policy in achieving the government's national security and international policy objectives by 2025, stating that cross-border migration is expected to increase due to global population growth, climate change, instability, and economic factors and that this will have consequences for the UK. It also suggests that the new migration policy should involve "taking full control of borders" as part of the UK's efforts to address international challenges in the post-Brexit, post-COVID-19 era (Cabinet Office, 2021).

In line with the *2025 UK Border Strategy* announced in December 2020, building an "efficient," "smart," "primed to flex to changing circumstances," and "responsive" border has been seen to enhance "the long-term prosperity" and "security for a global United Kingdom" (Cabinet Office, 2020: 10; Cabinet Office 2021). The 2025 *UK Border Strategy* highlights an ambition to create "the most effective border in the world" (Cabinet Office, 2020: 6). "More than a line on the map," the UK's framing of "border" represents a "combination of policies, processes, and systems delivered by both public and private organisations across more than 270 recognised crossing points and many other smaller entry points across the UK" (Cabinet Office, 2020: 10).

The UK has a long history of migration, and as the Integrated Review emphasises, migration through safe, legal routes can bring economic benefits to both host countries and countries of origin through remittances. To continue to benefit from migration during the post-Brexit period, the UK would secure talented migrants for key sectors, including science and technology, which are seen as vital for productivity and jobs across the country (Home Office, 2021).

The new policy on migration, as mentioned in the *Global Britain* approach, claims to tackle irregular migration while protecting refugees as well as asylum seekers. In the framework of the post-Brexit migration policy of the UK, this chapter further analyses the point-based system and the Rwanda Asylum plan as the two cases to discuss the *Global Britain* vision's (in)consistency with the new migration policy.

The Post-Brexit Migration Policy of the UK

The Point-Based Migration System and the New Asylum Plan

Migration was "central" to the political debates of pre-Brexit, and it was "peripheral" to economic debates about its probable consequences (Portes, 2022; Portes and Forte, 2017). As Portes (2022) argues, during pre- and immediate post-referendum, the "UK's decision was frequently presented as a trade-off between the political advantages of leaving free movement and regaining 'control' over immigration on the one hand, and the economic costs of escalating trade frictions between the UK and EU on the other." However, the EU citizens' migration statistics to the UK have changed throughout time: Following the EU's 2004 enlargement, it reached its first significant high and ended in 2008 with the financial crisis. Before the Brexit referendum, between 2013 and 2015, net migration from EU citizens increased once more, reaching a peak of over 280,000 in the year ending in March 2016 (Sumption and Walsh, 2022). After the Brexit referendum in 2016, there was a sharp decline in EU immigration, but until early 2020, "the net migration of EU citizens was still positive." On the other hand, the effect of COVID-19 on EU immigration is still unclear, although the data points to negative net migration, with more people leaving than coming in, of EU nationals in 2020 (Sumption and Walsh, 2022).

The end of free movement as of January 1, 2020, has been framed as "taking back control of borders" by the government. EU citizens migrating to the UK are now subject to more restrictive immigration rules, the same as for citizens from non-EU countries. Any person, regardless of their nationality, moving to the UK to live or work will require a visa (Sumption and Walsh, 2022), and visas are granted based on points (GOV.UK, 2021). This new policy, introduced as the "point-based immigration system," focuses on "skilled workers and the best global talent, with skills and salary thresholds and an English-language requirement" (Cabinet Office, 2022a: 5). The government claims that its system has allowed bringing in "thousands of workers with the skills necessary to support the domestic labour market in the UK," including doctors, scientists, butchers, and bricklayers, amid work to recover from the COVID-19 pandemic (Cabinet Office, 2022a: 5).

However, Sumption and Walsh (2022) argue that long-term EU migration decreased "even before any new policies restricting it came into force." For them, the reasons include the decrease in the value of the pound, political instability due to Brexit, and the fact that EU migration would have fallen anyway since it has been unusually high in the pre-referendum period (Sumption and Walsh, 2022).

The Migration Observatory at the University of Oxford's (2022) data shows that "the post-Brexit immigration system continued not to attract substantial numbers of EU citizens in the first quarter of 2022." According to the same data, "only 7% of skilled work visa applications were from EU citizens. The share was particularly low for health and social care roles (1%)" (The Migration Observatory, 2022).

Considering the new asylum programme, the UK government formally stated on April 14, 2022, that it will deport those who enter the country seeking asylum to the Republic of Rwanda (Prime Minister's Office, 2022). Qualified by the media as a "one-way ticket to Rwanda" (Adams, 2022), the policy is officially known as the Migration and Economic Development Partnership (Walsh, 2022). Being presented as the "world's first partnership to tackle the global migration crisis" by the government, it announced the aim as "to address the shared international challenge of illegal migration and break the business model of people smuggling gangs" (Home Office, 2022a). Moreover, the government sees the Rwanda scheme as an "innovative solution" to the global migration challenge with the ambition to "set a new international standard" (Pursglove, 2022).

Home Secretary Priti Patel expressed the need for such an initiative, saying: "The global migration crisis and how we tackle illegal migration requires new world-leading solutions." She also argued that since existing responses to this global challenge have failed and the "global approach to asylum and migration is broken," as a "world-leading" partnership this would "help break the people smugglers' business model and prevent loss of life while ensuring protection for the genuinely vulnerable" (Home Office, 2022a).

Furthermore, Patel, "whose family fled persecution in Uganda" (Prime Minister's Office, 2022), claimed that "at the heart of this approach is fairness" since "access to the UK's asylum system must be based on need, not on the ability to pay people smugglers" (Home Office, 2022b). While trying to justify the government's decision to the public, she underlined that "The demands on the current system, the cost to the taxpayer, and the flagrant abuses are increasing. The British public have rightly had enough." Similarly, Johnson expressed that "we can't ask the British taxpayer to write a blank cheque to cover the costs of anyone who might want to come and live here" since immigration "creates unmanageable demands" on the health system and the welfare state, "it overstretches (our) local schools, (our) housing and public transport, and creates unsustainable pressure to build on precious green spaces" (Prime Minister's Office, 2022).

Critics of the UK's New Migration Policy

The point-based system and the Rwanda Asylum plan have raised criticism from a broad range of sectors and actors, both domestic and international. The UK-Rwanda Migration and Development Partnership, seen as controversial, has been criticised for its "legality, practicality, and value for money" (Gower and Butchard, 2022: 6). The critics of the point-based system, on the other hand, mostly focus on its business and economic impacts and access to the benefits system with fewer rights.

As Portes (2022) emphasises, compared to free movement during EU membership, the point-based policy significantly restricts immigration from the EU. In theory, immigrants are no longer allowed to enter the country to take lower skilled or lower paid jobs. Even if they do meet the requirements, their potential employers must apply for them, pay high fees, and EU migrants have fewer rights similar to non-EU migrants in the past (Portes, 2022). The new system also raises concerns about its practicality. For instance, Michael O'Leary, Ryanair's boss, urges the British government "to take a more practical, common-sense approach to post-Brexit policy, to allow more workers from Europe to fill vacancies" (David, 2022). He also underlines that "he could hire people from continental Europe for jobs that he cannot fill with British workers but is unable to get visas for them," although "facilitating such visas would help ease disruption to air travel" (David, 2022).

Moreover, the COVID-19 pandemic has highlighted the crucial role played by migrant workers in the UK's economy, especially in sectors such as healthcare, social care, and agriculture. Thus, the pandemic revealed an old debate on the importance of migrants as "key workers" or "essential workers" for key industries and sectors (Anderson et al., 2021; OECD, 2020). Migrant workers have been on the frontlines of the pandemic, risking their lives to provide essential services to the UK. They have been vital in keeping the healthcare system running, caring for the elderly and vulnerable, and ensuring that the country's food supply chain remains intact. However, the pandemic has also exposed the vulnerabilities of migrant workers in terms of access to healthcare, welfare benefits, and protection from exploitation. Many migrant workers do not have access to adequate healthcare or welfare benefits, leaving them at risk of falling through the cracks of the system. They are often forced to work in precarious and exploitative conditions, with little protection or support from their employers or the government. As Anderson et al. (2021) argue, the pandemic has made migrant workers' role clear for the labour market and the society as a whole, and thus an attentive policy response is required.

Regarding the new asylum plan, one of the criticisms has been on the precondition that asylum seekers reach the UK through "safe and legal" routes. While announcing the "world-leading asylum system," Johnson said he wants to allow "thousands" to settle in the UK through "safe and legal routes." However, Zoë Abrams, executive director at the British Red Cross, argues that Johnson "doesn't say how many, from where and by when" (Abrams, 2022). Abrams underlines that there are only a few safe routes available, and they are concentrated on specific crises like the one in Afghanistan or Ukraine. Even in cases where these pathways do exist, accessing and using them can be challenging, as witnessed with the Ukraine visa programmes. Many asylum seekers have to embark on perilous journeys, especially because "the UK's refugee family reunion criteria is limited to spouses/partners and children under 18," frequently via people smugglers, to reach the UK (Abrams, 2022).

In the same vein, "The Rwanda scheme is wrong in principle and in practice," argues Diane Abbott, the Labour MP for Hackney North and Stoke Newington (2022). She criticises the government's policy for not respecting international responsibilities such as respect for human rights, being too costly, and being far from a real solution. Her first point is on the UK's international responsibility to follow the European Court of Human Rights (ECHR) decision on blocking the flight carrying refugees to Rwanda. Her second point is about the cost-effectiveness of the policy, for which the UK has already spent "hundreds of thousands of pounds for the flight that was blocked and £120 million as a down payment to Rwanda." And third, her criticism focuses on the government's claim that the "sole motivation for the Rwanda policy is to stop people traffickers taking advantage of asylum seekers." Instead of this unpractical policy, she rather proposes the government "arrange for those asylum claims to be heard in France." She says that "since three-quarters of these asylum claims are upheld, there can be no sense in sending people thousands of miles to have their claims processed" (Abbott, 2022).

Finally, the goal of being a "reliable global partner," one of the objectives of the *Global Britain* vision, seems in danger because of regional and structural changes, including the loss of free movement since Brexit (Niblett, 2021). Niblett emphasises that "There are few things more damaging to a country's international reputation than the perception of double standards" (2021: 54). He also argues that "The UK has lost its reputation as one of the countries that are most open and welcoming to immigration, not only from the EU but also from around the world" (Niblet, 2021: 54). The new migration and asylum policies raise concerns about being "increasingly seen as a harsh country that closes its borders to refugees and asylum seekers from conflict-afflicted countries," including the ones fleeing Ukraine (Niblet, 2021: 54). Accordingly, Abrams (2022) argues that, in line with the *Global Britain* vision, the UK would and must afford more than the current asylum system "with people stuck in hotels and too many having to wait months, if not years, for a decision on their claim" or "trying to send people halfway around the world."

Concluding Remarks

This chapter aimed to discuss the UK's post-Brexit migration policy in the aftermath of the COVID-19 outbreak. Using the international migration-pandemic-security nexus as a theoretical framework, the chapter aimed to reveal how the borders are instrumentalised and secured through the government's policy. The study first analysed the restrictions and measures introduced by lockdowns and border closures since the outbreak of the coronavirus. Second, it elaborated on the new point-based post-Brexit migration framework to take control of who passes through the borders. Third, it put into perspective the Rwanda Asylum plan as a policy to not allow asylum seekers through the borders. All three of these border control policies are discussed considering the *Global Britain* approach. It, therefore, questioned the post-Brexit migration policy's consistency with the *Global Britain* approach, announced as a roadmap to become a global power with an increased capacity to respond to transnational challenges during post COVID-19 period.

As a result, this study concludes that *Global Britain's* migration approach matches the current migration policy in several aspects. On the other hand, the study also finds that the current migration and asylum policies need reconsideration for a more comprehensive vision. The matching aspects include more strengthened border management to take over the control, the freedom to decide who comes to the country based on the skills people have to offer, and the return of asylum seekers reaching the UK via irregular routes to a third country. For instance, when the *Integrated Review* emphasises that "following our departure from the EU, we will use our new points-based immigration system to ensure we can secure the talent we need for key sectors in our economy," it's consistent with the current scheme. While "the UK is also committed to tackling irregular migration because it endangers lives, often those of the most vulnerable, and places burdens on host countries," it's also consistent with the current policy based on the Rwanda plan. In the same vein, when it claims to "work with European and other partners to manage the movement of people within Europe's wider neighbourhood, including towards the UK – whether they are pursuing economic opportunities overseas or escaping instability at home," it seems partly consistent because it excludes European partners while introducing the new asylum plan.

Furthermore, this study reveals that the new migration policy is more pragmatic and opportunist rather than respecting international norms. Therefore, it does not match the ambition of becoming a global power, at least in the framework of migration, one of the transnational challenges of the post-COVID-19 era. On the other hand, the *Global Britain* approach emphasises that the UK "will also build capacity upstream for enforcement, including to address organised immigration crime, which exploits the vulnerable," and it "will protect the most vulnerable, including by offering support to the victims of trafficking, modern slavery, and exploitation." At first sight, since the Rwanda Asylum plan's main objective has been announced as targeting smugglers, this objective seems consistent. In this sense, the Rwanda plan seems consistent with the Integrated Review as it already announced that the UK would "return people without the right to remain in the UK to their countries of origin or another safe country, rebalancing the asylum system to disincentivise specific illegal routes and strengthening the returns process" and that it would "also increase the capability to tackle the migrant challenge in the Channel, including ending the dangerous, illegal, and unnecessary small boat crossings, through collaboration with France and other near neighbours." However, as previously analysed in detail, because of the concerns and criticism raised on the rights of asylum seekers trying to reach the British shores, the UK's policy does not seem protective towards migrants nor sensitive to international norms, even though it seems consistent with the *Integrated Review*.

Last but not least, while drafting the final version of this chapter, Johnson resigned, and the two candidates for the Prime Ministry announced that they would follow the same line on migration and asylum policies as Johnson. However, considering that migration will not be the only challenge in the post-COVID international order, the *Global Britain* vision requires reconsideration. To protect its international reputation in a competitive and fragmented international order, a more comprehensive approach must be taken concerning international law, international norms, and respect for human rights, rather than focusing on the cost-benefits of migration in the short run.

References

Abbott, D. (2022). *The Rwanda scheme is wrong – the British courts should strike it down completely*. Politics Home. Available at: https://www.politicshome.com/thehouse/article/the-rwanda-scheme-is-wrong-the-british-courts-should-strike-it-down-completely (Accessed: August 10, 2022).

Abrams, Z. (2022). *As Global Britain we can and should have a more generous asylum system*. Politics Home. Available at: https://www.politicshome.com/thehouse/article/as-global-britain-we-can-and-should-have-a-more-generous-asylum-system (Accessed: July 20, 2022).

Adams, C. (2022). Rwanda: We're committed to asylum plan, says Priti Patel. *BBC News*. 15 June. Available at: https://www.bbc.com/news/uk-61808120 (Accessed: August 10, 2022).

Akgül Açıkmeşe, S. (2014). 'Güvenlik, Güvenlik Çalışmaları ve Güvenlikleştirme'. In: E. Balta (ed.), *Küresel Siyasete Giriş*. İstanbul: İletişim.

Anderson, B. (2019). 'New Directions in Migration Studies: Towards Methodological De-nationalism'. *Comparative Migration Studies*, 7(1), pp. 1–13. doi:10.1186/s40878-019-0140-8.

Anderson, B., Poeschel, F. and Ruhs, M. (2021). 'Rethinking Labour Migration: Covid-19, Essential Work, and Systemic Resilience'. *Comparative Migration Studies*, 9(1). doi:10.1186/s40878-021-00252-2.

Benson, M., Sigona, N., Zambelli, E. and Craven, C (2022). 'From the State of the Art to New Directions in Researching What Brexit Means for Migration and Migrants'. *Migration Studies*, 10(2), pp. 374–390.

Booth, K. (1991). 'Security and Emancipation'. *Review of International Studies*, 17(4), pp. 313–326. doi:10.1017/s0260210500112033.

Boucher, A., Hooijer, G., King, D., Napier, I. and Stears, M. (2021). 'COVID-19: A Crisis of Borders'. *PS: Political Science & Politics*, 54(4), pp. 617–622. doi:10.1017/s1049096521000603.

Buzan, B. (1983). *People, States and Fear: The National Security Problem in International Relations*. Chapel Hill, NC.: University of North Carolina Press.

Buzan, B., Waever, O. and De Wilde, J. (1998). *Security: A New Framework for Analysis*. Boulder, CO: Lynne Rienner.

Cabinet Office (2020). *2025 UK border strategy*. GOV.UK. Available at: https://www.gov.uk/government/publications/2025-uk-border-strategy (Accessed: July 1, 2022).

Cabinet Office (2021). *Global Britain in a competitive age: The integrated review of security, defence, development and foreign policy CP 403*. Available at: https://assets.publishing.service.gov.uk/government/uploads/system/uploads/attachment_data/file/975077/Global_Britain_in_a_Competitive_Age-_the_Integrated_Review_of_Security__Defence__Development_and_Foreign_Policy.pdf (Accessed: April 1, 2022).

Cabinet Office (2022a). *Benefits of BREXIT: How the UK is taking advantage of leaving the EU*. Available at: https://assets.publishing.service.gov.uk/government/uploads/system/uploads/attachment_data/file/1054643/benefits-of-brexit.pdf (Accessed: July 15, 2022).

Cabinet Office (2022b). *COVID-19 Response: Living with COVID-19*. Available at: https://assets.publishing.service.gov.uk/government/uploads/system/uploads/attachment_data/file/1056229/COVID-19_Response_-_Living_with_COVID-19.pdf. (Accessed: July 15, 2022).

CNN (2022). *Travel to the UK during COVID-19: What you need to know before you go*. CNN. Available at: https://edition.cnn.com/travel/article/uk-travel-COVID-19/index.html (Accessed: August 14, 2022).

David, D. (2022). Ryanair's Michael O'Leary wants 'practical' immigration approach. *BBC News*. July 21. Available at: https://www.bbc.com/news/business-62221544 (Accessed: August 15, 2022).

Department for Levelling Up, Housing and Communities (2022). *Levelling up the United Kingdom*. GOV.UK. Available at: https://www.gov.uk/government/publications/levelling-up-the-united-kingdom (Accessed: August 10, 2022).

Frelick, B., Kysel, I. and Podkul, J. (2016). 'The Impact of Externalization of Migration Controls on the Rights of Asylum Seekers and Other Migrants'. *Journal on Migration and Human Security*, 4(4), pp. 190–220. doi:10.14240/jmhs.v4i4.68.

GOV.UK (2021). *The UK's points-based immigration system: An introduction for employers*. GOV.UK. Available at: https://www.gov.uk/government/publications/uk-points-based-immigration-system-employer-information/the-uks-points-based-immigration-system-an-introduction-for-employers (Accessed: July 1, 2022).

Gower, M. and Butchard, P. (2022). *UK-Rwanda Migration and Economic Development Partnership*. Research Briefing. Available at: https://researchbriefings.files.parliament.uk/documents/CBP-9568/CBP-9568.pdf (Accessed: August 1, 2022).

Home Office (2021). *Immigration statistics data tables, year ending September 2021*. GOV.UK. Available at: https://www.gov.uk/government/statistical-data-sets/immigration-statistics-data-tables-year-ending-september-2021#asylum-and-resettlement (Accessed: August 1, 2022).

Home Office (2022a). *Memorandum of Understanding between the government of the United Kingdom of Great Britain and Northern Ireland and the government of the Republic of Rwanda for the provision of an asylum partnership arrangement*. GOV.UK. Available at: https://www.gov.uk/government/publications/ (Accessed: July 1, 2022).

Home Office (2022b). *World first partnership to tackle global migration crisis*. GOV.UK. Available at: https://www.gov.uk/government/news/world-first-partnership-to-tackle-global-migration-crisis (Accessed: July 10, 2022).

Kirk, J. and McDonald, M. (2021). 'The Politics of Exceptionalism: Securitization and COVID-19'. *Global Studies Quarterly*, 1(3). doi:10.1093/isagsq/ksab024.

Landler, M and Castle, S. (2020). U.K.'s Johnson faces a growing revolt over his coronavirus policy. *The New York Times*. November 2. Available at: https://www.nytimes.com/2020/11/02/world/europe/britain-johnson-coronavirus-revolt.html (Accessed: August 1, 2022).

Mathews, J.T. (1989). 'Redefining Security'. *Foreign Affairs*, 68(2), p. 162. doi:10.2307/20043906.

Meyers, E. (2000). 'Theories of International Immigration Policy-A Comparative Analysis'. *International Migration Review*, 34(4), pp. 1245–1282. doi:10.2307/2675981.

Mix, D.E. (2021). *The United Kingdom: Background, Brexit, and relations with the United States*. Available at: https://crsreports.congress.gov/product/pdf/RL/RL33105 (Accessed: July 2, 2022).

Niblett, R. (2021). *Global Britain, Global Broker A Blueprint for the UK's Future International Role*. London: The Royal Institute of International Affairs Chatham House.

OECD (2020). *COVID-19 and Key Workers: What Role Do Migrants Play in Your Region?* Paris: OECD Publishing.

Palm, E. (2020). 'Externalized Migration Governance and the Limits of Sovereignty: The Case of Partnership Agreements between EU and Libya'. *Theoria*, 86(1), pp. 9–27. doi:10.1111/theo.12224.

Panebianco, S. (2020). 'The EU and Migration in the Mediterranean: EU Borders' Control by Proxy'. *Journal of Ethnic and Migration Studies*, 48(6), pp. 1–19. doi:10.1080/1369183x.2020.1851468.

Portes, J (2022). 'Immigration and the UK Economy after Brexit'. *Oxford Review of Economic Policy*, 38 (1), pp. 82–96.

Portes, J and Forte, G. (2017). 'The Economic Impact of Brexit-Induced Reductions in migration'. *Oxford Review of Economic Policy*, 33(suppl 1), pp. S31–S44. doi:10.1093/oxrep/grx008.

Prime Minister's Office (2022). *PM speech on action to tackle illegal migration: 14 April 2022*. GOV.UK. Available at: https://www.gov.uk/government/speeches/pm-speech-on-action-to-tackle-illegal-migration-14-april-2022 (Accessed: July 10, 2022).

Pursglove, T. (2022). *The Rwanda scheme is an innovative solution to a broken asylum system*. Politics Home. Available at: https://www.politicshome.com/thehouse/article/rwanda-scheme-innovative-solution-to-a-broken-asylum-system (Accessed: August 10, 2022).

Rumelili, B. and Karadağ, S. (2017). 'Göç ve güvenlik: Eleştirel yaklaşımlar'. *Toplum ve Bilim*, 140, pp. 69–93.

Sumption, M. and Walsh, P.W. (2022). *EU Migration to and from the UK – Migration Observatory*. Migration Observatory. Available at: https://migrationobservatory.ox.ac.uk/resources/briefings/eu-migration-to-and-from-the-uk/ (Accessed: August 1, 2022).

Teitelbaum, M. (1984). 'Immigration, Refugees, and Foreign Policy'. *International Organization*, 38 (3), pp. 429–450.

The Migration Observatory (2022). *Share of successful asylum claims reach a 30-year high, new Home Office data reveal*. Migration Observatory. Available at: https://migrationobservatory.ox.ac.uk/press/share-of-successful-asylum-claims-reach-a-30-year-high-new-home-office-data-reveal/ (Accessed: August 1, 2022).

Wæver, O., Buzan, B., Kelstrup, M. and Lemaitre, P. (1993). *Identity, Migration, and the New Security Agenda in Europe*. London: Pinter Publishers.

Walsh, P.W. (2022). *Q&A: The UK's policy to send asylum seekers to Rwanda*. Migration Observatory. Available at: https://migrationobservatory.ox.ac.uk/resources/commentaries/qa-the-uks-policy-to-send-asylum-seekers-to-rwanda/ (Accessed: July 10, 2022).

15 Post-Pandemic World Order and Russia

Fırat Purtaş

Introduction

Since the first days of the COVID-19 outbreak, many predictions have been made regarding the post-pandemic world. Many claimed that the world would not be the same, including that the balance of power in the world could change in favour of those who emerged stronger after the pandemic, the US-led international system is likely unsustainable, a bipolar world order could emerge with the rise of China, an increase of protectionist could be seen due to the food crisis, economic difficulties could intensify after the pandemic, and the end of globalisation and the rise in popularity of the Chinese model statist capitalism against the liberal system could also be seen (Bordachev, 2020).

The Russia-Ukraine war, which started at the end of the pandemic's peak, further strengthened the pessimistic forecasts. Although it is not clear how the pandemic will change the international system, the Euro-Anglo-Saxon alliance has shown strong solidarity against Russia's invasion of Ukraine and emerged as a new power bloc. The European Union (EU) has preferred to be a part of the North Atlantic Treaty Organization (NATO), the Group of Seven (G-7), and liberal financial institutions at the expense of its role as a global actor. In the current circumstances, it can be claimed that NATO continues to keep the United States (US) inside, Russia outside, and Germany down in line with its founding philosophy.

Russia will not accept being an ordinary state in the system and refuses to give up its great power status. It continues to oppose a West-centred international system led by the US. Moscow took steps such as the Georgian war in 2008, the annexation of Crimea in 2014, and the intervention in Syria in 2015 as preventive measures against American hegemony and NATO's expansion. It then went further and prepared a new move during the COVID-19 pandemic. Russia offered a new agreement to the US and NATO after amassing troops on the Ukrainian border from the beginning of 2021 but when its demands were not met, it launched a military assault against Ukraine on February 24, 2022. Russian President Vladimir Putin defined the year 2022, in which tens of thousands of soldiers and civilians lost their lives and millions of people had to migrate from their place of residence, as a year in which Russia made significant gains in terms of full sovereignty and providing a strong social consolidation (Novogodnee obreshenie k grazhdanam Rossii, 2022).

DOI: 10.4324/9781003377597-17

This chapter will focus on Russia's fight within the international system, its claim to the world order, Russia-West relations, Russia's fragile partnership with its neighbours and allies, and the effects of all these on the post-COVID-19 world order. The main thesis of the study is that Russia is on the verge of a transformation, as in 1917 and 1990, along with the world, which entered a rapid transformation process with the COVID-19 pandemic. Soviet Russia, which provided new territorial gains in Europe after World War II and legitimised them in 1975, soon experienced a great disintegration. Historical references indicate that the annexation of Crimea and the subsequent developments may have a heavy cost to Russia in the medium and long term.

Moscow's Unending Divisive Syndrome and Putin's Russia

Russia has experienced tides between the West and the East throughout history and has continued its existence as a Eurasian empire since its establishment. It experienced two major disintegrations, the first in 1917 and the second in 1991, leading to a "disintegration syndrome" and the problem of nations was evaluated in the same context. Due to its multinational and multicultural population, the regulation of relations between ethnic groups has always been one of the most important agenda topics of Russia. On the other hand, each disintegration took place simultaneously with major political transformations and then caused new rifts.

The Bolsheviks, who described Russian tsarism as a prison of nations and promised freedom to the captive nations, put into practice the political theory pioneered by Karl Marx by starting a revolution during World War I. During the Paris Peace Conference, where the rules of the post-war order were determined and the new borders of Europe were drawn, the civil war in Russia was underway. For this reason, the Soviet Union, which was established only at the end of 1922, was among those excluded from the Paris order. Soviet Russia turned into a union state consisting of federal republics on paper at the end of the era of empires and continued for 70 years as an ideological empire with a strictly centralised administration.

By the end of the Cold War, Mikhail Gorbachev's *glasnost* and *perestroika* reforms proved unsuccessful in holding the Soviet Empire together, and in this process, Boris Yeltsin, who accused Gorbachev of not being reformist enough, established the Russian Federation by giving "as much sovereignty as they could bear." The "young Turks" in Yeltsin and his team aimed to turn Russia away from the imperial mentality and turn it into a Western, civilised, developed "normal state." However, the first Chechnya War between 1994 and 1996 and the second between 1999 and 2003 greatly hindered the normalisation of Russia. Developments such as the 1998 economic crisis and NATO's intervention in Serbia in 1999 were also effective in Russia's re-emergence.

Despite the fact that after the collapse of the Soviet Union Russia has had a homogeneous population structure and a strong administration with the support of the overwhelming majority of the people, the disintegration syndrome of Russia has reached its peak today. In the 2010s, objections were voiced at the anti-Putin rallies held in Moscow, saying "It's enough to feed the Caucasus." Putin's response to this was that he annexed Crimea in the spring of 2014, leaving such questions meaningless. With the special military operation launched in February 2022, the Putin administration expanded its territory and population by annexing the regions of Donbas and Zaporegia. However, as it can be understood from the speech he made at the beginning of the year 2023, the fear of Russia's disintegration has reached an extreme level. According to Putin, the war front in Ukraine is aimed at protecting Russia's independence against the attacks of the West (Novogodnee obreshenie k grazhdanam Rossii, 2022).

Launched on February 24, 2022, Russia labelled its invasion of Ukraine as a "special military operation" that it said had two officially declared aims: to ensure the security of civilians in the separatist Donbas region, which wants to leave Ukraine and unite with Russia and has been fighting for this since 2014, and to overthrow the Zelenskyy administration, which it sees as illegitimate, by defining it as neo-Nazi. In addition, it was emphatically emphasised that the Ukrainian people were not targeted by the operation and that this war was started to eliminate the West's threat to Russia, which made Ukraine a prisoner, and to defend Russia. However, even towards the end of 2022, the actual purpose of the war still remained unclear. As the war drags on, along with the belief that Russia has failed, the "special military operation" has turned into Russia's struggle for existence against the West. On the other hand, fractures in Russian society on the legitimacy of the war have become more visible. Particularly, the reaction of Russian society against the partial mobilisation announced in September 2022 revealed the weakness of Russian public opinion.

The weapons aid and support provided to Ukraine by the Western alliance, especially the Anglo-Saxon world, shows that the crisis created by Russia is not only related to Ukraine. The Western alliance considers Russia's invasion of Ukraine an attack by an authoritarian power on liberal democratic values and a reflection of Russia's revisionist policies on the field. The historical references of the views on this are also strong because Russia's objections to American hegemony and the Western-oriented world order started in the late 1990s. Russia, which strongly opposed NATO's intervention in Serbia in 1999, took China with it at the Shanghai Five Summit held in the same year and jointly opposed the US hegemony. In 2004, NATO made the biggest enlargement in its history and became a neighbour with Russia, further increasing the discomfort in Moscow. In his speech at the Munich Security Conference in 2007 for the first time, Putin described the enlargement of NATO as a threat to Russia and declared that they would take every step to protect their national security. The "5-Day War" between Russia and Georgia, which started on August 8, 2008, was evaluated as the reflection of Putin's speech on the field. After serving as prime minister between 2008 and 2012, Putin's "grand strategy" in the third presidential term, which was extended to six years with the constitutional amendment, was to establish the Eurasian Union. Described as the revival of the Soviet Union, the Eurasian Union was planned as a move against the enlargement of the EU and NATO. At the end of 2013, the step of the pro-Russian Yanukovych administration to remove Ukraine from its partnership with the EU and to include it in the Eurasian Union sparked the Russia-Ukraine conflict that continues until today. Considering the historical process and the statements made by Western and Russian leaders in this period, the new Cold War between Russia and the Western alliance, which started in the late 1990s, turned into a proxy war with a predominant hybrid nature with a front opened in Ukraine in 2013.

The Conservative Russia against the Liberal West

Putin is a leader who describes himself as a conservative. Especially with Putin's third presidential term, which started in 2012, he adopted conservatism as the main ideology of his domestic and foreign policy. In his speech at the 2013 meeting of the Valdai Club, which is held every year, Putin focused on Russia's national identity. Putin disregarded the national, cultural, religious, and even gender-related moral and traditional values of the Euro-Atlantic countries; he said instead of believing in God they believed in Satan. In this speech, Putin explained that the Eurasian Union project has clear priorities and that this project aims to preserve the identity of the nations in the historical Eurasian area in a new century in the new world (Meeting of the Valdai International Discussion Club, 2013). Neo-Eurasianism, which emerged as a reaction to Yeltsin's reforms in the early 1990s, is another name for Russian conservatism.

Russian conservatism has its origins in Slavyanophiles. Slavism, Orthodoxy, and a centralised administration form the basis of Russian conservatism. Conservatives in Russia argue that Russians with their own history should go their own way as a Eurasian society, neither Western nor Eastern. Returning to Russia during the Perestroika period, Nobel Prize-winning sociologist Alexander Solzhenitsyn laid the foundations of modern Russian conservatism. According to Solzhenitsyn, Russia, which needs to get over the Soviet hump, should use its resources for the development of Russian culture and Orthodoxy by establishing a new empire that gathers the Slavs. Solzhenitsyn, who died in 1999, is the philosopher that Putin most refers to in his speeches. When Putin's statements about Belarus, Ukraine, and Kazakhstan are analysed, it is seen that Solzhenitsyn's "Rebuilding Russia" thesis, which was tried in 1991 but was not successful, is still valid (Coalson, 2014).

There are different evaluations regarding the reflections of conservative thought on Russian foreign policy. According to Leonid Polyakov, conservative foreign policy was an approach compatible with Russia's return to Asia (Polyakov, 2015: 4). On the other hand, according to Timofey Bordachev, Russia's conservative foreign policy ideology is a response to the international order imposed by the West (Bordachev, 2021). However, Vera Ageeva draws attention to the low level of religious practices in Russian society and the weak ground for the arguments based on the high divorce rates. Another point that Ageeva emphasised is that the Russian doctrine of conservatism, as an ideology export, has contradictions and uncertainties within itself. The opposition to democratic institutions and strong statism, security, and authoritarian administration practices are considered obstacles to the export of Russian conservatism (Ageeva, 2021).

The "National Security Strategy of the Russian Federation," which entered into force on July 2, 2021, clearly shows how conservative thinking has changed the understanding of national security in Russia. One of the titles in Russia's new

National Security Strategy is "Preservation of Russia's Traditional Spiritual-Moral Values, Culture and Historical Memory." Compared to previous national security doctrines, "Preservation of Russia's Traditional Spiritual-Moral Values, Culture and Historical Memory" is organised under a separate heading for the first time. In the document, it is noted that the US and its allies, as well as multinational corporations, foreign non-governmental organisations (NGOs), religious, extremist groups, and terrorist organisations actively attack Russia's traditional spiritual, moral, cultural, and historical values. It is pointed out that the culture has been Westernised and the cultural dominance of Russia has been damaged by the psychological warfare carried out. It is stated that historical facts and historical memory have been eliminated through the distortion of Russian and world history, the fuse of conflicts between nations and religions has been ignited, and the state-founding people have been weakened.

Among the spiritual and moral values of Russia are patriotism, service to the country, high moral ideals, strong family ties, labour, the superiority of the spiritual over the material, humanism, compassion, justice, collectivism, mutual aid and respect, historical memory, the continuation of the legacy of generations, and unity of the people of Russia. It is stated that these values unite the multi-national and multi-religious country.

These issues, which are a manifesto against Western-style liberalism, are a defence developed by Russia against the imposing liberalism of the Euro-Atlantic alliance. Within the framework of the National Security Doctrine, the decree on the Protection and Strengthening of Traditional Russian Spiritual-Moral Values was enacted by Putin on November 9, 2022. With this decree, liberalism was defined as a destructive ideology. The institution of marriage based on the marriage of men and women and the preservation of traditional family values are among the objectives of state policy.[1]

Post-COVID World and Russia

Another dimension of Putin's conservatism is the defence of the international system, in which sovereign nation-states are the main actors, against globalisation. Putin and his circle oppose the hegemony of the US and argue that the Western-centred international system should also change. During the coronavirus pandemic, which has turned into a global problem throughout 2020, the helplessness of international organisations and the vaccine nationalism of Western countries have played a role in strengthening Russia's thesis. Based on these developments, Andrey Kortunov claimed that Russia will be one of the architects of the post-COVID world order (Kortunov, 2020).

Sergey Karaganov, in the article he published in May 2020, claimed that the international system under the dominance of the West that emerged in the 20th century (Westphalia) was coming to an end. Karaganov claims that a great depression like the 1929 world economic crisis to be experienced after the pandemic will further intensify the competition between the US, China, and Russia, and the risk of a third world war in which nuclear weapons will be used after the pandemic increases (Karaganov and Suslov, 2020).

On the other hand, the restrictions put into effect due to the pandemic caused a decrease in production in all countries. This decrease brought about a decrease in energy prices. During this period, Russia had to sell oil below its cost. These challenging economic conditions made it difficult for Russia's military presence and operations in countries such as Syria, Libya, and Mali (Isaev and Zaharov, 2020). The increasing economic difficulties with the pandemic after the Western sanctions have led to estimates that the public's support for foreign policy may decrease. However, Russia's invasion of Ukraine on February 24, 2022, has proven that Russian decision-makers do not care much about public support.

During the first wave of the pandemic, Putin published an article on the occasion of the 75th Anniversary of Victory, and in this article, he focused on the ineffectiveness of the League of Nations in resolving the crises in the period leading up to World War II. Putin emphasised the necessity of maintaining the Security Council structure for the UN system to work effectively (Putin, 2020a). Putin also published an article with similar content in the National Interest magazine at the same time, stressing that it would be irresponsible to abolish the veto right in the UN Security Council (Putin, 2020b). Therefore, even though they are not satisfied with the current order and international relations, the Russian administrators have a negative approach to changing the UN system. From the Russian point of view, besides the UN, organisations such as the BRICS (Brazil, Russia, India, China, and South Africa), Shanghai Cooperation Organisation (SCO), and the Association of Southeast Asian Nations (ASEAN) are organisations that can play a key role in the construction of a pluralistic and democratic international system.

With the pandemic, the security perceptions of states have also changed. Global health issues topped the threat ranking. This shift changed Russia's position as the number one threat to European security. However, Russia, preparing for a large-scale military action against Ukraine in the summer of 2021, turned down the opportunity to reconcile with the West by itself. From the Russian point of view, the West caused this invasion by not meeting the ultimatum demands sent to the US and NATO at the end of 2021.[2]

Dmitri Medvedev's predictions regarding the post-COVID world order are striking. According to Medvedev, the world order has completely changed. As the West ignores Russia's security expectations and sensitivities, a new order can only be established on the brink of a third world war and nuclear disaster. According to Medvedev, the United States and NATO members rejected Russia's demands that Ukraine not become a member of NATO and supported the fascists in Ukraine to destroy Russia and the Russian world. Westerners see Russia as separate from the Western world, and Russia's trust in the Anglo-Saxon world has disappeared. Under these conditions, there is no longer any interlocutor in the West for Russia to talk to and reconcile with (Medvedev, 2022).

Conclusion

Russia's annexation of Crimea in 2014 and then Russia's direct intervention in the Syrian crisis a year later started the "New Cold War" discussions in world politics.

UN Secretary-General Antonio Guterres, in his speech at the Munich Security Conference, held four days before Russia started military action against Ukraine, stated that the threats to global security are more complex and at a higher level compared to the Cold War era (Munich Security Brief, 2022). The war between Russia and Ukraine, which started on February 24, 2022, has developed beyond a regional conflict. By invading Ukraine, Russia has clearly demonstrated that it will not be an ordinary state, that it will not abandon its imperial past, that it will not be subject to the global hegemony of the US, that Russia will follow its own path, and that it will be a balancing factor in global politics.

On February 10, 2023, NATO and EU leaders issued a joint declaration on EU-NATO cooperation. This declaration is the third declaration to strengthen the strategic partnership in the Euro-Atlantic area after the solidarity declarations signed in 2016 and 2018. This declaration, which was signed while Russia's aggression continued, also strengthened the common stance against Russia and emphasised support for Ukraine's self-defence. In the declaration, it is emphasised that authoritarian actors threaten democratic values by using political, economic, technological, and military tools (Joint Declaration on EU-NATO Cooperation, 2023).

The NATO 2022 Strategic Concept adopted by NATO at the Madrid Summit in June 2022, the US National Security Strategy put into effect in October 2022, the UK's Global Strategy for Britain in a Competitive Age, and the EU's Strategic Compass for Security and Defence described Russia as the biggest threat to European security and have described China as the number one state threatening the rule-based international system. The two states, which are described as a threat by the Euro-Atlantic alliance, define their cooperation as a partnership without borders[3] (Joint Statement of the Russian Federation and the People's Republic of China on the International Relations Entering a New Era and the Global Sustainable Development, 2022). The similarity and divergence in the threat perceptions of the partners without borders will shape the size of the alliance between them. The asymmetrical balance between Russia and its ally China is the most important factor limiting the alliance. Based on the thesis that Russia is gradually turning into a part of a China-centred bloc, Dmitri Trenin argues that Russia can maintain its status and prestige by developing its relations with major economic and financial players, especially with European countries, India, and Japan (Trenin, 2020). On the other hand, while the COVID-19 pandemic continues, the joint leaders' summit of the SCO and the CSTO held in Dushanbe in September 2021 was evaluated as a signal of a possible new political bloc (RFE/RL's Tajik Service, RFE/RL's Kyrgyz Service, RFE/RL's Kazakh Service, 2021).

The ideological basis of the new polarisation policy, which is carried out through the separation of democratic and authoritarian governments, is shaped as conservatism against liberalism. While defending the rights of the LGTB community is accepted as the criterion of democracy, defending the traditional family structure and religious values is considered authoritarian. At this point, Russia has already declared itself as the pioneer of the conservative world. However, Russia's attempt to destroy Ukraine's territorial integrity in clear violation of international law has left its allies and neighbours in a difficult situation. The world is going through a process of intertwined complexities and contradictions. In an environment where black and white cannot be distinguished, Russia seems to have made a clear choice. Russia's persistence and resilience in its choice, rather than whether it is right or wrong, will be decisive in shaping the new international system.

Notes

1 Ukaz Prezidenta Rossiiskoi Federatsii Ob Utverzhdenii Osnob Gosuderstvennoi Politiki po Sohraneniu i Ukrepleniu Traditsionnıh Rossiiskih Duhovno-Nravstvennih Tsennostei, Moskova, Kremlin, 9 November 2022. http://static.kremlin.ru/media/events/files/ru/qcDRpNRKdqbKAX8mD0TP9z02hAhAJAT4.pdf
2 Russian Deputy Foreign Minister S. Ryabkov presented two draft agreements, one with the United States and the other with NATO, that included Russia's security guarantees to the US Deputy Secretary of State K. Donfrid on December 15, 2021, in Moscow. The USA and NATO submitted their negative responses to these drafts in writing on January 26, 2022. Three basic demands came to the fore in the comprehensive draft presented by Russia: Ban on Ukraine entering NATO and a limit to the deployment of troops and weapons to NATO's eastern flank, in effect returning NATO forces to where they were stationed in 1997, before an eastward expansion.
3 "The sides call for the establishment of a new kind of relationship between world powers on the basis of mutual respect, peaceful coexistence, and mutually beneficial cooperation. They reaffirm that the new inter-state relations between Russia and China are superior to the political and military alliances of the Cold War era. The friendship between the two states has no limits, there are no 'forbidden' areas of cooperation, strengthening of bilateral strategic cooperation is neither aimed against third countries nor affected by the changing international environment and circumstantial changes in third countries." Please see: Joint Statement of the Russian Federation and the People's Republic of China on the International Relations Entering a New Era and the Global Sustainable Development, February 4, 2022. http://en.kremlin.ru/supplement/5770

References

Ageeva, V. D. "The Rise and Fall of Russia's Soft Power", Russia in Global Affairs, No. 1, 2021. https://eng.globalaffairs.ru/articles/rise-fall-russias-soft-power/
Bordachev, T. "Bipolarnoe Rasstroistvo", 2020. https://profile.ru/columnist/bipolyarnoe-rasstrojstvo-271423/
Bordachev, T. "Origins and Challenges of Putin's Conservative Strategy", 2021. https://valdaiclub.com/a/highlights/origins-and-challenges-of-putin-s-conservative-str/
Coalson, R. "How a Famous Soviet Dissident Foreshadowed Putin's Plan-in 1990", The Atlantic, 2014. https://www.theatlantic.com/international/archive/2014/09/how-a-famous-soviet-dissident-foreshadowed-putins-planin-1990-russia-ukraine/379467/
Joint Declaration on EU-NATO Cooperation, 2023. https://www.nato.int/nato_static_fl2014/assets/pdf/2023/1/pdf/230110-eu-nato-joint-declaration.pdf
"Joint Statement of the Russian Federation and the People's Republic of China on the International Relations Entering a New Era and the Global Sustainable Development", 2022, http://en.kremlin.ru/supplement/5770
Kortunov, A. "Covid-19 Presents Both Opportunities and Threats to Russia's Foreign Policy", 2020. https://russiancouncil.ru/en/analytics-and-comments/analytics/covid-19-presents-both-opportunities-and-threats-to-russia-s-foreign-policy/

RFE/RL's Tajik Service, RFE/RL's Kyrgyz Service, RFE/RL's Kazakh Service. Leaders of Russia, "China-Led Security Blocs Meet to Discuss Afghanistan", 2021. https://www.rferl.org/a/sco-csto-afghanistan-taliban/31462890.html

Isaev, L. and Zaharov, A. (2020), Vliyanie Pandemii Covıd-19 na politiku Rossii na Blizhnem Vostoke i v Sirii, Geneva Centre for Security Policy, Haziran, 2020. https://www.hse.ru/mirror/pubs/share/416767943.pdf

Medvedev, D. "Nashi Lyudi, Nasha Zemlya, Nasha Pravda", Rossiiskaya Gazeta, 2022. https://rg.ru/2022/12/25/nashi-liudi-nasha-zemlia-nasha-pravda.html

Munich Security Brief, "Unity in a Time of Upheaval", 2022, s.4. https://securityconference.org/assets/01_Bilder_Inhalte/03_Medien/02_Publikationen/2022/MSB_Readout_UnityinaTimeofUpheaval_MSC22.pdf

"Meeting of the Valdai International Discussion Club", 2013. http://en.kremlin.ru/events/president/news/19243

"Novogodnee obreshenie k grazhdanam Rossii", 2022. http://kremlin.ru/events/president/news/70315

Polyakov, L. "Concervatism in Russia: Political Tool or Historical Choice?", Russie.Nei. Visions No.90, 2015, p. 4. https://www.ifri.org/sites/default/files/atoms/files/ifri_rnv_90_eng_poliakkov_protege.pdf

Putin, V. "75 let Velikoy Pobedı: Obshaya Otvestvennost Pered İstoriey i Budushim", RG, 2020a. https://rg.ru/2020/06/19/75-let-velikoj-pobedy-obshchaia-otvetstvennost-pered-istoriej-i-budushchim.html

Putin, V. "The Real Lessons of the 75th Anniversary of World War II, National Interest", 2020b. https://nationalinterest.org/feature/vladimir-putin-real-lessons-75th-anniversary-world-war-ii-162982?page=0%2C5

Karaganov, S. and Suslov, D. (2020), "Rossia v Mire Posle Koronovirusa: Novıe idei dlya Vnreshnei Politiki, Rossiya v Globalnoi Politike", No. 3, 2020. https://globalaffairs.ru/articles/rossiya-mir-koronavirus-idei/#_ftn1

Trenin, D. "How Russia Can Maintain Equilibrium in the Post Pandemic Bipolar World", 2020. https://carnegiemoscow.org/commentary/81702

Ukaz Prezidenta Rossiiskoi Federatsii Ob Utverzhdenii Osnob Gosuderstvennoi Politiki po Sohraneniu i Ukrepleniu Traditsionnıh Rossiiskih Duhovno-Nravstvennih Tsennostei, Moskova, Kremlin, November 9, 2022. http://static.kremlin.ru/media/events/files/ru/qcDRpNRKdqbKAX8mD0TP9z02hAhAJAT4.pdf

16 South Caucasus and COVID-19

Vulnerabilities, Setbacks, Responses

F. Didem Ekinci

Introduction

Pandemics have taken their toll on the world since at least the Plague of Athens in the fifth century B.C. (Gugushvili and McKee, 2021; History.com, 2019; Piret and Boivin, 2021). Their impact can be more severe on certain regions, such as the post-Soviet geographies, which still struggle with long-standing inadequacies. The situation in the South Caucasus since the outbreak of the COVID-19 pandemic is a case in point. Although the worst phases of the pandemic have been left behind, the chances for a desirable human security environment to emerge in the region remain quite dim due to the lingering setbacks and vulnerabilities. Indeed, the pandemic exacerbated vulnerabilities in the region, reflecting the need to provide human security, wherein people can be free of wants and where they can find themselves in an environment free from all sorts of threats, as Booth (1991) argues. The necessity to explore the regional background, current conditions, and the responses throughout the pandemic is obvious. Accordingly, an inquiry into the Armenia, Azerbaijan, and Georgia cases is in order.

Vulnerabilities and Setbacks at a Glance: Before the Pandemic

The COVID-19 pandemic has spotlighted several common vulnerabilities and setbacks peculiar to the post-Soviet South Caucasus. Since the foremost challenge has to do with the pandemic itself, the weak health capacity in the region inherited from the Soviet era should be discussed first. Second, the already troubled economic conditions of the actors – perhaps except Azerbaijan – suggested further deterioration with the pandemic outbreak. On a side note, false narratives about the virus and criticism of authoritarianism also meant more problems to deal with. As substantial determinants of the pandemic, these all unfolded in their own way, imprinting on the region's states and people throughout the ordeal.

First, it must be pointed out that the most important factor, weak health systems in the region, dates back to the Soviet era. This issue substantially shaped the course of the pandemic, making it necessary to discuss the system's peculiarities.

Following the Bolshevik Revolution, Moscow established a centralised (Kilani, 2021) and integrated healthcare system, known as the Semashko system, named

DOI: 10.4324/9781003377597-18

after Nikolai Semashko, the Soviet Union's first People's Commissar of Public Health. The Soviet Constitution (1936) ensured all citizens were entitled to free medical care. By the mid-1950s, the system had remarkably improved but deteriorated in the 1970s due to insufficient funding from the central government (Hohmann and Lefevre, 2014; Kazatchkine, 2017). Although medical service was supposedly egalitarian, it was divided into socio-economic clusters (Hohmann and Lefevre, 2014), which meant, for instance, nomenklatura and employees of priority industries (Shishkin, 2017); also, some regions such as the Far North and Siberia received different treatment (Hohmann and Lefevre, 2014). The economic crisis in the late 1980s and 1990s deteriorated the healthcare systems, and the World Bank counselled fee-for-service payments to South Caucasian states (Hohmann and Lefevre, 2014).

While reforms introduced in the 1990s in Armenia formalised fee-for-service payments, others introduced in the early 2000s were mainly about maternal and child health (Hohmann and Lefevre, 2014). Despite the reforms, the healthcare system in Armenia remains incapable of meeting basic healthcare needs due to "misdistribution of infrastructure and human resources, weak government oversight, socio-economic imbalance, and low public financing" and the country "… for the last three decades … suffered from lack of vision, inchoate strategic planning, poor quality, … corruption and nepotism" (Shekerdimian, 2021). Quantitative improvements concerning medical equipment, medical personnel, and access to healthcare are not likely to automatically solve all of the problems, and it has been suggested that quality healthcare services should be provided (Shekerdimian, 2021).

Similarly, in Soviet Azerbaijan, the problems concerning health services were an inefficient health sector, state monopoly, financing based on a quantitative emphasis on the number of beds, prioritisation of hospitals rather than primary healthcare for financing, and a Soviet-style vertical organisation that prioritised cities (World Health Organization, 1996). The post-1991 healthcare system, which started as a quite centralised system, degenerated immensely due to a lack of funding, managerial capacity, interruption of the Soviet health network and supplies, and inadequate population coverage (World Health Organization, 1996). Hohmann and Lefevre (2014) state that after 1991, large oil companies introduced their health systems for their personnel, which had their roots in the Soviet system, and private healthcare was legalised in 2001 (2014). While some decentralisation took place in healthcare policies, governmental decisions ultimately shape the system. The free-of-charge universal health coverage was introduced in April 2021 (Rehimov, 2021), and its impact remains to be seen.

In Soviet Georgia, the central government managed the healthcare system, as in the cases of Armenia and Azerbaijan. By 1995, Georgia introduced compulsory public health insurance and a co-payment system for important medicines, which formalised payment by both the state and the patient. However, both the production and distribution of medication were privatised in 1996. Optional private health insurance schemes were introduced later (Hohmann and Lefevre, 2014). Most primary healthcare services continued to exist in the provincial areas as a remnant of the Soviet period (Hohmann and Lefevre, 2014). The Rose Revolution brought about significant changes in the health sector. Almost all hospitals were privatised, many primary healthcare facilities were shut down, and a new insurance programme for the poor was implemented. The programme worked based on taxes and was managed by private insurance companies (Hohmann and Lefevre, 2014). Citizens covered by the programme were entitled to receive complete health services without paying out of pocket; however, most medications were not covered (Hohmann and Lefevre, 2014). By 2013, the new government targeted universal health coverage (Richardson and Berdzuli, 2017). In 2015, the "Government of Georgia adopted Decree N724 'Georgian Healthcare System State Concept 2014-2020' ... The Concept defines state policy in the field of healthcare for the following years, which is directed to increase the population's life expectancy, reduce maternal and child mortality, improve health status and quality of life" (UN Human Rights Office of the High Commissioner, n.d.).

Second, the economy matters. Although the three states became independent after 1991, their development indicators in the immediate aftermath of independence were quite dim since the Soviet Union's development indicators had been faltering for quite a long time. Except for resource-rich Azerbaijan, the other two states had to struggle after independence. Table 16.1 shows the overall development indicators concerning the three actors from 1990 until 2021.

The above account allows one to assert that multiple weaknesses in healthcare infrastructures and the economic picture inherited from the Soviet era reflect continuity rather than a grassroots change for the better at present, perhaps except for Azerbaijan. In particular, the immediate aftermath of the Cold War in the region saw more, and not less, predicaments. The outbreak of the pandemic exacerbated grievances, leaving its imprint on the three states. How it unfolded and put the regional actors to the test after the first reported case requires analysis.

Vulnerabilities and Setbacks at a Glance: During and After the Pandemic

Armenia

Although the first case in Armenia was confirmed on March 1, 2020 (Sargsyan, 2020), the government had already taken steps to form a task force to prevent the virus from spreading, suspended the visa-free regime with China, and closed the Armenian-Iranian border because Iran already had a high number of cases. The first case in Armenia was a person who arrived from Tehran (Sargsyan, 2020). Armenia declared a state of emergency and a lockdown on March 16, 2020, before Azerbaijan and Georgia did so (Grigoryan, 2020; Sammut, 2020), and started bringing Armenian citizens back from states in lockdown (Avedissian, 2020). The constitutional referendum scheduled on April 5 was postponed (Aliyev, 2020). Online education began, and state employees began working from home. Travel between Armenia and Georgia was banned (Avedissian, 2020). Strict amendments were introduced in case of a breach of the lockdown (Grigoryan, 2020). However, since the public practices were lax, the number of cases was the highest in the

Table 16.1 Country profiles of Armenia, Azerbaijan, and Georgia

Country Profile	Armenia				Azerbaijan				Georgia			
	1990	2000	2010	2020	1990	2000	2010	2020	1990	2000	2010	2020
World view												
Population, total (millions)	3.54	3.07	2.88	2.96	7.18	8.05	9.05	10.09	4.8	4.08	3.79	3.72
Population growth (annual %)	0	−0.6	−0.4	0.2	0.7	0.8	1.2	0.7	0	−1.9	−0.7	0.1
Poverty headcount ratio at national poverty lines (% of the population)	—	—	—	27	—	49.6	9.1	—	—	—	37.3	21.3
Poverty headcount ratio at $1.90 a day (2011 PPP) (% of the population)	—	14.4	1	0.4	—	2.6	—	—	—	19.2	12	4.2
GNI, Atlas method (current US$) (billions)	1.06	2.03	9.99	12.52	0.83	5.11	49	45.21	3.67	3.22	12.14	15.86
GNI per capita, Atlas method (current US$)	310	660	3,470	4,220	110	630	5,410	4,480	750	790	3,210	4,260
GNI, PPP (current international $) (billions)	9.44	8.4	22.67	38.83	24.19	26.73	124.95	145.21	12.55	12.8	28.14	52.28
GNI per capita, PPP (current international $)	2,670	2,740	7,880	13,100	3,230	3,320	13,800	14,390	2,580	3,140	7,430	14,040
People												
Income share held by the lowest 20%	—	7.7	9.1	10.2	—	7.4	—	—	—	5.4	5.7	7
Life expectancy at birth, total (years)	68	71	73	75	65	67	71	73	70	70	71	74
Births attended by skilled health staff (% of total)	100	97	100	—	97	81	99	99	97	96	100	99
Mortality rate, under 5 (per 1,000 live births)	49	31	18	11	95	74	37	19	48	37	14	9
Economy												
GDP (current US$) (billions)	2.26	1.91	9.26	12.64	8.86	5.27	52.91	42.69	7.75	3.06	12.24	15.84
GDP growth (annual %)	−11.7	5.9	2.2	−7.4	−0.7	11.1	5	−4.3	−14.8	1.8	6.2	−6.8
Inflation, GDP deflator (annual %)	79.4	−1.4	7.8	2	83.5	12.5	13.5	−7.4	22.2	4.7	14.2	7.3
Agriculture, forestry, and fishing, value added (% of GDP)	—	—	18	11	27	16	6	7	30	21	8	7
Industry (including construction), value added (% of GDP)	—	—	28	27	30	43	60	42	31	21	17	21

(Continued)

Table 16.1 (Continued)

Country Profile	Armenia				Azerbaijan				Georgia			
	1990	2000	2010	2020	1990	2000	2010	2020	1990	2000	2010	2020
Exports of goods and services (% of GDP)	35	22	20	30	44	40	54	36	40	23	33	37
Imports of goods and services (% of GDP)	46	50	45	40	39	38	21	36	45	40	50	57
Gross capital formation (% of GDP)	47	22	39	19	27	21	18	24	31	27	21	24
Revenue, excluding grants (% of GDP)	–	–	22.6	24.1	–	17.6	46.8	42.8	–	14.3	23.1	24.9
States and markets												
Tax revenue (% of GDP)	–	–	17.1	21.9	–	12.7	12.2	14.2	–	11.4	21.4	21.4
Global links												
Total debt service (% of exports of goods, services, and primary income)	1.2	8.7	29.7	34.9	–	6.4	1.4	10.8	–	12.7	17.5	35.3
Personal remittances, received (current US$) (millions)	–	182	1,669	1,327	–	57	1,410	1,403	–	206	1,184	2,110
Foreign direct investment, net inflows (BoP, current US$) (millions)	2	104	529	47	0	130	3,353	507	0	131	921	534
Net official development assistance received (current US$) (millions)	2.7	215.9	320.3	105.6	0.3	140.6	156.5	121.3	0.2	171.9	588.9	1,040.90
Source: World Development Indicators database												

Source: Data extracted from the World Bank's (2021a, 2021b, 2021c) website
Armenia country profile, https://databank.worldbank.org/views/reports/reportwidget.aspx?Report_Name=CountryProfile&Id=b450fd57&tbar=y&dd=y&inf=n&zm=n&country=ARM;
Azerbaijan country profile, https://databank.worldbank.org/views/reports/reportwidget.aspx?Report_Name=CountryProfile&Id=b450fd57&tbar=y&dd=y&inf=n&zm=n&country=AZE;
Georgia country profile, https://databank.worldbank.org/views/reports/reportwidget.aspx?Report_Name=CountryProfile&Id=b450fd57&tbar=y&dd=y&inf=n&zm=n&country=GEO (all accessed on July 12, 2022)

initial phases in the region (Avedissian, 2020). This resulted in the extension of the lockdown until March 13, 2020 (Meister, 2020). There were also allegations that some citizens did not report their symptoms (Stronski, 2020). Reportedly, Armenia had the highest number of cases (3,500+) as of May 2020 in the South Caucasus (Grigoryan, 2020), but its hospital bed capacity was only between 3,000 and 4,000. The number of cases started dropping in August 2020 (Avedissian, 2020).

The situation led to criticism of the measures, emanating from the fear of the unknown. As Gramada and Done (2020) maintain, civil society grew concerned about media restrictions and the implementation of reforms. The regional civil society denounced campaigns sharing fake news, conspiracy theories about the virus, and/or supporting authoritarian state decisions. As Grigoryan (2020) explains, the strict measures caused some NGOs and other organizations associated with former President Robert Kocharyan and the son-in-law of former President Serzh Sargsyan, Mikayel Minasyan, as well as other media outlets to target Prime Minister Nikol Pashinyan and his aides. Allegations ranged from the government's mismanagement of the pandemic and the vaccination process to doubts regarding the actual number of cases and casualties, as well as rumours that speculated Pashinyan would give concessions on the Karabakh issue (Grigoryan, 2020).

A closer look reveals that such an atmosphere was already ripe for misinformation and disinformation regarding the contagion. To start with, although tackling such a pandemic should have been the business of medical personnel and state authorities, public discourse reflected narratives on traditional treatment methods, allegations that the virus spread from bananas, that the reason why the officials mandated masks was to profit from their sale, or that the pandemic was a plot to implant chips in humans for controlling them (Papyan, 2021). It was also asserted that the COVID-19 vaccination was a plot of the World Health Organization (WHO), Bill Gates, and the Global Alliance for Vaccines/and Immunization (GAVI) to reduce Armenia's population. Narratives claiming American bio-laboratories existed in former Soviet states were also circulating (Papyan, 2021). However, when the 44-day war shifted the attention to security issues between September and November 2020, observation of the hygiene rules became less important (Papyan, 2021) and the war became the top concern.

Interestingly, though Iranians went to Armenia to get the first shot because it was not available in Iran, Armenia's vaccination rates remained rather low (3%) by July 2021. Moreover, although Armenia was offered Pfizer vaccines, it rejected the offer since it lacked the necessary cold storage infrastructure (Lehmann, 2021). In addition, the public grew suspicious of the AstraZeneca vaccine following the death of a nurse in Georgia after receiving that vaccine.

To add to the predicament, the outbreak of war in Karabakh caused the relocation of its residents to Armenia, which overwhelmed the flawed healthcare system. Many people were put into crowded basements, and some infected medical personnel continued to work in the capital of Karabakh due to a shortage of staff (Balalian et al., 2021). The number of cases increased sevenfold in the weekly average of new cases daily at the beginning of the war, which exceeded Armenia's bed and oxygen supply capacity (Balalian et al., 2021).

By the end of the war, the government reported more than 2,900 casualties due to the conflict and stated that the number of cases by November 28, 2020, had increased by 172%, amounting to 85,194. This placed Armenia 10th in the global rankings of cases per million people (Markosian et al., 2022). People living close to borders were at higher risk due to limited medical services (Markosian et al., 2021).

The economic toll of the pandemic on Armenia reflects regress, efforts of internal improvement, and external assistance. Armenia's economy deteriorated in 2020 due to the compound effect of the pandemic and the war, leading to a 7.4% fall in GDP, but it had begun to recover by 4.4% as of January 2021. Foreign finance was received from the IMF as a Eurobond worth $750 million. Armenia continued anti-corruption reforms in 2021 (EBRD, 2021). Depreciation followed as of November 2020, but the exchange rate stabilised by early 2021. Inflation rose from 1.2% to 8.9% in September 2021. The external sector remained relatively stable due to remittances and external actors' transfers in the first half of 2021. After a 3.3% decrease in the first quarter of 2021, the economy presented a relative 5% growth in the first half of the same year. Yet, overall, the low vaccination rates and geopolitical risks still showed a bleak picture (EBRD, 2021).

Regarding aid, Armenia introduced packages worth up to 12.3 billion drams for businesses and families. The farming sector and those who lost their jobs were provided financial assistance. The EU provided 92 million euros to assist Armenia in obtaining medical equipment and support its business sector. However, tourism and copper prices declined due to the closure of borders with Georgia and Iran (Aliyev, 2020). In tandem with the pandemic period strategies, in 2020, assistance was given to sectors such as tourism and agriculture, as well as the private sector, to the small and medium-sized enterprises (SMEs) in the form of subsidised loans, grants, and social assistance programmes (EBRD, 2021). Armenia also introduced a centralised register of citizens' bank accounts (EBRD, 2021).

It is estimated that restrictions in Armenia caused half of the slowdown in growth and regress in the entertainment and hospitality sectors (UNDP, 2021). Amid dim prospects, the United Nations Development Programme (UNDP) (2021) stated, "Cutting back on spending, widening the tax base, minimizing tax avoidance; an examination of loss-making state-controlled assets" would be required for a strong fiscal structure. Last but not least, the recent imbroglio in Ukraine is less likely to debilitate Armenia's economy since the regress in the Russian economy due to the war in Ukraine implies a drop in remittances coming from Russia (Polláková, 2020).

Azerbaijan

The first case in Azerbaijan was reported on February 28, 2020. This caused public criticism that the state was late closing its borders with Iran (Avedissian, 2020). Following violations of lockdown measures (as of March 24), Azerbaijan introduced stricter measures in April 2020 (Aliyev, 2020; Stronski, 2020). Large gatherings were cancelled. The authorities repatriated citizens from abroad (Aliyev, 2020). Mobile tracking began. These precautions enabled the state to hospitalise everyone who tested positive, and the number of cases and casualties decreased for a certain period. Azerbaijan closed schools and universities as soon as the WHO declared the COVID-19 pandemic (on March 11, 2020). Due to its partnership with Microsoft, Azerbaijan swiftly switched to online education (Valiyev and Valehli, 2021).

However, the pandemic hit the health sector because the latter began just when the government was about to move to compulsory health insurance and leave behind the remnants of the Soviet system. Thirty-five hospitals in the country were arranged to provide treatment for COVID-19. The state allocated $57 million to the State Agency for Compulsory Medical Insurance to supply medical equipment (Valiyev and Valehli, 2021). Although the number of cases was higher than in Armenia and Georgia, the number of recoveries was also higher, but the number of casualties was lower in Azerbaijan. Likewise, almost 50% of the population received two vaccines as of July 2022 (Our World in Data, 2022). In this respect, the country was leading in the South Caucasus. Had the vaccination rate reflected lower figures, Azerbaijan could have faced a double crisis of an unseen magnitude due to its higher population, whose recovery would have implied a longer period than estimated amid the war conditions.

A striking observation concerning the country was the previous excessive confidence in the sustainability of gas and oil sales and their prices (Giragosian, 2020). Although the 30% fall in April 2020 in global oil demand caused concern in Baku, Ivana Duerte, the European Bank for Reconstruction and Development (EBRD) head of the mission in Azerbaijan, stated that "after the 2014 economic crisis, the economy was growing at a moderate pace, the exchange rate in real terms barely changed and authorities embarked on improving the business environment and diversifying to non-oil sectors" (Bagirova and Antidze, 2020). Still, to what extent this statement mitigated worries amid the contagion is debatable because, on the negative side, the lockdown increased unemployment, and cuts in income, with the daily losses amounting to 120–150 million manats. To help mitigate the impact of the economic downturn, Azerbaijan introduced a support package for unemployed people and SMEs, issued state guarantees for bank deposits, and produced a bail-out package worth 2.5 million manats. The tax code was amended to assist the enterprises most affected by the pandemic. Likewise, value added tax (VAT) was exempted from food and medical security goods and services; the government gave $5 million to the COVID-19 fund and received medical aid from Türkiye and China (Abaslı, 2020).

The pressing economic issues included too much dependence on hydrocarbons, declining oil production and prices, and the country's not-so-robust banking and finance systems (Abaslı, 2020). Regarding external aid, Azerbaijan received support from the EU, US, China, and Russia and sent aid worth 5 million manats to Iran and medical assistance to China in April 2020 (Alili, 2020). In 2021, the EBRD report on Azerbaijan stated that economic recovery could be facilitated through non-hydrocarbon and hydrocarbon sectors and that a new vision for a development named "Azerbaijan 2030" had been formulated. The same report also introduced a digitalisation and finance-related COVID-19 response package (EBRD, 2021).

Last, mutual criticism from the public and the government was also present. The authorities' responses included an accusation that opponents were the fifth column, which led to their detention due to the spreading of negative information. Some opponents were blocked on social media. The critics ultimately claimed that the state used lockdowns to crack down on opponents (Polláková, 2020; Samadov, 2020).

Georgia

The first case in Georgia was confirmed on February 26, 2020, after which education switched to online platforms, transportation was suspended, and foreigners' entry was restricted. A state of emergency was announced on March 21, 2020, and curfews began. Before the pandemic, the government and the opposition had been facing off in the political arena, but with the COVID-19 outbreak, both sides prioritised the importance of health measures (Meister, 2020). After the initial accusations accusing the government of not imposing strict measures and intentionally importing the virus, criticism that was meant to gain points with the public, on April 3, 2020, many opposition parties supported the government's decision to get external financial assistance (Anjaparidze, 2020). The state of emergency was criticised by civil society groups, and restrictions strengthened the conservatism of the ruling elite (Gamkrelidze, 2021).

In fact, in these initial phases, Georgia was likened to the Netherlands in terms of its success in keeping the number of cases low (Hauer, 2020). However, the Church did not obey the distancing measures at the outset (Meister, 2020) and was criticised (Aliyev, 2020) for holding Easter services (Stronski, 2020). Reportedly, most cases emanated from places where anti-lockdown protests took place (Avedissian, 2020).

Georgia was relatively successful in keeping the number of cases, casualties, and spread level low in the early phases (Gamkrelidze, 2021) due to the issuance of necessary preventative information to the public (Stronski, 2020). Contact with infected people was tracked, and those who travelled abroad were required to quarantine for two weeks upon arrival. Mass testing was impossible due to a lack of resources (Gamkrelidze, 2021).

The UK donated personal protective equipment, Germany sent RNA extraction kits, Slovenia allocated funds worth 44,198 euros, and China sent humanitarian aid (Aliyev, 2020). In early 2021, the Parliament amended the Law on Public Health, making the state responsible for any harm resulting from imported vaccines (Avetisyan et al., 2021). As in Armenia, false narratives about the vaccines emerged, claiming that they would cause autism or harm children's health in the future. In March 2021, the Ministry of Health tried to counter this disinformation and hesitation among medical personnel and the elderly to persuade them to get the vaccine (Avetisyan et al., 2021). In general, the main factors that hampered rapid and sufficient vaccination in Georgia can be listed as hesitation due to false narratives, the death of a nurse after getting the AstraZeneca vaccine, and the insufficient number of vaccines.

In July 2021, the government eased mask requirements and lifted the curfew, but the number of cases was higher than in the other two states, and the vaccination rate was only around 3.9% (Lehmann, 2021). As of August 2022, the completed vaccination rate was slightly above 34% (Vaccination rate in Georgia, 2022).

The economic and financial regress in the country urgently called for new policies. Thus, an anti-crisis economic plan was announced by Prime Minister Giorgi Gakharia on April 24, 2020, to assist the tourism sector, particularly. A financial aid package was formulated to support the economy, the health sector, the poorest, and those who lost their jobs (Eradze, 2020). As a state dependent on foreign goods, foreign capital, and foreign currency, Georgia had also been wrestling with a 42% trade deficit when the pandemic started. The fact that 90% of external debt in Georgia is denominated by foreign currency necessitated a new strategy (Eradze, 2020). Amid this imbroglio, the most affected sectors were, again, tourism, entertainment, food services, and transportation. (Aliyev, 2020). Moreover, Georgia lost revenue as an energy transit country (Giragosian, 2020) due to the fall in the demand for energy resources.

According to the EBRD's 2021 assessment, slow but new economic momentum and lingering risks, such as a low vaccination rate, co-existed in Georgia. In addition, unresolved business sector vulnerabilities are among the issues addressed. To this end, a 10-year socio-economic development vision has been formulated. In line with these concerns, boosting governing standards, advancing education, and state-owned enterprise reform is important, while the GDP is forecast to accelerate to 5.5% in 2022 (EBRD, 2021).

Conclusion and Recommendations

The pandemic took its toll on the entire world. The South Caucasus was also tested, laying bare chronic impediments, inadequacies, and weaknesses in healthcare and the economy – all inherited from the Soviet era. Such common background conditions in Armenia, Azerbaijan, and Georgia showcased approximately similar – if not identical – vulnerabilities, setbacks, and responses to the pandemic.

From a human security perspective, the inadequate healthcare and economic infrastructures, financial regress, and lingering geopolitical issues meant that chances for a swift and robust recovery would remain low. This was because the responses were too varied and multifold to be managed once and for all, including traditional security measures such as border closures, declarations of a state of emergency, closures of schools and universities, switching to online education, repatriation of citizens, travel bans, the introduction of fines for violations of measures, mobile tracking, false narratives and conspiracy theories about the virus, reactions from opponent factions, media censures, anti-vaccination propaganda, an accusation of the governments for ineptness, detention of opponents, lack of accurate statistics on the number of cases, lax practices such as refusal to wear masks and participation in large gatherings, and the accusation of governments for authoritarianism.

Therefore, how the vulnerabilities, setbacks, and responses unfolded seems to point to an unstable human security environment in the short term. However, the worst-case scenarios have been left behind in the region. This situation prompts certain recommendations from a human security perspective.

First, the pandemic in the South Caucasus attests to the fact that new international assistance rules and practices need to be developed to mitigate and eradicate the economic and financial weakness in conflict-bound post-Soviet geographies during pandemics and/or other disasters. Novel international frameworks with a robust legal basis should be devised swiftly to alleviate the plight of people in this region as soon as possible. The unsystematic delivery of external assistance in crises, based on goodwill, may continue to confine these actors within legal and practical barriers in the future, resulting in only a temporary impact. In this endeavour, the primary actor in charge should be the UN.

Second, and related to the first, the pandemic lays bare the urgent need for more multilateralism since the capacities of the actors in question regarding healthcare, economic, and political capacity require improvement. This prevents these actors from taking steps and mobilising popular action. Above all, such multilateralism should make a difference in emergencies, such as pandemics, based on a new set of global rules.

Third, the pandemic functioned as a stimulus that put into perspective the critical importance of digitalisation. It made the need for efficient digitalisation crystal clear when lockdowns began. Provision of and access to accurate statistics, sharing them with the public, and digitalising public services can reinforce the governance capacities of states and ultimately provide good leadership. The impossibility of good decision-making in the absence of required data is obvious. Among all other needs, the need for South Caucasian states to go "more digital" was never more vital than during the pandemic period. Since access to accurate data in governance structures is critical in emergencies such as the COVID-19 pandemic, the region needs assistance for capacity development in this sector. That, again, implies multilateral effort. In the final analysis, the need to reconfigure the regional order in the post-pandemic world, based on the understanding of security three years after the outbreak, dictates a powerful response based on these concerns. Whether the region, aided by the external actors, will succeed in achieving this remains to be seen.

References

Abaslı, I. (2020) 'The socio-economic impact of COVID-19 and oil price fluctuations in Azerbaijan'. Available at: https://ge.boell.org/en/2020/09/15/socioeconomic-impact-covid-19-and-oil-price-fluctuations-azerbaijan (Accessed: June 7, 2022).

Alili, A. (2020) 'Analysis: Covid-19 is an important test for Azerbaijani unity'. Available at: https://www.commonspace.eu/analysis/analysis-covid-19-important-test-azerbaijani-unity (Accessed: July 19, 2022).

Aliyev, V. (2020) 'Covid-19 and the South Caucasus'. Available at: https://www.academia.edu/43107739/Covid_19_and_the_South_Caucasus (Accessed: May 20, 2022).

Anjaparidze, Z. (2020) 'The political implications of COVID-19 in Georgia'. Available at: https://jamestown.org/program/the-political-implications-of-covid-19-in-georgia/ (Accessed: May 30, 2022).

Avedissian, K. (2020) 'Understanding the region: COVID-19 response in the South Caucasus'. Available at: https://evnreport.com/understanding-the-region/understanding-the-region-covid-19-response-in-the-south-caucasus/ (Accessed: May 3, 2022).

Avetisyan, A, Gıyasbaylı, H, & Kincha, S. (2021) 'Global perspectives on Covid-19 vaccination - Covid-19 vaccine access in the South Caucasus countries: Armenia, Azerbaijan and Georgia'. Available at: https://eu.boell.org/en/covid-19-vaccines-south-caucasus (Accessed: June 30, 2022).

Bagirova, N, & Antidze, M. (2020) 'Coronavirus, low oil prices to hit Azeri economy'. Available at: https://www.reuters.com/article/health-coronavirus-azerbaijan-economy-idUSL8N2BV2PI (Accessed: June 7, 2022).

Balalian, A. A., Berberian, A., & Chiloyan, A. et al. (2021) 'War in Nagorno-Karabakh highlights the vulnerability of displaced populations to COVID-19', *Journal of Epidemiology and Community Health*, 75(7), pp. 605–607.

Booth, K. (1991) 'Security and emancipation', *Review of International Studies*, 17(4), pp. 313–326.

EBRD (European Bank for Reconstruction and Development) (2021) Transition report 2021-22 system upgrade: delivering the digital dividend. Available at: https://www.ebrd.com/publications/transition-report-202122-eastern-europe-and-the-caucasus (Accessed: May 2, 2022).

Eradze, I. (2020) 'Corona pandemic as an amplifier of socio-economic crises in Georgia', *Caucasus Analytical Digest*, 115, pp. 3–7. Available at: https://css.ethz.ch/content/dam/ethz/special-interest/gess/cis/center-for-securities-studies/pdfs/CAD115.pdf (Accessed: June 30, 2022).

Gamkrelidze, T. (2021) 'COVID-19 in Georgia: State emergency as political non-law and its impact on pluralism', *Democracy and Security*, pp. 1–23. doi: https://doi.org/10.1080/17419166.2021.1972288 (Accessed: June 12, 2022).

Giragosian, R. (2020) 'Bracing for impact - shifting geopolitics in the South Caucasus'. Available at: https://neweasterneurope.eu/2020/07/07/bracing-for-impact-shifting-geopolitics-in-the-south-caucasus/ (Accessed: July 20, 2022).

Gramada, A, & Done, C. G. (2020) 'The civil society's response to the coronavirus pandemic in the Central-South-Eastern Europe and the Caucasus'. Available at: https://www.esga.ro/wp-content/uploads/2020/10/Policy-Brief-Desinformation-2.pdf (Accessed: May 5, 2022).

Grigoryan, A. (2020) 'Armenia: Difficult choice ahead as socio-economic risks loom', *Caucasus Analytical Digest*, 115, pp. 7–11. Available at: https://css.ethz.ch/content/dam/ethz/special-interest/gess/cis/center-for-securities-studies/pdfs/CAD115.pdf (Accessed: June 30, 2022).

Gugushvili, A., & McKee, M. (2021) 'The COVID-19 pandemic and war', *Scandinavian Journal of Public Health*, 50(1), pp. 1–3. Available at https://www.researchgate.net/publication/349497490_The_COVID-19_pandemic_and_war (Accessed: May 6, 2022).

Hauer, N. (2020) 'A deceptive dream? Georgian government hopes early coronavirus success results in ballot box success'. Available at: https://www.rferl.org/a/a-deceptive-dream-georgian-government-hopes-early-coronavirus-success-results-in-ballot-box-success/30579803.html (Accessed: July 24, 2022).

History.com (2019) 'Pandemics that changed history'. Available at: https://www.history.com/topics/middle-ages/pandemics-timeline (Accessed: May 6, 2022).

Hohmann, S., & Lefevre, C. (2014) 'Post-Soviet transformations of health systems in the South Caucasus', *Central Asian Affairs*, 1, pp. 48–70.

Kazatchkine, M. (2017) 'Health in the Soviet Union and in the post-soviet space: From utopia to collapse and arduous recovery', *The Lancet*, 390, pp. 1611–1612. Available at: https://www.thelancet.com/journals/lancet/article/PIIS0140-6736(17)32383-8/fulltext (Accessed: May 8, 2022).

Kilani, A. (2021) 'An interpretation of reported COVID-19 cases in post-Soviet states', *Journal of Public Health*, 43(2), pp. 409–410. Available at: https://www.researchgate.net/publication/350719394_An_interpretation_of_reported_COVID-19_cases_in_post-Soviet_states (Accessed: May 10, 2022).

Lehmann, D. (2021) 'South Caucasus COVID-19 update'. Available at: https://www.caspianpolicy.org/research/energy-and-economy-program-eep/south-caucasus-covid-19-update-13139 (Accessed: May 3, 2022).

Markosian, C., Khachadourian, V., & Kennedy, C. A. (2021) 'Frozen conflict in the midst of a global pandemic: Potential impact on mental health in Armenian border communities', *Social Psychiatry and Psychiatric Epidemiology*, 56, pp. 513–517.

Markosian, C., Layne, C. M., & Petrosyan, V. et al. (2022) 'War in the COVID-19 era: Mental health concerns in Armenia and Nagorno-Karabakh', *International Journal of Social Psychiatry*, 68(3), pp. 481–483.

Meister, S. (2020) 'Covid-19 in the South Caucasus – fast reactions and authoritarian reflexes'. Available at: https://ge.boell.org/en/2020/04/07/covid-19-south-caucasus-fast-reactions-and-authoritarian-reflexes (Accessed: May 2, 2022).

Our World in Data (2022) Coronavirus (COVID-19) vaccinations. Available at: https://ourworldindata.org/covid-vaccinations?country=OWID_WRL (Accessed: July 20, 2022).

Papyan, A. (2021) 'The COVID-19 infodemic'. Available at: https://freedomhouse.org/sites/default/files/2021-06/Disinformation-in-Armenia_En-v3.pdfpp (Accessed: May 3, 2022).

Piret, J., & Boivin, G. (2021) 'Pandemics throughout history', *Front. Microbiol.* Available at: https://www.frontiersin.org/articles/10.3389/fmicb.2020.631736/full (Accessed: May 6, 2022).

Polláková, L. (2020) 'South Caucasus states set to diverge further due to COVID-19'. Available at: https://www.chathamhouse.org/2020/06/south-caucasus-states-set-diverge-further-due-covid-19 (Accessed: July 12, 2022).

Rehimov, R. (2021) 'Azerbaijan starts universal health coverage'. Available at: https://www.aa.com.tr/en/health/azerbaijan-starts-universal-health-coverage-/2195287 (Accessed: May 14, 2022).

Richardson, E., & Berdzuli, N. (2017) 'Georgia: Health system review – Health systems in transition', *The European Observatory on Health Systems and Policies* 19(4), pp. 1–90. Available at: https://apps.who.int/iris/bitstream/handle/10665/330206/HiT-19-4-2017-eng.pdf?sequence=7&isAllowed=y (Accessed: May 14, 2022).

Samadov, B. (2020) 'Azerbaijan – COVID-19 and a divided opposition', *Caucasus Analytical Digest*, 115, pp. 12–15. Available at: https://css.ethz.ch/content/dam/ethz/special-interest/gess/cis/center-for-securities-studies/pdfs/CAD115.pdf (Accessed: June 30, 2022).

Sammut, D. (2020) 'The impact of COVID-19 on the EU's neighbourhood: the South Caucasus'. Available at: https://www.epc.eu/en/Publications/The-impact-of-COVID-19-on-the~30d9dc (Accessed: June 22, 2022).

Sargsyan, L. (2020) 'Observations about Armenia's COVID-19 response'. Available at: https://evnreport.com/covid-19/observations-about-armenia-s-covid-19-response/ (Accessed: June 30, 2022).

Shekerdimian, S. (2021) 'Transforming Armenia's healthcare system: from quantitative misconceptions to qualitative sustainability'. Available at: https://evnreport.com/magazine-issues/transforming-armenia-s-healthcare-system-from-quantitative-misconceptions-toqualitative-sustainability/ (Accessed: May 12, 2022).

Shishkin, S. (2017) 'How history shaped the health system in Russia', *The Lancet*, 390, pp. 1612–1613. Available at: https://www.thelancet.com/journals/lancet/article/PIIS0140-6736(17)32339-5/fulltext (Accessed: May 8, 2022).

Stronski, P. (2020) 'Coronavirus in the Caucasus and Central Asia'. Available at: https://carnegieendowment.org/2020/07/08/coronavirus-in-caucasus-and-central-asia-pub-81898 (Accessed: May 2, 2022).

UNDP (2021) 'COVID-19 and the countries of South Caucasus, Western CIS and Ukraine'. Available at: https://www.undp.org/eurasia/publications/covid-19-and-countries-south-caucasus-western-cis-and-ukraine (Accessed: July 12, 2022).

UN Human Rights Office of the High Commissioner (n.d.) 'Response of the Government of Georgia to the questionnaire on the application of the technical guidance on the application of a human rights-based approach to the implementation of policies and programmes to reduce preventable maternal mortality and morbidity'. Available at: https://www.ohchr.org/sites/default/files/Georgia.pdf (Accessed: May 15, 2022).

Vaccination rate in Georgia (2022) Available at: https://www.google.com/search?q=georgia±vaccination±rate±tbilisi&ei=eO73YpeMF5G-xc8PzbCUsAI&oq=georgia±vaccination±rate±&gs_lcp=Cgdnd3Mtd2l6EAEYAzIECAAQEzIICAAQHhAWEBMyCAgAEB4QFhATMggIABAeEBYQEzIICAAQHhAWEBMyCAgAEB4QFhATMggIABAeEBYQEzIICAAQHhAWEBMyCAgAEB4QFhATMgsIABAeEMkDEBYQE0oECEEYAUoECEYYAFDbAljbAmCvI2gBcAB4AIABhwGIAYcBkgEDMC4xmAEAoAEBwAEB&sclient=gws-wiz (Accessed: August 13, 2022).

Valiyev, A. & Valehli, F. (2021) 'COVID-19 and Azerbaijan: Is the system resilient enough to withstand the perfect storm?', *Problems of Post-Communism*, 69(1), 1–12.

World Bank (2021a) 'Country Profile Armenia'. Available at: https://databank.worldbank.org/views/reports/reportwidget.aspx?Report_Name=CountryProfile&Id=b450fd57&tbar=y&dd=y&inf=n&zm=n&country=ARM (Accessed: July 12, 2022).

World Bank (2021b) 'Country Profile Azerbaijan'. Available at: https://databank.worldbank.org/views/reports/reportwidget.aspx?Report_Name=CountryProfile&Id=b450fd57&tbar=y&dd=y&inf=n&zm=n&country=AZE (Accessed: July 12, 2022).

World Bank (2021c) 'Country Profile Georgia'. Available at: https://databank.worldbank.org/views/reports/reportwidget.aspx?Report_Name=CountryProfile&Id=b450fd57&tbar=y&dd=y&inf=n&zm=n&country=GEO (Accessed: July 12, 2022)

World Health Organization (1996) 'Health care systems – Azerbaijan'. Available at: https://apps.who.int/iris/bitstream/handle/10665/108421/E73099.pdf?sequence=1&isAllowed=y1996 (Accessed: May 14, 2022).

Part III

Global Responses to COVID-19

17 Human Impact on the Environment and the Increased Likelihood of Pandemics

Ana-Belén Soage

Introduction

Fears of a pandemic started growing in the 1990s in the context of the spread of AIDS and the emergence of new diseases like the Creutzfeldt-Jakob disease (CJD), popularly known as "mad cow disease." As early as 1993, Stephen Morse edited the collective work *Emerging viruses*, which warned about the threat posed by zoonotic viruses, i.e., those able to jump from non-human animals to humans. The following years saw the publication of Richard Preston's non-fiction bestseller *The Hot Zone*, which was included in *American Scientist*'s 1999 list of "The 100 or so Books that Shaped a Century of Science," and of two works of scientific journalism, Laurie Garrett's *The Coming Plague* and Robin Marantz Henig's *Dancing Matrix*.

Those fears are being realised, and new pathogens have appeared more frequently in the last 30 years. We have witnessed four pandemics, i.e., diseases affecting many people across multiple countries: SARS in 2003, swine flu in 2009–2010, MERS in 2012, and the ongoing COVID-19 pandemic. There have also been epidemics that seriously affected a certain region but did not spread beyond it: several outbreaks of the Nipah virus in Southeast Asia since 1997, Ebola in West Africa in 2013–2016, and Zika fever in Central and South America in 2015–2016. Why is this happening, and what can be done about it?

To answer those questions, we need to look at COVID-19 and similar outbreaks as part of a larger phenomenon. A growing number of scientists have started to refer to the current geologic era as the Anthropocene, which is characterised by the fact that human activity has a significant impact on the planet. Many advocates of the term warn that we are transgressing planetary boundaries, i.e., exceeding Earth's capacity to continue providing an environment where we can thrive (Rockström et al., 2009). Pandemics are part of that story.

In this chapter, the anthropogenic factors that are increasing the risk of pandemics will be reviewed: Human disruption of the environment brings us into contact with new pathogens and makes it more likely for those pathogens to emerge. Urbanisation creates conditions where viruses may proliferate, while globalisation spreads them faster than ever before. Animal farming represents a challenge due to its potential to enhance the pathogenicity of viruses and to the abuse of antibiotics

DOI: 10.4324/9781003377597-20

in megafarms. Finally, climate change intensifies the problem, i.e., by expanding the range of species that act as vectors for zoonoses. Needless to say, those factors are interconnected and should be considered jointly.

Finally, this chapter will examine the need to broaden our notion of security to include its ecological and socio-economic dimensions. This means adopting approaches that examine the dynamic interconnections between people, animals, and plants within an ecosystem and considering the impact of cities, trade, travel, food production, and land management. The chapter concludes by arguing that we need to change our economic development model and introduce radical changes to our lifestyles.

Anthropogenic Factors and Their Impact

Human Disruption of the Environment

The origin of the COVID-19 pandemic is disputed, and we may never know how it started, but the most credible hypothesis is that it spilled over from animals to humans in a wet market in Wuhan, China, possibly multiple times (Mallapaty, 2021). As such, it is part of a pattern. According to a 2008 study, over 60% of emerging infectious diseases are zoonoses, and nearly 72% of these originate in wildlife (Jones et al., 2008). Human encroachment on natural habits results in contact with reservoir species, i.e., animals inside of which a pathogen can live and reproduce, often without harming its host.

Bats are major reservoirs of viruses, probably because there are so many different species and they have developed a unique immune system, but most zoogenic pathogens are hosted by several species owing to cross-species transmission. Furthermore, the most common source of transmission to humans is commensal or domestic animals such as rats, pigs, cattle, or dogs (Keesing and Ostfeld, 2021). MERS and Nipah virus have their natural reservoir in bats, but they spread to humans via camels and pigs, respectively. Moreover, viruses can evolve to become transmissible human-to-human. This is rare in the case of MERS, SARS, avian flu, and swine flu, but it is the main form of transmission for COVID-19 and monkeypox.

The exploitation of wild animals in unsanitary conditions can lead to the transmission of pathogens, as in Asian wet markets. In West Africa, bushmeat consumption has been linked to the emergence of HIV-1 and HIV-2 and instances of Ebola. The trade of wildlife across regions can also help pathogens spread; for instance, the American bullfrog has become an invasive species in South America, Western Europe, and East and Southeast Asia and is one of the vectors for the spread of the fungus *Batrachochytrium dendrobatidis*, which has decimated global amphibian populations.

Other disruptive activities that bring humans in contact with virus reservoirs include logging, mining, the development of infrastructures, and agricultural expansion. This is especially the case in tropical areas that are rich in biodiversity. For example, animal agriculture is a major driver of deforestation in the Amazon rainforest because the land is frequently cleared to provide pastures or plant crops that are used to feed animals. Rapid deforestation in the Amazon has provoked malaria outbreaks, while in Central and West Africa, it may have led to the Ebola virus spilling over from fruit bats to people.

Another consequence of the degradation, fragmentation, and destruction of natural habitats is that animals are forced to live closer together, which may make them stressed and, therefore, more prone to disease. Infections propagate easier and more rapidly in reduced habitats, and ecosystems filled beyond carrying capacity become unsuitable for some species to survive, causing a loss of biodiversity. Recent research indicates that biodiversity loss increases the likelihood of zoonoses spreading to humans in two ways: It weakens the so-called dilution effect, whereby biodiversity decreases the risk of transmission of pathogens (Ellwanger and Chies, 2021). And potentially zoonotic species are more likely to proliferate in habitats that have been disturbed by humans, whereas they are less numerous in areas with natural biodiversity (Keesing and Ostfeld, 2021).

A final, neglected aspect of wildlife-human interaction is pathogens being introduced into the wild by humans or by domestic or commensal species. Those pathogens can infect wild animals, sometimes leading to die-offs or even extinction, such as canine distemper in lions in the Serengeti. The international community has been slow to respond to this ecological catastrophe. Still, growing awareness should prompt more legislation, like the 2016 United States (US) ban on importing salamanders to protect native species from a new fungus killing European captive and wild salamanders (Cunningham et al., 2017).

Urbanisation and Globalisation

A form of human encroachment on the environment that requires special attention in our discussion is urbanisation. It has been one of the key population trends since the mid-19th century, with huge economic, social, and environmental impacts. In 1950, only 30% of the global population, or 751 million people, lived in urban areas. In 2009, the world reached an inflexion point, with more people living in cities than in rural areas for the first time in history; city dwellers were then 3.42 billion people. By 2050, it is estimated that two-thirds of the population will live in cities, i.e., 2.5 billion more than today.

Urbanisation brings humans in contact with new pathogens. SARS is thought to have originated in the wild in Southern China. Nipah virus was first documented among bats in Malaysia, and Hantavirus is named after the river in South Korea where it was first observed. Ebola comes from a river near a village in the Democratic Republic of Congo, where it was first identified. At the same time, Zika is the forest in Uganda where that virus was first isolated. On the other hand, cities may provide the conditions for species to change their behaviour. *Aedes aegypti* mosquitos, which spread dengue fever, yellow fever, and Zika virus, are thought to have evolved their human biting habits in circumstances of high population density, developing a preference for human odour (Rose et al., 2020).

Demographic concentration makes it easier for diseases to spread, but cities can be unhealthy in other ways. Over a billion city dwellers live in overcrowded slums lacking basic services such as access to water, sanitation, healthcare, and education. Nine out of ten breathe air that does not meet WHO guidelines, provoking respiratory illnesses (World Health Organization, 2019). Emissions cause the premature death of up to 8.8 million people annually, according to a study published in 2016 (GBD 2015 Risk Factors Collaborators, cited in Burnett et al., 2018). And as we saw with the COVID-19 pandemic, people with underlying medical problems have more chances of developing serious illnesses and of dying.

Urbanisation also poses a threat to biodiversity. Wildlife is subjected to manufactured physiological stress and may be threatened by new predators. It is exposed to diseases transmitted by humans and by domestic and commensal species with often catastrophic effects, as mentioned in the previous section. Infrastructures fragment habitats into small, unconnected patches, and some animals may no longer find their natural food sources. Moreover, the waste and pollution produced by cities harm the environment far beyond, especially in countries of the Global South, which often lack appropriate waste management and disposal systems. Stress and reduced biodiversity are thought to lower resistance to pathogens and increase the chances of their proliferation as seen above.

Furthermore, cities are better connected than ever before and play a leading role in the interaction and integration processes that characterise globalisation. The movement of goods and people has always been a driver for the spread of disease, from the Antonine plague in the second-century Roman Empire, thought to have been brought back from the Near East by soldiers, to smallpox and measles, which decimated native populations in the American continent beginning in the 15th century. Global modern transit networks by land, sea, and air have only made the process wider and faster.

Air travel has particularly seen a marked rise over the last two decades. The number of airline passengers doubled between 2000 and 2019, from less than 2 billion to over 4.5 billion. A vector may survive travel in the cabin or cargo hold of a plane and infect people at or near an airport at the destination, as in so-called "airport malaria," but it is unlikely that this will set off an outbreak because that would require a significant number of vectors and their finding suitable conditions. An infected human encountering a vector able to establish local transmission is a more plausible scenario. In cases of diseases transmissible from human to human, like COVID-19, that vector is the local community.

Animal Husbandry

Growing populations and incomes have contributed to another risk factor: Greater demand for animal products. A 2012 report found that 13 zoonotic diseases are responsible for 2.2 million deaths yearly, mainly in poor or middle-income countries. Many cases are a result of people living close to farm animals (Grace et al., 2012). Regular human-animal contact potentially enhances pathogenicity, as seen in triple-reassortant swine influenza viruses, which contain genes from human, swine, and avian influenza A viruses (Dawood et al., 2009). In addition, live transport can spread disease across regions, countries, and continents. It is thought to have led to Rift Valley fever travelling to Saudi Arabia and Yemen in 2000 (Tucker et al., 2021).

The first documented instance of the Nipah virus in Malaysia in 1997 originated in pigsties in the proximity of mango trees and the bats that fed on them. The bats' saliva, faeces, and urine fell on the pigsties and spread the virus to pigs, causing them a mild respiratory illness. Repeated contamination of pigs made it possible for the virus to persist and spread to people, who can develop acute respiratory disease and fatal encephalitis. The virus travelled beyond bat habitats when infected pigs were sold to other farms or sent for slaughter. It may have been transmitted by air between adjacent farms due to high pig farm density (Pulliam et al., 2012). The outbreak was contained after a million pigs were culled. Still, since then Nipah virus has killed hundreds of people in Southeast Asia, and outbreaks occur almost every year in India and Bangladesh.

There are other recent examples: Q fever, transmitted from goats, cattle, and sheep to humans; an outbreak in the Netherlands in 2007 infected thousands of people and killed dozens. H1N1, or swine flu, which is endemic in pigs, may have killed over half a million people during the WHO-declared pandemic between June 2009 and August 2010. The forms of avian influenza H5N1 and H7N9, first detected in humans in 1997 and 2013, respectively, have left hundreds dead in over a dozen Asian countries and, in the case of H5N1, also in Africa. After the fifth outbreak of H7N9 was declared in 2016, a report published by *Smithsonian* magazine hypothesised that a future pandemic might start in China and be provoked by contact with poultry (Liu, 2017).

In intensive farming, animals are generally kept in overcrowded, unsanitary conditions, which makes it easier for disease to emerge and for pathogens to mutate. Their genetic diversity is low, which facilitates infection. To prevent it, it is common practice to use huge amounts of antibiotics; it is estimated that over two-thirds of those consumed worldwide are used on farm animals. The overuse of antibiotics leads to the appearance of drug-resistant bacteria popularly known as "superbugs." Antimicrobial resistance already kills 700,000 people a year, and the WHO has warned that by 2050 the number could rise to 10 million (IACG 2019). Apart from this overuse of antibiotics, there are communicable diseases often acquired from animal products that have developed antibiotic-resistant strains, such as *E. coli* and salmonella.

In the wake of the COVID-19 pandemic, there was a flurry of warnings that intensive farming may set off another pandemic, and studies on the issue received wide coverage.[1] However, a report argued that intensive farming could reduce pandemics because alternatives require more land, resulting in the disruptions and risks discussed above (Bartlett et al., 2022). The scientists who carried out the study did consider the possibility of dramatically reducing meat consumption to lower the risks of infectious diseases, but they dismissed it as "extremely challenging."

We should add that the excessive consumption of animal products has been linked to type-2 diabetes, cardiovascular diseases, obesity, and, in the case of red or processed meat, even some cancers (HSPH, 2015). Those conditions reduce the ability to fight infections and increase the likelihood of complications, as the COVID-19 pandemic showed.

Climate Change

All the issues we have dealt with in this chapter are major contributors to climate change. Animal agriculture is one of the largest; livestock alone is estimated to release nearly 15% of global greenhouse gas emissions, according to the Food and Agriculture Organization (FAO) (2019: 1). In the case of international trade, container ships alone are responsible for 3% of greenhouse gas emissions (Northam, 2021). Air travel represents around 2.5% of global annual CO_2 emissions but 3.5% of effective radiative forcing, which takes into account non-CO_2 climate impacts (Ritchie, 2020)[2] – and this, even though at present only around a fifth of the world population, can afford to fly. These percentages may not sound like much, but if they were countries, they would occupy positions sixth and seventh on the global CO_2 emissions ranking between Japan (3.5%) and Germany (2.2%).

Human activities generate carbon emissions while reducing the global carbon sink, leading to a further rise in temperatures. This weakens and reduces natural habitats, e.g., by rising sea levels, worsening wildfires, or limiting water availability, and they become less resilient and healthy. In addition, it expands transition zones in which species can interact, making it more likely for pathogens to jump species. It also extends the geographical range of vector species, such as mosquitoes, increasing the number of people exposed to the disease. Models have predicted that within decades malaria and dengue could reach central Europe and North America (Colón-González et al., 2021).

Furthermore, global warming affects the migration of animals such as bats. This is important due to the strong correlation between bat species richness in an area and the number of coronaviruses. A 2021 study suggests climate change has led to a proliferation of bat species in the Chinese province of Yunnan and neighbouring regions in Myanmar and Laos. This probably played a role in the SARS and COVID-19 epidemics (Beyer et al., 2021).

A more far-fetched, not impossible scenario is that melting glaciers could release pathogens and bacteria that have been dormant for thousands of years. Some precedents: In 2016, there was an Anthrax outbreak in Siberia when spores surviving in frozen animal remains were released by a thaw, causing the death of thousands of reindeer and the hospitalisation of dozens of nomadic herders, one of whom died (Ezhova et al., 2021). In a recent study, scientists analysed ice samples from glaciers on the Tibetan Plateau and found 33 viruses and nearly a thousand microbial species. Twenty-eight viruses and around 98% of microbial species were completely new to science (Zhong et al., 2021). Some of them could infect humans, although it is doubtful that they will come back to life spontaneously.

On the other hand, climate change and associated phenomena affect people's overall health and well-being, making them more vulnerable to disease. Air pollution can induce the onset of respiratory illnesses such as asthma and exacerbate others, like chronic obstructive pulmonary disease (Jiang et al., 2016). It also limits the solar UVB that reaches the earth's surface, thereby decreasing the capacity of the human skin to synthesise vitamin D. Vitamin D deficiency is already widespread. It's known to lead to osteoporosis but has also been linked to brain dysfunction and autism (Hosseinpanah et al., 2010; Lee et al., 2021; Wang et al., 2022).

Besides these health problems, climate change compromises our ability to feed ourselves by reducing the land usable for cultivation and decreasing its fertility, threatening pollinators, and provoking severe droughts and extreme precipitation. It is already displacing 20 million people annually, according to a 2019 report (Oxfam, 2019). Most of those people move to the nearest city, reinforcing the trend towards urbanisation and its complications, which illustrates the compounding nature of our problems.

Compounding Problems Demand Holistic Solutions

Tackling the problems discussed above will demand a wide range of measures aimed at lowering emissions, restoring damaged or destroyed ecosystems, preserving biodiversity, controlling the trade and consumption of wildlife, setting animal standards in farms, transport, and markets, implementing health policies that emphasise sanitation, and developing programmes to discover new pathogens that may spread from nature. This requires going beyond the focus on human health and considering human activities and behaviours, and how they harm the natural systems we depend on for survival.

There is a need for interdisciplinary, cross-sectoral approaches that recognise that human health is closely related to that of non-human animals and the environment and cannot be divorced from discussions of sustainability and human development. Several such approaches have emerged over the last few decades: One Health, EcoHealth, Planetary Health, One Medicine, Zoobiquity, One Welfare... These are evolving concepts, but Lerner and Berg (2017) have tried to identify the defining features of the first three approaches and have come up with a classification that looks at their core values and the number of scientific areas they bring together.

One Health is the most successful of the three approaches, having been adopted by international institutions like the World Health Organization (WHO), the FAO and the Davos Global Risk Forum, and the EU and the US Centers for Disease Control and Prevention (CDC). It has evolved from a narrow focus involving human medicine and veterinary to encompass, among other things, ecology, conservation, epidemiological modelling, immunology, field biology, agriculture, and social sciences such as anthropology and economics. It has moved closer to EcoHealth, which links the health of humans, animals, and the ecosystem to environmental sustainability and socio-economic stability.[3] Finally, Planetary Health is the more anthropocentric of the approaches analysed because it contemplates biodiversity and ecological sustainability from a utilitarian perspective.

Each approach is underpinned by philosophical assumptions regarding the intrinsic value of living creatures and the natural world, so our approach will depend on our stand on that issue. However, they all represent a step towards the mindset needed to prevent future pandemics and move towards a fairer, healthier world. More will have to be done for them to be adopted at the policy and governance levels so that the relevant government ministries (most notably, Health, Agriculture, Environment, and Forestry) work jointly to confront the challenges we face (Cunningham et al., 2017).

In addition, there is an increasing awareness that our current development model, based on encouraging production and pursuing economic growth at all costs, is incompatible with efforts to protect the environment and curb global warming. In the first year of the pandemic, World Economic Forum Chairman Klaus Schwab called for a "great reset" of global capitalism that prioritised environmental protection and reduced inequality (Schwab, 2020). He was encouraged by the measures taken to tackle COVID-19, which showed that we could radically change our lifestyle and were willing to make sacrifices when needed. Unfortunately, the looming economic crisis and the Russian invasion of Ukraine in 2022 have again pushed those concerns into the background to the detriment of our long-term survival.

Notes

1 For instance, Nedelman (2019), Saner (2019), and Barrett (2020).
2 Radiative forcing measures the difference between energy absorbed by Earth's system and energy radiated back to space. If the former is greater than the latter, the atmosphere becomes warmer. In the case of planes, less than half the warming they cause comes from CO_2, while two-thirds is due to non-CO_2 forcings, especially contrails.
3 There have been calls for the two approaches to be merged. However, One Health has a more individualistic approach whereas EcoHealth considers aggregations of individuals in an ecosystem (Lerner & Berg 2017: 5).

References

Barrett, A. (2020) 'Disease transfer in intensive farming poses "huge public health risk"', *BBC Science Focus Magazine* (May 5). Available at: https://www.sciencefocus.com/news/disease-transfer-in-intensive-farming-poses-huge-public-health-risk/

Bartlett, H., Holmes, M. A, Petrovan, S. O, Williams, D. R., Wood, J. L., & Balmford, A. (2022) 'Understanding the relative risks of zoonosis emergence under contrasting approaches to meeting livestock product demand', Royal Society Open Science. Available at: http://doi.org/10.1098/rsos.211573

Beyer, R. M., Manica, A., & Mora, C. (2021) 'Shifts in global bat diversity suggest a possible role of climate change in the emergence of SARS-CoV-1 and SARS-CoV-2', *Science of the Total Environment*, 767, p. 145413. Available at: http://doi.org/10.1016/j.scitotenv.2021.145413

Burnett, R., Chen, H., Szyszkowicz, M., Fann, N., Hubbell, B., Pope, C. A., Apte, J. S., Brauer, M., Cohen, A., Weichenthal, S., Coggins, J., Di, Q., Brunekreef, B., Frostad, J., Lim, S. S., Kan, H., Walker, K. D., Thurston, G. D., Hayes, R. B., & Spadaro, J. V. (2018) 'Global estimates of mortality associated with long-term exposure to outdoor fine particulate matter', Proceedings of the National Academy of Sciences, 115(38), pp. 9592–9597. Available at: https://doi.org/10.1073/pnas.1803222115 (Accessed: October 24, 2022).

Colón-González, F. J., Sewe, M. O., Tompkins, A. M., Sjödin, H., Casallas, A., & Rocklöv, J. et al. (2021) 'Projecting the risk of mosquito-borne diseases in a warmer and more populated world: a multi-model, multi-scenario intercomparison modelling study', *The Lancet Planetary Health*. Available at: https://doi.org/10.1016/S2542-5196(21)00132-7

Cunningham, A. A., Daszak, P., & Wood, J. L. N. (2017) 'One health, emerging infectious diseases and wildlife: Two decades of progress?', *Philosophical Transactions: Biological Sciences*, 372(1725). Available at: https://doi.org/10.1098/rstb.2016.0167

Dawood, F. S., Jain, S., Finelli, L., Shaw, M. W., Lindstrom, S., Garten, R. J., Gubareva, L. V., Xu, X., Bridges, C. B., & Uyeki, T. M (2009). 'Emergence of a novel swine-origin influenza a (H1N1) virus in humans', *The New England Journal of Medicine*, 360(25), pp. 2605–2615.

Ellwanger, J. H, & Chies, J. A. B. (2021) 'Zoonotic spillover: Understanding basic aspects for better prevention', *Genetics and Molecular Biology*, 44 (June 4). Available at: https://doi.org/10.1590/1678-4685-GMB-2020-0355

Ezhova, E., Orlov, D., Suhonen, E., Kaverin, D., Mahura, A., Gennadinik, V., Kukkonen, I., Drozdov, D., Lappalainen, H. K., Melnikov, V., Petäjä, T., Kerminen, V. M., Zilitinkevich, S., Malkhazova, S. M., Christensen, T. R., & Kulmala, M. (2021). 'Climatic factors influencing the anthrax outbreak of 2016 in Siberia, Russia', *Ecohealth* 18(2), pp. 217–228. Available at: 10.1007/s10393-021-01549-5 (Accessed: October 24, 2022).

FAO (2019) 'Five practical actions towards low-carbon livestock', Rome. Available at: https://www.fao.org/3/ca7089en/CA7089EN.pdf

Grace, D., Mutua, F., Ochungo, P., Kruska, R., Jones, K., Brierley, L., Lapar, L., Said, M., Herrero, M., Phuc, P. M., Thao, N. B., Akuku, I., & Ogutu, F. (2012) 'Mapping of poverty and likely zoonoses hotspots. Zoonoses Project 4', Report to the UK Department for International Development. Nairobi, Kenya: ILRI. Available at: https://hdl.handle.net/10568/2116

Hosseinpanah, F., Hashemipour, S., Heibatollahi, M., Moghbel, N., Asefzade, S., & Azizi, F. (2010) 'The effects of air pollution on vitamin D status in healthy women: A cross sectional study', *BMC Public Health*, 10(519). Available at: https://doi.org/10.1186/1471-2458-10-519

HSPH (Harvard School of Public Health) (2015) 'WHO report says eating processed meat is carcinogenic: Understanding the findings', *Harvard University*. Available at: https://www.hsph.harvard.edu/nutritionsource/2015/11/03/report-says-eating-processed-meat-is-carcinogenic-understanding-the-findings/

IACG (Ad Hoc Interagency Coordination Group on Antimicrobial Resistance) (2019) 'No time to wait: Securing the future from drug-resistant infections', Report to the Secretary-General of the United Nations (April). Available at: https://www.who.int/docs/default-source/documents/no-time-to-wait-securing-the-future-from-drug-resistant-infections-en.pdf

Jiang, X. Q., Mei, X. D., & Feng, D. (2016) 'Air pollution and chronic airway diseases: What should people know and do?', *Journal of Thoracic Disease*, 8(1), pp. E31–E40. Available at: https://doi.org/10.3978/j.issn.2072-1439.2015.11.50 (Accessed: October 31, 2022).

Jones, K. E., Patel, N. G., & Levy, M. A. et al. (2008) 'Global trends in emerging infectious diseases', Nature (February 21). Available at: https://www.nature.com/articles/nature06536

Keesing, F., & Ostfeld, R. S. (2021) 'Impacts of biodiversity and biodiversity loss on zoonotic diseases', *Proceedings of the National Academy of Sciences of the United States of America*, 118(17). Available at: https://doi.org/10.1073/pnas.2023540118

Lee, B. K., Eyles, D. W., & Magnusson, C. et al. (2021) 'Developmental vitamin D and autism spectrum disorders: Findings from the Stockholm Youth Cohort', *Molecular Psychiatry*, 26, pp. 1578–1588. Available at: https://doi.org/10.1038/s41380-019-0578-y

Lerner, H., & Berg, C. (2017) 'A comparison of three holistic approaches to health: One health, EcoHealth, and planetary health', *Frontiers in Veterinary Science*, 4(163). Available at: https://doi.org/10.3389/fvets.2017.00163

Liu, M. (2017) 'Is China ground zero for a future pandemic?', *Smithsonian Magazine* (November). Available at: https://www.smithsonianmag.com/science-nature/china-ground-zero-future-pandemic-180965213/

Mallapaty, S. (2021) 'Did the coronavirus jump from animals to people twice?', *Nature* (September 16). Available at: https://www.nature.com/articles/d41586-021-02519-1

Northam, J. (2021) 'Shipping industry is pressured to cut pollution caused by merchant fleet', *NPR* (December 1). Available at: https://www.npr.org/2021/12/01/1060382176/shipping-industry-is-pressured-to-cut-pollution-caused-by-merchant-fleet

Nedelman, M. (2019) 'Eat healthier, and you'll help save the planet, report says', *CNN* (August 8). Available at: https://edition.cnn.com/2019/08/08/health/ipcc-report-healthy-eating-climate-diet/

Oxfam (2019) 'Forced from home: Climate-fuelled displacement', *Oxfam International* (December 2). Available at: https://oxfamilibrary.openrepository.com/bitstream/handle/10546/620914/mb-climate-displacement-cop25-021219-en.pdf

Pulliam, J. R., Epstein, J. H., Dushoff, J., Rahman, S. A., Bunning, M., Jamaluddin, A. A., Hyatt, A. D., Field, H. E., Dobson, A. P., & Daszak, P. (2012) 'Agricultural intensification, priming for persistence and the emergence of Nipah virus: A lethal bat-borne zoonosis', *Journal of the Royal Society Interface*, 9(66), pp. 89–101. Available at: http://doi.org/10.1098/rsif.2011.0223 (Accessed: October 24, 2022).

Ritchie, H. (2020) 'Climate change and flying: What share of Global CO_2 emissions come from aviation?', *Our World in Data*. Available at: https://ourworldindata.org/co2-emissions-from-aviation

Rockström, J., Steffen, W., Noone, K., Persson, Å., Chapin, F. S., Lambin, E., Lenton, T. M., Scheffer, M., Folke, C., Schellnhuber, H., Nykvist, B., De Wit, C. A., Hughes, T., van der Leeuw, S., Rodhe, H., Sörlin, S., Snyder, P. K., Costanza, R., Svedin, U., Falkenmark, M., Karlberg, L., Corell, R. W., Fabry, V. J., Hansen, J., Walker, B., Liverman, B., Richardson, K., Crutzen, P., & Foley, J. (2009) 'Planetary boundaries: Exploring the safe operating space for humanity', *Ecology and Society*, 14(2), p. 32. Available at: http://www.ecologyandsociety.org/vol14/iss2/art32/

Rose, N. H., Sylla, M., Badolo, A., Lutomiah, J., Ayala, D., Aribodor, O. B., Ibe, N., Akorli, J., Otoo, S., Mutebi, J.-P., Kriete, A. L., Ewing, E. G., Sang, R., Gloria-Soria, A., Powell, J. R., Baker, R. E., White, B. J., Crawford, J. E., & McBride, C. S. (2020) 'Climate and urbanization drive mosquito preference for humans,' *Current Biology* 30(18), pp. 3570–3579. Available at: https://doi.org/10.1016/j.cub.2020.06.092

Saner, E. (2019) 'Should meat be banned to save the planet?', *The Guardian* (September 23). Available at: https://www.theguardian.com/environment/shortcuts/2019/sep/23/should-meat-be-banned-save-planet-new-laws-environment

Schwab, K. (2020) 'Now is the time for a 'great reset', *World Economic Forum*. Available at: http://www.weforum.org/agenda/2020/06/now-is-the-time-for-a-great-reset/

Tucker, C. J., Melocik, K. A., Anyamba, A., Linthicum, K. J., & Fagbo, S. F. et al. (2021) 'Reanalysis of the 2000 Rift Valley fever outbreak in southwestern Arabia', *Plos One*, 16(3), p. e0248462. Available at: https://doi.org/10.1371/journal.pone.0248462

Wang, J., Huang, H., Liu, C., Zhang, Y., Wang, W., Zou, Z., Yang, L., He, X., Wu, J., Ma, J., & Liu, Y. (2022) 'Research progress on the role of vitamin D in autism spectrum Disorder', *Frontiers in Behavioral Neuroscience*, 16, p. 859151. Available at: https://doi.org/10.3389/fnbeh.2022.859151

World Health Organization (2019) 'New report calls for urgent action to avert antimicrobial resistance crisis', April 29. Available at: https://www.who.int/news/item/29-04-2019-new-report-calls-for-urgent-action-to-avert-antimicrobial-resistance-crisis

Zhong, Z P., Tian, F., & Roux, S. et al. (2021) 'Glacier ice archives nearly 15,000-year-old microbes and phages', *Microbiome*, 9(160). Available at: https://doi.org/10.1186/s40168-021-01106-w

18 The World Health Organization and the COVID-19 Pandemic

Haydar Karaman and Burak Güneş

Introduction

The United Nations (UN) was founded 75 years ago to address global threats through multilateral action. The World Health Organization (WHO), which is now striving for a healthier world, was to be established in accordance with the UN Charter, which was signed on June 26, 1945 (Mathers, 2020: 1–13). The UN system works to bring about a cosmopolitan vision of a global society that will serve as the basis for cross-border cooperation to improve global health. The UN General Assembly has conducted high-level special sessions on communicable and non-communicable diseases. However, the coronavirus pandemic has posed unprecedented challenges to this multinational system. This global phenomenon has been fast and widespread.

COVID-19 has presented the globe with a scenario that began as a health catastrophe and progressed into a societal disaster in less developed nations. The reason for this disaster is that neither nations nor the WHO studied or planned for a catastrophic scenario, despite the breakout of SARS in 2003. Therefore, the world community has found itself unarmed against this pandemic, and many unpredicted results and unplanned steps have occurred. In other words, the world struggled to deal with such a pandemic and indicated a need for a centralised enforcement mechanism, which was pictured as the role and duty of the UN, especially the WHO. Additionally, there has been a gradual effort to indicate and emphasise the UN's legislative role, particularly after the Cold War. According to Cronin and Hurd, the UN Security Council did not hesitate to implement legislative resolutions created to impose binding regulations for all states. In other words, "They are acts of international legislation that establish new binding rules of international law rather than commands relating to a particular situation" (Cronin and Hurd, 2008: 81).

This step raises doubts about whether the UN Security Council will replace itself with international treaties by imposing binding regulations over the community of states. The states have long created these binding regulations in the form of treaties. Alvarez highlights this diverse view over the legislative role of the international organisation by pointing out the dilemma and deadlock that international organisations pose as they become more centralised. The UN itself can be a good example

DOI: 10.4324/9781003377597-21

considering the role of the Security Council (see Articles 103, 24, and 25 of the UN Charter) and the sovereignty of states expected in Article 2 of the UN Charter (Alvarez, 2001: 106–107). For instance, it is fair to question the legal consequences if the Security Council authorises the WHO in accordance with Article 39 of the UN Charter to impose binding resolutions over states to fight against the pandemic (Hurd, 2014: 296).

The WHO faced harsh criticism during the COVID-19 pandemic as it was deemed ineffective in dealing with it. Thus, this chapter evaluates the role of the WHO during and after the COVID-19 pandemic and discusses the organisation's financial difficulties, technical capacity, legitimacy, and political positioning. Before touching upon the criticism directed at the WHO, this chapter briefly gives an overview of the legal base that the WHO uses.

WHO Is Stuck between Objectives and Achievement

The epidemic of COVID-19 will affect the 21st century. COVID-19 has become a worldwide sensation and continues to exist as a *"global spectre."*[1] Similar to previous pandemics and crises, it may permanently and irrevocably impact the development of human life. Undoubtedly, the COVID-19 pandemic has introduced challenges and critics. Paradoxically, even though combating the disease required increased national isolation, eradicating it required international collaboration. This issue has implications for global organisations such as the WHO. Since the primary function of the WHO, as stated in Worldwide Health Regulations (IHR) Art. 2., is "to prevent, protect against, control and provide a public health response to the international spread of disease," its role has been questioned considering its objectives and aspirations.

With its specialised institutions, funds, and programmes, the UN goes far beyond being simply an international organisation. It has in fact crossed the line into a system. International cooperation and standardisation are crystallised in the body of the UN, stretching from west to east and north to south. As seen throughout history, global governance has gained an important pivotal place in human history in the name of cooperation among states. There are plenty of reasons why the need for and importance of global governance, which is different from the world government, has been coined and praised. According to Karns et al., globalisation, technological developments, the end of the Cold War, and enhancement in transnationalism are subjects that caused a proliferation of subject matters in world politics and promoted complexity, which inevitably paved the way for better governing efforts (Karns et al., 2015: 4). Therefore, the UN found itself on the brink of change and transformation, without which the UN would fail to couple with the world's problems and maintain international peace and security.

The new challenges to international peace and security have arisen and need to be tackled with new methods. Therefore, international organisations have modified their operations in line with these recent and rapid changes. The WHO is among the international organisations expected to adapt to new situations. As Mingst and

Karns have stressed, the WHO has three major areas on its agenda. Taking its legacy from the previous international organisations, the WHO has long been at the forefront of fighting against "the spread of communicable diseases" (Mingst and Karns, 2012: 265). At the beginning of the second half of the 20th century, four diseases – namely yellow fever, cholera, plague, and smallpox – were mentioned in the International Health Regulation issued by the WHO in 1951. Over the years, due to the acceleration of globalisation and other factors that created newly emerged viruses and diseases, the WHO adopted new legal frameworks to deal with them effectively. Ebola, West Nile virus, HIV/AIDS, and avian flu were at the top of the list for the WHO to tackle. A better and more effective legal framework, which could be labelled as the updated version of its predecessor introduced in 1951, was released by the WHO in 2006 (Mingst and Karns, 2012: 265).

The second duty of the WHO is to help governments with technical, medical, and bureaucratic means to annihilate already existing viruses and diseases in the form of programmes. Malaria is one of the best examples among other conditions that the WHO, with the support of NGOs and charities, has worked hard to end in Nigeria and has made progress in eliminating the disease (Mingst and Karns, 2012: 266).

Finally, the WHO is responsible for regulating the pharmaceutical market to enhance justice in drug allocation, increasing the quality of medicines, and monitoring states' behaviour to help prevent the further spread of possible pandemics. For instance, in 1981, the WHO adopted the "Code of Marketing for Breast-Milk Substitutes" (WHO, 1981) to encourage states to prohibit advertisements that discourage mothers from breastfeeding (Mingst and Karns, 2012: 267).

Being an international organisation, the WHO is governed by the rules created by the state parties in line with the formal inner procedures of the organisation. Moreover, the WHO may adopt recommendations and organise international conferences resulting in international treaties, which the Health Assembly may adopt. The normative power of the WHO comes from three basic legal documents: conventions, regulations, and recommendations.

As for the WHO's constitution, the World Health Assembly has the authority and right to determine and draft "regulations" dealing with worldwide health problems, especially pandemics and quarantines. Regarding its binding force over states, Article 21 of the WHO Constitution (WHO, 2020: 1–20) authorises the Health Assembly to make decisions regarding procedures, standards, regulations, and requirements, all related to public health. Among these documents, rules binding member states have a pivotal place. According to Article 22, "Regulations adopted according to Article 21 shall come into force for all Members after due notice has been given of their adoption by the Health Assembly except for such Members as may notify the Director-General of rejection or reservations within the period stated in the notice." In other words, if a member state does not express its objection, the regulation is automatically binding for that state. Therefore, as written on the official website of the WHO, regulations have binding power over states, and states shall fulfil the requirements of these legal instruments unless they express their grievances or reject them (Burci and Toebes, 2018; Samancı, 2014, 2016).

The first International Health Regulation (IHR) was introduced in 1951 and has faced deep and considerable revisions. In 2005, the most recent IHR came into effect, aiming to provide standardisation, coherence, and centralised health politics around the globe (WHO, 2016). The very nature and scope of the latest IHR went beyond its ancestors, "addressing the public health aspects of any international spread of disease regardless of origin or source" and potentially covering "the health response to a nuclear or chemical accident or even a bioterrorist attack, leads to a broad range of potential interactions between a dedicated health instrument and other international legal regimes" (Gian L. Burci and Cassels, 2016: 458).

Conventions (or agreements) are drafted and adopted by the Health Assembly in accordance with the constitution of the WHO. As Burci and Cassels point out, the WHO Framework Convention on Tobacco Control has the privilege of being called the only international agreement adopted thus by the Assembly in May 2003 and entered into force in February 2005 (Gian L. Burci and Cassels, 2016: 456). Finally, the WHO, with its non-binding instruments called "soft law instruments," has long been contributing to directing and shaping national health policies with the aim of global standardisation. These are, without doubt, for some commentators, the most compelling and shortcut way to set an international legal framework (Gian L. Burci and Cassels, 2016: 458).

According to Toebes, having adopted "one treaty, two regulations, and a range of non-binding recommendations," the WHO was a disappointment compared to the International Labour Organization (ILO) (Burci and Toebes, 2018: 10). Indeed, it is not an exaggeration to say that the WHO has long been criticised for failing to create a worldwide health regime that is binding over states and generally accepted standards regarding public health. Behind the curtain, there may be some logic legitimising these critics.

Decoupled Political Cooperation of COVID-19

The local context divides the pandemic's worldwide effects into two distinct categories. While developed and underdeveloped countries encountered various catastrophes, nations' readiness for any such epidemic led to a political challenge. Additionally, nationalist and internationalist attitudes contribute to disagreements on emergency response plans.

Nationalist states have damaged global health governance in response to COVID-19, in contrast to the cosmopolitan idea of global unity through international organisations. The isolationist policies imposed by nationalist countries hinder global unity. As governments worldwide rapidly enforced travel bans and prohibited trade, several countries practised medical protectionism and hampered medical supply movement in the early stages of the epidemic (Wang, 2021: 25–30). Nationalist methods pitted governments against one another, weakened international attempts to stop the pandemic, and brought the globe to a standstill rather than uniting it against a common threat.

These beliefs have damaged authority and prevented a coordinated UN response. These challenges to international law and institutions have escalated the pandemic threat (Gostin et al., 2020). When governments position the WHO in the centre of political power conflicts, they paralyse the UN and isolate themselves in a globalising world, rendering global governance ineffective. This is obvious in member state attacks on WHO leadership and a refusal to meet financial responsibility to the WHO's pandemic response programmes to withdraw completely from the WHO (Leal Filho et al., 2020).

It is evident in the Sino-American conflict; political polarisation influenced the WHO's action. Donald Trump, then the president of the United States of America (US), has said that the WHO leadership is inefficient and has allowed itself to be controlled by the Chinese government. The Trump administration attributed the outbreak to China, calling it the "China virus," to deflect attention from Washington's shortcomings (Boylan et al., 2021: 25–36). The US government has abdicated the responsibility for global health among nationalist movements. Then, Trump terminated US contributions to the WHO finances. The Trump administration's suspension of US assistance amid a pandemic was a wholly inappropriate step and avoiding collective action during a pandemic hindered the global response. It places the ship's helm at the mercy of the storm because the US is one of the WHO's largest donors.[2] Additionally, the UN Security Council has been hampered by disagreements between China and the US on the pandemic's origins and the appropriateness of the first response. China, which asserts vehemently that it has dealt with the domestic problem well, has pointed to its comprehensive surveillance network and population control as a model for all other nations. However, China was perceived to have originally concealed the emergence of the virus. As a result, permanent political tensions have paralysed the UN and WHO, preventing them from coordinating a worldwide response (Gostin et al., 2020: 1616). Consequently, the Security Council did not adopt a resolution on COVID-19 for six months.

"Insufficient Funds": The Problem of Financial Contribution

Contrary to what was first expected, rather than the credibility of the WHO eroding, numerous nations (Canada, Germany, France, and Italy) declared their support for the WHO, raised their financial contributions, and reaffirmed their positions. Nevertheless, the agency was pushed into a dire financial situation. The international health governance authority found a solution to this economic collapse by bringing together non-governmental groups with the WHO through voluntary involvement and funding despite their lack of legitimacy (Thomas et al., 2020). For instance, the Bill and Melinda Gates Foundation donated millions of dollars to the WHO. There are other privately funded agencies; all have health specialists (Shamasunder et al., 2020: 1083–1089). Most of them have faster administrative procedures and decision-making timelines, and, most crucially, nearly all have superior funding than the WHO. Another concern is the WHO's weak technical competence. It cannot afford to pay the best technical workers, who find better opportunities and greater compensation with other organisations, groups, or the private sector. Second, the WHO has already limited operational capabilities compared with NGOs.

One may assume that there is a unanimous agreement that the WHO should be more aggressive in seeking engagement with NGOs, leading the partnership to include the dynamics of government and civil society and accrediting NGOs to engage with member states. However, Brazil and India were against the efforts, noting that they may compromise the WHO's independence and integrity and offer unnecessary access to vital information. Therefore, integrating non-governmental organisations into international organisations blurs the distinction between purchasing a chocolate bar in a store and renting an office in Geneva. The pandemic illustrates the WHO's ambiguous character. The WHO is a giant as the UN's health-related decision-making agency but a dwarf owing to its financial dependence.

Legitimacy

Despite its conceptual variability, legitimacy is commonly defined as another actor's recognised right to act, rule, or govern. Therefore, legitimacy is the consensual acceptance of an actor's identity, interests, behaviours, or the WHO's norms, rules, and guiding principles (Tallberg and Zürn, 2019). However, the WHO's legitimacy challenge during the coronavirus pandemic occurred at the same time as the virus's massive devastation effect and the organisation's inability to form a worldwide response. Granted, the WHO has already undergone some (legitimacy) crises, not least because of its inconsistent performance during global health emergencies (Zürn, 2021: 45–51). During the HIV/AIDS pandemic as well as the SARS, 2009 H1N1 influenza, and Ebola outbreaks, the WHO was under the spotlight and often heavily criticised (Yi-chong and Weller, 2020: 50–56).

The COVID-19 outbreak has reignited this passionate and enduring debate over legitimacy. The legitimacy debate surfaced at two different moments. COVID-19 became entangled in the power struggle between China and the US. The US accuses the group of pandering to Beijing and failing to act fast and appropriately. The WHO has lost credibility due to Trump administration critiques, concurrent politicisation of the institution, and highlighting of its fundamental issues. However, the Trump administration's broad legitimisation of the WHO spurred others to rally around it and inspired attempts to legitimise it by further financing and support from others. With aid, the organisation overcame legitimacy difficulties.

Nonetheless, in the second stage, the WHO's technical/technocratic approach exhibited great variation. Some health specialists criticised the agency's reluctance to encourage mask use and ambiguity regarding the risk of asymptomatic and airborne transmission (Morawska and Milton, 2020). It destroyed the organisation's technical legitimacy. Some national governments view the agency technocrats, scientific committees, and authorities as scapegoats for their delay and lack of readiness. Consequently, the legitimacy of the organisation remains in question.

The WHO cannot escape being depicted as a tool of imperialist states by some observers. Sometimes rooted in conspiracy theories, some say that large, million dollars NGOs are serving not ordinary people but higher purposes. The Gates Foundation, according to advocates of this idea, is most of the time given as an example (Levich, 2015). Other scholars have pointed to powerful states' jargon during the pandemic as an example of the dialogue of imperialism, which inherently reproduces itself by referencing the term "war" (Connolly, 2020). Generally speaking, the WHO and its donor states, which can be called superpowers, are criticised as being a tool for exploitation, i.e., imperialism, labelling it a "West-centred" organisation (Denk, 2015: 339).

Capacity Issue

It is asserted that the WHO prioritises procedure over action and is blamed for lacking the necessary authority to intervene in emergencies due to the WHO's poor technical capabilities. It cannot afford to pay the best technical personnel, who pursue better career possibilities and higher incomes in other agencies, organisations, or the private sector. Other privately financed organisations, such as the Bill and Melinda Gates Foundation, employ their health professionals. Most of them have quicker administrative procedures and decision-making timelines, and most crucially, nearly all have superior funding than the WHO.

As a result, the WHO was subjected to scathing criticism for its inadequate response to the COVID-19 outbreak. This difficulty was reflected in the availability of vaccinations against COVID-19. While high-income nations paid money to gain early COVID-19 vaccine candidate pledges for their domestic needs, low-income countries could not. Other nations, particularly low- and middle-income nations that rely more on the WHO's technical guidance and operational help, have suffered from the organisation's lack of capacity (Santos Rutschman, 2020).

Additionally, its limited operational capability must be aligned with its member states' political mandate. This issue cannot be resolved just by reformulating its aims and mandates; it is also necessary to optimise and increase the amount of collaboration and information sharing across governmental, corporate, and non-profit entities.

Conclusion

There are two lessons to be learnt from the COVID-19 pandemic. The first is that functional or technical cooperation is more successful and valuable than political cooperation. The second lesson is that separating politics and function may result in polarised globalisation. Since the pandemic's start, there has been no clear distinction between animal and human health; this must be reconsidered first. Considering these facts, health is one of the most important factors. Health in this more holistic sense (one health policy) necessitates reorganising its governance (Mackenzie and Jeggo, 2019: 1–5). Reformulating its aims and mandates is required, and the public, private, and civil actors must optimise and increase their collaboration and information sharing. However, the most significant issue remains before us. International inequities are growing, while the most disadvantaged people's access to health care is deteriorating. Health care used to be viewed as an inherent right for everyone. Still, as it has been changed towards privatisation and commercialisation, it has become a market-based good that is vulnerable to cost and profit. For the WHO, this makes the problem a structurally complicated one.

Due to these factors, if we accept wealth and development inequalities, everything else being equal, there may be a proposal to reformulate the organisation in certain ways. First, the disparity between North and South technical assistance should be addressed. The organisation should also be maintained apart from state conflicts of interest. The slow, burdensome, and strict procedures should be replaced with more efficient ones. Last and foremost, when earlier pandemics (Ebola and SARS) and the coronavirus are examined, there is no longer a clear distinction between animal and human health. Health should be expanded more holistically (one health policy), necessitating restructuring its governance.

Notes

1 The sentence alludes to the introductory sentence in Marx and Engels' (2019) Communist Manifesto, p. 9.
2 The United States has been one of the main donors to the WHO. It donated almost $700 million, making it the third largest in 2020–2021. See World Health Organization (2022), United States of America: Partner in global health, available at https://www.who.int/about/funding/contributors/usa (Accessed: December 14, 2022).

References

Alvarez, J. E. (2001). The constitutional interpretation in international organizations. *In:* -M. Coicaud and V. Heiskanen (eds) *The Legitimacy of International Organizations*. Tokyo: United Nations University Press.

Boylan, B. M., McBeath, J., & Wang, B. (2021). US–China relations: Nationalism, the trade war, and COVID-19. *Fudan Journal of Humanities and Social Sciences*, 14(Commission), 23–40.

Burci, G. L., & Toebes, B. (2018). *Research Handbook on Global Health Law*. Cheltenham: Edward Elgar Publishing Limited.

Connolly, C. (2020). War and the coronavirus pandemic. *Third World Approaches to the International Law Review*, 2020 (1).

Cronin, B., & Hurd, I. (2008). *The UN Security Council and the Politics of International Authority*. London: Routledge.

Denk, E. (2015). *Uluslararası Örgütler Hukuku: Birleşmiş Milletler Sistemi*. Ankara: Siyasal Kitabevi.

Gian, L. Burci, & Cassels, A. (2016). Health. *In:* J. Katz Cogan, I. Hurd, and I. Johnstone (eds) *The Oxford Handbook of International Organizations*. New York: Oxford University Press.

Gostin, L. O., Habibi, R., & Meier, B. M. (2020). Has global health law risen to meet the COVID-19 challenge? Revisiting the international health regulations to prepare for future threats. *The Journal of Law, Medicine & Ethics*, 48(2), 376–381.

Gostin, L. O., Moon, S., & Meier, B. M. (2020). Reimagining global health governance in the age of COVID-19. *American Journal of Public Health*, 110(Commission), 1615–1619.

Hurd, I. (2014). *International Organizations: Politics, Law, Practice*. Cambridge: Cambridge University Press.

Karns, M. P., Mingst, K. A., & Stiles, K. W. (2015). *International Organizations: The Politics and Processes of Global Governance.* Boulder: Lynne Rienner Publishers.

Leal Filho, W., Brandli, L. L., Lange Salvia, A., Rayman-Bacchus, L., & Platje, J. (2020). COVID-19 and the UN sustainable development goals: Threat to solidarity or an opportunity? *Sustainability*, 12(13), 5343.

Levich, J. (2015). The Gates Foundation, ebola, and global health imperialism. *American Journal of Economics and Sociology*, 74, 704–742.

Mackenzie, J. S., & Jeggo, M. (2019). The one health approach—Why is it so important? *Tropical Medicine and Infectious Disease*, 4(2), 85–88.

Marx, K., & Engels, F. (2019). The communist manifesto. *Ideals and Ideologies.* London: Routledge.

Mathers, C. D. (2020). The history of the global burden of disease assessment at the World Health Organization. *Archives of Public Health*, 78(Commission), 1–13.

Mingst, K. A., & Karns, M. P. (2012). *The United Nations in the 21st Century.* Boulder: Westview Press.

Morawska, L., & Milton, D. K. (2020). It is time to address the airborne transmission of coronavirus disease 2019 (COVID-19). *Clinical Infectious Diseases*, 71(Commission), 2311–2313.

Samancı, U. (2014). Uluslararası Sağlık Tüzüğü (2005) ve hukuki niteliği. *Dokuz Eylül Üniversitesi Hukuk Fakültesi Dergisi*, 16, 113–169.

Samancı, U. (2016). Dünya Sağlık Örgütü ve Normatif İşlevi. *Dokuz Eylül Üniversitesi Sosyal Bilimler Enstitüsü Dergisi*, 18, 55–89.

Santos Rutschman, A. (2020). The reemergence of vaccine nationalism. *Georgetown Journal of International Affairs (Online), Saint Louis U. Legal Studies Research Paper No.* (2020–16), 1–3. https://papers.ssrn.com/sol3/papers.cfm?abstract_id=3642858.

Shamasunder, S., Holmes, S. M., Goronga, T., Carrasco, H., Katz, E., Frankfurter, R., & Keshavjee, S. (2020). COVID-19 reveals weak health systems by design: Why we must re-make global health in this historic moment. *Global Public Health*, 15(7), 1083–1089.

Tallberg, J., & Zürn, M. (2019). The legitimacy and legitimation of international organizations: Introduction and framework. *The Review of International Organizations*, 14(4), 581–606.

Thomas, S., Sagan, A., Larkin, J., Cylus, J., Figueras, J., & Karanikolos, M. (2020). *Strengthening Health System Resilience: Key Concepts and Strategies.* Copenhagen (Denmark): The European Observatory on Health Systems and Policies.

Wang, Z. (2021). From crisis to nationalism? *Chinese Political Science Review*, 6(Commission), 20–39.

WHO (1981). *International Code of Marketing of Breast-Milk Substitutes.* Geneva: the World Health Organization.

WHO (2016). *International Health Regulations (2005), 3rd.* France: World Health Organization.

WHO (2020). *Basic Documents: Forty-Ninth Edition (Including Amendments Adopted up to May 31 2019).* Geneva: the World Health Organization.

The World Health Organization (2022). United States of America: Partner in global health. Available at https://www.who.int/about/funding/contributors/usa (accessed December 14, 2022).

Yi-chong, X., & Weller, P. (2020). International organizations and state sovereignty: The World Health Organisation and COVID-19. *Social Alternatives*, 39(2), 50–59.

Zürn, M. (2021). COVID-19 and the legitimacy crisis of global governance 1. *The Crises of Legitimacy in Global Governance* (pp. 37–52). London: Routledge.

19 The COVID-19 Pandemic as a Security Issue and Its Implications for NATO

Arif Bağbaşlıoğlu

Introduction

Spreading globally since February 2020, the COVID-19 pandemic has had immediate, concrete effects in many areas, from economic and political relations to social and cultural relations and from individuals' daily habits to states' foreign policies. States have had to resort to intense countermeasures within their national borders to control the pandemic through their efforts. The international society also needed to cooperate to control the pandemic and overcome the resulting economic problems. When the pandemic first appeared, however, international organisations could not achieve the required international solidarity to fight the spreading pandemic. These included the United Nations (UN), the World Health Organization (WHO), which was expected to exhibit a leading global role in the combat against the pandemic as a specialised UN agency, and supranational organisations like the European Union (EU). These developments provoked discussions questioning the belief and respect for the effectiveness and legitimacy of international organisations operating for decades.

Indeed, the COVID-19 pandemic encouraged new discussions regarding the functions of states and international organisations and the norms, rules, and other institutions they have jointly created, such as diplomacy and international law. Although this does not determine whether international society is a myth or a reality when theorising international relations, the pandemic has revealed the lack of solidarity in existing international society. For example, the EU, which supposedly symbolises European integration, experienced "mask wars" between member states; China allegedly hid the scope of the pandemic due to economic and political concerns, and the United States of America (USA) cut its contribution to the World Health Organization in the middle of the pandemic.

Such actions remind us of former UK Prime Minister Margaret Thatcher's statement – albeit in a completely different context in 1987: "There's no such thing as society. There are individual men and women, and there are families (Keay, 1987)." Similarly, we can ask whether there is an international society or whether there are only states and their interests. There are good reasons to ask such questions. Elena Alekseenkova (2020), for example, argues that the pandemic has confirmed that there are no global responses to global challenges. Given the nature

DOI: 10.4324/9781003377597-22

of the COVID-19 pandemic, including its effects on human security and public health, and remembering the previous inadequacies of international organisations during international crises, global expectations that international organisations could combat the pandemic were not based on history. Nevertheless, this does not mean that international cooperation and solidarity and international organisations have lost their functions (Bağbaşlıoğlu, 2020: 97–98). Rather, it highlights the need to increase reform efforts to make international organisations more effective and sensitive to global problems.

The COVID-19 pandemic has risen as a non-military human security problem that transcends national borders and threatens everyone regardless of status. This suggests that the health sector should be considered a component of the security sector (Bağbaşlıoğlu, 2021: 30–31). The pandemic revealed the vulnerabilities of North Atlantic Treaty Organization (NATO) members' infrastructure and supply chains. Although NATO rapidly took measures to compensate for the pandemic's negative effects on its activities, we cannot say that NATO was prepared enough for the pandemic posing security threats to international institutions.

Accordingly, this study investigates whether the COVID-19 pandemic affected internal solidarity within NATO and encouraged members to solve NATO's existing problems. There are two main allegations of this study. First, the pandemic has increased the visibility of existing problems within NATO and accelerated ongoing efforts to solve them. Second, despite some difficulties and shortcomings in NATO's crisis management response, the COVID-19 pandemic has strengthened NATO's solidarity.

This chapter first considers the issues under discussion within NATO when the pandemic started and then evaluates how the pandemic affected these discussions. It then considers how the pandemic has affected NATO solidarity, burden sharing, and new strategic concept studies within NATO.

NATO's Agenda When COVID-19 Started

In response to the Cold War's evolving requirements, NATO has transformed its activities due to the changing international conjuncture and security environment in the post-Cold War era. During this transformation process, which can be considered a product of NATO's ability to adapt to changes in the international security environment, NATO has expanded its appreciation of the threats and risks against itself and established relations with the countries of Central Asia, the North East Africa, the Middle East, and the Asia Pacific Region. In this context, the Alliance has developed policies in many different areas, such as ensuring energy, maritime, human, and cyber security.

Since the 2010 Lisbon Summit, at which the third post-Cold War strategic concept of NATO was published, various significant international and regional developments have required a reassessment of NATO's security and defence policies. The Ukraine crisis in 2014 has had more visible and significant consequences for NATO's official discourse and practice. They started a process that has made collective defence missions and deterrence more pronounced. These were the original reasons for establishing NATO. NATO has treated the Ukraine crisis as a global problem that tests NATO's deterrent power – its core function. In addition, for the first time in NATO history, China is now a topic of political debate within NATO regarding its security approach regarding trade wars, the economy, technology, espionage, and cyber warfare.

Before the COVID-19 pandemic, there was much debate about the international system and organisations. These discussions included predictions of the collapse of the international liberal order and the end of the EU's dream of political integration, given the effects of Brexit. Critics also argued that international organisations had lost prestige because of the need to reform the UN system, particularly regarding the unrepresentativeness of the UN Security Council. Within NATO itself, the most fundamental debate was concerned with internal solidarity. NATO members have not always been able to form a common stance in addressing issues affecting their agenda for international politics. There have been disagreements among NATO members regarding the measures to be taken against Russia after the annexation of Crimea and the policies to be implemented in relations with China within the framework of the Syrian crisis or the discourse on trade wars. The disagreement within NATO about these issues generally arises from the differences in the geopolitical priorities of the NATO members. European members of NATO have repeatedly expressed their concern and dissatisfaction with US decisions regarding Afghanistan, Iraq, or Syria. The most visible form of this dissatisfaction is French President Emmanuel Macron's "brain death" comment, and his criticism of the lack of consultation among NATO member states in his interview with The Economist on November 7, 2019 (Macron, 2019). The problem of burden sharing, which has remained on the agenda at various times since the establishment of the Alliance, has been kept on the agenda more intensely by the US administrations, especially in the Trump Administration. European allies have been accused of being free riders (Birnbaum and Rucker, 2018). In fact, behind both the "brain death" comment and the burden-sharing problem lie the divergences among NATO member countries in terms of security understanding and threat perception. These have become more visible in recent years.

The COVID-19 pandemic broke out when these issues were on the agenda within NATO. The last NATO summit before the pandemic became global took place on December 3–4, 2019 in London. Because of the international environment described above, it is significant that the principles of "solidarity, unity and cohesion" are NATO's cornerstones in the first article of the Summit Declaration. According to the Summit Declaration, an evaluation process was initiated to strengthen consultation and improve cohesion. As a result of this process, the NATO 2030 Report, released on November 25, 2020, proclaimed a new perspective, including priorities and the need to broaden NATO's security approach. Thus, when the COVID-19 pandemic started, NATO had already held discussions and strengthened internal solidarity.

NATO's Response to the COVID-19 Pandemic

NATO faced an "invisible enemy," in the words of NATO Secretary General Jens Stoltenberg (NATO, 2020a), and the defence structure built against conventional threats was insufficient in the fight against this kind of enemy. Like many international organisations, NATO was caught unprepared for the COVID-19 pandemic, and NATO was criticised for its inability to provide sufficient cooperation and coordination during the initial outbreak, particularly with two European member states, Italy and Spain. It is worth noting that the pandemic did not hit all European countries simultaneously and with the same intensity after February 2020. At the beginning of the pandemic among NATO member states, we observed a lack of mutual assistance and the absolute superiority of sovereign governments in dealing with this security threat (Jović-Lazić, 2021: 150). Consequently, since NATO member states had differing perceptions and experiences of the threat, this resulted in a late realisation of the pandemic's devastating potential (De Mario, 2020: 3). It has become increasingly clear that NATO has to adapt and develop its effectiveness in detecting and countering such non-military global health threat.

In its public pandemic discourse, NATO has highlighted its experience with crisis management tasks such as strategic airlift, which proved beneficial during the COVID-19 outbreak (Baciu, 2021: 265). NATO foreign ministers ordered the Supreme Allied Commander Europe to coordinate the air transport of medical supplies and personnel (Rodihan and Mcpartland, 2020). During the pandemic, various parts of NATO's organisational structure ensured coordination among member states, such as the Euro-Atlantic Disaster Response Coordination Centre (EADRCC) and the Committee of the Chiefs of Military Medical Services in NATO (COMEDS) (Jones, 2020: 1–3).

As well as these NATO mechanisms, member-state governments also acted bilaterally. For example, Poland and Albania sent doctors to Italy; Germany's air force flew COVID-19 patients from Italy and France to German hospitals; the US delivered medicines to Italy; Estonia sent face masks and disinfectants to Spain and Italy; and Czechia sent face masks to the Republic of North Macedonia (Willa and Olszanecka, 2021: 276). EADRCC provides a clearinghouse to coordinate assistance requests and offers from seven NATO members and nine partner nations, as well as from the United Nations Office for the Coordination of Humanitarian Affairs (EADRCC, 2020: 1). According to Iftimie (2020: 51), the confidence in NATO's regional deterrence and defence mechanisms by both members and partners in recent crises, particularly in the EADRCC's response to the COVID-19 pandemic, is critical for NATO's ability to prevent, pursue, and prepare for the spread of biological agents and other weapons of mass destruction.

In addition to the mechanisms described above, NATO commissioned scientific research on the future impacts of COVID-19 on itself and its member states. For example, the NATO Systems Analysis Studies Specialist Team assessed the potential strategic and operational military short-term (1–6 year) impacts of the COVID-19 environment to provide national and NATO planners and decision-makers with high-level recommendations. Several alternatives were proposed in this study, distinguished primarily by the time required to develop a viable vaccine and overcome the impact of the pandemic.[1] The basic assumption of this study, which adopted the scenario analysis approach, was that although the future cannot be precisely predicted, scenarios can help make predictions about several possible futures. NATO uses such methods to make important decisions, such as preparing its strategic concepts.

However, despite these positive mechanisms and efforts, NATO could not rapidly develop a system to share medical supplies and personnel among its member countries. To exemplify, Poland (where the pandemic was manageable) only sent 15 doctors to Italy, which faced a much more serious situation, and nine doctors to the US, where the crisis reached dramatic proportions (Willa and Olszanecka, 2021: 277).

In addition to the lack of coordination and due to the independent state actions, it is also important to evaluate the pandemic's implications for NATO operations and exercises. To prevent the pandemic from affecting its military readiness, NATO concentrated primarily on maintaining the continuity of its activities while safeguarding its troops. Most of the NATO missions were held with a few briefly discontinued exceptions (De Mario, 2020: 1). Because NATO troops are vulnerable to COVID-19, military drills were redesigned. For example, after having started as scheduled in early February 2020, Defender-Europe 20 was significantly reduced in size and scope by mid-March due to the health risks of large-scale movements of personnel (De Mario, 2020: 4). These developments also raised the issue of troop security and medical security. NATO, therefore, established a COVID-19 Task Force to coordinate the provision of medical assistance within and outside the territory of member states. Although these NATO activities were relatively limited in scope, they provided important evidence of NATO's reactive capability and member states' solidarity.

COVID-19 and NATO's Burden-Sharing Issue

When the pandemic's effects on the global economy were most intense, studies conducted during 2020 and 2021 predicted that NATO's European members' military expenditure would fall as they prioritised health over military spending. This was expected to intensify discussions about burden sharing, a familiar problem within the Alliance, given repeated complaints by US administrations (Gvosdev, 2020). However, Russia's attack on Ukraine in February 2022 increased NATO solidarity, at least officially, and forced NATO's European members to increase their military spending.

Within NATO, burden sharing refers to the equitable distribution of costs and risks among member states while accomplishing its goals (Bağbaşlıoğlu, 2021: 32). The key criteria are that member states' defence spending should not be less than two per cent of gross domestic product (GDP). That member states should spend more than 20 per cent of their defence budgets on important equipment purchasing, including research and development.[2] Between 2013 and 2020, NATO made significant progress in increasing defence spending, both as a share of GDP and in real terms, with the number of member states achieving the two per cent target increasing from three to ten.

According to Willa and Olszanecka (2021: 277–278), NATO state governments have prioritised defence spending cuts to prevent social discontent, so most members are still struggling to meet their two per cent commitment. As Vanholme (2020) notes, if defence spending falls below the required planned level, NATO will have a difficult time building mutual trust among its member states, which may negatively influence the United States' military involvement in Europe. Gjoreski (2020: 89) predicts that although most NATO members will probably maintain their current defence spending levels or even increase it significantly as a percentage of GDP, the largest decline in defence spending is expected to occur after 2023 when adjustments to the burden-sharing methodology could be announced. This would involve varying the desired percentage of GDP allocated to defence spending.

After Russia attacked Ukraine in February 2022, statements by NATO leaders and decisions taken at the Summit on March 24, 2022 indicated renewed solidarity within NATO. Russia's attack was described as a "full-scale invasion" and "the gravest threat to Euro-Atlantic security in decades" at the virtual NATO Heads of Government and State meeting held on February 25 2022, one day after the invasion. Russia and Belarus, which contributed to this invasion, were condemned in the strongest possible terms. Apart from this joint declaration, all NATO members condemned Russia's actions as unacceptable. Significantly, on February 27, Chancellor Olaf Scholz announced that Germany would establish a €100 billion special fund for defence spending (Connolly, 2022). This was very important concerning NATO's burden-sharing problem. With this announcement, Germany can be one of the states that will fulfil its two per cent commitment. At this point, it should be remembered that NATO members increased their defence expenditures after the 2014 Ukraine crisis; however, although these increases were not uniform, they were generally made by countries geographically close to Russia, such as the Baltic countries and Poland. In addition to these developments, with the referendum held in Denmark on June 1, 2022, Denmark has been incorporated into the EU security and defence policy (Henley, 2022). In addition to the efforts mentioned by NATO members regarding the increase to their individual and collective defences, Sweden and Finland's application for membership to NATO is valuable in terms of being concrete indicators of the rise in solidarity within the Alliance of the Russia-Ukraine War.

At this point, it should be highlighted that Russia's invasion has started a period in which NATO increased the defence spending of European countries, thereby contradicting earlier predictions that the pandemic's effects would force a reduction. COVID-19 has created many dilemmas and severely challenged even the most economically powerful NATO members, who are expected to take more responsibility for the burden sharing. However, the lessons learnt from the 2008–2009 financial crisis indicate that there will be no drastic reductions in defence spending in the near future.

NATO 2030 Report and NATO 2022 Strategic Concept

The pandemic has also accelerated the efforts to rectify the obvious lack of dialogue and solidarity among NATO member states, such as decisions taken at the first NATO Heads of State Summit since the pandemic began, held in London in December 2019. More specifically, by the decisions, the Secretary General of NATO charged the Reflection Group, made up of ten distinguished individuals, with formulating suggestions for enhancing Allied unity and political consultation. On November 25, 2020, the Reflection Group released its NATO 2030 Report to offer a fresh viewpoint on the Alliance's security assessment (NATO, 2020b). The document covers issues such as threats to NATO, the policies of Russia and China, the effects of developing technologies on security, terrorism, developments in the Mediterranean, arms control and nuclear deterrence, as well as climate change, human security, pandemics, and natural disasters. The 2021 NATO's Brussels Summit announced various decisions in line with the report.

At the Madrid Summit held on June 28–30, 2022, a new strategic concept was adopted, in which the threats against NATO in the current international conjuncture and the methods for combating these threats are identified. The NATO 2022 Strategic Concept, the fourth strategic concept of the Alliance declared after the Cold War, is divided into four chapters that cover the Alliance's key missions, the current strategic environment, NATO's goals and guiding principles, and the conditions necessary to assure continuing success (NATO, 2022). The "Strategic Environment" section describes an international conjuncture that differs significantly from the adoption of the previous strategic concept that NATO announced at the Lisbon Summit in 2010. In contrast to NATO's three previous post-Cold War strategic concepts, the 2022 concept marks a significant shift in the Alliance's official discourse by stating that the Euro-Atlantic region is not at peace and identifying the Russian Federation as the most important and direct threat to NATO members.

For this reason, it can be stated that the document makes it a fundamental priority to increase the Alliance's capabilities in NATO's defence and deterrence issues. NATO's new Strategic Concept can be considered the roadmap for the Alliance's future course of action. The core tasks of the Alliance are linked to the new Strategic Concept of "investing in technical advancements, climate change, human security, women, peace, and security," which were excluded from the previous strategic concept. The text highlights that better steps would be taken to guarantee member states' safety in situations involving public health, climate change, and food insecurity.

Conclusion

The COVID-19 pandemic has demonstrated that the current understanding, norms, decision-making processes, and institutions are insufficient worldwide. In this regard, the pandemic has made it clear again that security cannot be managed solely from a state-oriented and military-based perspective, and health is actually a security issue. During the pandemic, NATO was compelled to alter its order of importance to establish a new norm. NATO's mission to build resilience has become an integral part of the Alliance's official discourse and was often emphasised in its response to the pandemic. NATO can be an effective force in the fight against threats like the pandemic that require global cooperation and solidarity. However, it has faced problems demonstrating its capacity due to differences in the geopolitical priorities of its member countries. As discussed in this chapter, these existed before the pandemic.

Since its establishment, NATO has worked to implement policies that redefine and counter security threats and risks within the framework of changes in the international conjuncture. For example, the COVID-19 pandemic emerged when security and international actors' security perceptions were changing. NATO's ability to adapt to these changes over 74 years has enabled it to transform itself from the original 12-member regional collective defence organisation into a global security organisation of 30 members and partnerships with 41 countries. NATO's transformation, resulting from the changes in the international security environment and security perceptions, has also expanded the Alliance's field of struggle and intervention. Although NATO included health risks as a security threat in its last strategic concept published in 2010, the COVID-19 pandemic showed that NATO, at least during the first phase of the pandemic, was not prepared enough and could not achieve the desired level of cooperation and coordination with European members, particularly Italy and Spain, when the pandemic first emerged. This led to criticism of NATO, raised doubts among NATO members about NATO's strategic concept and readiness to counter security threats, and necessitated a re-evaluation of its ability to identify non-military global threats to human security to take appropriate countermeasures.

By constituting a breakpoint in the traditional security approach, the COVID-19 pandemic stimulated new discussions regarding how to define the roles of institutions and organisations responsible for state security, territorial control, border and coast guard operations, counterterrorism, and public order. The pandemic has revealed that it is not enough to respond to global problems with only local/national policies and the importance of international cooperation in the fight against such problems.

Notes

1 For more detail, see Adlakha-Hutcheon and Johnston (2020).
2 According to NATO data, by 2022, 11 (Estonia, Greece, France, Poland, Romania, Latvia, Lithuania, Norway, Slovakia, the United Kingdom, and the USA) out of 30 NATO members complied with the two-percent commitment. Thus, member states are trying to meet their commitments. For more information, see NATO (2019b: 3). Overall, NATO member countries' defence spending has increased since 2013.

References

Adlakha-Hutcheon, G. and Johnston, P. (2020) "The Future Impacts of COVID-19 on the North Atlantic Treaty Organization—a Futures Framework", DRDC Canada. https://cradpdf.drdc-rddc.gc.ca/PDFS/unc349/p812285_A1b.pdf

Alekseenkova, E. (2020) "Corona as a Crown of (Neo) Modernism". https://valdaiclub.com/a/highlights/corona-as-a-crown-of-neo-modernism-/

Baciu, C. (2021) "Beyond the Emergency Problematique. How Do Security IOs Respond to Crises-A Case Study of NATO Response to COVID-19", *Journal of Transatlantic Studies*. 19 (3), pp. 261–281.

Bağbaşlıoğlu, A. (2020) "Koronavirüs Salgınının Uluslararası Örgütlerin Meşruiyeti Ve Etkinliğine Yönelik Yansımaları: NATO Örneği", *Turkish Studies*. 15 (4), pp. 95–108.

Bağbaşlıoğlu, A. (2021) "NATO Burden-Sharing in the COVID-19 Era: A Diminishing US Appetite for Security Guarantees for Europe?", *Perceptions: Journal of International Affairs*. 26 (1), pp. 29–53.

Birnbaum, M. and Rucker, P. (2018) "At NATO, Trump Claims Allies Make New Defense Spending Commitments After He Upends Summit", The Washington Post. https://www.washingtonpost.com/world/europe/trump-upends-nato-summit-demanding-immediate-spending-increases-or-he-willdo-his-own-thing/2018/07/12/a3818cc6-7f0a-11e8-a63f-7b5d2aba7ac5_story.html

Connolly, K. (2022) "Germany to Set up €100bn Fund to Boost Its Military Strength", The Guardian. https://www.theguardian.com/world/2022/feb/27/germany-set-up-fund-boost-military-strength-ukraine-putin

De Mario, G. (2020) "NATO's Response to COVID-19: Lessons for Resilience and Readiness", The Brooking Institution. https://www.brookings.edu/research/natos-response-to-covid-19-lessons-for-resilience-and-readiness/

EADRCC (2020) *EADRCC Situation Report 19 on COVID-19*. Brussels: NATO. https://www.nato.int/nato_static_fl2014/assets/pdf/2020/7/pdf/200702-EADRCC-0107_sitrep19.pdf

Gjoreski, I. (2020) "NATO Burden Sharing Policy and COVID 19 Implications on Defence Expenditures", *Contemporary Macedonian Defense*. 20 (39), pp. 69–91.

Gvosdev, N. K. (2020) "The Effect of COVID-19 on the NATO Alliance", Foreign Policy Research Institute. https://www.fpri.org/article/2020/03/the-effect-of-covid-19-on-the-nato-alliance/

Henley, J. (2022) "Denmark Votes Overwhelmingly to Join EU's Common Defence Policy". https://www.theguardian.com/world/2022/jun/01/denmark-votes-on-joining-eus-common-defence-policy

Iftimie, I. A. (2020). "The Implications of COVID-19 for NATO's Counter-Bioterrorism". *In*: Thierry Tardy (ed.) *COVID-19: Report Subtitle: NATO in the Age of Pandemics*. NATO Defense College.

Jones, K. (2020) "From Smart Defence to Strategic Defence: Pooling and Sharing from The Start", NATO Parliamentary Assembly, Science and Technology Committee.

Jović-Lazić, A. (2021) "The COVID-19 Pandemic and Its Impact on NATO". *In*: Sanja Jelisavac Trošić and Jelica Gordanić (eds) *International Organizations and States' Response to COVID-19*, pp. 145–161. University of Belgrade.

Keay, D. (1987) "Interview for Woman's Own ('No Such Thing as Society')". https://www.margaretthatcher.org/document/106689

Macron, E. (2019) "Emmanuel Macron in His Own Words". *The Economist*. https://www.economist.com/europe/2019/11/07/emmanuel-macron-in-his-own-words-english.

NATO (2019) "London Declaration". https://www.nato.int/cps/en/natohq/official_texts_171584.htm

NATO (2020a) "Coronavirus Response to Top NATO Ministerial Agenda". https://www.nato.int/cps/en/natohq/news_174785.htm

NATO (2020b) "NATO 2030: United for a New Era". https://www.nato.int/nato_static_fl2014/assets/pdf/2020/12/pdf/201201-Reflection-Group-Final-Report-Uni.pdf

NATO (2022) "NATO 2022 Strategic Concept". https://www.nato.int/nato_static_fl2014/assets/pdf/2022/6/pdf/290622-strategic-concept.pdf

Rodihan, C. and Mcpartland, C. (2020) "NATO in the Fight against Coronavirus: Coordinating, Contributing, Controlling and Communicating", The Atlantic Council. https://www.atlanticcouncil.org/blogs/new-atlanticist/nato-in-the-fight-against-coronavirus-coordinating-contributing-controlling-and-communicating/

Vanholme, R. (2020) "How COVID-19 May Impact the European Defence", FINABEL European Army Interoperability Centre. https://finabel.org/how-COVID-19-may-impact-the-european-defence/

Willa, R. and Olszanecka, N. (2021) "NATO: Building a Security Community in the Face of Covid-19 Pandemic", *European Research Studies Journal*. 24 (1), pp. 269–280.

20 Post-Pandemic Effects on the Realisation of Sustainable Development Goals (SDGs) for OECD Countries

R. Arzu Kalemci and Mehmet Güray Ünsal

Introduction

In September 2015, 193 United Nations (UN) member countries adopted 17 Sustainable Development Goals (SDGs), scheduled for completion by 2030, to end poverty worldwide and ensure that all people on the planet can peacefully enjoy equal well-being. In line with this plan, the Organisation for Economic Cooperation and Development (OECD), established in 1961, supports the UN in ensuring the success of the 2030 Agenda for Sustainable Development (Lamichhane et al., 2021). However, in 2015, when the SDGs were adopted, the world was unaware of the emerging pandemic. The pandemic has greatly affected the three dimensions of sustainable development: economic, social, and environmental. Indeed, following the emergence of the COVID-19 pandemic, for the first time since the adoption of the SDGs in 2015, the global average SDGs Index score for 2020 decreased from the previous year (Sachs et al., 2020). The success of the SDGs is directly related to sustainable economic growth and globalisation. The COVID-19 process has had a contractionary effect on the global economy. At this point, industrialised countries struggling to support their citizens may face the threat of being unable to finance the development of others. The effects of future pandemics may worsen their impact on the SDGs (Naidoo and Fisher, 2020). In addition, achieving the SDGs is important for our preparation for future pandemics. Indeed, according to the World Health Organization (WHO), from 2011 to 2017, 1,307 outbreaks occurred in 172 countries, with an average of one epidemic event every two days (Kam, 2020).

With an analytical approach, this study aims to reveal to what extent the pandemic has affected OECD countries, which play important roles in realising the SDGs. Since the SDGs were adopted, a series of studies have been conducted to show the performance of countries based on each SDG. One of them is the annual reports published by the Bertelsmann Stiftung and the Sustainable Development Solutions Network, one of the leading collaborative organisations of the UN Sustainable Development Information Platform. These reports provide critical information on countries' overall performance in achieving the 17 SDGs. In the current study, we examine the pre-pandemic and post-pandemic performance of OECD countries with the data envelopment analysis (DEA) method by

DOI: 10.4324/9781003377597-23

considering the reports published between the years of 2018–2021 (Sachs et al., 2018; Sachs et al., 2019; Sachs et al., 2020; Sachs et al., 2021). The study starts with the introduction of 17 SDGs briefly and then analyses how the pandemic may have affected the realisation of the SDGs in OECD countries. Then the study continues with methodology, data analysis, and findings. Finally, the results are evaluated in the conclusion.

Sustainable Development Goals (SDGs)

The UN accepted the SDGs in 2015 as a universal call to action, perhaps agreed upon by all countries with a high level of participation and motivation. In this context, 17 SDGs have been identified. The goals are stated by the United Nations as follows: Goal 1: No Poverty; Goal 2: Zero Hunger; Goal 3: Good Health and Well-Being; Goal 4: Quality Education; Goal 5: Gender Equality; Goal 6: Clean Water and Sanitation; Goal 7: Affordable and Clean Energy; Goal 8: Decent Work and Economic Growth; Goal 9: Industry, Innovation, and Infrastructure; Goal 10: Reduced Inequalities; Goal 11: Sustainable Cities and Communities; Goal 12: Responsible Consumption and Production; Goal 13: Climate Action; Goal 14: Life Below Water; Goal 15: Life on Land; Goal 16: Peace, Justice and Strong Institutions and Goal 17: Partnership for the Goals.

Pandemic, SDGs, and the OECD Countries

The situation was very different for the whole world in 2015 when the UN adopted 17 SDGs. An infectious disease that is believed to have started in China in December 2019 and is defined as a coronavirus (SARS-CoV-2) quickly spread worldwide (Zhou et al., 2020). On March 11, 2020, the World Health Organization (WHO) declared that the number of cases worldwide had reached 118,319, of which 4,292 were fatal, and it was a pandemic. Afterwards, terms such as "quarantine," "curfew," and "social distance" entered people's lives (Nundy et al., 2021). Much research has been done on the effects of the pandemic in the scientific field. Some of these studies have revealed how quarantines and social distancing associated with COVID-19 have affected national economies, business life, tourism, education, political relations, etc. (Ahimi et al., 2020; Brown et al., 2020; Ghosh et al., 2020). Naidoo and Fisher (2020) have provided a framework for the effects of COVID-19 on the SDGs for how each SDG will be affected. According to their framework, almost all SDGs are under threat. COVID-19 has particularly affected SDG 1 (No Hunger), SDG 2 (Zero Hunger), and SDG 8 (Decent Work and Economic Growth). For example, in the aftermath of COVID-19, extreme poverty increased in sub-Saharan Africa and other parts of the world in 2020, pushing an additional 120 million people into extreme poverty, mostly in low- and middle-income countries. In the long term, it is estimated that COVID-19's impact on SDG 4 (Quality Education), SDG 5 (Gender Equality), SDG 6 (Clean Water and Sanitation), SDG 7 (Affordable and Clean Energy), and SDG 9 (Industry, Innovation, and Infrastructure) can have very significant effects on the realisation of the goals. It was also predicted that with schools closed for months during the pandemic, countries without a digital infrastructure to realise distance education would see a decline in the quality of teaching. This situation will be difficult to compensate for in the long run (Sachs et al., 2021).

The consequences of this disease have inevitably started to threaten the successful realisation of the SDGs. While the global economy is expected to decrease by at least 5% with the effects of COVID-19, it poses an important threat, especially for industrialised countries, which have a significant share in the realisation of these 17 SDGs (Naidoo and Fisher, 2020). For the first time since the SDGs were adopted in 2015, the global average SDGs Index score for 2020 fell from the previous year due to rising poverty rates and unemployment (Sachs et al., 2021). On the other hand, in the realisation of goal 17, goal 17.2, that is, "developed countries should commit at least 0.7% of gross national income overseas for developing and 0.15% to at least-developed nations" should be emphasised for the OECD countries after COVID-19 (Naidoo and Fisher, 2020). The OECD, established in 1961, supports the UN in ensuring the success of the 2030 Agenda for Sustainable Development (Lamichhane et al., 2021). OECD countries have an important role in the effective realisation of the SDGs. OECD member countries work with partner organisations and stakeholders for policymaking, communication, and economic, social, and technological development for sustainable economic development and welfare (Singh et al., 2012).

OECD partnerships provide a strong support mechanism as a buffer between private and public, local and international sectors, and country resources (Sachs et al., 2018). However, in 2015, when the SDGs were adopted, there was no pandemic worldwide. Frankly, the pandemic significantly impacted three dimensions of sustainable development: economic, social, and environmental. Under normal circumstances, OECD member countries are closer to reaching the goals than other countries. Still, due to COVID-19, the importance of strengthening health systems, including in the OECD countries, is clear, which SDG 3 also points out (Sachs et al., 2021). Despite the improvement in average living conditions in OECD countries over the last decade, the pandemic has caused them to lag (OECD, 2020a).

In 10 OECD countries, a quarter of households do not have a personal computer. In 2018, 85% of households in 29 OECD countries had access to broadband internet services. Internet access is below 60% in Mexico, 70% in Japan, and 80% in New Zealand, Greece, Portugal, Australia, the United States, Lithuania, Latvia, the Slovak Republic, and Poland (OECD, 2020b). As a matter of fact, the SDGs call for strengthening the capacity of all countries, especially developing countries, to be prepared for pandemics, reduce risks, and manage national and global health risks. On the other hand, current funding efforts are insufficient to respond to crises of the magnitude of COVID-19. Crises greatly affect both developed and developing countries and sufficient funding is an important source of strength for countering COVID-19 and future pandemics. Therefore, multilateral systems and forums for coordinating development assistance, such as the OECD Development Assistance Committee (DAC), designing a better coordinated and more efficient response and pooling resources have become more important than ever. In most OECD countries, excessive indebtedness is more common among middle-income households than low- and high-income households, affecting around 11% of middle-income households on average. While the average household disposable income in the OECD region has increased by 6% cumulatively since 2010, it remained below 2010 in Spain and Italy, which were most affected by COVID-19. Therefore, in the current situation, considering that COVID-19 isolated the entire population in their homes and brought almost all sectors of the economy to a standstill, it is predicted that the transfer of low gross domestic product (GDP) to lower household income may be faster than the situation in 2008. Thus, considering that one out of every three people in the OECD is financially insecure, it is a fact that the incomes of young people will decrease, and less educated people will inevitably increase (OECD, 2020c).

Methodology

DEA is one of the most popular methods in the literature for efficiency measurement. Both being a non-parametric method and having no limitations for the number of inputs and outputs in the production process, DEA is one of the most commonly used methods for the efficiency measurement of the units. These units are called decision-making units (DMUs) in the DEA methodology.

In DEA methodology, many models can be used to measure efficiency, and these models are based on the ratio of the weighted sum of outputs to the weighted sum of inputs (Charnes et al., 1978). At the end of the efficiency evaluation process, DEA supplies advantages such as benchmarking, classification, ranking, and projection for DMUs in the analysis. DEA models are also classified into different structures according to their orientations and return to scales. If the projection feature of the models is for the production of fixed output values by decreasing the inputs, these models are called input-oriented models. Moreover, basic DEA models include constant returns to scale (CRS or CCR) or variable returns to scale (VRS or BCC) in the production process. CRS or CCR ideas express that output value can only change by the same proportion as input value is changed in the production process (Banker et al., 1984).

In general terms, the efficiency of a DMU can be represented as a ratio of the weighted outputs to the weighted inputs, where maximum efficiency scores are restricted to 1; a DMU is considered efficient if its efficiency score is equal to 1, and a DMU is regarded as inefficient one if its efficiency scores are less than 1 (Cooper et al., 2011). The efficiency scores of inefficient countries are greater than 1 in output-oriented models, which will be discussed in this study. It is possible and easy to set all efficiency scores to the 0–1 range with a suitable transformation. Therefore, although the output-oriented model is used in this study, the values of the efficiency scores are converted into the 0–1 range to conform to this definition.

In Model 20.1, x_{ij} $(i=1,\ldots,m)$ and y_{rj} $(r=1,\ldots,s)$ represent the input and output values of DMU_j $(j=1,\ldots,n)$, respectively. Here, v_i $(i=1,\ldots,m)$ and u_r $(r=1,\ldots,s)$ are decision variables, which are the weights of input and output variables, respectively. Naturally, it is aimed to determine the set of weights that optimise the objective function giving the efficiency score of the relevant DMU. Due to the output and input variables that will be explained in the next section, an output-oriented CCR model will be used in the analysis of this study. DMU_o represents the DMU under evaluation. According to these basic explanations, the efficiency of DMU_o based on the output-oriented CCR or CRS (constant returns to scale) model is calculated as given below (Cooper et al., 2011):

Model 20.1

$$\text{Min } \phi_o = \sum_{i=1}^{m} v_i x_{io}$$

$$s.t. \sum_{r=1}^{s} u_r y_{ro} = 1$$

$$\sum_{r=1}^{s} u_r y_{rj} - \sum_{i=1}^{m} v_i x_{ij} \leq 0, \ j=1,\ldots,n$$

$$u_r \geq 0, \ r=1,\ldots,s$$

$$v_i \geq 0, \ i=1,\ldots,m$$

Model 20.1 is known as the multiplier (or primal) model of the input-oriented CCR. The dual form of the multiplier model is known as the envelopment model, and it can be given in Model 20.2 (Cooper et al., 2011).

Model 20.2

$$\text{Max } z_o = \theta_o$$

$$s.t. \ x_{io} - \sum_{r=1}^{n} x_{ij} \lambda_j \geq 0$$

$$\sum_{r=1}^{n} y_{rj} \lambda_j \geq \theta_o y_{ro}$$

$$\lambda_j \geq 0, \ i=1,\ldots,m \quad r=1,\ldots,s \quad j=1,\ldots,n$$

In DEA, DMUs are also benchmarked, classified, and ranked according to efficiency scores obtained in the analysis.

Efficiency Evaluation of OECD Countries Based on Sustainable Development

This section includes the efficiency evaluation of OECD countries. In this part of the study, it is necessary to discuss the selected outputs and inputs in the application part of this study. In DEA, variables need to be separated as input and output. The determination process of variables as input and output is due to their effect on the DMU in the evaluation (Unsal and Orkcu, 2017). Retzlaff-Roberts (1996) proposes that it is appropriate to consider the concept of positive and negative effectiveness instead of input and output variables. It is suggested that variables whose increase (positive effective) provides a better evaluation of the DMU are taken as outputs. On the other hand, variables whose decrease (negative effective) provides a better assessment of the DMU are taken as inputs (Retzlaff-Roberts, 1996).

As mentioned in Section 2 of the study, the 16 goals related to the sustainable development report are classified under three main subheadings: *Economy*, *Equality*, and *Sustainability*. By following this concept of Retzlaff-Roberts (1996), it is clear that the scores of countries obtained from each subheading can be considered one of the outputs in the sustainable development efficiency measurement of OECD countries. This is because the meaning of high scores to be obtained from these three subheadings can be interpreted as countries getting better in terms of development. Thus, the total scores obtained from these three subheadings can represent three output variables for each OECD member country. To make the analysis completely equitable and fair, the input value can be fixed to be the same numerical value for all countries. It is possible to frequently come across such use of inputs in the literature (Alp, 2006). So, the evaluation process has three outputs and one fixed input for each country. The output variables are the total score in the *Economy* subheading, the *Equality* subheading score, and the *Sustainability* subheading score. As a scaling feature, the input value is taken as 100 for each DMU (country) in the analysis.

Data Description

In the study, the reports published by Bertelsmann Stiftung and the Sustainable Development Solutions Network in 2018, 2019, 2020, and 2021 are taken as a data set. In the mentioned reports, OECD countries are classified as on track, moderately increasing, stagnating, decreasing, and data unavailable based on SDGs. The current study coded on track as 4, moderately increasing as 3, stagnating as 2, decreasing as 1, and data not available as 0 for the 16 SDGs rather than 17 SDGs as the 17th goal "partnership for the goals" thought to be the general description. As related literature highlighted, all the SDGs are also classified as Economy, Equality, and Sustainability, as the pandemic has greatly affected the three dimensions

Table 20.1 Classification of Goals*

Goals	Description	Classification
Goal 1	No poverty	Economy
Goal 2	Zero hunger	Economy
Goal 3	Good health and well-being	Equality
Goal 4	Quality education	Equality
Goal 5	Gender equality	Equality
Goal 6	Clean water and sanitation	Sustainability
Goal 7	Affordable and clean energy	Sustainability
Goal 8	Decent work and economic growth	Economy
Goal 9	Industry, innovation and infrastructure	Economy
Goal 10	Reduced inequalities	Equality
Goal 11	Sustainable cities and communities	Sustainability
Goal 12	Responsible consumption and production	Sustainability
Goal 13	Climate action	Sustainability
Goal 14	Life below water	Sustainability
Goal 15	Life on land	Sustainability
Goal 16	Peace, justice and strong institutions	Equality

*17th goal "partnership for the goals" is excluded from the classification as it has a general description.

of sustainable development: economic, social, and environmental (Heggen et al., 2020). The classification approach of each goal can be seen in Table 20.1.

According to this classification, Likert scale type (0–4) scores given to each goal are formed by summing within themselves for each classification title. A Likert score is assigned for each item in a questionnaire to evaluate the respondent's response in a quantitative value on the item with the level of agreement/disagreement. In this study, output variables are calculated as the summation of the Likert scale scores of goals for each classification title.

As an extra finding in the data description, Figures 20.1–20.3 indicate the countries that decreased the output values calculated after the pandemic process. Australia, Austria, Belgium, Chile, Colombia, Estonia, Hungary, Lithuania, Mexico, the UK, and the US are notable for decreasing values of the *Economy* subheading after the pandemic process. Similarly, the Czech Republic, Denmark, Finland, France, Ireland, Italy, Türkiye, and the US decrease their *Equality* subheading values after the pandemic. In the *Sustainability* subheading, Denmark, Finland, Hungary, Spain, Sweden, Switzerland, and the UK are the countries that decrease their values. To see whether their relative efficiencies will be affected due to these decreasing values in their data, the analysis results in subsection 4.2 have to be investigated.

Evaluation of the Efficiency Scores over the Years

The application data of OECD countries belong to 2018–2021. The term from 2018 to 2021 is adequate to observe the efficiency changes before and after the pandemic process related to the COVID-19 global health problem. According to the results of

234 *R. Arzu Kalemci and Mehmet Güray Ünsal*

Figure 20.1 The countries which are shown a decrease in the *Economy* subheading.

Post-Pandemic Effects on the Realisation of the SDGs 235

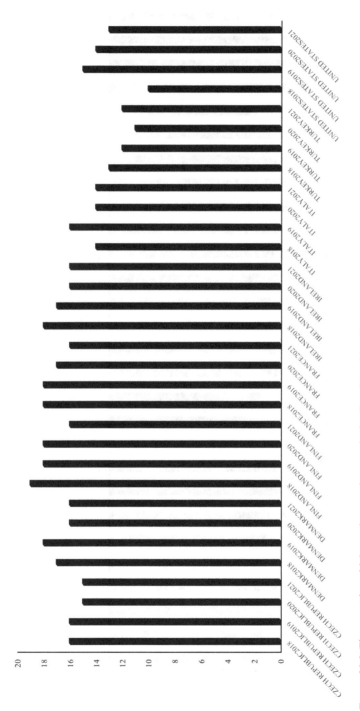

Figure 20.2 The countries which are shown a decrease in the *Equality* subheading.

236 *R. Arzu Kalemci and Mehmet Güray Ünsal*

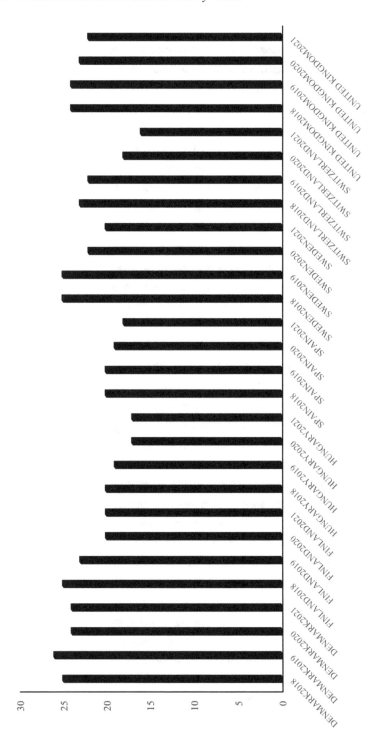

Figure 20.3 The countries which are shown a decrease in *Sustainability* subheading.

Table 20.2 Efficiency Scores of Each Country from 2018 to 2021

Countries	CCR (2018)	CCR (2019)	CCR (2020)	CCR (2021)
Australia	0.867	0.871	0.879	0.782
Austria	0.933	0.968	0.933	0.875
Belgium	0.939	1.000	0.933	0.969
Canada	0.842	0.887	0.933	1.000
Chile	0.933	0.871	0.846	0.846
Colombia	0.933	0.852	0.958	0.807
Czech Republic	0.933	0.935	0.933	0.933
Denmark	1.000	1.000	1.000	1.000
Estonia	0.765	0.890	0.943	0.906
Finland	1.000	0.984	1.000	0.938
France	0.970	0.968	0.947	0.938
Germany	1.000	0.988	0.981	0.974
Greece	0.760	0.890	0.886	0.875
Hungary	0.800	0.877	0.867	0.737
Iceland	0.947	0.933	1.000	0.969
Ireland	1.000	0.952	0.933	0.938
Israel	0.800	0.933	0.824	1.000
Italy	0.840	0.897	0.904	0.867
Japan	0.800	0.933	0.942	1.000
Korea Republic	0.733	0.933	1.000	0.844
Latvia	0.818	0.880	0.841	0.859
Lithuania	1.000	0.871	0.841	0.875
Luxembourg	0.933	0.704	0.933	0.813
Mexico	0.867	0.800	0.833	0.731
Netherlands	1.000	1.000	1.000	1.000
New Zealand	0.867	0.933	0.933	0.933
Norway	0.947	1.000	1.000	1.000
Poland	0.842	0.871	0.933	0.933
Portugal	0.840	0.880	0.933	0.938
Slovak Republic	0.800	0.868	0.867	0.875
Slovenia	0.960	0.919	0.933	1.000
Spain	0.800	0.898	0.885	0.938
Sweden	1.000	1.000	1.000	1.000
Switzerland	0.920	0.846	1.000	0.875
Turkey	0.733	0.733	0.800	0.800
United Kingdom	0.960	0.988	0.958	0.917
United States	0.867	0.933	0.867	0.800
Mean	0.891	0.910	0.924	0.905

the output-oriented CCR model (in Models 20.1 and 20.2), the efficiency scores of each country are obtained from 2018 to 2021 in Table 20.2.

According to the classification ability of DEA models, the countries are separated into two groups each year, efficient and inefficient countries. In Table 20.2, the three most remarkable countries are Denmark, Netherlands, and Sweden, according to their performances. These three countries are efficient in all periods from 2018 to 2021. Efficient countries by years, in 2018, are Denmark, Finland, Germany, Ireland, Lithuania, Netherlands, and Sweden. In 2019, Belgium, Denmark,

Netherlands, Norway, and Sweden are efficient countries. According to the results in 2020, Demark, Finland, Iceland, the Republic of Korea (South Korea), the Netherlands, Norway, Sweden, and Switzerland are efficient countries. Canada, Denmark, Israel, Japan, the Netherlands, Norway, Slovenia, and Sweden are efficient countries in 2021. Furthermore, DEA models can benchmark the countries according to their efficiency scores. For instance, Belgium showed a better performance than Australia in 2018 because its efficiency score was higher (0.939 > 0.867). Similar comments can be made for the other countries regarding efficiency scores each year.

According to the ranking ability of DEA models, the countries can be ranked in descending order according to their efficiency scores each year. In Figures 20.4–20.6, the performance of the countries can be seen visually by considering the mean value of each year as a threshold value in the line graphs. In these figures, countries above and below the average efficiency scores can be observed more clearly.

The average level of efficiency scores in 2018 is calculated as 0.891. In Figure 20.4, the countries that fall under the grey line have lower efficiency scores than the average efficiency value of OECD countries in 2018. These countries are Australia, Canada, Estonia, Greece, Hungary, Israel, Italy, Japan, the Republic of Korea, Latvia, Mexico, New Zealand, Poland, Portugal, Slovak Rep., Spain, Turkey, and the US.

In Figure 20.5, the countries that fall under the grey line have lower efficiency scores than the average efficiency value of OECD countries in 2019. The average level of efficiency scores in 2019 is calculated as 0.910. The countries below the average level are Australia, Canada, Chile, Colombia, Estonia, Greece, Hungary, Italy, Latvia, Lithuania, Luxembourg, Mexico, Poland, Portugal, the Slovak Republic, Spain, Switzerland, and Türkiye. Unlike in 2018, Chile, Colombia, Lithuania, Luxembourg, and Switzerland fell below the average in 2019.

In Figure 20.6, the results belong to the year 2020. As mentioned in Figures 20.4 and 20.5, the grey line represents the average efficiency score (0.924) level of the OECD countries in 2020. If the results in 2020 are compared with the results of the two previous years, similar countries fall under the average line, such as Australia, Chile, Greece, Hungary, Israel, Italy, Latvia, Lithuania, Mexico, the Slovak Republic, Spain, Türkiye, and the US. 2020 is a year in which the effects of the COVID-19 pandemic were felt. Thus, it should be examined in more detail. In 2020, Israel and the US returned to the level of countries that fell below the average after a one-year hiatus. Another interesting point is the attention of the Republic of Korea (South Korea). Despite the pandemic, it has become one of the most efficient countries and has reached the highest level of efficiency in a four-year period.

In 2021, the average level of efficiency score was 0.905. The countries below the average level are Australia, Austria, Canada, Chile, Colombia, Greece, Hungary, Italy, the Republic of Korea, Latvia, Lithuania, Luxembourg, Mexico, Poland, the Slovak Republic, Switzerland, Türkiye, and the US. 2021 was a year in which the effects of the pandemic continued in the world. In Figure 20.7, it is seen that the Republic of Korea joins the countries under the average efficiency level

Post-Pandemic Effects on the Realisation of the SDGs 239

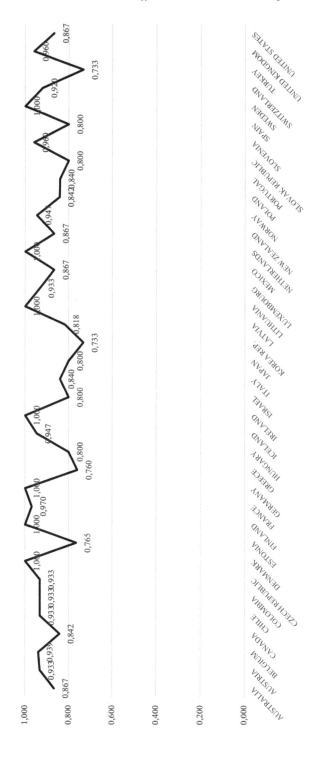

Figure 20.4 Line graph of efficiency scores of each country in 2018.

240 *R. Arzu Kalemci and Mehmet Güray Ünsal*

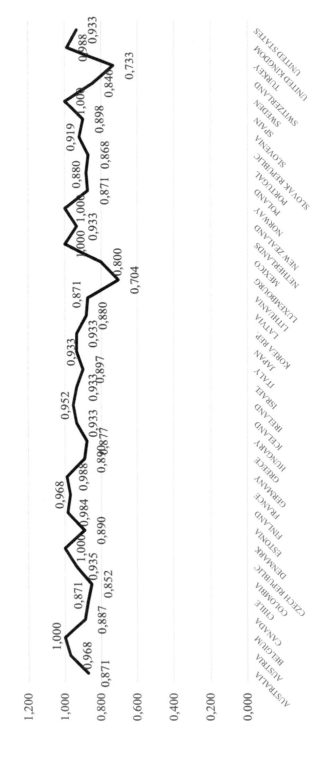

Figure 20.5 Line graph of efficiency scores of each country in 2019.

Post-Pandemic Effects on the Realisation of the SDGs 241

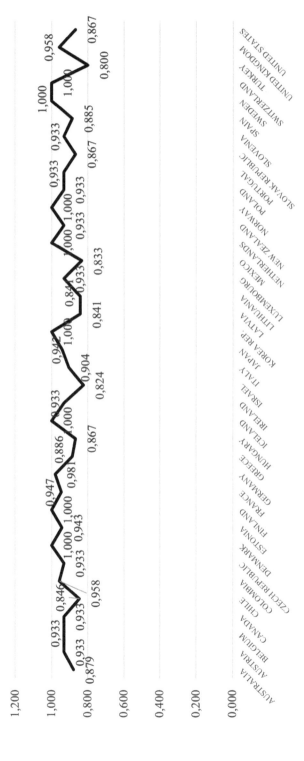

Figure 20.6 Line graph of efficiency scores of each country in 2020.

242　*R. Arzu Kalemci and Mehmet Güray Ünsal*

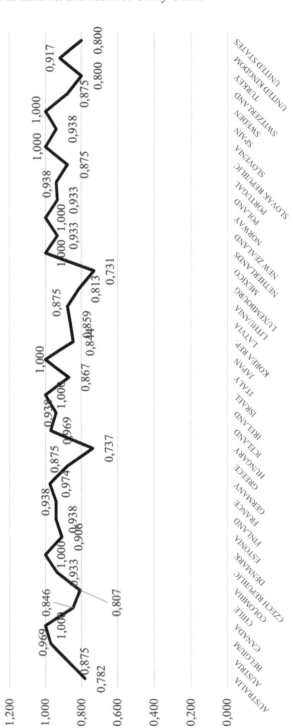

Figure 20.7 Line graph of efficiency scores of each country in 2021.

again. Another interesting point is that Spain stayed above the average efficiency level for the first time.

Evaluation of the Efficiency Scores of Countries Before and After the Pandemic

To more visually describe the pre- and post-pandemic process, mappings are made over the average values of each country in the 2018–2019 and 2020–2021 terms in Figures 20.8 and 20.9, respectively. The average efficiency scores of countries and mappings can be seen in Table 20.3 and Figures 20.8 and 20.9.

According to the efficiency scores in Table 20.3, due to the decrease in the average efficiency scores, the countries that are adversely affected by the pandemic in terms of satisfying the sustainable development criteria are Australia, Australia, Belgium, Chile, Colombia, the Czech Republic, Finland, France, Germany, Hungary, Ireland, Italy, Lithuania, Mexico, the UK, and the US.

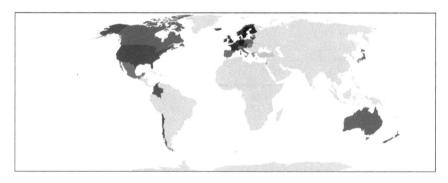

Figure 20.8 Mapping for average efficiency values of countries in 2018–2019.

Map source: © Australian Bureau of Statistics, GeoNames, Microsoft, Navinfo, OpenStreetMap, TomTom, Wikipedia, Zenrin

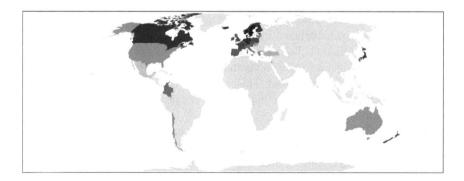

Figure 20.9 Mapping for average efficiency values of countries in 2020–2021.

Map source: © Australian Bureau of Statistics, GeoNames, Microsoft, Navinfo, OpenStreetMap, TomTom, Wikipedia, Zenrin

Table 20.3 Average (Mean) Efficiency Scores of OECD Countries in 2018–2019 and 2020–2021

Countries	MeanBP*	MeanAP*	Countries	MeanBP	MeanAP
Australia	0.869	0.831	Korea Rep.	0.833	0.922
Austria	0.951	0.904	Latvia	0.849	0.850
Belgium	0.970	0.951	Lithuania	0.936	0.858
Canada	0.865	0.967	Luxembourg	0.819	0.873
Chile	0.902	0.846	Mexico	0.834	0.782
Colombia	0.893	0.883	Netherlands	1.000	1.000
Czech Republic	0.934	0.933	New Zealand	0.900	0.933
Denmark	1.000	1.000	Norway	0.974	1.000
Estonia	0.828	0.925	Poland	0.857	0.933
Finland	0.992	0.969	Portugal	0.860	0.936
France	0.969	0.943	Slovak Republic	0.834	0.871
Germany	0.994	0.978	Slovenia	0.940	0.967
Greece	0.825	0.881	Spain	0.849	0.912
Hungary	0.839	0.802	Sweden	1.000	1.000
Iceland	0.940	0.985	Switzerland	0.883	0.938
Ireland	0.976	0.936	Turkey	0.733	0.800
Israel	0.867	0.912	United Kingdom	0.974	0.938
Italy	0.869	0.886	United States	0.900	0.834
Japan	0.867	0.971			

*BP: Before pandemic, AP: After pandemic.

The results can be seen in Figures 20.8 and 20.9 before and after the pandemic, respectively.

Projection for Inefficient Countries for the Most Recent Year, 2021

Table 20.2 shows that Canada, Denmark, Israel, Japan, the Netherlands, Norway, Slovenia, and Sweden were efficient countries in 2021. As mentioned in Section 3, one of the most important features of DEA methodology is the projection ability of the models, and the output-oriented CCR model is used in this study. If the projection feature of the models is for the use of fixed input values by increasing the outputs, these models are called output-oriented models. For this reason, the aim is to determine the projected (goal) numerical value levels for outputs of inefficient countries that should be increased. This will provide guidance on how inefficient countries can reach the levels of efficient ones. The projected (goals) values can be seen in Table 20.4.

As seen in Table 20.4, some projection values have decimal places. Since it is not possible to have a decimal value for any variable measured in the Likert scale, the goal values with decimal values are rounded up in Table 20.4. It is very easy and practical to make comments about projection values. Some examples can be given through some of the countries identified as inefficient ones in 2021. For instance, Australia has to increase its output values from 11, 14, and 18 to 15, 18, and 24 for Economy, Equality, and Sustainability, respectively. As another example,

Post-Pandemic Effects on the Realisation of the SDGs 245

Table 20.4 The Projected (Target) Numerical Value Levels for Outputs of Inefficient Countries

Countries	Outputs	Original Value	Projected (Target) Value	Countries	Outputs	Original Value	Projected (Target) Value
Australia	Economy	11	14.066 (15)	Korea Rep.	Economy	12	14.222 (15)
	Equality	14	17.902 (18)		Equality	15	17.778 (18)
	Sustainability	18	23.016 (24)		Sustainability	18	23
Austria	Economy	12	13.714 (14)	Latvia	Economy	12	13.970 (14)
	Equality	16	18.286 (19)		Equality	15	17.463 (18)
	Sustainability	18	23		Sustainability	20	23.284 (24)
Belgium	Economy	14	14.452 (15)	Lithuania	Economy	12	13.714 (14)
	Equality	17	17.548 (18)		Equality	16	18.286 (19)
	Sustainability	21	23		Sustainability	19	23
Chile	Economy	12	14.182 (15)	Luxembourg	Economy	12	14.769 (15)
	Equality	14	16.545 (17)		Equality	14	17.231 (18)
	Sustainability	20	23.636 (24)		Sustainability	17	23
Colombia	Economy	10	13.549 (14)	Mexico	Economy	10	13.684 (14)
	Equality	14	17.352 (18)		Equality	13	17.789 (18)
	Sustainability	19	23.549 (24)		Sustainability	17	23.263 (24)

(Continued)

Table 20.4 (Continued)

Countries	Outputs	Original Value	Projected (Target) Value	Countries	Outputs	Original Value	Projected (Target) Value
Czech Rep.	Economy	14	15	New Zealand	Economy	14	15
	Equality	15	17		Equality	13	17
	Sustainability	20	23		Sustainability	20	23
Estonia	Economy	12	13.241 (14)	Poland	Economy	14	15
	Equality	17	18.759 (19)		Equality	15	17
	Sustainability	20	23		Sustainability	19	23
Finland	Economy	14	14.933 (15)	Portugal	Economy	14	14.933 (15)
	Equality	16	17.067 (18)		Equality	16	17.067 (18)
	Sustainability	20	23		Sustainability	19	23
France	Economy	14	14.933 (15)	Slovak Rep.	Economy	13	14.857 (15)
	Equality	16	17.067 (18)		Equality	15	17.143 (18)
	Sustainability	21	23		Sustainability	17	23
Germany	Economy	14	14.378 (15)	Spain	Economy	14	14.933 (15)
	Equality	15	16.378 (17)		Equality	16	17.067 (18)
	Sustainability	23	23.622 (24)		Sustainability	18	23

(Continued)

Post-Pandemic Effects on the Realisation of the SDGs 247

Table 20.4 (Continued)

Countries	Outputs	Original Value	Projected (Target) Value	Countries	Outputs	Original Value	Projected (Target) Value
Greece	Economy	13	14.857 (15)	Switzerland	Economy	13	14.857 (15)
	Equality	15	17.143 (18)		Equality	15	17.143 (18)
	Sustainability	20	23		Sustainability	16	23
Hungary	Economy	11	14.929 (15)	Turkey	Economy	12	15
	Equality	12	16.929 (17)		Equality	12	17
	Sustainability	17	23.071 (24)		Sustainability	18	23
Iceland	Economy	14	14.452 (15)	UK	Economy	12	14
	Equality	17	17.548 (18)		Equality	13	16
	Sustainability	19	23		Sustainability	22	24
Ireland	Economy	14	14.933 (15)	USA	Economy	12	15
	Equality	16	17.067 (18)		Equality	13	17
	Sustainability	21	23		Sustainability	18	23
Italy	Economy	13	15				
	Equality	14	17				
	Sustainability	19	23				

Türkiye has to increase its output values from 12, 12, and 18 to 15, 17, and 23 for Economy, Equality, and Sustainability, respectively. As the last example, Iceland has to increase its output values from 14, 17, and 19 to 15, 18, and 23 for Economy, Equality, and Sustainability, respectively. Similar comments can be considered for all inefficient countries in Table 20.4.

Conclusion

This study examines the performances of OECD countries in realising the SDGs between 2018 and 2021 under the headings of *Economy, Equality,* and *Sustainability*, both before and after the pandemic. Accordingly, there are countries whose values have decreased after the pandemic. Among the countries that showed a decline after the pandemic in the *Economy* category are Australia, Austria, Belgium, Chile, Colombia, Estonia, Hungary, Lithuania, Mexico, the UK, and the US. In addition, the Czech Republic, Denmark, Finland, France, Ireland, Italy, Türkiye, and the US decrease their *Equality* values after the pandemic. Finally, Denmark, Finland, Hungary, Spain, Sweden, Switzerland, and the UK are the countries that decrease their *Sustainability* values. The current study's findings show us that even Denmark and Sweden, which were efficient ones in almost all years (Tables 20.2 and 20.3), had a post-pandemic decline in *Sustainability*.

This may lead us to conclude that the SDGs, which were planned before the pandemic, should undergo post-pandemic updates because we have seen that some goals may become more urgent with the presence of COVID-19[32]. For this reason, redesigning the SDGs to include management prepared for COVID-19 and similar pandemics becomes important. In fact, in a relatively stagnant global economy, countries with limited connections with each other should clarify which goals can be achieved more clearly. For example, making energy affordable and clean may require extra investment and financing to support industries and infrastructure to create new markets. Indeed, even before COVID-19, the SDGs were allotted $2.5 trillion in funding. Naidoo and Fisher (2020) argue that the UN should put some important issues on its agenda for preventing COVID-19 in low-income countries, such as the provision of universal health coverage, supporting the health workforce, and strengthening the capacity of early warning systems for global health risks. They share the view that, in this way, the effects of COVID-19 and similar pandemics will decrease. In addition, Kam (2020) stated that the SDGs could be organised into 4Ps: planet, people, prosperity, and partnership. The first P denotes the planet, emphasising that urbanisation must now occur with its effects on nature, water, and life on land. The second P refers to people, meaning that in cities where poverty, hunger, and gender inequality are less, there will be fewer vulnerable populations who need extra help in disaster situations. The third P is well-being associated with prosperity. But given current circumstances, prosperity should be driven by affordable and clean energy development rather than economic growth. Finally, just like SDG 17, the fourth P represents partnership. However, unlike the SDGs, a proactive partnership in preparation for pandemics and similar disasters is mentioned.

The current study uses the projection feature of the DEA methodology and thus presented the estimated values that OECD countries should increase to be efficient in terms of *Economy, Equality,* and *Sustainability.* Thus, it has created a projection framework for OECD countries to realise the SDGs (Table 20.4). It is thought that the current study will make an important contribution in this respect. Finally, in addition to other studies in this field, we share the idea that SDGs, which were designed unaware of the looming pandemic, should be redesigned. In this sense, given the importance of the partnership of OECD countries in the effective realisation of the SDGs, OECD countries should make new arrangements to prepare for future crises.

References

Ahimi, A. E., Ahimi, E., Soheil, D., Ani Esfa, A., Ni, H. A. and Ebrahimi, S. (2020) 'COVID-19 Could Change Medical Education Curriculum', *Journal of Advances in Medical Education & Professionalism* 8, pp. 144–145. https://doi.org/10.30476/jamp.2020.86090.1217

Alp, İ. (2006) 'Performance Evaluation of Goalkeepers of the World Cup', *GU Journal of Science.* 19 (2), pp. 119–125.

Banker, R. D., Charnes, A. and Cooper, W. W. (1984) 'Some Models for Estimating Technical and Scale Inefficiencies in Data Envelopment Analysis', *Management Science.* 30 (19), pp. 1078–1092.

Brown, S. M., Doom, J. R., Lechuga-Peña, S., Watamura, S. E. and Koppels, T. (2020) 'Stress and Parenting during the Global COVID-19 Pandemic', *Child Abuse and Neglect.* 110. https://doi.org/10.1016/j.chiabu.2020.104699.

Charnes, A., Cooper, W. W. and Rhodes, E. (1978) 'Measuring the Efficiency of Decision Making Units', *European Journal of Operational Research.* 2, pp. 429–444.

Cooper, W. W., Seiford, L. M. and Zhu, J. (2011) 'Data Envelopment Analysis History. Models and Interpretations (Chapter 1)', Part of the International Series in Operations Research and Management Science Book Series (ISOR. volume 164).

Ghosh, A., Nundy, S., Ghosh, S. and Mallick, T. K. (2020) 'Study of COVID-19 Pandemic in London (UK) from Urban Context', *Cities.* 106, p. 102928. https://doi.org/10.1016/j

Heggen, K., Sandset, T. and Engebretsen, J. E. (2020) 'COVID-19 and Sustainable Development Goals', *Bulletin of the World Health Organization.* 98 (10), p. 646. http://dx.doi.org/10.2471/BLT.20.263533

Kam, M. (2020) 'Sustainable Development Goals (SDGs) and Pandemic Planning', *Planning Theory and Practice.* 21 (4), pp. 507–512.

Lamichhane, S., Eğilmez, G., Gedik, R., Bhutta, K. M. S. and Erenay, B. (2021) 'Benchmarking OECD Countries' Sustainable Development Performance: A Goal-Specific Principal Component Analysis approach', *Journal of Cleaner Production.* 287, p. 125040.

Naidoo, R. and Fisher, B. (2020) 'Sustainable Development Goals: Pandemic Reset', *Nature.* 583, pp. 198–201.

Nundy, S., Ghosh, A., Mesloub, A., Albaqawy, A. G. and Alnaim, M. M. (2021) 'Impact of COVID-19 Pandemic on Socio-Economic, Energy-Environment and Transport Sector Globally and Sustainable Development Goal (SDGS)', *Journal of Cleaner Production.* 312, p. 127705.

OECD (2020a) *COVID-19: Protecting People and Societies, OECD Policy Responses to Coronavirus (COVID-19).* Paris: OECD Publishing. https://doi.org/10.1787/e5c9de1a-en

OECD (2020b) *How's Life? 2020: Measuring Well-Being*. Paris: OECD Publishing. https://dx.doi.org/10.1787/9870c393-en

OECD (2020c) *Strengthening health systems during a pandemic: The role of development finance. OECD Policy Responses to Coronavirus (COVID-19)*. Paris: OECD Publishing. https://doi.org/10.1787/f762bf1c-en.

Retzlaff-Roberts, D. L. (1996) 'Relating Discriminant Analysis and Data Envelopment Analysis to One Another', *European Journal of Operational Research*. 23, pp. 311–322.

Sachs, J., Kroll, C., Lafortune, G., Fuller, G. and Woelm, F. (2021) *The Decade of Action for the Sustainable Development Goals: Sustainable Development Report 2021*. Cambridge: Cambridge University Press.

Sachs, J., Schmidt-Traub, G., Kroll, C., Lafortune, G. and Fuller, G. (2018) *SDGS Index and Dashboards Report 2018*. New York: Bertelsmann Stiftung and Sustainable Development Solutions Network (SDSN).

Sachs, J., Schmidt-Traub, G., Kroll, C., Lafortune, G. and Fuller, G. (2019) *Sustainable Development Report 2019*. New York: Bertelsmann Stiftung and Sustainable Development Solutions Network (SDSN).

Sachs, J., Schmidt-Traub, G., Kroll, C., Lafortune, G., Fuller, G. and Woelm, F. (2020) *Sustainable Development Report 2020: The Sustainable Development Goals and Covid-19 Includes the SDG Index and Dashboards*. Cambridge: Cambridge University Press.

Singh, R. K., Murty, H. R., Gupta, S. K. and Dikshit, A. K. (2012) 'An Overview of Sustainability Assessment Methodologies', *Ecological Indicators*. 15 (1), pp. 281–299.

Unsal, M. G. and Orkcu, H. H. (2017) 'Ranking Decision Making Units with the Integration of the Multi-Dimensional Scaling Algorithm into PCA-DEA', *Hacettepe Journal of Mathematics and Statistics*. 46 (6), pp. 1187–1197.

Zhou, P., Yang, X. L. and Wang, X. G. (2020) 'A Pneumonia Outbreak Associated with a New Coronavirus of Probable Bat Origin', *Nature*. 579, pp. 270–273.

21 The African Union and COVID-19

Regional Coordination and Solidarity

Bilge Sahin

Introduction

In Africa, the first COVID-19 case was reported on January 28, 2020, in Nigeria. The disease has since spread throughout the continent. African Union (AU) member states reported 12,109,663 COVID-19 cases and 256,086 deaths by November 2022. This determination constitutes 2% of all cases and 4% of all deaths recorded worldwide (Africa CDC, 2022a). Regarding the overall COVID-19 cases and death statistics, it seems Africa has not been affected by the pandemic to the same extent as other continents. Some argue that the experience in combating many diseases and viruses has provided African countries with the necessary knowledge and preparedness to deal with COVID-19 efficiently (Fagbiyo and Ndidiamaka, 2021: 184; Oloruntoba, 2021: 57). However, others explain the low number of COVID-19 cases through the changing surveillance and testing capabilities among African countries. Not all countries publish COVID-19-related data regularly, which might have distorted estimates of growth rates, active cases, and test-per-case ratios. Additionally, different testing techniques were utilised by countries to identify COVID-19. For example, some countries adopted fast antigen tests to detect cases on a limited basis, which might result in more false negative findings (Salyer et al., 2021: 1272–1273). Hence, the overall statistics regarding COVID-19 may be significantly understated.

Early in the COVID-19 pandemic, African countries decided to close borders and restrict trade to control the spread of the virus, resulting in achieving national interests as a trade-off for commitments regarding regional integration in the continent (Atta, 2020: 5). However, the need for disease management also encouraged strong African cooperation and the commitment to collaboration among African governments. The AU implemented various policies to deal with COVID-19 and promoted continent-wide collaboration and solidarity to challenge this global crisis. Crises such as the COVID-19 pandemic provide the major players in regional integration with new opportunities to strengthen cooperation, unity, and other advanced forms of regionalism, which might expand the regional authority's capabilities to accomplish successful outcomes (Melo and Papageorgiou, 2021: 59).

This chapter examines the AU's responses to the COVID-19 pandemic. It questions to what extent the AU could create and control a continent-wide response to

DOI: 10.4324/9781003377597-24

the pandemic. For this purpose, the AU's policies and strategies on health, economy, education, and security are analysed together with the political and economic problems it encountered to achieve and implement these strategies. Later, the AU policies on acquiring and delivering vaccines are examined. The AU showed a strong focus on coordination and harmonisation built on understanding the necessity for global solidarity and a continent-wide specialised and technical response (Patterson and Balogun, 2021: 152–153). This chapter argues that the AU strengthened African leadership and ownership of the pandemic response through continent-wide policies and strategies.

Continental Responses to COVID-19

In 2002, the AU was established following the Organization of African Unity's decision to be replaced by a new continental organisation to expand its activities. The main objectives of the AU are to establish political and economic integration of the continent and create solidarity among African countries and their people. Promoting security, which includes good governance and living standards for people, is also recognised under the AU authority. The AU's approach to security goes beyond traditional state security and encompasses security issues such as disease prevention and promoting good health on the continent (AU, n.d.). The AU member states' cooperation on health priorities has advanced significantly in recent years. The Africa Health Strategy 2016–2030 serves as the main guiding document. It identifies two main goals: establishing universal health coverage through improved social determinants of health and strengthened health systems and reducing morbidity and preventable mortality from communicable and non-communicable diseases. It also suggests strengthening research and innovation, institutional capacity development, enhancing disaster planning and response mechanisms for the health sector, and focusing on infectious and non-communicable diseases (AU, 2021b). The AU should thus be considered the leading actor in creating and implementing a continent-wide response in health security.

The health systems in most African countries have experienced epidemics, like Ebola and the Lassa virus. Moreover, Africa has been dealing with endemic diseases for decades. Although these diseases created severe health crises, they were also seen as opportunities to gain experience in pandemic management (Osseni, 2020: 49). The monitoring and planning processes have significantly improved due to these experiences. The AU facilitated the establishment of health centres that provide training for medical professionals and public health preparedness (Melo and Papageorgiou, 2021: 65). Following the Ebola crisis of 2014–2016, the AU formed the Africa Centres for Disease Control and Prevention (Africa CDC) in January 2017 to prevent infectious disease outbreaks and enhance monitoring and emergency responses. National infection prevention and control plans were developed, with task teams established to coordinate infection control activities. Evidence-based methods for effective patient treatment and the deployment of public health initiatives were developed. Furthermore, the AU has acknowledged the need for community involvement in bridging cultural divides and distributing information to implement all initiatives (Osseni, 2020: 50).

During the COVID-19 pandemic, the AU Commission and Africa CDC organised an emergency ministerial meeting after the World Health Organization (WHO) announced an international public health emergency over COVID-19 on January 30, 2020. The gathering aimed to inform member states about COVID-19. Participants discussed and agreed to adopt a continent-wide strategy to respond to the potential spread of COVID-19 in Africa (Africa CDC, 2020b). The cooperation between the AU member states has facilitated the capacity of the continent to lessen the epidemic's effects. The virus has no sense of national boundaries; therefore, regional coordination and collaboration are crucial to eradicating it in Africa and globally (Wetzel, 2020). The principle of Pan-African unity was emphasised by the then AU Chair Cyril Ramaphosa to deal with COVID-19 (Ettang, 2021: 314; Loembé et al., 2020: 999).

The pandemic response governance has been set up on a continental basis, with the Africa CDC handling any technical issues and the AU coordinating the political responses (Engel and Herpolsheimer, 2021: 9). The AU has supported its member states in policy, advocacy, and coordination. It regularly convened meetings with African leaders and developed and disseminated documents providing policy guidelines on several technical aspects of managing the COVID-19 epidemic, such as easing lockdowns, social isolation, mobility restrictions, surveillance, and infection prevention and control (AU, 2021a). The policies and strategies employed by the AU implemented global strategies following the specificities of the continent. The reaction to and management of COVID-19 is considered the conception of African citizenship because the borders dividing African countries are considerably permeable, historically arbitrary, and artificial. This enables undocumented workers, particularly those close to borders, to visit surrounding countries regularly and spread the disease through cross-border commerce and travel. Therefore, a regional strategy to regulate COVID-19 was necessary due to the porous nature of these boundaries (Oloruntoba, 2021: 59).

The AU mobilised the Africa CDC before any recorded cases on the continent. In January 2020, the African CDC urged member states to increase their monitoring for severe acute respiratory infections and to pay attention to any unusual patterns in infected patients (Aidi, 2020: 21). On January 27, 2020, the Africa CDC launched its Emergency Operations Center for COVID-19 after at least four Asian countries reported cases. It also regularly published press briefings. In addition, it organised weekly virtual coordination meetings with Africa CDC Regional Collaborating Centres, Ministries of Health, and National Public Health Institutions to ensure swift dissemination of information about the evolving outbreak. The Regional Collaborating Centres improved communication between the five African regions (North, East, West, South, and Central Africa) by allowing countries to verify warnings and reports (Loembé et al., 2020: 1000; Salyer et al., 2021: 1265).

On February 22, 2020, during an AU Commission meeting where African health ministers were gathered, it was decided to create the Africa Taskforce on Coronavirus Preparedness and Response (AFTCOR). AFTCOR is a continent-wide strategy for COVID-19 that supports the development of monitoring systems and processes for laboratory diagnosis, surveillance of border activities, infection prevention, treatment for COVID-19 cases, and supplying vaccines (Osseni, 2020: 48–49). The main objective of AFTCOR is to support continental initiatives to share knowledge and best practices, develop technical ability, make effective policy decisions, and coordinate detection and control activities at borders (Ettang, 2021: 316).

Following these developments, the Africa Joint Continental Strategy for COVID-19 Outbreak was released in March 2020 by the AU and the Africa CDC. Since transmission across the continent was unlikely to be prevented, the focus was on delaying and reducing the pandemic's peak by improving how well health services handle the influx of patients and how well communities adjust to the interruption of social, cultural, and economic activities. It required coordination between the member states, AU institutions, the WHO, and other partners. Moreover, the African CDC was obligated to offer its member states technical assistance, basic supplies, and training. This continent-wide strategy encouraged using evidence-based public health practices for COVID-19 surveillance, prevention, diagnosis, treatment, and control (Africa CDC, 2020a: 2–6). The initial efforts under this strategy were about strengthening the AU member states on case monitoring and containment (Loembé et al., 2020: 1000). Some countries had difficulties identifying COVID-19 cases due to insufficient testing capacity. Therefore, the AU Commission and Africa CDC established the Partnership to Accelerate COVID-19 Testing: Trace, Test, and Track on April 21, 2020. This initiative sought to increase Africa's capacity to test for COVID-19, focusing on countries in urgent need. It resulted in testing at least 10 million Africans in six months, who would not have been tested otherwise (ElAteek et al., 2021: 630; Osseni, 2020: 48–49). The Africa CDC also provided technical and logistical support and established a protocol to streamline sampling designs and detection methods for African countries (Tessema and Nkengasong, 2021: 469). This proved vital to receive reliable results from the countries and have a clear overview of the COVID-19 situation in the continent (Africa CDC, 2022b). In 2021, The Africa CDC adopted another Africa Joint Continental Strategy for COVID-19 Pandemic to enhance the previous one's prevention, monitoring, and treatment policies (Africa CDC, 2021b).

Various African countries, international health organisations, and donors recognised Africa CDC's contribution to the pandemic response and provided economic resources to support continental-wide efforts against COVID-19. The Ethiopian government and the Chinese Jack Ma Foundation have donated medical equipment to every African country. In addition, the Bill and Melinda Gates Foundation has pledged $20 million to support strengthening medical centres, surveillance, contact tracing, and isolation. Furthermore, the German government donated an extra 500,000 COVID-19 test kits to the Africa CDC through the Federal Ministry for Economic Cooperation and Development. The AU also received 10 million euros from the EU, providing access to about 1.4 million kits for detecting COVID-19 infections (Africa CDC, 2020c).

Additionally, the AU launched the COVID-19 Response Fund, which supports the Africa CDC in assisting Africa's public health and healthcare delivery systems with equipment, training, and guidance (Loembé et al., 2020: 1000–1001). On April 12, 2020, Ramaphosa appointed several former African ministers of finance as special envoys of the AU to gather international financial support (Africa CDC,

2020d; Engel and Herpolsheimer, 2021: 10–11). Furthermore, the AU formed the Africa Medical Supplies Platform on June 18, 2020, to organise the logistical distribution of medical supplies and mobilise international support for African states. This initiative assisted African countries in addressing the scarcity and high costs of essential medical procurements by fostering economies of scale (AU, 2021a, para 8; ElAteek et al., 2021: 630; Engel and Herpolsheimer, 2021: 12).

To prevent and control COVID-19, the AU also emphasised the distribution of information and awareness-building. The AU has thoroughly investigated social and popular media as platforms for raising awareness of the virus and disseminating information, including daily updates on the number of infections, hospitalisations, and fatalities (Fagbiyo and Ndidiamaka, 2021: 193; Witt, 2020). The Africa CDC also released a guideline on community physical distancing during the COVID-19 pandemic in May 2020. The goal was to implement policies that fit local conditions and requirements and sustain benefits for public health while minimising adverse effects on people's physical, mental, and financial well-being (Africa CDC, 2020d). The Africa CDC organised the Target COVID-19 Campaign to disseminate important messages about prevention and combat false information about COVID-19 among various African populations. In addition, the Africa CDC started the Africa Infodemic Response Alliance, in partnership with the WHO, to coordinate efforts to prevent false information concerning COVID-19 and vaccinations and to increase knowledge of public health emergencies in Africa (Africa CDC, 2021a).

Casting a Wide Net: Security Issues beyond Health

The COVID-19 pandemic also triggered other security issues. In addition to the technical and medical security threats dealt with through Africa CDC initiatives, the AU also promoted policies and strategies for other pandemic-related problems. These policies often have a long-term focus and contribute to the post-pandemic recovery.

The pandemic affected the economy of the continent. It has simultaneously caused a demand shock, wherein rising unemployment and increased uncertainty lower consumption and investment spending, as well as a supply-side shock that has spread along value chains due to the interruption of corporate operations and escalating trade frictions. Lockdowns and border closures as part of the COVID-19 measures led to a decrease in oil consumption and hampered tourism. Both resulted in a considerable economic deficit for countries dependent on these sectors (Ettang, 2021: 313). In addition, the pandemic crisis affected Africa's key commercial partners (such as China, the EU, the US, and India), which has decreased their imports from Africa and led to significant trade disruptions. African trade has developed an intriguing pattern, with most of the continent choosing international trade over intraregional trade due to the nearly twofold increase in transaction costs inside the region compared to outside the region (Obayelu et al., 2021: 45–49). Boosting intra-African trade is seen by the AU as the primary vehicle for development and economic recovery in a future post-pandemic period. For this purpose, the AU prioritises the implementation of the African Continental Free Trade Agreement (AfCFTA), a free trade area encompassing most of Africa. The AfCFTA came into effect on May 30, 2019; however, free trading only started on January 1, 2021, due to a delay caused by COVID-19 (Signé, 2022). The AfCFTA aims to create a continental market that allows for the free movement of people, capital, goods, and services, essential for advancing economic integration and fostering industrialisation, agricultural growth, and structural economic transformation. By 2040, the AfCFTA is projected to increase intra-African trade in products and services by up to 25%. Over the next 5–15 years, the trade agreement will erase at least 90% of the tariff lines on commodities manufactured in Africa (Diallo, 2022).

Issues in the economy further affected food security in the continent. Food insecurity worsened because of the economic repercussions and the disruption of the agri-food supply chains (caused by labour shortages, transportation issues, and mobility issues), particularly in countries that import food (Anyanwu and Salami, 2021: 7; Medinilla et al., 2020: 5). The AU created a Taskforce on COVID-19's Impact on Food Security and Nutrition in Africa in May 2020. The Taskforce was established to implement the decisions the African Ministers of Agriculture made on addressing food security due to the pandemic and the steps taken to control it. It comprises representatives from the AU Commission, the AU Development Agency-New Partnership for Africa's Development, the Food and Agriculture Organization, the European Commission, the World Bank, and the African Development Bank (Fagbiyo and Ndidiamaka, 2021: 192–193).

Another problem was access to education. During COVID-19, the digital divide became visible. While students in rich countries were learning remotely through online learning resources, public schools in Africa, from elementary schools to university institutions, remained closed (Ujunwa et al., 2021: 3). As a result, the availability of education has been severely hampered since many families cannot afford to purchase e-learning resources for their children (Fagbemi and Asongu, 2020: 7). The AU works on the education sector with its Specialized Technical Committee on Education, Science, and Technology and the technology giant Hewlett-Packard for its continental education strategy. An education strategy was put forward in 2021 to ensure that learning is available to young people. To address the effect of COVID-19 on the education of girls in Africa, the AU has teamed up with UNESCO, multilateral funding platforms such as the Global Partnership for Education, civil society organisations, and traditional and religious leaders (AU, 2021a, para 30–31).

Moreover, the pandemic disproportionately affected women and girls at the societal level. Women have been more likely to get sick since they are the primary carers. Women suffered the most financially from various lockdowns as they make up the bulk of workers in the informal sector, perform domestic work, and provide childcare. Sexual and gender-based violence crimes have also increased due to lockdowns, restricted freedom of movement, and financial loss (Aidi, 2020: 24–25; Ettang, 2021: 313). Concerned about how COVID-19 would affect the advancement of gender equality and women's empowerment in Africa, the Office of the Special Envoy on Women, Peace and Security and the Women, Gender and Development Directorate of the AU Commission held several consultation meetings to bring these concerns to light. The AU adopted guidelines on gender-sensitive responses to COVID-19 to enhance the integration of gender equality and women's engagement in COVID-19 responses in Africa (AU, 2021a, para 30–31).

Another critical issue to address was the ongoing conflicts in the continent. Dealing with violence and conflict in Africa became more complex during COVID-19 due to the restrictions and fragility of the security situation on the continent. The UN Security Council (UNSC) urged a 90-day ceasefire in all armed conflicts, including the Democratic Republic of the Congo, Libya, and South Sudan, on July 1, 2020, in its first resolution on the pandemic. The AU Peace and Security Council (PSC) stressed this measure a month before the UNSC resolution. The PSC has been dealing with ongoing armed conflicts, military coups, terrorism, violent extremism, and peacekeeping missions. It has consistently highlighted the effects of the epidemic on these security issues. The PSC focused on the COVID-19 pandemic at half of its 14 sessions from April 14 to June 17, 2020. These meetings discussed how the virus affects specific vulnerable populations, including peacekeepers, migrants, children, and internally displaced people. The PSC noted that terrorists, armed groups, criminals, and cyber-criminals are taking advantage of the situation (Engel and Herpolsheimer, 2021: 5–6).

The AU demonstrated a substantial level of mobilisation to organise a coordinated response on the continent, used the technical expertise gained in other crises, and took early action to restrict the spread of COVID-19. The organisation's efforts and the Africa CDC's effectiveness demonstrated a break from the fragmented ways of previous fights with infectious diseases and display a feasible pan-African strategy. However, the AU continues to be an intergovernmental organisation that depends on member state direction, involvement, and foreign aid, raising concerns about its competence and competency to handle a major crisis (Melo and Papageorgiou, 2021: 66). Firstly, the refusal of some AU member states to follow the continental agenda on social exclusion, infection reporting, airspace closure, and respect for fundamental human rights was a significant obstacle. In Tanzania, the government put restrictions on media freedom and free speech by suspending a journalist for six months for covering COVID-19 (Fagbiyo and Ndidiamaka, 2021: 205). Fundamental rights are suppressed, undermining AU standards for democratic administration and raising the likelihood of political unrest and conflicts in member states (ibid.). Secondly, although a continental framework has been established, its application varies based on the capacity and responsiveness of national health systems and the logistical and coordination difficulties. As regional and global response mechanisms gain momentum, national health systems need to be adapted, necessitating significant short- and long-term financial inputs (Medinilla et al., 2020: 8). Finally, there are not enough people and financial resources for the AU and the Africa CDC to successfully fight the infection. Even though the AU has taken the initiative to establish financial arrangements for the Africa CDC and its initiatives, the organisation still heavily depends on outside funding. Such dependency leaves organisations vulnerable to changes since donors may decide to curtail or cease giving aid (Fagbiyo and Ndidiamaka, 2021: 206; Witt, 2020).

Vaccine Policies

An equitable distribution of COVID-19 vaccinations across and within African countries is crucial to establish herd immunity and containing the pandemic. This will enable the reconstruction of societies and the economy in a future post-pandemic period. The creation of regional and national strategies that guarantee equitable and fair vaccine distribution should be guided by knowledge of the pandemic's nature, the health system's needs, and the sociodemographics of African countries. By implementing such strategies, the continent will be less likely to experience life-threatening shortages, affordability issues, the marginalisation of those most vulnerable, and inefficient resource usage (Africa CDC, 2021d). To achieve herd immunity, the AU vaccine strategy seeks to immunise at least 60% of the population. This goal is based on scientific evidence that an infectious disease cannot spread when a sizable portion of a population is immune to it (AU, 2021b, para 5). Currently, 54 member states are administering COVID-19 vaccinations to the public. Eritrea is the only AU member state that has not yet begun the COVID-19 immunisation rollout. In Africa, 626.6 million doses have been delivered, with 318.1 million people receiving the first dose and 276.5 million inoculated with two doses. However, Africa has a very uneven vaccination rate, ranging from 30 countries with coverage levels of less than 1% to the continent's most immunised country, Seychelles, with 66%. Overall, the vaccination rate is substantially low, with only 19.6% of people on the continent receiving all recommended vaccinations (Africa CDC, 2022a).

The United Nations-led COVAX initiative provides Oxford/AstraZeneca and Pfizer/BioNTech vaccines to African states. This initiative was established to allow universal access to COVID-19 vaccines and aims to distribute doses to low- and medium-income countries, and to immunise 20% of their population, prioritising medical professionals and the most vulnerable populations in 2021 (Loembé and Nkengasong, 2021: 1353). As part of this programme, Africa received almost 270 million vaccines by January 2022 (Statista, 2022). Despite investing in COVAX, the Global North has prioritised national access ahead of global equity. A few wealthy countries have reduced the number of vaccines accessible to the Global South by establishing pre-purchase agreements with producers and hoarding sufficient doses to vaccinate their people several times. The infamous events of unequal access to HIV medicines or the stockpiling of H1N1 vaccine doses by a few during the 2009 pandemic are being repeated concerning vaccine availability in Africa today (Loembé and Nkengasong, 2021: 1353).

As a result, the AU created the African Vaccine Acquisition Task Team (AVATT) to facilitate vaccine procurement and support COVAX (Tessema and Nkengasong, 2021: 469). Recognising the worldwide objective of immunising 60% of the African population, AVATT and COVAX complement each other's efforts to assist African countries in achieving their immunisation objectives. Africa has independently acquired 250 million extra vaccine doses from AstraZeneca, BioNTech, and Johnson and Johnson through the AVATT. Payments are facilitated by the African Export-Import Bank (Afreximbank), which offers advance acquirement guarantees of up to $2 billion to the suppliers on behalf of the member states (Loembé and Nkengasong, 2021: 1362). Additionally, AVATT and Johnson and Johnson had an agreement under which all member states would have received 220 million doses, with the option to acquire up to 180 million additional doses (ElAteek et al., 2021: 632). Several African countries have also been securing their doses of the COVID-19 vaccine. Additionally, "vaccine diplomacy" led by African states turned increasingly to countries such as China, Russia, and India to support immunisation campaigns. This was frequently done before the vaccines were listed on the WHO Emergency Use Listing and with limited efficacy and safety information publicly available (Adepoju, 2021; Loembé and Nkengasong, 2021: 1353–1354).

Equally, the AU and Africa CDC also work on distributing the vaccines to African countries and populations. The Africa CDC (2021d) defines its framework for vaccine distribution through African traditions and liberal principles. In traditional African communities, neither individual nor collective subjectivity is dominant since they are mutually constitutive. The traditional value system strongly emphasises social cohesion and the fair allocation of resources among all group members. The framework for fair, equitable, and timely access to COVID-19 is based on a created framework that combines African traditions and liberal principles, promoting human rights and ensuring human dignity and inclusion of all members of society. This suggests that weak and disadvantaged people in remote and rural regions, urban slums, and conflict zones should not be excluded from receiving a COVID-19 vaccination in Africa. Everyone should have access to vaccinations regardless of gender, religion, sexual orientation, or political affiliation (Africa CDC, 2021d).

Despite these efforts, there are various obstacles to these vaccination strategies. Firstly, there is still a long wait for vaccinations in Africa, while COVID-19 immunisation rates in high-income countries highlight the presence of inequity in global health. The acceptance of fair access to vaccinations and calls for countries to give up vaccine nationalism have mostly gone unheeded. The WHO warned that vaccine nationalism might lengthen rather than end the outbreak (Adepoju, 2021). Other factors contributing to unequal access include manufacturers' refusal to waive vaccine patents, even temporarily. The AU has endorsed an earlier appeal by South Africa and India to waive intellectual property rights for COVID-19 vaccines and medications (Fagbiyo and Ndidiamaka, 2021: 195).

Furthermore, the logistical constraints of shipping, storing, and delivering vaccinations are other obstacles to immunising African populations. Another barrier to the rapid and widespread distribution of COVID-19 vaccinations is the fragility of African healthcare infrastructures. A countrywide deployment and vaccination plan, priority target population definition, logistics and cold chain set-up, safety surveillance and adverse effect monitoring protocols, and vaccination team training are necessary to manage vaccine distribution (Loembé and Nkengasong, 2021: 1355–1356).

Finally, vaccine hesitancy and resistance among communities are important obstacles. Four out of five respondents (79%) in 15 African countries who participated in a recent study conducted by the Africa CDC (2020a) stated that they were willing to be immunised. The study attributed reluctance to disinformation regarding COVID-19, including claims that it is not real, does not represent a significant threat, or can be treated with safer alternative treatments, as well as concerns about the vaccinations' efficacy and safety. In Benin, Liberia, Niger, Senegal, and Togo, according to Afrobarometer's nationally representative polls, just four out of ten individuals indicated they would be inclined to attempt to be immunised. Most people claim they do not trust their government to ensure the safety of immunisation. Also, many argued that COVID-19 was a conspiracy orchestrated by foreign actors to use people in Africa in vaccine trials (Seydou, 2021). Community health professionals are crucial to raising awareness in communities and providing vaccinations. A review of the data on Rwanda's national immunisation programme revealed that local ownership, including roles for community health workers that include immunisation education, community mobilisation, and data collection on immunisation status, was crucial to the country's immunisation coverage. In Kenya, Lwala Community Alliance provided community health workers with digital tools to register young children, track their immunisation status, and send household reminders about missed vaccine appointments. As a result, the communities where these community health professionals worked experienced 95% immunisation coverage. This shows that strengthening community health workers and providing approaches on the local level can increase immunisation coverage (Africa CDC, 2021c). Active community participation fosters accountability and ownership of the decisions made about allocation, allowing for authenticity, and building trust. Active community participation is required to combat vaccination reluctance, uphold public confidence, and concurrently manage the epidemic (Africa CDC, 2021d).

To strengthen vaccination policies, the AU and Africa CDC also work on producing vaccines in Africa. An important meeting on vaccines was organised by the AU and the Africa CDC on April 12–13, 2021. The leaders of the AU pledged to improve the proportion of vaccines produced on the continent to 60% by 2040, emphasising the crucial role that vaccine production plays in ensuring public health security in Africa. Moreover, the Africa CDC launched the Consortium for COVID-19 Vaccine Clinical Trials to promote regional initiatives on research and development of vaccines suitable to the African context (i.e., cold chain free storage for widespread immunisation programmes in remote areas) (Loembé and Nkengasong, 2021: 1358). Vaccine trials are also taking place in South Africa (Ettang, 2021: 316). However, regulatory frameworks often obstruct the effective and safe deployment of COVID-19 vaccines in Africa. The Africa CDC, in collaboration with the AU Development Agency, the African Medicines Regulatory Harmonization Initiative, and the WHO, developed the Africa Regulatory Task Force to quickly approve novel vaccinations for emergency commercialisation during a pandemic (Loembé and Nkengasong, 2021: 1361). The AU also established the Partnerships for African Vaccine Manufacturing in 2021 to support the African vaccine industry to develop, produce, and deliver more than 60% of the doses needed on the continent by 2040, as there is a need for local manufacturing to overcome dependency on foreign aid regarding vaccines and promote ownership (Africa CDC, 2022c).

Conclusion

COVID-19 poses a serious threat to Africa and has tested the abilities of the AU to manage this complex health crisis. The Constitutive Act of the AU and various agendas accepted on the continent give a leading role to the AU in creating and implementing a continent-wide response to health crises. Experiences dealing with diseases for decades strengthened the AU's preparedness to develop regional infection prevention and control plans, public health initiatives, and community involvement programmes. Regarding COVID-19, the AU and Africa CDC have been deemed efficient since they have contributed significantly to resource mobilisation and provided advocacy, coordination, expertise, and technical support to its member states. The AU and Africa CDC have also worked on issues other than health to deal with the consequences of COVID-19. They disseminated information to raise awareness, created an emergency, resilience, and recovery action plan to mitigate socio-economic issues, employed an education strategy to facilitate access to education, adopted guidelines to enhance the integration of gender equality and women in COVID-19 responses, created a taskforce for food security, and worked on the impacts of the pandemic on ongoing conflicts. The AU and Africa CDC have also organised and mobilised resources to boost vaccine availability, deal with the competition for vaccines and unequal distribution between developed and underdeveloped countries, address vaccination hesitancy issues, and promote increasing local production of COVID-19. However, the AU continues to be an intergovernmental organisation that depends on member states' capacities and involvement of foreign aid, both of which create obstacles to achieving and implementing continent-wide strategies to deal with COVID-19.

Nevertheless, the AU provided measures to control the pandemic and demonstrated its ability to handle a crisis. The Africa CDC has quickly gained prominence and established itself as a leader in crisis management at the continental level. The AU played an essential role in responding to COVID-19 by creating solidarity, cooperation, and collaboration between various local, regional, and international actors. The COVID-19 pandemic provided the AU with new opportunities to strengthen its authority to accomplish results and advance regionalism successfully.

References

Adepoju, P. (2021) 'Africa Prepares for COVID-19 vaccines', *The Lancet*. 2 (2), e59.

Africa CDC (2020a) Africa Joint Continental Strategy for COVID-19 Outbreak. Available at: https://africacdc.org/download/africa-joint-continental-strategy-for-covid-19-outbreak/ [Accessed: July 17, 2022].

Africa CDC (2020b) Report of an Emergency Meeting of Africa Ministers of Health on 22 February 2020 Addis Ababa, Ethiopia, the COVID-19 Outbreak. Available at: https://africacdc.org/download/report-of-an-emergency-meeting-of-africa-ministers-of-health-on-the-covid-19-outbreak/ [Accessed: June 3, 2022].

Africa CDC (2020c) Team Europe: Germany and European Union Jointly Support African Union's Response to COVID-19. Available at: https://africacdc.org/news-item/team-europe-germany-and-european-union-jointly-support-african-unions-response-to-covid-19/ [Accessed: May 19, 2022].

Africa CDC (2020d) Guidance on Community Physical Distancing during Covid-19 Pandemic. Available at: https://africacdc.org/download/guidance-on-community-social-distancing-during-covid-19-outbreak/ [Accessed: May 31, 2022].

Africa CDC (2021a) Annual Progress Report 2020. Available at: https://africacdc.org/download/annual-progress-report-2020/ [Accessed: May 31, 2022].

Africa CDC (2021b) Adapted Africa Joint Continental Strategy for COVID-19 Pandemic. Available at: https://africacdc.org/download/adapted-africa-joint-continental-strategy-for-covid-19-pandemic/ [Accessed: May 31, 2022].

Africa CDC (2021c) The Critical Role of Community Health Workers in COVID-19 Vaccine Roll Out. Available at: https://africacdc.org/download/the-critical-role-of-community-health-workers-in-covid-19-vaccine-roll-out/ [Accessed: June 2, 2021].

Africa CDC (2021d) Framework for Fair, Equitable and Timely Allocation of COVID-19 Vaccines in Africa. Available at: https://africacdc.org/download/framework-for-fair-equitable-and-timely-allocation-of-covid-19-vaccines-in-africa/ [Accessed: June 2, 2022].

Africa CDC (2022a) Outbreak Brief #148: Coronavirus Disease 2019 (COVID-19) Pandemic. Available at: https://africacdc.org/download/outbreak-brief-148-coronavirus-disease-2019-covid-19-pandemic/ [Accessed: November 24, 2022].

Africa CDC (2022b) Covid-19 Rapid Antigen Self-testing: Interim Guidance to African Union Member States. Available at: https://africacdc.org/download/interim-guidance-on-covid-19-rapid-antigen-selftesting-to-african-union-member-states/ [Accessed: June 2, 2022].

Africa CDC (2022c) Partnerships for African Vaccine Manufacturing (PAVM) Framework for Action. Available at: https://africacdc.org/download/partnerships-for-african-vaccine-manufacturing-pavm-framework-for-action/#:~:text=The%20Framework%20for%20Action%20answers,vaccine%20needs%20locally%20by%202040 [Accessed: June 3, 2022].

Aidi, H. (2020) 'Public Trust, Capacity and Covid-19: Early Lessons from Africa', *Policy Centre for the New South*, Policy Brief, pp. 20–45. https://www.policycenter.ma/sites/default/files/2021-01/PB_20-45_Aidi.pdf

Anyanwu, J. C., & Salami, A. O. (2021). 'The Impact of COVID-19 on African Economies: An Introduction', *African Development Review*. 33 (Suppl 1), S1–S16.

Atta, F. K. (2020) 'Examining the Challenges of the COVID-19 Pandemic for Regional Integration in Africa', *Research Journal in Advanced Humanities*. 1 (4), pp. 44–53.

AU (2021a) Report on the Implementation of Africa Joint Continental Strategy for Covid-19 Response, EX.CL/1256 (XXXVIII).

AU (2021b) Report on the COVID-19 Vaccine Financing Strategy, EX.CL/1256 (XXXVIII) Annex 2.

African Union (AU) (n.d.) About the African Union. Available at: https://au.int/en/overview [Accessed: July 15, 2022].

Diallo, A. (2022) Boosting Intra-African Trade Will Power Post-COVID-19 Recovery and Foster Food Security. Africa Renewal. https://www.un.org/africarenewal/magazine/august-2022/boosting-intra-african-trade-will-power-post-covid-19-recovery-and-foster-food [Accessed: November 24, 2022].

ElAteek, A., Heikal, S. A., Rozanova, L. and Flahault, A. (2021) 'Between Ambitious Strategies and Reality: The African Union Strategy on COVID-19 Vaccine', *Epidemiologia*. 2, pp. 621–638.

Engel, U. and Herpolsheimer, J. (2021) 'African Regional and Inter-Regional Health Governance: Early Responses to the Covid-19 Pandemic by ECOWAS and the African Union', *African Security*. 14 (4), pp. 1–23.

Ettang, D. (2021) 'New Opportunities and Threats: Reimagining Africa's International Relations in the Midst of COVID-19', *Politikon*. 48 (2), pp. 312–330.

Fagbemi, F. and Asongu, S. (2020) 'Covid-19 and Socioeconomic Crises in Africa: Overview of the Prevailing Incidents', *Regional Economic Development Research*. https://papers.ssrn.com/sol3/papers.cfm?abstract_id=3755217

Fagbiyo, B. and Ndidiamaka, U. (2021) 'Crisis as Opportunity: Exploring the African Union's Response to COVID-19 and the Implications for Its Aspirational Supranational Powers', *Journal of African Law*. 65, pp. 181–208.

Loembé, M. M. and Nkengasong, J. N. (2021) 'COVID-19 Vaccine Access in Africa: Global Distribution, Vaccine Platforms, and Challenges ahead', *Immunity*. 54, pp. 1353–1362.

Loembé, M. M., Tshangela, A., Salyer, S. J., Varma, J. K., Ouma, A. E. O. and Nkengasong, J. N. (2020) 'COVID-19 in Africa: the Spread and response', *Nature Medicine*. 26, pp. 996–1008.

Medinilla, A., Byiers, B. and Apiko, P. (2020) 'African Regional Responses to COVID-19', *The European Centre for Development Policy Management (ECDPM)*, Discussion Paper No. 272.

Melo, D.S.N. and Papageorgiou, M. (2021) 'Regionalism on the Run: ASEAN, EU, AU and MERCOSUR Responses Mid the Covid-19 Crisis', *PArtecipazione e COnflitto PACO*. 14 (1), pp. 57–78.

Obayelu, A. E., Edewor, S. E., & Ogbe, A. O. (2021). 'Trade Effects, Policy Responses and Opportunities of COVID-19 Outbreak in Africa', *Journal of Chinese Economic and Foreign Trade Studies*. 14 (1), pp. 44–59.

Oloruntoba, O. (2021) 'Unity Is Strength: Covid-19 and Regionalism in Africa', *The International Spectator*. 56 (2), pp. 56–71.

Osseni, I. A. (2020) 'COVID-19 Pandemic in Sub-Saharan Africa: Preparedness, Response, and Hidden potentials', *Tropical Medicine and Health*. 48, pp. 48–50.

Patterson, A. S. and Balogun, E. (2021) 'African Responses to COVID-19: The Reckoning of Agency?' *African Studies Review*. 64 (1), pp. 144–167.

Salyer, S. J., Maeda, J., Sembuche, S., Kebede, Y., Tshangela, A., Moussif, M., Ihekweazu, C., Mayet, N., Abate, E., Ouma, A. O. and Nkengasong, J. (2021) 'The First and Second Waves of the COVID-19 Pandemic in Africa: A Cross-Sectional Study', *The Lancet*. 397, pp. 1265–1275.

Seydou, A. (2021) 'Who Wants COVID-19 Vaccination? In 5 West African Countries, Hesitancy Is High, Trust Low', *Afrobarometer,* Dispatch No. 432. https://africaportal.org/wp-content/uploads/2023/05/ad432-covid-19_vaccine_hesitancy_high_trust_low_in_west_africa-afrobarometer-8march21-1.pdf

Signé, L. (2022) Understanding the African Continental Free Trade Area and How the US Can Promote Its Success. Available at https://www.brookings.edu/testimonies/understanding-the-african-continental-free-trade-area-and-how-the-us-can-promote-its-success/ [Accessed: November 24, 2022].

Statista (2022) Number of Administered Coronavirus (COVID-19) Vaccine Doses per 100 People in Africa as of 10 July, 2022, by Country. Available at: https://www.statista.com/statistics/1221298/covid-19-vaccination-rate-in-african-countries/ [Accessed: July 12, 2022].

Tessema, S. K. and Nkengasong, J. N. (2021) 'Understanding COVID-19 in Africa', *Immunology*. 21, pp. 469–470.

Ujunwa, A. I., Ujunwa, A. and Okoyeuzu C. R. (2021) 'Rethinking African globalisation agenda: Lessons from COVID-19', *Research in Globalization*. 3, 100055. https://doi.org/10.1016/j.resglo.2021.100055

Wetzel, D. (2020) 'Pandemics Know No Borders: In Africa, Regional Collaboration Is Key to Fighting COVID-19', *World Bank Blog*. Available at: https://blogs.worldbank.org/africacan/pandemics-know-no-borders-africa-regionalcollaboration-key-fighting-COVID-19 [Accessed: May 25, 2022].

Witt, A. (2020) 'An Island of Internationalism: The African Union's Fight against Corona', *PRIF BLOG*. Available at: https://blog.prif.org/2020/04/07/an-island-of-internationalism-the-african-unions-fight-against-corona/ [Accessed: May 20, 2022].

22 Europe in the Post-Pandemic World Order

A Human Rights Perspective

Ebru Demir

COVID-19 and Human Rights in Europe

Europe's initial response to the COVID-19 pandemic was fragmented and uncoordinated (Alemanno, 2020: 308). European states developed their national risk responses instead of coming together and building one (ibid: 313). Such reactions to the COVID-19 pandemic resulted in questions about European solidarity. The research conducted by Cicchi et al. (2020: 1) shows that the "nation first, neighbour next" approach was common across Europe during the pandemic and solidarity was viewed by European citizens "as a reciprocal benefit rather than a moral or identity-based obligation." Especially at the outset of the outbreak of the COVID-19 pandemic, many criticised the EU's lack of action and posed serious questions about European solidarity in times of crisis.

This chapter examines the extent the European Court of Human Rights (ECtHR or the Court) can effectively address fundamental human rights and freedoms violated by Council of Europe (CoE) member states during the pandemic (1952). It stresses that the ECtHR should pay sufficient attention to the differences among the CoE member states and consider each state's specific circumstances that could influence its responses to the COVID-19 pandemic. The chapter examines the recent jurisprudence of the ECtHR on the COVID-19 pandemic and also brings forward the case law of the Court that is related to the pandemic.

What makes the COVID-19 pandemic different from other pandemics in history is that it is the first pandemic to "occur in a period of human history where human rights play such a primordial role in public discourse" (Tzevelekos and Dzehtsiarou, 2020: 146). At a time when human rights instruments, human rights NGOs, and monitoring bodies "boomed" all over the world, states suddenly started taking severe measures to restrict fundamental rights and freedoms due to the COVID-19 pandemic. As UN Special Rapporteur Selam Gebrekidan (2020) pointed out, this created a chance for autocrats and democrats to grab even more power. As a result, governments used the pandemic "as a pretext to grab power" (Forman and Kohler, 2020: 549), resulting in serious human rights abuses and violations.

Governments have enacted severe restrictions that were "previously unknown to European democracies" as a response to the COVID-19 pandemic (Cathaoir, 2021: 47). Belgium, for instance, recorded ethnic profiling and took discriminatory

DOI: 10.4324/9781003377597-25

measures that disproportionately affected ethnic minorities (Šeško, 2021). Poland used the pandemic as an "opportunity" to suspend the freedom of assembly under the guise of protecting health – except for religious gatherings – to restrict mass protests on the abortion ban (Krajewska, 2021). Hungary also became an often-cited example of "the authoritarian wave in Europe" during the pandemic. The Hungarian government imposed a general and complete ban on public assemblies and increased military presence on streets and hospitals. It severely restricted freedom of expression and media freedom (Kovács, 2021). Such examples show that European governments limited the exercise of fundamental human rights and freedoms by taking discriminatory, disproportionate, and unconstitutional measures.

The CoE stressed the importance of proportionality and necessity while responding to the crisis. In a toolkit that it prepared for member states, the CoE (2020: 2) underlined "Europe's founding values of democracy, the rule of law and human rights" and called on all CoE institutions to "use the tools and resources of the Organisation to share information, good practices and lessons learnt among all stakeholders, including authorities, civil society and citizens, to find common responses to the challenges" (2020: 9). The CoE maintains that even though throughout its 70-year history it has served as a pan-European organisation setting a leading example for the rest of the world, CoE institutions are now "more relevant than ever" amid the ongoing unprecedented crisis (ibid).

ECtHR in Times of COVID-19: "More Relevant than Ever"

The uncoordinated and fragmented responses had repercussions on European states' legal responses to the human rights violations that occurred during the pandemic. States developed various policies and strategies to respond to the pandemic and restricted fundamental human rights and freedoms to different extents. While the differences in responses might seem to cause a solidarity deficit, this chapter argues that when it comes to human rights responses, there cannot (and in fact should not) be a unique strategy for all European states. The COVID-19 pandemic created varying effects that required varying measures and restrictions by the CoE member states. Even within the countries, different standards and restrictions were necessary due to regional specificities. As Scheinin and Molbæk-Steensig (2021: 29) argued, "differences between viruses, rates, and means of contagion, probability of population immunity, the proportion of infections resulting in death or permanent disability, the impact on national health services, and availability of vaccination and medication" have a part in individual states' responses to the COVID-19 pandemic. Therefore, judicial bodies, while monitoring states' responses to the pandemic, should be vigilant regarding the factors that might have been involved in states' strategies to combat the pandemic.

As the main human rights monitoring mechanism within the CoE, the ECtHR is responsible for monitoring the CoE member states' compliance with the ECHR, even in the most difficult circumstances. However, according to Article 15, the contracting states can derogate from their obligations under the Convention "in time of war or other public emergency threatening the life of the nation." The expression

Europe in the Post-Pandemic World Order 267

"or another public emergency" allows various exceptional circumstances, other than war, to be considered an emergency. When states face extraordinary circumstances, they can use derogations to buy time to confront crises (Hafner-Burton et al., 2011). According to Wallace (2020: 774), the ongoing pandemic is a textbook example of an emergency since "there is an identifiable, extraordinary threat which requires exceptional, temporary measures outside the normal law." Undoubtedly, the COVID-19 pandemic met the conditions for a valid derogation from the Convention. Still, the ECtHR can examine the proportionality and necessity of the COVID-19 measures taken by the CoE member states.

Before examining the ECtHR's relevant case law, it should be underlined that it is witnessing a new crisis. While some analogies could be made with other exceptional circumstances, such as armed conflicts or terrorist activities, the COVID-19 pandemic has unique circumstances. One can argue that it is an ambitious attempt to create analogies between COVID-19 and other emergencies. However, as Jovičić (2021: 559) argues, emergent circumstances have common features. Namely, they all threaten the life of the nations and make it difficult for states to function as usual. Therefore, the ECtHR's case law can easily be applied to the current COVID-19 crisis (ibid: 550).

ECtHR's Evaluation of COVID-19 Measures

A of December 2022, the number of confirmed COVID-19 cases globally has declined, and the number of COVID-19-related deaths has sharply decreased. European countries, including Germany, Britain, France, and Italy, have completely lifted their COVID-19 measures and restrictions. Mask requirements, travel restrictions, and vaccine checks have been abandoned across Europe. Although COVID-19's long-term effects are unknown, it seems that vaccines are effective against the virus and nationwide vaccination programmes across Europe enabled the return to "normal."

The ECtHR will be hearing COVID-19-related cases in "normal times." This means that the Court will evaluate the proportionality and necessity of the CoE member states' COVID-19 measures and restrictions in a post-COVID world – if other conditions remain the same. When one considers the outbreak of the pandemic and the states' initial and extreme responses to it, these responses might seem excessive and unreasonable through a post-COVID lens. This might raise important questions regarding the Court's evaluation of COVID-19 measures, and CoE member states might doubt the fairness of the Court's assessment. At this point, the Court's earlier jurisprudence can guide and reassure member states. In *Ireland v United Kingdom* (1969), the Irish Government argued that the extrajudicial deprivation of liberty that the UK Government used as a "counter-terrorism" policy was ineffective. According to the Irish Government, the policy failed to "put a break on terrorism but also had the result of increasing it" (para 214). While examining the proportionality and necessity of the UK Government's measures, the Court concluded that it does not deliver a judgment in the light "of a purely retrospective examination of the efficacy of those measures, but of the conditions and circumstances reigning when they were originally taken and subsequently applied" (para 214). The Court, therefore, argued that the (in)effectiveness of the "counter-terrorism" policies could not be anticipated by the UK Government *at the time*, i.e. before the policies were implemented. This decision can assure states that the ECtHR will not assess the COVID-19 measures and restrictions retrospectively. In its assessment of the measures, the Court would consider its case law and consider the conditions when the CoE member states took the measures and restrictions if those measures were proportionate or necessary.

During the initial stages of the COVID-19 pandemic, European governments took strict measures and imposed curfews, lockdowns, and severe restrictions, flights were cancelled, and many European governments imposed travel bans. For specific age groups, more severe measures were taken. For instance, Türkiye set a curfew for those aged 65 and older (Bilgic, 2020). Although these measures seem excessive retrospectively, they might be found reasonable by the ECtHR due to "the unknown characteristics of the new virus and the lack of adequate preparedness and response" (Jovičić, 2021: 559).

In the Court's assessment of CoE member states' measures and restrictions, vaccines will have an important place. Although "national immunisation" strategies' targets are often infants and children (Sheikh et al., 2018), in their battle with the COVID-19 virus, European states aimed to reach a wider population to immunise people of all ages through vaccines to achieve herd immunity. Some European states imposed vaccine mandates. For instance, Greece declared that older people who were not vaccinated would face monthly fines (Joly, 2022). Italy similarly reported that it would implement a mandatory vaccination programme for people aged 50 and above (Amante et al., 2022). In addition, for certain categories of workers, COVID-19 vaccines were obligatory. Germany, Greece, France, Italy, Latvia, and Hungary stated that healthcare or public service workers were required to vaccinate to continue exercising their professional activities (Crego et al., 2022). Estonia allowed employers to ask their employees to be vaccinated to continue working (ibid).

The ECtHR, on August 19, 2021, received an application from 672 members of the French fire service about the mandatory vaccination programmes. The applicants claimed that the French law, which required public employees to be vaccinated, breached Articles 2 (right to life) and 8 (right to respect for private and family life) of the ECHR. The applicants requested that the ECtHR suspend the French Government's requirement to be vaccinated to exercise their occupation (ECtHR, 2021). Under Rule 39 of the Rules of Court, the ECtHR might request CoE member states to take interim measures and suspend the application of the law immediately. However, in this case, the Court did not find interim measures necessary and rejected them. It maintained that "[T]he Court grants such requests only on an exceptional basis when the applicants would otherwise face a real risk of irreversible harm" (*Abgrall and 671 others v France*).

On September 2, 2021, the Court received two similar applications against Greece brought by 30 health professionals working independently or in public health institutions. The applicants claimed that the Greek law, which required health sector professionals to be vaccinated, breached Articles 2 (right to life), 3 (prohibition of inhuman or degrading treatment), 4 (prohibition of slavery and forced labour), 5 (right to liberty and security), 6 (right to a fair hearing), 8 (right to respect for private and family life), and 14 (prohibition of discrimination) of the ECHR. The applicants requested the Court apply interim measures under Rule 39 of the Rules of Court and suspend the application of the Greek law concerned. Similarly, the Court concluded that suspension from work did not create a real risk of irreversible harm; therefore, the request for interim measures fell outside the scope of Rule 39 of the Rules of Court (*Kakaletri and others v Greece*; *Theofanopoulou and others v Greece*).

It should be emphasised, however, that in these three applications, the ECtHR did not examine the legitimacy, necessity, and proportionality of compulsory vaccination as an anti-COVID-19 measure. In other words, these applications have yet to be heard on their merits. Therefore, the ECtHR might still declare the admissibility of these (and similar) applications concerning the compatibility of such domestic laws with the ECHR (Gibelli, 2022: 6). Traditionally, the Court requested that CoE member states take interim measures when the applicant faced an immediate danger of torture or death or a flagrant denial of justice (Dzehtsiarou and Tzevelekos, 2021: 3) When the cases in which the Court granted interim measures are compared with these three applications at stake, the rejection of provisional measures is unsurprising (Vinceti, 2021: 2).

Mandatory Vaccination in Europe: Looking at the ECtHR's Case Law

In April 2021, amid debates concerning compulsory vaccination, the ECtHR delivered its first judgment about mandatory vaccination against childhood diseases: *Vavřička and Others v the Czech Republic*. Although the case was not specifically related to the COVID-19 virus, the Court, albeit quite slightly, engaged with the anti-vaccination arguments and vaccine hesitancy in this case. The Court could not but be affected by the ongoing COVID-19 pandemic while delivering a decision on compulsory vaccination. The Court is highly likely to follow its precedent established by previously decided cases; therefore, the decision can inform us about the Court's view on compulsory vaccination policies and gives us a sense of the discussions that will take place in future COVID-19-related cases.

In *Vavřička*, six Czech nationals challenged the domestic regulations concerning the vaccines against childhood diseases such as diphtheria, tetanus, whooping cough, and measles. According to these regulations, "day-care facilities for children up to the age of three and other types of preschool facilities (…) may only accept children who have received the required vaccinations, or who have been certified as having acquired immunity by other means" (para 73). The regulations also imposed a fine – that may only be charged once – on those who refused compulsory vaccination for themselves and their children for whatever reason.

The applicants claimed that, with the compulsory vaccination scheme, the Czech Government breached Articles 8 (right to respect for private and family life), 9 (freedom of thought, conscience, and religion), 2 (right to life), 6 (right to a fair trial), 13 (right to an effective remedy), and 14 (prohibition of discrimination) of the ECHR and Article 2 of Protocol No. 1 (right to education). The ECtHR declared all the complaints under Articles 9, 2, 6, 13, and 14 inadmissible and held that there was no need to examine the complaints under Article 2 of Protocol No. 1. The complaints under Article 8, however, were declared admissible. In the case, the Court established that compulsory vaccination schemes interfere with the right to respect private and family life. Having shown that, the Court moved on to examine whether the interference, in this case, was justified. The Court's discussions on the necessity and proportionality of the compulsory vaccination scheme in the Czech Republic are especially relevant for future COVID-19-related cases.

While determining the necessity of the mandatory vaccination programmes, the Court examined various European states' practices and observed that "there is a consensus among the Contracting Parties (…) that vaccination is one of the most successful and cost-effective health interventions" (para 277). *Vavřička* concerns the mandatory childhood vaccination, which has been scientifically proven to be one of the most effective public health strategies to control and prevent diseases such as diphtheria, tetanus, and measles for many years. Therefore, the Court's statement is valid for childhood vaccinations. COVID-19 vaccinations, compared to childhood vaccinations, are quite new, and their long-term impacts are unknown. An analogy between childhood vaccinations and COVID-19 vaccinations seems far-fetched on this issue. *Vavřička* shows that while determining whether mandatory COVID-19 vaccinations for some professions or age groups are proportionate and necessary, the Court will have to evaluate the vaccinations' success and effectiveness, among other factors. Indeed, compulsory vaccination schemes can only be proportional and essential if they are supported by extensive scientific evidence proving the effectiveness of the vaccines (Paris, 2021: 293).

Having recognised the importance and efficacy of childhood vaccination, the Court proceeded to examine the mandatory nature of vaccination. It underlined that the states' parties "are under a positive obligation (…) to take appropriate measures to protect the life and health of those within their jurisdiction" under Articles 2 (right to life) and 8 (right to respect for private and family life) of the ECHR (para 282). Importantly, to delve into the positive obligations of the state party at stake, the ECtHR engaged with the Czech medical authorities' views and submissions on the mandatory vaccination programme in the Czech Republic and questioned whether the relevant and expert bodies, in fact, considered these programmes necessary. The recommendations demonstrated that,

> In the Czech Republic, the vaccination duty represents the answer of the domestic authorities to the pressing social need to protect individual and public health against the diseases in question and to guard against any downward trend in the rate of vaccination among children (para 284).

The Court's attention to the medical experts' views "on the ground" is quite significant. Although childhood vaccinations are supported by strong scientific evidence, the Court additionally paid attention to the specific circumstances that might have shaped the Czech Republic Government's decision on compulsory vaccination schemes in its territory. The ECtHR acknowledged the public health rationale underlying the Czech Republic Government's policy choice (para 285). Rather than a general ban or permit for mandatory vaccination across Europe, the Court underlined the importance of the specific circumstances in the concerned countries. In COVID-19-related cases, too, the Court must pay attention to European states' particular circumstances, which might have influenced their responses to the COVID-19 pandemic.

In *Vavřička*, another important issue was the vaccines' side effects, which have been considerably discussed in the context of COVID-19. The Court was informed by the Czech Government that "out of approximately 100,000 children vaccinated annually in the Czech Republic (representing 300,000 vaccinations), the number of cases of serious, potentially lifelong damage to health stood at five or six" (para 301). On this important matter, the Court underlined that the state parties must take necessary precautions and check each case for possible serious side effects before vaccination (para 301). Having observed that medical professionals in the Czech Republic efficiently studied each individual before vaccinating, the Court held that the state at stake took the necessary precautions for any serious side effects. Therefore, the state parties' positive obligations to protect public health through vaccines encompass the protection of people from the vaccines' side effects. The state parties might be held accountable before the ECtHR unless they take due precautions.

Similar issues have also been discussed for COVID-19 vaccines. Although the effectiveness of the COVID-19 vaccines – in the short term – is evident and scientifically proven, rare cases of COVID-19 vaccine-related deaths or serious side effects were reported (Lamptey, 2021). Extremely rare cases of blood clots, for instance, after the Oxford-AstraZeneca COVID-19 vaccines were reported in the UK (Gallagher, 2021). To tackle the side effects of the COVID-19 vaccines, the World Health Organization (WHO) recommended that health workers, who administer the vaccine, ask people to wait for 15–30 minutes at the vaccination site to be monitored for any possible contraindication (WHO, 2021). This has been one of the most commonly used precautions across Europe.

In contrast to childhood vaccinations' side effects, it is difficult to identify the number of COVID-19 vaccine-related deaths or serious health problems. In the COVID-19 era, in addition to the issue seen with reporting, a great deal of misinformation and misleading claims were also witnessed (Wadman, 2021). Therefore, in COVID-19-related cases, the ECtHR will first need to establish the extent to which deaths and serious health problems occurred due to the vaccines and later, based upon this, decide which precautions would have been sufficient.

COVID-19 Measures: Leave Them to States' Discretion?

In *Vavřička*, the Czech Republic did not administer any vaccines contrary to the will of the applicants (para 302) but imposed fines on parents choosing not to vaccinate their children against diseases. According to the ECtHR, the administrative penalty was not excessive (para 304), and it concluded that:

> The Czech authorities remained within their wide margin of appreciation in this area. The Court concludes that they did not exceed their margin of appreciation, so the impugned measures can be regarded as "necessary in a democratic society" (para 310).

As a result, no violation of Article 8 of the ECHR was found. The Court granted the state party at stake a wide margin of appreciation for compulsory childhood vaccination.

Nilsson criticises the ECtHR for not sufficiently engaging with the reasons for vaccine hesitancy in *Vavřička* (Nilsson, 2021: 336). This is important criticism that underlines the necessity of understanding the reasons for vaccine hesitancy and rejection of a vaccine in the COVID-19 era. Compared to childhood vaccines, COVID-19 vaccines are quite new and scientific unknowns still exist about their efficacy. Besides, there is more than one COVID-19 vaccine in the world. The ones who are authorised by the WHO are BioNTech, Oxford-AstraZeneca, Sinopharm BIBP, Moderna, Janssen, Sinovac, Covaxin, Novavax, and Convidecia. COVID-19 anti-vaxxers worry about "the newness and safety of the vaccine as well as potential side effects" (Paul, 2021: 2). Research shows that the most common reasons to refuse vaccines relate to safety; a vaccine produced in such a short time is not considered safe by vaccine refusers (Troiano and Nardi, 2021). Low confidence in government measures and the health service responses and lack of consistent and reliable information provided have also been effective for vaccine refusers (Soares et al., 2021). Some worries are directly connected with the vaccines' "brand." The COVID-19 era created "corona orientalism" (Debeuf, 2020), and bias towards certain (non-Western) vaccines emerged. Thus, some anti-vaxxers denied not all but certain vaccines. Vaccines developed by countries in the Global South were compared with Western vaccines, and their effectiveness was constantly questioned on social media platforms (Çankal, 2021). Thus, there are reasons for COVID-19 vaccine hesitancy, and the ECtHR might have to pay more attention to these in the future.

In future cases regarding mandatory COVID-19 vaccination brought before the ECtHR, the hesitancy might have originated from the vaccine's brand that the state was administering, and the applicants might be hesitant to not all but one specific vaccine brand. In cases concerning vaccine hesitancy, unlike *Vavřička*, the ECtHR should elaborate more on the underlying reasons for vaccine hesitancy and rejection. In addition, the Court might hold the state parties responsible for communicating with the public about vaccines in future cases. Amid misinformation and misleading and fabricated comments (Eck and Hatz, 2020), the Court might maintain that the state's parties did and do have positive obligations to coordinate education and outreach efforts to inform the public about the effectiveness and safety of the vaccines.

Alekseenko (2022: 86) suggests that *Vavřička* reveals the Court's position in cases concerning the COVID-19 vaccination. Indeed, *Vavřička* has become an example of future COVID-19-related issues that could be brought before the ECtHR. The approach in *Vavřička* is highly likely to be seen in COVID-19-related cases. Therefore, the Court might consider a mandatory COVID-19 vaccination policy for certain occupations and age groups proportionate and necessary if vaccines are not administered against applicants' will and sanctions for refusing the vaccines are not excessive and unreasonable. On this issue, a wide margin of appreciation will likely be granted to the state's parties.

Whereas *Vavřička* gives us a sense of future discussions on COVID-19-related cases, there are certain issues concerning the COVID-19 vaccines not tackled in *Vavřička*. *Vavřička* concerned with childhood vaccination, and the applicants are children represented by their parents in this case. However, in Europe, COVID-19 vaccines have been mandatory for adults from certain professions and age groups. Thus, there will be additional considerations in COVID-19-related cases. For instance, Alekseenko (2022: 88) notes that adults might have undergone vaccination to keep their jobs and to provide for themselves and their families. In such scenarios, it is open to debate whether people who volunteered to be vaccinated to keep their jobs were free to decide and not forcibly vaccinated. The Court might have to consider additional issues examining "free choice" in COVID-19-related cases (ibid).

Another additional issue that the ECtHR might have to tackle is travel restrictions. In the era of COVID-19, European states classified countries as "high-risk" or "low-risk" countries and implemented different limits for people from these risk categories. After vaccination rates increased, the EU started implementing the EU Digital COVID Certificate, so-called "vaccine passports." In June 2021, 16 European states began using vaccine passports (McDonagh, 2021), and this became more common in Europe. Such measures were considered necessary at the time. European government officials stated that they did strike a fair balance in enforcing these measures since those without access to a vaccine would submit a negative coronavirus test to travel to Europe (Chini, 2021).

However, there were many problems in practice, and some of these problems directly interfered with the fundamental rights and freedoms under the ECHR, such as Article 8 (right to respect for private and family life), 2 of Protocol No. 4 (freedom of movement), and 14 (prohibition of discrimination). For instance, Southeast Asian tourists were unable to travel to Europe for a long time as their vaccine certificates or Sinovac and Sinopharm BBIP shots were not considered valid by European governments (Hutt, 2022). In India, those who "received AstraZeneca shots produced by India's Serum Institute" were not allowed to travel to Europe since the EU Digital COVID Certificate did not recognise these shots as valid (Berger, 2021). The vaccines donated to many African countries were also not identified; therefore, those vaccinated had difficulties travelling to Europe (Dean et al., 2021). In short, countries in the Global South had problems accessing the same vaccines. In addition to access issues, the commodification of vaccines pushed these countries into debt and reproduced national inequalities (Skelala et al., 2021). The COVID-19 pandemic exposed such inequalities and injustices (Davis, 2021). Human rights scholars called for "a decolonial framing of human rights and public law" that could address systemic injustices worldwide (ibid).

Cases concerning travel restrictions, vaccine nationalism, and vaccine discrimination might be brought before the ECtHR shortly. The Court might have to examine whether the state parties' vaccine distribution has been fair and non-discriminatory. Especially considering vaccine shortages, it becomes important to question who gets the vaccine and why. In May 2022, in a judicial seminar, the Court stated that "[p]rocedures developed for vaccine distribution within the groups, as defined by the prioritisation process, must be non-discriminatory in design and impact" (ECtHR, 2022). Thus, the distribution of vaccines in a non-discriminatory manner was recommended to the state parties by the Court. However, the extent to which the prohibition of discrimination (Article 14 of the ECHR) will play a role in COVID-19-related cases is yet to be seen.

Conclusion

The ECtHR might have to tackle several complex legal and moral issues soon. The Court's case law regarding the COVID-19 pandemic will be quite novel and significant in international human rights law. It will be relevant for other international human rights courts and monitoring bodies. Will the Court be able to re-deliver the common European values within its legal space and provide effective remedies for human rights violations that have occurred in the COVID-era in Europe? It most certainly will, but to what extent? There are two options: The ECtHR might take a proactive role in its future case law on the COVID-19 pandemic, or the Court might prefer to remain modest.

If the Court prefers modesty, the state parties will be granted a wide margin of appreciation in their responses to the COVID-19 pandemic. However, modesty in international human rights law might hinder structural change and reinforce inequalities (Quintana and Uriburu, 2020: 688). If the Court takes a proactive approach at the expense of being accused of "judicial activism," it might "politicise the legal analysis of the pandemic" (ibid). Besides, the Court can also engage with the state parties' responses to the COVID-19 pandemic from a critical point of view. Issues regarding travel restrictions or vaccine discrimination might be considered and evaluated in the scope of wider structural inequalities. Therefore, the Court might identify many of the COVID-19 measures of European states as "deliberate choices" rather than "the only option."

References

Alekseenko, A. (2022) 'Implications for COVID-19 Vaccination Following the European Court of Human Right's Decision in *Vavřička* and Others v Czech', *Medical Law International*. 22 (1), pp. 75–89.

Alemanno, A. (2020) 'The European Response to COVID-19: From Regulatory Emulation to Regulatory Coordination?', *European Journal of Risk Regulation*. 11 (2), pp. 307–316.

Amante, A. et al. (2022) 'Italy extends COVID vaccine mandate to everyone over 50', *Reuters*, January 6. Available at: https://www.reuters.com/world/europe/italy-make-covid-jab-mandatory-over-50s-tighten-curbs-draft-2022-01-05/ (Accessed: December 2, 2022).

Berger, M. (2021) 'AstraZeneca vaccine doses produced in India not included in Europe's vaccine passport ahead of launch', *The Washington Post*, July 1. Available at: https://www.washingtonpost.com/world/2021/06/30/eu-vaccine-travel-passport-india/ (Accessed: December 2, 2022).

Bilgic, T. (2020) 'Turkey reimposes curfews for at-risk seniors as virus surges', *Bloomberg*, November 11. Available at: https://www.bloomberg.com/news/articles/2020-11-11/turkey-reimposes-curfews-for-at-risk-seniors-as-virus-surges#xj4y7vzkg (Accessed: December 2, 2022).

Çankal, G. (2021) 'Sosyal Medyada Turkovac Aşısına İlişkin Self-Oryantalist Söylemler', *Journal of Media and Religion Studies*. 4 (2), pp. 223–235.

Cathaoir, K. Ó. (2021) 'Human Rights in Times of Pandemic: Necessity and Proportionality'. In Kjaerum, M. et al. (eds) *COVID-19 and Human Rights*, pp. 35–51. New York: Routledge.

Chini, M. (2021) 'EU considers Covid-19 vaccination passport to travel', *The Brussels Times*, January 15. Available at: https://www.brusselstimes.com/149844/eu-considers-covid-19-vaccination-passport-to-travel-ursula-von-der-leyen-commission-germany-kyriakos-mitsotakis (Accessed: December 2, 2022).

Cicchi, L. et al. (2020) *EU Solidarity in Times of Covid-19*. Florence: European University Institute.

Council of Europe (CoE) (1952) *The European Convention on Human Rights*. Strasbourg.

Council of Europe (CoE) (2020) 'Respecting Democracy, Rule of Law and Human Rights in the Framework of the COVID-19 Sanitary Crisis: A Toolkit for Member States', SG/Inf(2020)11 (April 7, 2020).

Crego, D. A. et al. (2022) 'Legal issues surrounding compulsory Covid-19 vaccination', European Parliamentary Research Service Briefing (March 14). Available at: https://www.europarl.europa.eu/RegData/etudes/BRIE/2022/729309/EPRS_BRI(2022)729309_EN.pdf

Davis, M.F. (2021) 'The Human (Rights) Costs of Inequality: Snapshots from a Pandemic'. In Kjaerum, M. et al. (eds) *COVID-19 and Human Rights*, pp. 67–81. New York: Routledge.

Dean, S. et al. (2021) 'Many Covid vaccine doses donated to African countries are not recognised by EU travel certificate', CNN, July 1. Available at: https://edition.cnn.com/2021/06/29/africa/africa-eu-vaccine-passport-intl/index.html (Accessed: December 1, 2022).

Debeuf, K. (2020) '"Corona Orientalism": Nothing to Learn from the East?', *euobserver*, April 23. Available at: https://euobserver.com/health-and-society/148135 (Accessed: December 1, 2022).

Dzehtsiarou, K. and Tzevelekos, V. P. (2021) 'Editorial: Interim Measures: Are Some Opportunities Worth Missing?', *European Convention on Human Rights Law Review*. 2 (1), pp. 1–10.

Eck, K. and Hatz, S. (2020) 'State Surveillance and the COVID-19 Crisis', *Journal of Human Rights*. 19 (5), pp. 603–612.

ECtHR (2022) 'Human rights protection in the time of the pandemic: New challenges and new perspectives', Council of Europe Judicial Seminar 2022 – Background Document (May 17). Available at: https://www.echr.coe.int/documents/d/echr/Seminar_background_paper_2022_ENG

Forman, L. and Kohler, J. C. (2020) 'Global Health and Human Rights in the Time of COVID-19: Response, Restrictions, and Legitimacy', *Journal of Human Rights*. 19 (5), pp. 547–556.

Gallagher, J. (2021) 'Covid: Trigger of rare blood clots with AstraZeneca jab found by scientists', *BBC News*, December 2. Available at: https://www.bbc.com/news/health-59418123 (Accessed: December 1, 2022).

Gebrekidan, S. (2020) 'For autocrats, and others, coronavirus is a chance to grab even more power', *The New York Times*, March 30. Available at: https://www.nytimes.com/2020/03/30/world/europe/coronavirus-governments-power.html (Accessed: December 1, 2022).

Gibelli, F. (2022) 'COVID-19 Compulsory Vaccination: Legal and Bioethical Controversies', *Frontiers in Medicine*. 9, pp. 1–8.

Hafner-Burton, E. et al. (2011) 'Emergency and Escape: Explaining Derogations from Human Rights Treaties', *International Organization*, 65(4), pp. 673–707.

Hutt, D. (2022) 'EU dallies on recognizing ASEAN COVID vaccine passports', *DW*, May 9. Available at: https://www.dw.com/en/eu-dallies-on-recognizing-asean-covid-vaccine-passports/a-61732024 (Accessed: December 2, 2022).

Joly, J. (2022) 'COVID in Europe: Greece begins fining those over 60 who are unvaccinated', *Euronews*, January 17. Available at: https://www.euronews.com/2022/01/17/covid-in-europe-greece-begins-fining-those-over-60-who-are-unvaccinated (Accessed: December 2, 2022).

Jovičić, S. (2021) 'COVID-19 Restrictions on Human Rights in the Light of the Case-Law of the European Court of Human Rights', *ERA Forum*. 21 (4), pp. 545–560.

Kovács, K. (2021) 'Hungary and the pandemic: A pretext for expanding power' *Verfassungsblog*, March 11. Available at: https://verfassungsblog.de/hungary-and-the-pandemic-a-pretext-for-expanding-power/ (Accessed: December 2, 2022).

Krajewska, A. (2021) 'Connecting Reproductive Rights, Democracy, and the Rule of Law: Lessons from Poland in Times of COVID-19', *German Law Journal*. 22 (6), pp. 1072–1097.

Lamptey, E. (2021) 'Post-Vaccination COVID-19 Deaths: A Review of Available Evidence and Recommendations for the Global Population', *Clinical and Experimental Vaccine Research*. 10 (3), pp. 264–275.

McDonagh, S. (2021) 'These sixteen countries are now using the EU's COVID travel pass (EUDCC)', *Euronews*, June 16. Available at: https://www.euronews.com/travel/2021/06/16/eu-covid-19-digital-pass-countries-begin-using-new-travel-system (Accessed: December 1, 2022).

Nilsson, A. (2021) 'Is Compulsory Vaccination Compatible with the Right to Respect for Private Life? A Comment on *Vavřička and Others v. the Czech Republic*', *European Journal of Health Law*. 28 (3), pp. 323–340.

Paris, E. (2021) 'Applying the Proportionality Principle to COVID-19 Certificates', *European Journal of Risk Regulation*. 12 (2), pp. 287–297.

Paul, E. et al. (2021) 'Attitudes towards Vaccines and Intention to Vaccinate against COVID-19: Implications for Public Health Communications', *The Lancet Regional Health – Europe*, 1, pp. 1–10.

Quintana, F. and Uriburu, J. (2020) 'Modest International Law: COVID-19, International Legal Responses, and Depoliticization', *American Society of International Law*. 114 (4), pp. 687–697.

Scheinin, M. and Molbæk-Steensig, H. (2021) 'Human Rights-Based Versus Populist Responses to the Pandemic'. In Kjaerum, M. et al. (eds.) *COVID-19 and Human Rights*, pp. 19–34. New York: Routledge.

Šeško, Z. (2021) 'Eastern European countries adopting authoritarian measures in face of Covid', *The Guardian*, December 29. Available at: https://www.theguardian.com/world/2021/dec/29/eastern-european-countries-adopt-authoritarian-measures-covid (Accessed: December 2, 2022).

Sheikh, A. et al. (2018) 'A Report on the Status of Vaccination in Europe', *Vaccine*. 36(33), pp. 4979–4992.
Skelala, A. et al. (2021) 'Decolonising Human Rights: How Intellectual Property Laws Result in Unequal Access to the COVID-19 Vaccine', *BMJ Global Health*. 6(7), 1–9.
Soares, P. et al. (2021) 'Factors Associated with COVID-19 Vaccine Hesitancy', *Vaccines*. 9(3), pp. 1–14.
Troiano, G. and Nardi, A. (2021) 'Vaccine Hesitancy in the Era of COVID-19', *Public Health*. 194, pp. 245–251.
Tzevelekos, V. P. and Dzehtsiarou, K. (2020) 'Editorial: Normal as Usual? Human Rights in Times of COVID-19', *European Convention on Human Rights Law Review*. 1 (2), pp. 141–149.
Vinceti, S.R. (2021) 'COVID-19 Compulsory Vaccination and the European Court of Human Rights', *Acta Biomed*. 92 (S6), pp. 1–7.
Wadman, M. (2021) 'Antivaccine Activists Use a Government Database on Side Effects to Scare the public', *Science*, May 26. Available at: https://www.science.org/content/article/antivaccine-activists-use-government-database-side-effects-scare-public (Accessed: December 2, 2022).
Wallace, S. (2020) 'Derogations from the European Convention on Human Rights: The Case for Reform', *Human Rights Law Review*. 20 (4), pp. 769–796.
WHO, (2021) 'Getting the COVID-10 vaccine', March 31. Available at: https://www.who.int/news-room/feature-stories/detail/side-effects-of-covid-19-vaccines (Accessed: December 2, 2022).

Cases

Abgrall and 671 others v France App no 41950/21 (ECtHR, August 25, 2021).
Ireland v the United Kingdom App no 5310/71 (ECtHR, January 18, 1978).
Kakaletri and others v Greece App no 43375/21 (ECtHR, September 9, 2021).
Theofanopoulou and others v Greece App no 43910/21 (ECtHR, September 9, 2021).
Vavřička and Others v the Czech Republic App nos 47621/13 and 5 others (ECtHR, April 8, 2021).

23 Globalisation in the Era of Power Transition
Lessons Post-COVID-19 for China and the US

Matti Izora İbrahim, Büşra Yilmaz, and Murat Çemrek

Introduction

This chapter will discuss globalisation in the post-COVID-19 transition utilising Organski and Kugler's (1980) power transition theory (PTT). Parallel to the PTT, we trace power shifts in world politics from the 1800s to today, with one eye on the effects of globalisation while keeping the other eye on the post-COVID-19 era. The COVID-19 pandemic has accelerated the transformation of global politics, interestingly with the concomitant rise of China as the challenger vis-à-vis American hegemony. The geopolitical impasse between China and the United States (US) has provoked much dialogue among international relations (IR) scholars concerning the nature, interpretation, and possible outcomes stemming from a power rivalry between China and the US. Thus, the PTT provides valuable insights to explain the changing power relationships in world politics. With reference to Heraclitus' ages-old saying, "The only constant in life is change," we, the scientists, are always behind the independent variable to comprehend and so to explain the change.

Power Transition Theory (PTT)

Originally conceived by A.F.K. Organski and first published in his book, *World Politics* (1958), the PTT considers the nature of war and shifting power relations in international politics. It provides a method by which such structural changes in the international system can predict shifts in cooperative or hostile relationships and the probability of preserving peace or pursuing war depending on the situation and its steps as a process. Thus, hierarchy, power, and satisfaction are the primary components of the PTT (Tammen et al., 2011, 2017).

Three basic assumptions distinguish power transition from realist models: First, the PTT views the world order as hierarchical in nature, analogous to the domestic political system. However, opposed the anarchical character of the international system, as staunchly offered in the realist perspective. Second, the PTT views the rules governing domestic politics and the international systems as fundamentally similar. Thus, in that international arena, political actors, and states predominantly and continuously compete over scarce resources in the international system, much like domestic political actors. Third, competition among international actors is highly

DOI: 10.4324/9781003377597-26

motivated by potential net gains. As such, rather than seeking to maximise power in Morgenthau's (1948) balance-of-power theory, the PTT argues that the objective of nations is to maximise their potential net gains amassed either from conflict or cooperation. So, peaceful competition could be accomplished when nations agree that the net gains accrued from conflict outweigh the net benefits (Kugler & Organski, 1989).

However, from a theoretical perspective, IR scholars evaluate the PTT from both realist and idealist perspectives. For example, from the realist perspective, the PTT stands up to empirical tests and objective conclusions. Yet, because of its dynamic nature, in that it understands that policy interests are central to resolving disputes, many scholars conceptualise the PTT from an idealist perspective. However, since the PTT blends empirical evidence with established scholarly research and policy advice, some scholars, like Tammen (2000), prefer to view this theory through a rationalist perspective, already embedded structurally.

Debates

Organski (1958) predicted China's rise and the West's subsequent decline nearly 60 years ago. Accelerated by the pandemic, China's rise to power has thus caused IR scholars to revisit the PTT. Three scholars have investigated the impact of COVID-19 on the international system transformation considering the PTT: Duggan and Grabowski (2021) and Mitra (2022). The focus of Duggan and Grabowski's research centred on American hegemonic satisfaction compared to China's rising power dissatisfaction. In contrast, Mitra (2022) took an alternative approach considering the discontent with the US' hegemonic power compared to China's rising power satisfaction. Finally, Ikenberry (2008) addresses the relationship between the US and China in the context of the former's potential to maintain its current global position and the latter's rise to power enough to be able to challenge and replace the former.

Duggan and Grabowski (2021) considered the impact of the COVID-19 pandemic on the transformation of the global system and the relative power distribution between the US and China. To evaluate the pandemic's impact on the power distribution between China and the US, the researchers focused on Southeast Asia as a case study. Their research concluded that the external shock of the pandemic and the Trump administration's abandonment of regional agreements (e.g., the Trans-Pacific Partnership) and withdrawal from global institutions (e.g., the WHO) caused Southeast Asian policymakers to look to China for leadership rather than the US. However, the power vacuum created by the Trump administration that allowed China to assume a leadership role – at least during the early phase of the COVID-19 crisis – was only short-lived. Because China has failed in medical diplomacy, and Joe Biden's advent to power would cause policymakers in Southeast Asia to turn to the US for leadership as they did in the past.

The nature of the rising state's regime, the degree of dissatisfaction, and the character of the international order are three main factors determining how power transitions occur (Ikenberry, 2008). Accordingly, Yilmaz and Xiangyu (2019) utilised the framework of the PTT to determine whether China was a dissatisfied power, and, if so, aimed to determine what changes in the international system it sought to change. Did China desire a multipolar global order in nature? Their analysis concluded that China is not a completely dissatisfied power and truly believes in the principles of the Westphalian system, which is essential to the existence of the Chinese state. Yet, according to Yilmaz and Xiangyu, China is unhappy with the standards imposed upon itself by the West, specifically by the US. China believes that the current international order has imposed Western standards of normative values on the globe and strongly feels that different societal and political systems should also be recognised.

Ikenberry (2008) considered the relations between China and the US and how through reinforcing the rules and institutions in the current Western-led order, the US can mould the environment wherein China is compelled to make strategic choices. The task for the West, he argues, is to make the Western order "so all-encompassing and institutionalised" that China has no choice but to follow the rules and institutions that the US has already created in the post-World War II era. In this respect, Ikenberry makes two key points: First, China can overtake the US; however, it is far less likely for China to overtake the fully fledged Western order. Second, despite the US' global dominance decline, the international system can remain well under American hegemony into the 21st century. Ikenberry acknowledges that the unipolar moment is nearing an end and that the American grand strategy "should be driven by one key question: What kind of international order would the United States like to see in place when it is less powerful?" To answer this question, Ikenberry draws on the political philosophy of John Rawls, who argued that "political institutions should be conceived behind a 'veil of ignorance.'"

The limits of the present study were drawn within the framework of the PTT, explained above. To better understand the power struggle after the COVID-19 pandemic, the cornerstone of this chapter, we discuss Globalisation Before COVID-19, followed by an analysis of Globalisation and Transitioning World Order in the Post-COVID-19 Era.

Globalisation Before the COVID-19

History presents a future perspective, having witnessed all powers' rise and fall. *Pax Romana* lasted for centuries in Europe. Afterwards, there have been endless power transitions between the 16th and 17th centuries. In the 20th century, bloc movements emerged, and two world wars broke out, hosting the Great Depression and its effects in between as tumultuous years. World War II left its place in the Cold War until the end of the Soviets in 1991. During the Cold War era, the system was neither multipolar nor unipolar. It was a bipolar system consisting of two superpowers (the Soviets and the US). After the end of the Cold War, we have witnessed the rise of America as a hegemon state in every aspect, including economically, politically, and militarily. Globalisation has paved the path for new rivals to compete with American hegemony in various sectors (Naím, 2009: 30).

According to Modelski, globalisation "is the history of growing engagement between the world's major civilization," since it is a long-term historical process

(Held & McGrew, 2008: 71). Although globalisation means increasing the interaction of people, cultures, and states, it does not mean that this interaction occurs equally worldwide. According to Naím (2009: 30), it was never about Americanization though globalisation has been heavily equalised with that since the US has been the hegemonic power. According to Kellner (2002: 292), "it is important to present globalisation as a strange amalgam of both homogenising forces of sameness and uniformity and heterogeneity, difference, and hybridity, as well as a contradictory mixture of democratising and anti-democratising tendencies." On the one hand, globalisation involves homogenisation. People not living in the US can also consume hamburgers, interestingly German in roots, people not from China can also buy Chinese goods, while someone illiterate about India might like Bollywood movies, or anyone might want to learn Korean to understand the lyrics of their K-pop favourite band. Thus, people interact more and more through increased communication and transportation opportunities. On the other hand, globalisation involves maintaining heterogeneity. Besides hamburgers, symbolising our planet's transformation into *McWorld* (Barber, 1996) at some points, people continue to eat their cultural food, watch their television programmes, and support the singers and sports people of their own country.

Globalisation has not only created or deepened some problems but also brought others to the surface more than in the past, such as climate change, environmental problems, pollution, pandemic, migration, etc. Some of these problems affect less developed countries even more due to their underdeveloped technologies, such as climate change. As a current example, the COVID-19 pandemic has spread worldwide so fast but affected developed and underdeveloped countries in different proportions. States have taken significant precautions like lockdowns, but we all have concluded that global problems need global solutions rather than local, national, and regional solutions to help us partially.

Undoubtedly, since globalisation is multifaceted, it has economic, political, sociocultural dimensions and so on. Moreover, globalisation affects and gets affected by technological advancements. Globalisation directly affects the international system composed of nation-states and their military structures, the international division of labour, and the world capitalist economy (Held & McGrew, 2008: 84), which are also related to economy, politics, and culture. Globalisation is a huge ongoing process in human history, although globalisation started to get popularised in the 1980s. One can say that global values of governance, human rights, and international law are at least extensions of globalisation. Moreover, there are mainly three theoretical approaches to globalisation: sceptics, hyperglobalists, and transformationalists. Rather than these perspectives, for the sake of this chapter's focus, we will evaluate globalisation in the light of the PTT.

According to Friedman (2005), globalisation has three periods: Globalization 1.0 (1492–1800), Globalization 2.0 (1800–2000), and Globalization 3.0 (2000–present). Although globalisation is a principal process and a field of study that requires holistic analysis, Friedman's classification facilitates our comprehension of the effects of globalisation concerning the COVID-19 pandemic. Some turning points in the history of the world have greatly affected and shaped the current international relations system. One such remarkable event is undoubtedly 1492. In other words, "Ever since the American Revolution, historians have recognised the connections between the nation's history and the age of discovery" (Mancall, 1998: 27). As is known, of course, there were states or empires as hegemons or superpowers of their periods before the US became the world hegemon after the end of the Soviets. Even in ancient times, different and significant civilisations existed in different regions. The Roman Empire would probably best exemplify that. When we talk about the Age of Discovery, there were two important states of the era: Portugal and Spain. Although Portugal is considered the first state that erupted as a colonial empire, Spain became the most influential and expansionist state of the era (Uluerler, 2018: 56–59). These two states were followed by other European powers, such as France, England, and the Netherlands (Uluerler, 2018: 68). The colonial rivalries among these powers and the concomitant power transitions continued till the half of the 20th century resulting in two world wars, without mention the relatively low-profile ones. In other words, through Globalization 1.0, the world became a medium size from a size large, and the battles among competitive powers have fuelled globalisation as a process through race for resources and imperial conquest in that era (Friedman, 2005).

Through Globalization 2.0, we see the world is getting smaller and transforming powers such as economic, cultural, soft, smart, and sticky, as well as hard power more common in Globalization 1.0. Thus, power transitions have also gained transparency. In other words, power transitions between states happen not only via hard power use but also in economic terms. This will be explained further under "Globalization and Transitioning World Order in the COVID-19 Era," the section specific to China and the US. Briefly, Globalization 2.0 made the world small (Friedman, 2005). Therefore, the war strategies between the Soviets and the US during the Cold War also reveal this power transformation.

Globalisation 3.0 has kept shrinking the world from a size small to a size tiny (Friedman, 2005). With the spread of the Internet in the 1990s, the peak of American hegemony, our world has entered a new era. The flow of information, money, goods, services, and even people has increased as ever in history. American political and economic hegemony erupted in this period, especially its cultural attractiveness. However, the 9/11 attacks were a decisive moment in global terms (Walker, 2007: 16). After 9/11, the US has not only prioritised its security problems but also globalised them through then-President George W. Bush's address to a joint session of Congress on September 20, 2001, "Every nation, in every region, now has the decision to make. Either you are with us, or you are with the terrorists."

We can indicate that "the Western-dominated Globalization 2.0 gave way to Globalization 3.0, it may have been when China acceded to WTO membership on December 11, 2001" (Walker, 2007: 20). As we stated before, globalisation has several dimensions: economy, military, technology, politics, and even geography. Regional integrations and nation-states' policymaking processes are also other aspects of globalisation. Besides 9/11, COVID-19 has hit the world, affecting all our routines and transforming power transitions.

Globalisation and Transitioning World Order in the COVID-19 Era

What distinguishes COVID-19 from other pandemics in human history is that globalisation has occurred on a much greater scale than in any past period. This interconnectivity of our planet through transportation, tourism, and trade has allowed infectious diseases to occur more frequently, spread to greater distances, transmit more easily, even between humans and animals, and mutate into new and more virulent strains faster (Mack et al., 2010). By the time the WHO declared the COVID-19 pandemic on March 10, 2020, the novel coronavirus had already spread across the globe and disrupted every facet of modern life. The global pandemic crisis prompted modern history's largest and fastest decrease in international flows. It tragically exceeded 6 million lives in two years since the WHO first declared the pandemic (WTO, 2022).

As countries around the world imposed lockdowns, travel restrictions, and border closings, economic activities declined dramatically, leading to massive unemployment, income losses, and disruptions in the global economy. Seemingly overnight, COVID-19 disrupted supply chains, slowing the raw materials needed for finished products, including many pharmaceuticals and other critical medical supplies needed to combat the virus. By April 2020, every country had enforced restrictions on international travel, with 45% of countries having either partially or completely closed their borders to foreign visitors. The impact of the pandemic on world gross domestic product (GDP) growth was unprecedented, and, according to International Monetary Fund (IMF) figures, the global economy decreased by 3.2% in 2020, the sharpest contraction since the 2008 financial crisis and the Great Depression of 1930 (Gopinath, 2020).

Prompted by the pandemic, alliances and international cooperation were questioned, and governments began to consider reducing their economic interdependence and moving towards more protectionist policies, especially regarding medical supplies and food. Even though the pandemic has slowed or even reversed economic growth, it did not mark the end of globalisation (Irwin, 2020). Irwin explains that trade flows peaked in 2008 and then fell sharply, marking the Great Recession from 2008 until 2010. Then, in 2010, world trade bounced back but steadily declined. We are currently in a period that some economists have called "slowbalization." Several factors have contributed to slow growth rates, including that states have begun to turn inward to reduce their trade dependence. And so, globalisation slowed down even before the pandemic, and the pandemic merely added to the momentum of the deglobalisation trend.

Reactionary Populist Nationalism, Democratic Backsliding, and Authoritarian Consolidation

There are two main aspects of populism: The notion of a corrupt elite invoking dissatisfaction with the status quo and the belief that power should be restored to "the people." Populism presents itself as being democratic, but all too often, populism can gravitate towards authoritarianism and democratic backsliding. Some of the main features of populism are scepticism towards authorities, journalism, and science, an aversion to outgroups, anti-globalism, and nationalist sentiments (Graves & Smith, 2020). Although populist nationalistic sentiments were prevalent long before the coronavirus outbreak, growing populist nationalist feelings have been observed globally during the COVID-19 pandemic. Some populist leaders adopted destructive denialist approaches undermining any efforts to respond to the pandemic effectively (Greer et al., 2020). Other populist politicians rejected scientific evidence, ignoring the advice of experts to justify their actions or inactions (Williams et al., 2020), and some illiberal governments have used the pandemic as an excuse to expand their executive power to constrain the individual rights of their citizens or crackdown on political opponents to tighten their grip on power (Brown et al, 2020).

Stephen M. Walt has taken a rather pessimistic view of the post-pandemic world. He has argued that COVID-19 will "strengthen the state and reinforce nationalism." "In short," he says, "COVID-19 will create a less open, less prosperous, and less free world. It did not have to be this way, but the combination of a deadly virus, inadequate planning, and incompetent leadership has placed humanity on a new and worrisome path" (Walt, 2020).

Kindleberger Trap and Power Transition

"When the world leader ceases to play its role in the international system, the world becomes vulnerable to chaos and instability" (Bahi, 2021: 88). The pandemic took a geopolitical dimension when the US and China sought to take advantage of the crisis extension of the pandemic to elevate their international positions. Several scholars (e.g., Bahi, 2021; Freeman, 2021; Sachs, 2020) have argued that the world has slipped into a Kindleberger Trap (Kindleberger, 1981) because COVID-19 has defied and even collapsed global cooperation while the US, as the traditional leader in international collective efforts, failed to deliver public goods on its soil at a time of need and abandoned its role as the global leader. As the rising power, though keen to play a greater role in the international system, China lacked the capability to play the role (Zheng, 2020).

In terms of power transition, COVID-19 accelerated the Chinese rise to power in three major ways: The economic performance of both China and the US, American withdrawal from international organisations, and the lack of leadership in the global response to the shortage of personal protective equipment (Duggan & Grabowski, 2021).

The pandemic has impacted the economic performance of both the US and China. For example, in terms of international trade, the US was more negatively impacted than China (Fu et al., 2020; Tian, 2021), with its GDP growth falling from 2.2% in 2019 to –3.5% in 2020. Conversely, China's GDP grew to 2.3% in 2020, down from 5.9% in 2019. American exports were also negatively impacted by the pandemic dropping by 13.5%, in contrast to Chinese ones, having increased by 3.5% (Duggan & Grabowski citing WTO, n.d.).

The second way that China's rise was accelerated is when the Trump administration withdrew from important international organisations and treaties. In particular, by withdrawing funding for the WHO, the US opened a power vacuum that enabled China to work closely with this international medical organisation firmly in responding to the pandemic, especially in Asia and in the Global South. By taking on the leadership role, China increased its relative power within the international system (Duggan & Grabowski, 2021).

The third way China's rise was accelerated was through Chinese face masks and vaccine diplomacy. While pursuing its "America First" policy, the Trump administration demonstrated a lack of leadership in responding to the global need for personal protective equipment such as face masks, face shields, and other critical medical supplies like ventilators. In contrast, to project a positive image as a responsible global power, China used its soft power to pursue an aggressive campaign to provide face masks, medical equipment, and vaccines to the countries most impacted by the pandemic. Moreover, China sent its military to train other armies throughout Eastern Europe and Latin America to respond to the pandemic and engaged in direct military-to-military cooperation in countries like Asia, the Middle East, and Africa. Thus, by taking a leadership role, China increased its relative power within the international system (Duggan & Grabowski, 2021).

While some scholars have suggested that Chinese face masks and vaccine diplomacy increased its soft power in the Global South, others suggest quite the opposite. The China Power Project at the Centre for Strategic and International Studies (2021) found that China's mask and vaccine diplomacy were not targeted at the Global South but were commercially motivated.

Post-Pandemic World Order

So, what would a post-pandemic world order look like? What is certain is that the current world order will be faced with more challenges due to the changing dynamics and calculations between states. What is also certain is a more confident and aggressive China (Hussain, 2021) will be before us in the close future. Guided by the PTT, Hussain's (2021) meta-analysis offers us several possible scenarios for future post-pandemic world order. In the first instance, Hussain makes the case that China's rise to prominence as a global leader does not pose a threat to American hegemony. There is a consensus among IR scholars that even as China continues to grow in both economic and military terms, it does not necessarily mean that China is a threat to the Western-led world order. Scholars, like Beckley (2012) and Brooks and Wohlforth (2016), have reasoned that China places more importance on lifting its citizens out of poverty by strengthening its economy and trade relations. Moreover, even if Chinese economic performance outpaces American one, the US still exceeds China in terms of its global military dominance and, given the uncertainty of the trajectory of China's economy, China still has a long way to fill the gap. With respect to China's rapid economic growth, Beckley (2012) has put forth the argument that there is a misconception about China's economy catching up to the US. He says: "This focus on the growth rate, however, obscures China's decline relative to the US in all these categories. China's growth rates are high because its starting point was low. China is rising but it is not catching up" (Beckley, 2012: 43–44).

COVID-19 provided the perfect opportunity for China to assert itself to pursue its own interests in the international order when the US failed to take the leading role in responding to the pandemic. In the second scenario, Hussain describes a relatively declining US and a more confident China that will seize the opportunity to use its military capability to challenge American hegemony in the Asia-Pacific. American observers have anticipated that China would follow a foreign policy towards Asia like the American Monroe Doctrine. Mearsheimer (2014) articulated this point:

> My argument, in a nutshell, is that if China continues to grow economically, it will attempt to dominate Asia the way the United States dominates the Western hemisphere. The United States will, however, go to enormous lengths to prevent China from achieving regional hegemony ... the result will be security competition with considerable potential for war. (pp. 332–333)

In the third scenario, Hussain highlights the role of multilateralism with Chinese integration into the current Western-led order based on rules and norms of equality and non-discrimination. The COVID-19 pandemic highlighted how states were unable to cooperate in a time of need, behaving in "selfish ways" or, to say, self-help in realist theory. All these raised many doubts about what kind of order the international community should seek over the coming decades. But for multilateralism to be functionally viable, a global hegemon must be willing and able to uphold the structures and processes of institutions and regimes. The hegemon's willingness, however, hinges on the ability of collective structures and arrangements to serve its interests (Hussain, 2021). Although a hegemonic power plays a chief role in the efficient functioning of regimes and institutions, its decline does not lead to the failure of the regimes and institutions it upholds. Furthermore, although a declining hegemon's disengagement may threaten multilateralism's progress, it does not "shake its core" (Zerubabel et al., 2020, cited by Hussain, 2021). Hussain further points out that the institutions and structures of the Western-led order, based on rules and norms of non-discrimination, create an open and rules-based institution and an environment from which rising states can ascend. With its ascendancy and its economic influence growing, the hegemon's stance in the multilateral institutions strengthens, "making it an important stakeholder in the sustenance of these institutions" (p. 9). Thus, in this way, China has successfully integrated into the existing system and has been able to advance its political and economic goals.

Hussain makes some recommendations for the peaceful integration of China as a rising power, which can only be sustained if the US, as a leader in the current Western-led order, works to strengthen the institutions it upholds. Considering the American disengagement during the COVID-19 pandemic as it turned out to be a crisis, the US should work towards re-establishing its role as a benign global hegemon to instil trust and confidence in the institutions. Towards that end, the US should invest in these institutions, while at the same time urging the participation of other states. The US should also abstain from distancing itself from multilateral institutions and regimes and guard against resorting to unilateral actions, as resorting to unilateral actions. This would only weaken confidence in the efficacy of international organisations and regimes and create a vacuum to be filled by a rising state. This may lead to conflict between the declining hegemon and its rising challenger.

Conclusion

The rivalry and power transition between the US and China should be considered globalisation as a process. The American hegemony is undoubtedly related to 1492, urging us to discuss globalisation from a historical perspective, so starting it with that date. Guided by Organski and Kugler's (1980) PTT, this chapter has traced the power shifts in world politics from the 1800s to the present, focusing on the effects of globalisation regarding international politics through the current post-COVID-19 era.

There is a consensus among IR scholars that even as China continues to grow in economic and military terms, it does not necessarily mean that China is a threat to the Western-led world order. China has demonstrated that it is willing and able to take the lead in response to external shocks when the US is not willing or unable to do so. Hussain (2021) highlights the role of multilateralism with China integrating into the existing Western-led order based on rules and norms of equality and non-discrimination. He makes several recommendations for the peaceful integration of China as a rising power into the Western-led order, which can only be sustained if the US, as a leader in the current Western-led order, works to strengthen the institutions it upholds. Ikenberry (2008) makes two key points: First, China can overtake the US; however, China is far less likely to overtake the Western order. Second, despite the American decline of global dominance, the US-led international system can remain well into the 21st century as the leading order.

References

Bahi, R. (2021) 'The Geopolitics of COVID-19: US-China Rivalry and the Imminent Kindleberger Trap', *Review of Economics and Political Science. 6* (1), pp. 76–94.

Barber, B. (1996) *Jihad vs. McWorld: How Globalism and Tribalism Are Shaping the World.* New York: Ballantine Books.

Beckley, M. (2012) 'China's Century? Why America's Edge Will Endure', *International Security. 36* (3), pp. 41–78.

Brooks, S. and Wohlforth, W. (2016) 'The Rise and Fall of Great Powers in the 21st Century and the Fate of America's Global Position', *International Security. 40* (3), pp. 7–53.

Brown, F. Z., Brechenmacher, S. and Carothers, T. (2020) *How will the coronavirus reshape democracy and governance globally?* Carnegie Foundation. https://carnegieendowment.org/2020/04/06/how-willcoronavirus-reshape-democracy-and-governance-globally-pub-81470

China Power Team. (23 September 2021). *Is China's COVID-19 diplomacy succeeding?* Center for Strategic and International Studies. https://bit.ly/3PQFsIA

Duggan, N. and Grabowski, M. (2021) 'The Influence of COVID-19 on the Power Transition between the United States and China: The Case of Southeast Asia', *Irish Studies in International Affairs. 32* (1), pp. 83–102.

Freeman, C. P. (2021) 'Reading Kindleberger in Beijing: Xi Jinping's China as a Provider of Global Public Goods', *The British Journal of Politics and International Relations. 23* (2), pp. 297–318.

Friedman, L. T. (2005, April 3) *It's a flat world, after all.* The New York Times Magazine. http://www.nytimes.com/2005/04/03/magazine/its-a-flat-world-after-all.html

Fu, X., Zhang, J. and Wang, L. (2020) 'Introduction to the Special Section: The Impact of COVID-19 and Post-Pandemic Recovery: China and the World Economy', *Journal of Chinese Economic and Business Studies. 18* (4), pp. 311–319.

Gopinath, G. (2020) World economic outlook, April 2020: The great lockdown. International Monetary Fund. https://bit.ly/3GvpS0E

Graves, F. and Smith, J. (2020) 'Northern Populism: Causes and Consequences of the New Ordered Outlook', *The School of Public Policy Publications. 13* (15), pp. 1–37.

Greer, S. L., King, E. J., da Fonseca, E. M. and Peralta-Santos, A. (2020) 'The Comparative Politics of COVID-19: The Need to Understand Government Responses', *Global Public Health. 15* (9), pp. 1413–1416.

Held, D. and Mcgrew, A. (2008) 'Küresel Dönüşümler: Büyük Küreselleşme Tartışması'. Trans. Güngen, A. R., et al. Ankara: Phoenix.

Hussain, M. (2021) 'Reimagining the New World Order Post-COVID-19', *Qubahan Academic Journal. 1* (1), pp. 5–10.

Ikenberry, J. G. (2008) 'The Rise of China and the Future of the West', *Foreign Affairs, 87* (23), pp. 23–37. https://fam.ag/3lXx4Jt

Irwin, D. A. (2020) The pandemic adds momentum to the deglobalization trend. Real-time economic issues watch. Peterson Institute for International Economics. https://bit.ly/3lZwV8u

Kellner, D. (2002) 'Theorizing Globalization', *Sociological Theory, 20* (3), pp. 285–305. http://www.jstor.org/stable/3108613

Kindleberger, C. P. (1981) 'Dominance and Leadership in the International Economy: Exploitation, Public Goods, and Free Rides', *International Studies Quarterly. 25* (2), pp. 242–254.

Kugler, J. and Organski, A. F. K. (1989) 'The Power Transition: A Retrospective and Prospective Evaluation', In M. Midlarsky (ed.) *Handbook of War Studies.* Boston, MA: Unwin Hyman. pp. 171–194.

Mack, A., Choffnes, E. R. and Relman, D. A. (Eds.) (2010) *Infectious Disease Movement in a Borderless World: Workshop Summary.* Washington, DC: National Academies Press.

Mancall, P. C. (1998) 'The Age of Discovery', *Reviews in American History. 26* (1), pp. 26–53. http://www.jstor.org/stable/30030873

Mearsheimer, J. (2014) *The Tragedy of Great Power Politics.* New York, NY: W.W. Norton and Company.

Mitra, R. (2022) China in the World Order: A Critical Examination. *Institute of Chinese Studies*, p. 145.

Morgenthau, H. J. (1948). *Politics Among Nations: The Struggle for Power and Peace.* New York: A. A. Knopf.

Naím, M. (2009). 'Globalization', *Foreign Policy, 171*, pp. 28–34. http://www.jstor.org/stable/20684848

Organski, A. F. K. and Kugler, J. (1980) *The War Ledger.* Chicago and London: University of Chicago Press.

Organski, A. F. K. (1958) *World Politics.* New York: Alfred A. Knopf. pp. xii, 461.

Sachs, J. D. (2020) 'COVID-19 and Multilateralism', *Horizons: Journal of International Relations and Sustainable Development. 16*, pp. 30–39.

Tammen, R. L. (2000) *Power Transitions: Strategies for the 21st Century*. London: Chatham House.

Tammen, R. L., Kugler, J. and Lemke, D. (2011) *Power Transition Theory*. New York: Oxford University Press.

Tammen, R. L., Kugler, J. and Lemke, D. (2017). Foundations of Power Transition Theory. *Oxford Research Encyclopedia of Politics.* https://oxfordre.com/politics/view/10.1093/acrefore/9780190228637.001.0001/acrefore-9780190228637-e-296

Tian, W. (2021) 'How China Managed the COVID-19 Pandemic', *Asian Economic Papers. 20* (1), pp. 75–101.

Uluerler, S. (2018) 'Coğrafi Keşifler ve Avrupa'nın Yayılması'. In S. H. Özkan (Ed.) *Yeni ve Yakın Çağ Tarihi*, pp 45–78. İstanbul: İdeal Kültür Yayıncılık.

Walker, M. (2007) 'Globalization 3.0', *The Wilson Quarterly (1976-). 31*(4), pp. 16–24. http://www.jstor.org/stable/40262473

Walt, S. M. (2020) The Global Order after COVID-19. *Institute for Security Policy.* https://www.belfercenter.org/sites/default/files/files/publication/paper-for-institute-for-security-policy-austria.pdf

Williams, C. R., Kestenbaum, J. G. and Meier, B. M. (2020) 'Populist Nationalism Threatens Health and Human Rights in the COVID-19 response', *American Journal of Public Health. 110* (12), pp. 1766–1768.

World Health Organization. (2022) *WHO Coronavirus (COVID-19) Dashboard.* https://covid19.who.int/

Yilmaz, S. and Xiangyu, W. (2019) 'Power Transition Theory Revisited: When Rising China Meets Dissatisfied United States', *China Quarterly of International Strategic Studies. 5* (03), pp. 317–341.

Zheng, C. (2020) 'China's Global Governance Challenge and Domestic Reforms: Rethinking the 'Kindleberger Trap' and Its Implications for the Rise of China', *The Diplomat.* https://bit.ly/38ZxCLR

24 Conclusion

Per Aspera Ad Astra[1]

Erman Akıllı, Burak Güneş, and Ahmet Gökbel

The COVID-19 pandemic, which emerged in China at the end of 2019, is a global event likely to be a candidate for a turning point in world history. This pandemic has touched, influenced, and even transformed almost every field of human life, from politics to the economy, from social relations to daily life practices. International security, one of the leading research areas of international relations, has been affected by COVID-19 and has even mutated like the COVID-19 virus. While COVID-19 has become a security issue, it has also changed how pre-existing security issues are addressed. The pandemic, during which international cooperation is insufficient, inter-state solidarity has decreased, and the virus is defined as the number one security problem by the UN Secretary-General, appeared to end today. However, regarding its effects and results, COVID-19 keeps the World busy for a long time. During the pandemic, states adopted a self-help approach and tried to fight a global pandemic with local/national defence reflexes. Each state has accepted its national health infrastructure and capacity as a security reference point, and health-related issues have become an element of their basic security approaches.

However, cooperation among states appeared necessary if humans desired to be on this blue planet. Yet, some parts of the World understand the need for collaboration as reproducing the inequality among states. The Global South suffered the most in vaccine allocations, for instance, compared to Global North. The death rates indicated an urgent need for cooperation. A virus emerged due to the uneven distribution of wealth and the never-ending desire of human beings to exploit the blue planet. So, this book critically investigated and questioned the current situation as of 2023 and security understanding by considering the pandemic. Additionally, this book introduced new security challenges and new responses to these challenges.

Why a new book on the COVID-19 Pandemic? First and foremost, as in every academic field, the International Relations discipline has long been accustomed to this unique ballgame. Thus, we wanted to focus on how and to what extent the International Relations discipline (most notably security studies) deals with it. Secondly, we wanted to bring together scholars from different countries and, therefore, different academic backgrounds. By so, we tried to combine diverse, competing,

DOI: 10.4324/9781003377597-27

and peculiar manuscripts written specifically on subjects constructing their arguments on the framework of the COVID-19 shaped World.

Back to the scope, *Diplomacy, Society, and the COVID-19 Challenge* consisted of three parts focusing on the World in transformation during/post the COVID-19 era. The first section dealt with "Diplomacy and COVID-19" by touching upon various forms of diplomacy, such as humanitarian, digital, and virtual diplomacy. The second part, "National and Regional Responses to COVID-19", was constructed to evaluate the foreign policies of states and regional actors and the national/regional impacts of COVID-19. The third part, "Global Responses to COVID-19", was about global actors' responses shaped by the pandemic, stretching from NATO to the OECD. This section concerns international organisations and their response to COVID-19's transformative effect, which caused unrest in their regions and globally.

Diplomacy, Society and the COVID-19 Challenge, dedicated to International Relations shaped by extraordinary health conditions, gives an in-depth overview of an emerging area, i.e. "hot topic" such as the COVID-19 Pandemic. This book also introduced detailed case studies and provided a timely response to current affairs and policy debates by bringing different perspectives from different countries together.

After 2023, it will be clear that the COVID-19 pandemic's stranglehold over society and the world order is gradually slipping. In other words, we are beginning to experience the post-pandemic world order as of 2023. This book is an academic remark on societies, the challenges the pandemic posed to the world, and how societies and states dealt with those challenges through diplomacy during the pandemic. World politics remain unstable due to issues like the Ukraine-Russia War, global economic difficulties, climate change, and regional issues, even though the coronavirus is losing its catastrophic effects. Thus, one could wonder, *Quo Vadis?* The world will eventually recover from the political, economic, and sociological effects of COVID-19, but still, there is a long way to the stars.

Note

1 **Per Aspera Ad Astra:** Latin phrase meaning *"Through hardships to the stars."*

Index

Africa Centres for Disease Control and Prevention (Africa CDC) 77, 252
African Cooperation 251
African Union (AU) 11, 100, 252
AI in Foreign Policy 9
Anthropocene 197
ASEAN 10, 99, 101–106, 123–128, 176
ASEAN Way 124

Belt and Road Initiative/BRI 97, 99
benchmarking 230
Bertelsmann Stiftung and the Sustainable Development Solutions Network 227, 232
Bill and Melinda Gates Foundation 214, 254, 255
biodiversity 198–200, 203
border crossing 25, 131
Brexit 158–167
burden-sharing 219, 221, 222

capacity-building 73, 75
Central Asia 58, 69, 76, 131, 132, 134–139, 218
childhood vaccination 270–273
China Dream 97–98
classification 8, 114, 131, 203, 230, 233, 237
climate change 2, 4, 6, 11, 56, 162, 198, 202, 203, 223, 291
compulsory vaccination 269, 270, 271
constant returns to scale (CRS or CCR) 230
continent-wide strategy 253, 254
corona orientalism 272
Council of Europe 11, 265
cultural diplomacy 41, 48, 111, 112, 113
cultural nationalism 30–31

data envelopment analysis (DEA) 11, 227
decision-making units (DMUs) 230
digital diplomacy 40–54, 111
Diplomacy 4.0 9, 52
Diplomacy 3.0 9, 47
diversification 114, 136, 150, 154

EcoHealth 203–206
efficiency measurement 230, 232
ethnic nationalism 30–31
EU Digital COVID Certificate 273
EU security 30, 35–36, 222
Eurasia 10, 131–139, 172–174
European Court of Human Rights 11, 166, 265
extreme violence 30–33, 35

Far Right Movements 9, 30–36
financial contribution 212
foreign aid 11, 111, 149, 257, 260, 261

Global Britain 10, 158–163, 166, 167
globalisation 2, 6, 11, 12, 39, 41, 62, 72, 112, 114, 147, 171, 175, 197, 199, 200, 209, 210, 214, 227

Hallyu 110–119
Hallyu 1.0 114
Hallyu 2.0 114
Hallyu 3.0 114
Hallyu Content Cooperation Division 110
Health Silk Road (HSR) 97, 99
human security 69, 180, 189, 218, 223, 224

international migration 158, 159, 160, 166
international society 11, 111, 115, 117, 119, 217

isolationist policies 211

judicial activism 274

Korean Wave 113, 115
K-pop 114, 115, 116, 117

labour migrants 131, 137

mandatory vaccination 110, 268–271
margin of appreciation 272–274
Metaverse 1, 53, 54
migrant workers 126, 127, 132, 137, 159, 165

nation state 2, 5, 8, 69, 71, 72, 73, 74, 75, 78, 122, 124, 175
NATO 2030 Report 219, 222, 223
NATO 2022 Strategic Concept 177, 222, 223
NATO's solidarity 218
negotiation 39, 40, 41, 45, 70, 71, 72, 73, 78
new public diplomacy 113
non-traditional security 124, 127, 128
normalization 147, 148, 149, 154, 172

One Health 203, 204, 214, 215
Organization for Economic Co-operation and Development (OECD) 227
ownership 252, 260
Oxford-AstraZeneca 271, 272

Pan-Africa 253, 257
pivot to Asia 98, 102
Planetary Health 203
post-Brexit 10, 158–167
pre-pandemic 227, 90, 110, 118, 137
projection 20, 230, 244, 249
public diplomacy 20, 23, 40, 41, 42, 47, 48, 49, 51, 52, 53, 54, 110, 111, 112, 113, 116, 117, 119
public emergency 266, 267

racial nationalism 30, 31, 34, 35, 160
radicalisation 29, 30, 34, 36, 37
ranking 21, 22, 81, 101, 176, 186, 202, 230, 238
regional coordination 11, 58, 251, 253
regulation 59, 73, 84, 132, 138, 172, 208, 209, 210, 211, 269
rohingya 125
Russo-Ukrainian War 133

scenarios 45, 127, 136, 137, 154, 189, 220, 273
security threat 158, 218, 220, 224, 255
South China Sea 102, 104, 106, 125, 127, 128
Southeast Asia 9, 10, 97, 98, 101–106, 122, 126, 176, 197, 198, 201, 273
Sustainable Development Goals (SDGs) 11, 227, 228

technology 22, 39, 40, 41, 42, 43, 44, 45, 49, 50, 59, 100, 115, 162, 219
The New Hallyu (K-Culture) 114
The Security Council 18, 44, 176, 209, 212
The World Health Organization 7, 19, 51, 69, 86, 97, 110, 123, 148, 158, 185, 203, 208, 217, 227, 228, 253, 271

urbanization 11, 197, 199, 200, 203, 248

vaccination policies 260, 269
vaccine hesitancy 259, 269, 272
vaccine passports 273
variable returns to scale (VRS or BCC) 230
Vavřička 269–273
virtual diplomacy 8, 39–45, 47, 290, 291

World Trade Organization (WTO) 61, 97

Xi Jinping 97, 98, 99, 105